BERNIE BROS GONE WOKE

Studies in Critical Social Sciences Book Series

Haymarket Books is proud to be working with Brill Academic Publishers (www.brill.nl) to republish the *Studies in Critical Social Sciences* book series in paperback editions. This peer-reviewed book series offers insights into our current reality by exploring the content and consequences of power relationships under capitalism, and by considering the spaces of opposition and resistance to these changes that have been defining our new age. Our full catalog of *SCSS* volumes can be viewed at https://www.haymarketbooks.org/series_collections/4-studies-in-critical-social-sciences.

Series Editor
David Fasenfest (Wayne State University)

Editorial Board
Eduardo Bonilla-Silva (Duke University)
Chris Chase-Dunn (University of California–Riverside)
William Carroll (University of Victoria)
Raewyn Connell (University of Sydney)
Kimberlé W. Crenshaw (University of California–LA and Columbia University)
Heidi Gottfried (Wayne State University)
Karin Gottschall (University of Bremen)
Alfredo Saad Filho (King's College London)
Chizuko Ueno (University of Tokyo)
Sylvia Walby (Lancaster University)
Raju Das (York University)

BERNIE BROS GONE WOKE

Class, Identity, Neoliberalism

MARC JAMES LÉGER

Haymarket Books
Chicago, IL

First published in 2022 by Brill Academic Publishers, The Netherlands
© 2022 Koninklijke Brill NV, Leiden, The Netherlands

Published in paperback in 2023 by
Haymarket Books
P.O. Box 180165
Chicago, IL 60618
773-583-7884
www.haymarketbooks.org

ISBN: 978-1-64259-818-6

Distributed to the trade in the US through Consortium Book Sales and Distribution (www.cbsd.com) and internationally through Ingram Publisher Services International (www.ingramcontent.com).

This book was published with the generous support of Lannan Foundation and Wallace Action Fund.

Special discounts are available for bulk purchases by organizations and institutions. Please call 773-583-7884 or email info@haymarketbooks.org for more information.

Cover design by Jamie Kerry and Ragina Johnson.
Cover map: Congressional Districts of the 117th Congress of the United States, 2023. Courtesy of the United States Census Bureau.

Printed in the United States.

10 9 8 7 6 5 4 3 2 1

Library of Congress Cataloging-in-Publication data is available.

Contents

Acknowledgements VII
List of Figures IX

Introduction 1
1. Democratic Brocialism 4
2. Identity Politics Is Class Politics 7
3. Progressive Neoliberalism 11
4. Post-politics 13
5. Outline of the Book 17

1 What Does the Professional-Managerial Class Want? 22
1. From the New Deal to the New Democrats 25
2. A Stratum without an Ideology 36
3. The Fall of the Liberal Class and the Rise of the Far Right 42
4. Left Populism as Compromise Formation 49
5. The Wages of Wokeness 52

2 Bernie Beats Trump, Clinton and Obama Beat Bernie 59
1. Millennials Feel the Bern 63
2. Whose Revolution? Whose Party? 77
3. Malarkey 92

3 Elective Affinities 97
1. Your Candidate Here 98
2. I'm Bernie Sanders and I Approve This Message 103
3. The Difference That Universalism Makes 130

4 Less than Bernie 141
1. I Know There Is No Democracy, but I Choose to Ignore 142
2. I Can't Breathe 151
3. Sectarians, Splitters and Fellow Travelers 171
4. When I Hear the Word Culture, I Reach for the Political Economy 185
5. Role Model Ideology 195

Conclusion   218
1   The Bipartisan Endgame   220
2   Meanwhile, Back in Wokeville   238
3   Political Revolution Inside   246

Bibliography   251
Index   282

Acknowledgements

The work of an independent scholar is somewhat less hectic but also less exciting than that of a university professor. I have had the privilege of knowing both worlds. Since working outside the university, I have benefitted from a situation that allows for more intellectual independence than that required by the demands of a discipline-based career path. This autonomy has allowed me to branch out from art theory and criticism to film studies, communication studies and politics. The present study is not unrelated to a book I started researching in February 2018 and completed by Fall 2019 – a critical study of the official portraits of Michelle and Barack Obama. What started out as an essay became a short book and then a much longer book that examines what I refer to as "post-representational politics" and "woke aesthetics" in relation to "reverse neoliberal colorblindness," or the propensity to ignore someone's politics on the basis of their identity. Among the several subject areas that are developed, a chapter on "racialism and its discontents" examines the many political standpoints according to which it is possible to advance the race and class debate.

So as to contribute to the success of the Sanders campaign, I had hoped the Obama book would be published before the November 2020 election. Since that did not happen, and the book remains forthcoming, I wrote extensively about the 2020 nomination race. This research and commentary were prepared into a short book defined as a "campaign chronicle." Since I had already said a great deal about class and identity issues in the Obama book, I avoided repeating myself on many points in the Sanders book. In addition, I have at the same time worked on an edited volume titled *Identity Trumps Socialism*, which brings together the writings of leading radical left critics of identity politics. For that book I have written an introduction as well as a lengthy addendum that provides a class critique of identity politics, radical democracy, populism, privilege theory and intersectionality. The addendum also examines positions on the class and identity debate by conservatives, (neo)liberals, postmodernists, anarchists, social democrats and communists. That book is also forthcoming, as is a second volume of film studies, in this case comprised of essays that address the impact of Black Lives Matter and the MeToo movements on contemporary cinema. I refer readers of *Bernie Bros Gone Woke* who would like more information on the critique of the paradigms of intersectionality, privilege theory or radical democratic left populism to the aforementioned books.

I acknowledge here the stewardship of Studies in Critical Social Science editor David Fasenfest, who advised me on the transformation of the chronicle format into a monograph. This book would not have been possible without

David's thoughtful support. At Brill, thanks to Jason Prevost and thanks also to John Robinson at Team Bernie for the kind permission to use images from Sanders campaign ads. As ever, thanks to comrade Cayley for her invaluable support.

Figures

1. Barbara Smith endorsement ad for Bernie Sanders, February 3, 2020   106
2. Matt McGorry endorsement ad for Bernie Sanders, February 14, 2020   115
3. Pramila Jayapal on *Real Time with Bill Maher* in a Bernie Sanders post, February 16, 2020   117
4. Tom Blanchard, a farmer from Clinton, Iowa, in a Bernie Sanders ad, November 26, 2020   120
5. Jamie Margolin in a Bernie Sanders campaign ad, February 24, 2020   121
6. Activist Shaun King in a Bernie Sanders advertisement, February 18, 2010   124
7. Bernie Sanders campaign advertisement promoting HBCUs, February 28, 2020   126
8. Bernie Sanders campaign ad featuring Adbullah Hammoud, March 8, 2020   129
9. Victoria Dooley, Jennifer Epps-Addison and Nayyirah Shariff at Sanders Town Hall on Racial and Economic Justice, Flint, Michigan, March 7, 2020   132
10. Cornel West at Sanders Town Hall on Racial and Economic Justice, Flint, Michigan, March 7, 2020   138

Introduction

> Those who make revolution only halfway dig their own graves.
> SAINT-JUST

∴

In 2016, Bernie Sanders, the democratic socialist senator from Vermont, ran a left populist campaign for nomination to the leadership of the Democratic Party. There has been much speculation about the meaning of the 2016 United States presidential election. Hillary Clinton and Donald Trump, the two most unpopular candidates in American history, campaigned on whether or not the electorate wanted to continue with the policies of George W. Bush and Barack Obama or opt for something new. Whether one thinks that Trump won the election because of sexism, racism and xenophobia, or because disorganized workers in the Midwest bought into Trump's claims that he would 'Make America Great Again' through economic nationalism, one could not avoid the fact that what made the 2016 election remarkable was the perseverance of Bernie Sanders, whose campaign demonstrated that the hegemony of the neoliberal technocracy could be challenged from the left. Just as Trump upset the Republican apple cart, Sanders promised to do something similar within the Democratic Party. The point of overlap between all three factions, left, right and center, was the confusion over the role that identity politics should play in the new political arrangement. While the Republicans had many of their conservative values bowdlerized by their leader's white supremacy and anti-democratic transgressions, the Clinton team used identity to bait their opponents and evade policy matters. The Sanders campaign, for its part, adjusted to criticisms and geared up for another run.

The failure of the 2016 Sanders campaign to win the nomination had its 'external' and 'internal' critiques on the left. Representative of the radical social movement left, Jeffrey St. Clair railed against the strategy of voting for the lesser evil as well as Sanders' decision to ensconce himself in the Democratic Party, both before he lost the nomination and after (St. Clair 2016). The Sanders revolution, St. Clair argues, was defunct from the beginning. Knowing very well that the political system is rigged by multinational corporations, militarists and financial elites, Sanders squandered his chance to run as a genuine outsider. Wearing the mantle of the New Deal and the Great Society, he promised to make America the sort of place that working-class and middle-class voters could feel good about and contribute to as progressive members of society. However, with the leadership of the Democratic National Committee and Clinton insiders determined to defeat him by any means necessary, Sanders ultimately led the 'Sandernistas' into the same neoliberal snake pit he had warned them against. For St. Clair, the contradiction and fault line of the Sanders campaign was preaching socialism to a collapsing middle class. He writes:

> At one of those rare, epochal moments, when the nation, preoccupied by the nature of its identity and obsessed with its engagement with the world, seemed to be searching desperately for a new logic to its existence, Sanders was punching a collective ticket back to a past that never existed.
> ST. CLAIR 2016: 8

Because he kept the left locked inside a party that no longer and perhaps never represented its real interests, St. Clair suggests that Sanders was not worthy of his dedicated followers. One would have to have a short memory to think that Roosevelt's New Deal and Johnson's Great Society, whatever their limitations, did not represent gains for average Americans. Universal health care is hardly a pipe dream, nor is free college and the rest of the Sanders platform. In 2016 most Americans were preoccupied with paying their mortgage or rent. This is borne out by the fact that the 2016 exit polls show that concern about economic issues scored with more than half of the electorate. In comparison, identity issues bottomed out at around one percent. Americans were, in addition, concerned about their involvement in costly regime change operations in Eastern Europe, the Middle East, North Africa and Latin America. What St. Clair does not mention, and what this book argues, is that the way Americans relate to class and identity issues contributes to making the U.S. one of the most politically influential and problematic nations on the planet.

The question of radical class politics, social movement organizing and government elections finds an acute expression in Adolph Reed Jr.'s assessment of the 2016 Sanders nomination run. A labor organizer and supporter of the Sanders campaign, Reed acknowledges that lesser evil voting is to all extents and purposes, and since at least the 1988 campaign of Michael Dukakis, the only reason to vote Democrat (Reed in Gautney 2018: 11). Playing second fiddle to Republican extremism, the Democrats since Jimmy Carter have abandoned all pretense to being concerned about the growth of social inequality, that is, except for the celebration of diversity and support for anti-discrimination laws. Hillary Clinton's 'lean-in feminism' perfectly embodies this mix of gender politics and bipartisan attack on democracy in the interest of corporations and the billionaire class. The hope of the Sanders movement, according to Reed, was never defined by its fate within the Democratic Party but was always characterized by social movement organizing. Just as one should not be dazzled by every single-issue campaign that comes along, Reed argues that leftists should not be concerned with any single piece of legislation and should approach federal elections as an instrument for movement building. There are limits to the kinds of social policies that someone like Sanders could have achieved in office and so more needs to be done to raise the level of the political consciousness of Sanders supporters in relation to and beyond the labor movement. For this reason, Reed argues that the 2016 Sanders campaign was always a long shot and that it is counterproductive to argue about why Sanders failed to win the nomination. Against pointless speculation, Reed argues, it is better to discuss how the radical movement can build on the momentum that was generated by the campaign. Warning against aimless Twitter bickering and calling on leftists to offer a compelling and pragmatic political alternative, Reed argues that the self-indulgent identity-based left should stop hurling accusations of discrimination and expiating against selling out to a corporate party. Such pseudo-activity, he claims, does little to solve our problems and minimizes what we could have learned from our mistakes. Much less introspection can be expected from establishment liberals, he argues, who simply expect that progressives should support the Democrats without them having to do anything to earn their vote.

Part of what protects the Sanders 2016 and 2020 campaigns from critical scrutiny is not only unconditional support for progressive causes and for left politics more generally, but also support for the ideological cover that contemporary leftism gives to identity politics. To even say this is like walking a tightrope. However, if the left is serious about class struggle, it must understand the differences between the class war and culture wars, even if the two are inextricably linked. Reed argues that Barack Obama succeeded in 2008 and 2012 with a "redefined liberalism" that was focused on ascriptively defined constituencies – blacks, Hispanics, LGBTQ constituencies and allied people – within a neoliberal class politics of downward economic redistribution, militarism and climate catastrophe (Reed in Gautney 2018: 22). He is correct when he suggests that the demographics game is a "purely electoral gambit," even when the numbers add up to a majority (Reed in Gautney 2018: 22). Republican mobilization against multicultural diversity and centrist condemnations of the white working class only exacerbate the problems of identity and class that could be more effectively understood if they were approached from the perspective of emancipatory universalism rather than the failed politics of identity, diversity, radical democracy, postmodernism and neoliberalism.

1   Democratic Brocialism

In 2016, Hillary Clinton supporters attacked the Sanders movement by turning working Americans against one another. They did this by inventing the stereotype of the Bernie Bro. The journalist Glenn Greenwald reported that the idea was concocted by pro-Clinton journalists as a means to counteract the public's interest in class issues and to focus instead on the kind of identity politics that would privilege the election of the first woman president in U.S. history (Greenwald 2016).[1] The Bernie Bro attack meme was a strategic counterpoint to Sanders' argument that Americans should look past identity politics and vote for candidates who are willing to confront corporate power. Whereas postmodern academics who have been trained to 'interrogate the text' often assume that a symptom can be directly linked to a cause, the clinical understanding of a symptom is closer to the notion of a 'floating signifier' in the sense that it is not always possible to know the underlying cause of a symptom. In psychoanalysis, symptoms are especially obscure since their cause may be unknown to even the patient. If Trump is a symptom of the crisis of global capitalism, as we often hear stated on the left, so is the Bernie Bro meme.

The Bernie Bro epithet is perhaps a more direct symptom of the crisis of neoliberalism than Trump. The reason for this is somewhat counterintuitive. In traditional fascism, the conflict between capital and labor cannot be perceived directly due to fascism's projection of social conflict onto a scapegoat whose presence is thought to disturb the unity of organic community. Neoliberalism inverts this strategy by making anti-racism and anti-oppression the focus of social, cultural and political conflict. While anti-racism is without doubt preferable to racism, it also obscures the conflict between capital and labor. Anti-oppression social movements thereby satisfy the ideological needs of a post-political end-of-ideology discourse that defines socialist universalism as outmoded, whether as Eurocentrism, masculinism, class reductionism, or on the basis of some other normative privilege. The identitarian liberals who invented the 'brocialist' meme to slander the Sanders campaign were reinforced in their attack by the simultaneous disparagement of 'cultural

---

[1] Incidentally, the birther debate was incubated in the Hillary Clinton camp by the same people who invented the Bernie Bro stereotype. See Greenwald 2020. See also Beauchamp 2020.

Marxists' by the alt-right. Both liberals and conservatives work to dismantle the left when they reduce socialism to social justice activism. None of this was news in 2016. Trump's apotheosis was the result of a social counter-revolution that began with the retreat of the radical left in the 1960s and that has been facilitated by the neoliberalization of culture and knowledge industries since the 1980s.

The stereotype of the Bernie Bro was designed to obscure the fact that Sanders was considered by voters to be the only opposition candidate who could defeat Trump. It was applied to anyone who was critical of Clinton and neoliberal Democrats. As a well-conceived diversion, it erased from political consciousness the fact that the majority of women under the age of 45 were Sanders supporters. In June 2016, a writer for *The Daily Beast* nevertheless saw fit to characterize Bernie Bros as entitled white men who consider the defeat of Sanders to be an injustice and so have an irrational sense of victimhood that is unable to understand the perspectives of black, Latino and minority Americans. They are said to be frustrated by economic hardship and expect immediate gratification, which, when frustrated, takes the form of "white tribalism" (Pitner). After the Trump victory, a writer with *The Guardian* criticized Sanders for encouraging Americans to look beyond identity politics, in particular, by emphasizing over and again that it is not good enough to vote for a candidate on the basis of their identity and that what is needed are candidates who will confront corporate power (Arceneaux). The writer considers Sanders' defense of the interests of the working majority to be the kind of colorblind politics that separate class from gender and race. His argument is that democratic socialists ignore how identity plays into economic power and therefore serves the privileged. Sanders is said to inadvertently support the cause of white men who do not want to "share" and so voted for Trump. Another writer for *The Guardian* suggested that white men ignore why it is that Clinton lost to Trump when they argue that identity politics are divisive. His retort is that Trump did not win because he focused on economic issues, but because he also played the game of identity politics, which has always been an issue in American politics, as noticed by the bias towards white votes in the electoral college and almost everywhere else in American life where a white man has greater economic advantages. What has changed, the writer argues, is the fact that white men are now beginning to lose the identity game and so class is being transformed into a category of identity, not unlike race and religion (Freeman). A writer for *Vanity Fair* stated that all of this points to the emergence of an 'alt-left,' which, like the alt-right, rejects identity politics (Wolcott). In contrast to the previous author, who argued that Bernie Bros dislike divisiveness, this writer suggests that the purpose of the alt-left is to foster divisions among liberal-left progressives, who do not have problems with candidates like Hillary Clinton.[2] The alt-left, he argues, fantasizes about revolution and authoritarian personality cults. A writer at *Teen Vogue* revived these issues after Sanders launched his 2020 campaign (Sarmiento). Much has changed since 2016, she argues, and the image of Sanders as a "white savior" figure betrays what she claims is his unpopularity with black voters, which is due to his white privilege and his lack of solidarity when it comes to gender and race. He seems "dead set," she writes, "on taking up spaces that simply do not belong to him." The article includes screen grabs of tweets that say "Bernie's 'democratic socialism' is still settler colonialism" and "I have to laugh at how many of y'all actually believe that a privileged straight white cisgender man is going to liberate us." Offering these kinds of writers a reality check, an article in *Jacobin* suggested that despite paying lip service to identity issues, mainstream Democrats have an inconsistent and selective commitment to diversity (Marcetic 2019a). The author notes that if Sanders was to win the election in 2020, he would be the first Jewish president in American history. While his ethnicity was ignored by the mainstream press, many journalists emphasized the notion that he is an octogenarian white male.

The sum of these views is that Sanders is raced, racist and indifferent to race. Similarly, Trump is raced, racist and plays the game of identity politics against the identity politics that could be used against him. What was gained from all of this for the left was a greater awareness of the limitations of the anti-racist left, which was more apparent with regard to Sanders than Obama. The 2016 Sanders platform, Reed argues, was issue by issue a black platform, with calls for a living wage, infrastructure spending and employment, free post-secondary education, single-payer health care, bank regulation, criminal justice and immigration reform (Reed 2016a). Those black activists and intellectuals who criticized Sanders rather than the right wing of the Democratic Party were people who willingly ignore anti-left policies like NAFTA and Bill Clinton's omnibus crime bill. Those who criticized Sanders on the view that his class-first universalism is economically reductionist did not, because they cannot, argue that his platform would not disproportionately benefit black and Latino constituents. It is all the better, according to Reed, that identitarians exposed themselves as left-wing neoliberals who distort the basis of genuine socialist solidarity. They belong to the same camp as Hillary Clinton, who argued that ending Wall Street corruption would not end racism, sexism, homophobia and

---

2   Similar accusations were raised against leftist critiques of candidates like Kamala Harris and Cory Booker in the 2020 Democratic Party nomination race. See Gray 2017b.

xenophobia (Weigel). As an example of this, civil rights leader and congressman John Lewis accused Sanders of misleading people into thinking that they could get something for free. Against such counter-solidaristic identity politics, Sanders sought to unify the working class against the neoliberal consensus (Zamora).

2   Identity Politics Is Class Politics

Identitarianism dies hard. So does electioneering. Regardless of his claims that voters should look beyond a candidate's identity, Sanders' 2020 campaign gave greater attention to his personal background, his record of civil rights activism and his efforts to redress accusations of discrimination in his campaign. In his second run for the Democratic Party nomination, and in response to identity-oriented attacks and critiques, Sanders combined his progressive universalist platform with an identity politics approach to demographics. The 2020 Sanders campaign enhanced its call for economic justice by associating all of the above forms of discrimination with the Trump administration. In doing so, his campaign missed an opportunity to critique the neoliberal ideologization of diversity. In 2020, the first line of attack against Sanders was his age. This allowed his team to emphasize his long record of progressivism on matters of economic justice as well as civil rights, which readily contrasted with Joe Biden's record of cronyism and discrimination. Not surprisingly, little was made by the media and the establishment about Sanders' working-class background and his identity as the son of Jewish immigrants (Marcetic 2019a). All of these, however, were emphasized by his campaign team. As identity issues and intersectional politics were increasingly marketed by the Sanders team in the first few months of the 2020 primaries, it seemed like the identity and class approach that is favored by postmodern academia and the millennial left was likely to carry the day. At the critical point of his defeat, however, what became obvious was that Sanders' soft peddling of socialism and his "that's not radical" common sense reformism failed to redirect the politically confused rage that working Americans feel about their government and their condition. In addition, the Sanders campaign failed to make a bigger issue of the fact that identity is a marker of political difference and a category of social struggle in today's end of history post-politics.

Although there were many factors involved in Sanders' defeat, in the days before the South Carolina primary and before the Democratic Party establishment engineered the suspension of several unpopular candidates so as to create a clear choice between Sanders and Biden, it seemed as though Sanders was poised to win either a majority or a plurality of delegates going into the Democratic National Convention. After the South Carolina vote, and going against all of the polls available to the effect that only a Sanders-style left populism could challenge Trump's right-wing populism, the question of policy preferences switched to the question of electability, with a bumbling and often incoherent Biden winning the better part of the black vote. Until then, the mainstream media had done its best to depict Sanders as either a Cuba and Venezuela-loving communist, or, thanks to a cheap trick on the part of Elizabeth Warren's campaign team that earned her the enmity of the left, a sexist who did not think a woman candidate could beat Trump. And so the 2020 Democratic primaries turned into a repetition of sorts of 2016, when Clinton pinched the nomination from Sanders through negative attacks, appeals to diversity and a rigged DNC. When she claimed in January 2020 that "nobody likes him," she did so to media-manage the public perception of the only candidate with a progressive agenda and with an authentically democratic ground game on the campaign trail (Evelyn).

In terms of the left critique of identity politics, the first Sanders nomination race plays as tragedy and the second as farce. Given the fact that around 55 percent of Trump voters in 2020 were women, and 57 percent were people of color, with considerable wins among Hispanics, African Americans, Asian Americans and LGBT voters, the theory promulgated by liberals that Trump won in 2016 on account of entitled working-class white males who feel insecure about changing demographics and loss of privilege fell flat. Moreover, Trump's support among white men declined in 2020. Surprisingly, according to the 2020 exits polls, while 35 percent of voters identified the economy as their main reason for their vote decision, with 83 percent of this group supporting Biden, 20 percent identified racial inequality as their main concern, with 92 percent of this number supporting Biden. Without doubt these numbers were influence by the poll questions but also by the impact of the George Floyd protests in the summer of 2020 and the overwhelming support for Black Lives Matter and police reform by the general public, corporate America and the Democratic establishment. A frequently cited report by Micah English and Joshua Kalla, published in the journal *Race and Class* in April 2021, found that despite increasing awareness of racial inequality, the anti-racist framing of issues is unpopular with Americans of all backgrounds and therefore detrimental to public policy (Edsell; English & Kalla). According to the authors, class policies that are race-neutral fare better overall.

People who supported Sanders did not do so because they are white, male or straight, or because they are black, Latino, lesbian or transgender. By that kind of logic, we would be obliged to say that Asians are white supremacist since more Asians voted for Trump than Hillary Clinton in 2016. The fact that, proportionally speaking, more blacks switched over to Trump in 2016 than did whites should not lead one to conclude that blacks are more sympathetic to white supremacist ideas than whites. The shibboleth that the racial framing of issues is unpopular with racists especially should not be given more importance than the bugbear that many people want to pay less taxes. No amount of statistical research or polling data can substitute for what is specific to politics and what cannot be reduced to winning elections. Debates over colorblindness, which were first advocated by socialists and Civil Rights activists, and then reversed when conservatives gamed it to their advantage, have only muddled the problem. What today's left has to contend with is a new form of woke visibility, where someone's identity is foregrounded in a way that ignores or justifies the detrimental aspects of their neoliberal politics. What the left needs to become sensitive to is the difference between diversity and the neoliberal ideologization of diversity. One might think that a progressive movement that lost working-class support during the Reagan and Bush years would not make the same mistake again. Yet here we are. The fact that 24 percent of the members of Congress are women and 22 percent are people of color may be less significant than the fact that the overall median income of House representatives is 500 percent higher than the median income of the average American. Only two percent of legislators have working-class backgrounds. As Dustin Guastella argues, the division of the nation into identity-based "communities" rather than classes is by and large the doing of wealthy and educated cadres that comprise 13 percent of the electorate, which contrasts, at 77 percent, with the working-class base, many of whom dislike "out-of-touch liberal cultural appeals" and "chic activist demands" (Guastella 2021).

There is clearly a rift between the consciousness of the professional liberal mainstream and the public at large. One might say that with the rise of neofascist political forces in the U.S., U.K., France, Germany, Spain, Brazil, India, Israel, Hungary, Ukraine and elsewhere, the petty-bourgeois 'middle' class is undergoing extreme polarization. In 2016 there were only a few commentators on the left who fully appreciated the class character of the culture wars. If this has changed it is thanks largely to the Sanders presidential campaigns, which were the first since the 1970s to be understood as a challenge to global capitalist hegemony. There is now a more widespread appreciation of the critique of identitarian culture wars among left commentators especially. This implies a hard-won critique of not only neoliberalism, but also the depoliticizing aspects of postmodern micro-politics.

Two axioms structure the analysis that follows. The first holds that *identity politics is increasingly an anti-left politics of the middle class*, whose petty-bourgeois ideology is now distributed across all social classes. We can speak in this case of the professional-managerial class, as defined by Barbara and John Ehrenreich, or the executant petty bourgeoisie, as defined by Pierre Bourdieu (Barbara & John Ehrenreich 1979; Bourdieu). An even more critical assertion would not fail to find some similarities between contemporary identity politics and the conservative anti-Enlightenment and fascist ideologies of the past. The left critique of identity politics involves the recognition of material realities like the shift to a culture and knowledge-based economy, where the marketing and flexibilization of identity in conditions of social competition have become commonplace. As the postmodern cultural politics of difference have gone into crisis mode, and as protest movements carry on as if the more significant threats to human survival are not at the level of global capitalism and neoliberal governance, a universalist politics of solidarity beyond identitarian fragmentation remains to be organized.

Second, the notion that every fascism is a failed revolution means that both *leftists and liberal progressives must cease accepting the failures of neoliberalism by taking refuge in the real and imagined threat of right-wing authoritarianism.* Just as Bush Jr.'s failures are not an alibi for Obama, Trump's politics are not an alibi for Biden. The bipartisan endgame undermines the goal of human progress and only the left can salvage what is of value in the Enlightenment tradition. One must add to this point about authoritarianism the fact that the failures of twentieth-century communism are not, by themselves, an argument for economic nationalism as a comprehensive solution to the problems of global capitalism. Anyone who does not notice the uneven advantages of the developed world in this regard cannot seriously consider themselves leftists. On the other hand, the argument in favor of reformism as a means to gradually win popular support for more radical politics deserves some due. On this score, one could support Sanders without, at the same time, feeling obliged to ratify the Biden government.

Whatever its limitations, the 2020 Sanders campaign was not unlike the Jeremy Corbyn campaign a measure of the strength of the organized left and of the prospect of radicalizing a 'post-mass' of educated and relatively affluent voters. It also represented a concerted effort to shift left energies away from activist protest and alter-global horizontalism towards some needed verticality and institutional power. So-called prefigurative politics are mostly self-satisfied. We have a long way to go and next to no time to make progress. We no longer have the luxury to think as Mao Zedong did that it could take a thousand years before we reach communism.

3   Progressive Neoliberalism

The tripartite nature of modern politics, the struggle among socialists, liberals and conservatives, is suppressed in American electoral politics by the bipartisan nature of elections, where the two major parties have historically made third party challengers ineffective. Notwithstanding the impact of new social movements, structural political change is reflected in the changing dynamics of these parties. The political philosopher Nancy Fraser has captured the current realignment of U.S. politics with the terms 'authoritarian populism,' 'progressive neoliberalism' and 'progressive populism.' The disintegration of social democratic regimes in the last few decades and the reappearance of proto-fascist authoritarianism, she argues, is in part due to a global breakdown in political ideology and traditional class identifications. In addition to this political shift, economic and ecological crises lead to a general social crisis that affects all institutions. Trump, she says, is the poster boy of this crisis of hegemony, in particular, as class divisions and status hierarchies become undone and are reorganized around identity markers to create new hegemonic articulations.

What Trump accomplished, above all, was a disruption of *progressive neoliberalism*, which represents the hegemonic bloc that is constituted by the unlikely yet real alliance between the high-end symbolic and financial sectors of the U.S. economy – Wall Street, Silicon Valley and Hollywood – and the mainstream currents of New Left social movements – feminism, anti-racism, multiculturalism, environmentalism and LGBTQ rights. This neoliberal consensus combined the upward redistribution of wealth with a seemingly downward redistribution of social capital. "Only when decked out as *progressive*," Fraser writes, "could a deeply *regressive* political economy become the dynamic center of a new hegemonic bloc" (Fraser 2017: 49). Since the Bill Clinton administration, the New Democrats combined a progressive politics of recognition and superficial egalitarianism with social hierarchy and the kind of meritocratic rhetoric that Thomas Frank describes as the ethos of today's "high-born and well-graduated" technocrats – those who are brave on cultural issues but who claim to be powerless when it comes to the redistribution of wealth (Frank 2016: 25, 27). This liberal mainstream incorporates the largest segments of new social movement groups who are often associated with the Richard Florida concept of the 'creative class' (Florida). Third-way New Democrats won out against neoconservative politics by going along with its free trade agenda of de-industrialization, deregulation and financialization. It attacked labor rights while at the same time implementing a War on Drugs and War on Crime that increased social inequality.

With no party defending the interests of workers and preventing the decline of living standards for average Americans, Trump's agenda of *reactionary populism* filled the void that was created when progressive neoliberals abandoned political democracy in favor of economic austerity. After the 2008 banking crisis and Bush's disastrous wars in Iraq and Afghanistan, Obama could have mobilized support against neoliberalism. Instead, he defended the corrupt with 'too big to fail' and 'too big to jail' policies, allowing inequality and carnage to metastasize. He also ignored social forces like Occupy Wall Street in favor of celebrity hobnobbing. Campaigning on populist themes, Trump capitalized on social anger and economic nationalism. Once in office, Trump demonstrated that his right-wing populism was little more than hyper-reactionary neoliberalism. The alternative to all of this, as represented by the Sanders movement, is defined by Fraser as *progressive populism*. Sanders denounced the 'rigged economy' in egalitarian and universalist terms. His coalition included not only blue-collar and Rust Belt workers but also young college students, public sector workers, unionized teachers and nurses, as well as minority groups and immigrants.

Sanders' inclusive view of the working class contrasts with Trump's xenophobic and reactionary populism. Mainstream liberals, however, are on the whole more comfortable with the neoliberal politics of Clinton and Obama than with the socialism that they associate with Fidel Castro, Hugo Chávez and Joseph Stalin. The anti-communist tradition is accustomed to playing race against class, a tendency that now prioritizes opposition to white supremacy over and against class struggle. Militant anti-racist politics that are today combined with neoliberal policy objectives threaten to remake progressive neoliberalism into reactionary populism, a trend that is not limited to conservatives but that is also noticeable in 'woke' forms of race and gender separatism. With no consensus conceivable between Trump Republicans and Clinton-type Democrats, neither of which can solve the problems of global capitalist hegemony, progressive populism offers the best opportunity to solve the problems of economic redistribution and social recognition. According to Fraser, only progressive populism can unite the working class and align it with the progressive sectors of the middle class and professional-managerial class. Two problems stand in the way of such an alliance, she says. One is the view that Trump voters are irredeemably racist, sexist and homophobic deplorables. The other is the view that progressives are smug, moralistic elitists. Progressive populists weaken the left when they assume that cultural and intellectual pursuits are the prerogative of elitists. Philistinism has never been a characteristic of the revolutionary left. The assumption that the use of terms like Latinx by a small percentage of left academics is the reason why the Democrats are losing voters is worthy of ridicule (Illing). As for deflecting support for Trump, one should focus on political economy but also advance a revolutionary culture that appeals to people who are fully conscious of social problems.

Combating these two stereotypes is what Fraser recommends for building the strength of a left populist movement. Working women, immigrants and people of color need to be diverted from lures like lean-in feminism, corporate diversity and green capitalism. Working people who have been abandoned by the two parties must also be diverted from the illusions of militarism and ethno-nationalism. However, the question remains as to the status of identity politics and similar strands of cultural and intellectual production on the left. As mentioned previously, even discourses of anti-oppression obscure matters that are specific to political economy. The left needs a more thorough and consistent politics if it is to advance human culture beyond the neoliberal endgame. The thesis of this book is that the 2020 Sanders campaign failed on the question of how a radical left movement mediates issues of class and identity. In this regard, the Sanders campaign not only lost the nomination, it also failed to create the kinds of policies that would allow the progressive movement to reimagine a radical, universalist culture. In the Biden era, the conditions of post-Fordist competition and precarity, shored up by right-wing authoritarianism on one side and democratic neoliberalism on the other, fuel the worst forms of identitarian elitism, populism and separatism.

4   Post-politics

The laudable combination of social recognition with economic redistribution is a simplification of complex social phenomena. It may very well do as a modus operandi in social movement milieux, where getting along is as important as building power, but it is theoretically naïve, especially for a movement that calls itself socialist. The 'anything but Bernie' sentiment that made the case for Biden's greater electability, and the focus on BLM as the leading edge of the progressive agenda, are both related to the rejection of class analysis. Both are aspects of neoliberalism's post-ideological rejection of politics. In "For a Leftist Appropriation of the European Legacy," which was published in the *Journal of Political Ideologies* in February 1998, Slavoj Žižek reviews the work of Jacques Rancière to draw a distinction between the categories of universal, particular and singular (Žižek 1998). The particular becomes a *singular universal* when its struggle represents the principle of universality. In this instance, the particular are not simply a minority constituency, but constitute a "part of no-part" that is excluded from the formal space of universality. These are people whose status as political equals is denied and for this reason their demands for equality threaten the dominant social order. A number of obstacles stand in the way of any one group representing the singular universal. This includes: 1) abstract appeals to unity; 2) the channeling and depoliticization of demands back into the dominant social order; 3) the assumption that oppression is endemic, and that people do not share a common history, humanity and society; 4) the kind of reductionism that examines only the political economy and leaves out culture, politics and ideology.

According to Žižek, a structural gap emerged in postwar social theory between formal democracy and social reality. Even if the formal equality of human rights and political liberalism were initially oriented to serve the needs of propertied European men, they set in motion a process of politicization that later encompassed labor rights, women's rights, civil rights, gay rights, and so on. What is different today, in the era of postmodernity, is the difference between the realm of appearances and the realm of simulation. What is lost in simulation, Žižek argues, is not the referent and the dimension of the real. In simulation, all of the elements are accounted for. Simulation, in this sense, is anthropological, as argued by the Endnotes collective in their picturesque defense of the anti-politics of today's identitarian "non-movements," defined as "expressions" of illiberal and ungovernable regimes of capitalist disorganization and decline (Endnotes 2020). The natural ally of such destituent movements, Reed argues, is the ruling class (Reed 2021). What is lost in simulation is the dimension of appearance, which is always incomplete. In the Lacanian terms of Imaginary, Real and Symbolic, illusion is imaginary, and appearance is symbolic. The Lacanian symbolic order refers to language and the myriad rules of social interaction, the imaginary refers to the illusory sense that a subject has of itself and the world, and the Real defines that which escapes symbolization. In today's world, symbolic efficiency is disintegrating, which brings the imaginary closer to the Real. Since politics is a matter of appearance, the ability of the singular part of no-part to represent universal interests is conditioned by symbolic efficiency. The Sanders campaigns were, in these terms, caught up in a political situation that emphasizes identities and downplays democracy as something that has not been fully actualized.

Today's post-political regimes are characterized by the shift from symbolic efficiency to a postmodern order of simulation. Post-politics is a defense formation that negates the order of politics. Post-political regimes, Žižek argues, do no repress the masses so much as foreclose the realm of mass politicization. The hysterics of Trump supporters are some of the ways in which the Real of global capitalist violence re-emerges as a consequence of this foreclosure of politics. Instead of the direct ideological clash between capitalism and socialism, what we have instead is what Žižek refers to as "postmodern racism," the kind of diversity that has more to do with the needs of market forces than with political demands for universal rights. Each identity group wants its share of the multicultural ideology of late capitalism (Žižek 2006b). However, insofar as the political challenge to capitalism is foreclosed, we have the simulation of politics in terms of demographics. This can involve the very legitimate politics of recognition.

Post-politics gives rise to globalization rather than universalization. Globalization allows for the progressive dismantling of human rights because it effectively precludes the dimension of universality. We could add that this is why experiences like sexual violence, police violence and genocide are acquiring a pre-eminent role in political thinking. Fascination with "unrepresentable" subjects like the Holocaust and slavery, Žižek says, allows politicians, artists, academics and journalists to depoliticize the social sphere and warn *against* politics. Crimes against humanity have the status of an apolitical excess of politics, which compels us to subordinate politics to morality. This is why people like Trump are useful to both the post-political establishment and post-political activists. Like Alfred Jarry's Père Ubu, he is so unfathomably banal and amorally grotesque that nothing more needs to be said. The question then becomes: What is to be done about post-politics? Can the left make use of human rights, free speech and the claims of the excluded to advance an emancipatory universalist politics rather than neoliberal governance and contemporary forms of discursive historicism? Žižek writes:

> The postmodern identity-politics of particular (ethnic, sexual, etc.) lifestyles fits perfectly the depoliticized notion of society in which every particular group is 'accounted' for, has its specific status (as a victim) acknowledged through affirmative action or other measures destined to guarantee social justice.
> ŽIŽEK 1998

Postmodern identity politics is more a logic of resentment than of progressive universalization. For the sake of oppressed minority groups, post-representational post-politics is willing to weaken the rights and privileges of all. It endorses the system of neoliberal inequality in the name of equality. As Chelsea Manning has put it, it is a form of equal opportunity oppression. In this sense, the contemporary ideology of diversity has more in common with the conservative tradition than the radical tradition. This is the context in which multiculturalism is now the official ideology of the neoliberal technocratic establishment, pandering communitarian ethics as the only gauge of social progress. The underside of all this community representation is neo-feudalization, militarism and climate catastrophe. There are countless events and documents that form the background to this discussion. This makes the class and identity debate impossible to fit into an easy formula. A few theorems may nevertheless be ventured as a part of the modus operandi of this book. Various forms of oppression predate capitalism. These have been unevenly incorporated into capitalist social relations and ideology. Ellen Meiksins Wood's claim that racism and sexism are not constitutive of capitalism (Wood 1995) is accepted here but I add to it Žižek's counter-intuitive postulate, which states: "the plural contingency of postmodern political struggles and the totality of Capital are not opposed ... today's capitalism, rather, provides *the very background and terrain for the emergence of shifting-dispersed-contingent-ironic-and so on, political subjectivities*" (Žižek 2000:108). For Žižek, the mantra of 'race, class, gender and sexuality' actually represses class politics, making social difference stand in for this displaced class antagonism. Rather than the universal state imagined by Hegel, post-politics avoids the reality of capitalism as the concrete universal and seeks instead to solve partial problems of abstract universality and democratic gradualism. Anti-oppression politics paradoxically obscure the workings of contemporary neoliberal capitalism.

Also methodological is the postulate that labor and capital are inherently antagonistic in ways that gender difference and racial difference are not. The opposition of whites to blacks, or women to men, is a means to avoid politics, remaking social conflict into eternal opposites, myths, archetypes and similar clichés. The presumption of the innate difference between, and hierarchy among, different social types is part of the history of reactionary thought. So is the assumption that working-class, middle-class and upper-class members of the same identity group have more in common, in terms of political interests, than the members of the same class group who have different identities. This makes the notion of "class reductionism" anathema to actual Marxism, which in all matters seeks to provide a non-reductionist explanation of social and historical phenomena. One could nevertheless suggest that social democracy is class reductionist since the working class in this case insists on its particularity. Social democracy seeks to redistribute wealth and reduce economic inequality but it does not presume that the working class should disappear. Socialism, in contrast, insists on the centrality of class because it insists on the fact that capitalism is the dominant social relation and mode of production. Socialism seeks to abolish the wage relation and the dispossession of the majority by the few. In this sense the proletariat is conceived as the universal class that has an interest in replacing capitalism with something better. When the left abandons revolutionary theory, it expects the working class to take its place in the chain of equivalent radical democratic particulars.

Postmodern post-politics serves the needs of global capitalist markets, not emancipatory universalism. If intellectuals, artists, activists and journalists want to take up the slack on end-of-history woketivism, they need to break with the petty-bourgeois politics of the postwar generation and reinvent revolutionary ideology. The slim chance that such work can be undertaken inside the Democratic Party is what explains the reorientation of the 2016 Sanders campaign into the demographics and identity politics framework of the 2020 campaign. It is fair and accurate to say that this shift was only one dimension of a complex electoral strategy. Yet this is the dimension that this book seeks to understand and elucidate. The problems of post-politics are not limited to the high-spirited efforts of one candidate and his supporters. It is nevertheless necessary for the broader political left to understand this weakness of the 2020 Sanders campaign if it is not to repeat the same mistakes.

5 Outline of the Book

This is not a book about Bernie Sanders, his biography and his political career. It is not about everything that happened during the 2020 Democratic Party nomination race. I do not address the profiles of the twenty-some candidates who were stacked up to make it look as though Sanders was unfit for the nomination. This book is about the problem of identity politics as it was manifested in the 2020 Sanders campaign. It is written in solidarity with those who supported the Sanders nomination as the most tactically electable candidate to take the U.S. and the rest of the world on a course beyond the neoliberal quagmire. My focus on the intersectional thrust of the campaign's last weeks is meant to contribute to the debates that must be had on the relevance of identitarianism to the class politics that can bring about the system change we need. It is clear that the diversitarian approach has developed in tandem with new standards in academia, government, corporations and in the culture at large. One of the first reasons to resist this trend is that the government and corporate lip service that is given to diversity is directly related to the indifference of the corporate state to social welfare and to its singular concern with managing the conditions that make profit for property holders. What we are experiencing around these debates is less a crisis of civilization than it is a crisis of capitalism with implications for culture. The wokewashing of neoliberal capitalism will not save us, neither on Wall Street nor on Main Street.

The first chapter of this book develops the claim made by Adolph Reed and others that the anti-racist and racialist politics of progressive neoliberals, including other forms of anti-oppression discourse, is a politics of the professional-managerial class. In terms of the class analysis of postwar identity politics, the broader concern is the rise to hegemonic status of the ideology of classlessness of the petty bourgeoisie, which informs the left populism of the Sanders movement. Based on the work of Erik Olin Wright, class structure is shown to lead to variations in class formation, which means that the working class does not inevitably organize itself in ways that are class-conscious. The contradictory location of the new 'middle' class sometimes leads it to organize according to non-class lines like race and gender. Since the petty bourgeoisie is not, strictly speaking, a class in its own right but is divided between bourgeois and working-class interests, its role in the production process can contribute to class inequality.

A brief presentation of the shift from the New Deal era to the neoliberal policies of the New Democrats provides some historical reference points for the decline of labor struggle and the creation of concepts like institutional racism as part of the ideology of postwar liberalism. The rise through the ranks of the professional-managerial class of minority constituencies is shown to have been cultivated by the corporate state as a bulwark against radicalization. A review of the concept of the PMC through the writings of Barbara and John Ehrenreich defines its objectively antagonistic relation to the working class. Although the PMC shares with the working class a common condition of opposition to capitalist domination, its antagonism to the ruling class is mostly oriented towards the maintenance of professional expertise. After the PMC abandoned the radicalism of the 1960s, it supported the entrepreneurial and meritocratic ideology of Thatcher and Reagan, becoming by the 2000s the power-hungry managers of disaster capitalism. In the context of this death of the liberal center, the class aspects of the 2016 presidential election are shown to be a matter of struggle. Accounting for the re-emergence of the far right in class terms allows us to see the ways in which contemporary social justice movements encompass conservative and reactionary ideological tendencies. This then allows us to make some preliminary criticisms of radical democratic left populism, whose identity-based critique of 'class essentialism' reveals the class allegiance of the PMC with capitalist anti-communism and the ideology of the end of history.

A popular idea during the two Sanders campaigns was that only the Vermont senator's left populism was able to compete with Trump's appeal to economic nationalism. This perception was confirmed by national polls that showed Bernie beating other Democratic Party candidates in a match against Trump.

While one might think that Democratic Party insiders would have given their support to the candidate most likely to win, the economic interests of the plutocracy was given priority over Sanders' efforts to reform American politics. Over two campaigns, party insiders colluded to block Sanders' path to the nomination. The second chapter examines the uses of identity politics in this effort and the relative weakness of a left populist strategy that fails to defend emancipatory universalism. It begins with Hillary Clinton's skewed account of "what happened" in 2016 and corrects the record by looking at the Sanders platform in detail, which identifies the policy areas and social realities that Clinton-type New Democrats avoid. Source documents written by Sanders and his team provide useful insights into his campaign strategy. This includes small donations, an appeal to young voters and their appreciation for anti-oppression discourses, a direct appeal to demographic groups in specific counties in the primaries and an on-the-ground campaign of direct contact with voters through speech events and town hall meetings. After BLM activists petitioned candidates to do more to reform policing, Sanders responded with immediate changes to his platform. Despite corrupt dealings by the DNC, his 2016 campaign won 22 states and almost half of the pledged delegates – a much stronger showing than anyone had anticipated. In 2016 as in 2020, the influence of James Clyburn in South Carolina biased black voters against Sanders. Regardless, Sanders won a large share of the youth votes across all demographic groups.

After WikiLeaks published the hacked 2016 DNC emails, Sanders supporters were incensed at the unscrupulousness of the party establishment. Ready for another campaign, the Sanders movement set off in 2019 on a much firmer footing, only this time the party would put up more than two dozen opponents. In order to cover all the bases in terms of race and gender, the Sanders campaign placed women and people of color in all of its major campaign positions. This allowed Sanders to compete against progressive neoliberals with the same kind of virtue signaling, most of it aimed at Trump. So as to secure an easier opponent, Trump campaigned early on against Sanders through red-baiting anti-socialist rhetoric. He was ultimately outflanked in this by Jimmy Carter, Bill Clinton and Barack Obama, who lined up in favor of Biden at the eleventh hour and orchestrated a party coup against an all but a certain Sanders victory. For all of the fuss about identity and demographics, what determined the outcome in 2020 was the control of politics by the business elite. The hard-learned lesson of Super Tuesday was that even if diversity is popular, it is not the politics that matters in Washington D.C.

The third chapter presents ample evidence of woke identitarianism in the advertisements presented by the Sanders campaign in the first few months of 2020. It is prefaced with some insights into the similarities between political advertising and advertising in general. Since most uninformed and undecided voters in the U.S. receive their knowledge about candidates from television ads rather than television news, campaigns make effective use of advertising to influence voter behavior. However, a political system with a commercial, laissez-faire attitude towards political advertising has built-in problems, including: the mystification of politics, the dependence of political campaigns on donors to pay for expensive advertising rates, the desublimation of politics and its transformation into lifestyle individualism or partisan tribalism, the substitution of celebrity for integrity. Through the strategy of accepting small donations only, the Sanders team not only raised enough money to run a competitive ad campaign, it avoided many of the compromises that establishment candidates typically make in order to secure financing. This allowed Sanders to focus on serious problems and the needs of the majority of American people.

The main difficulty with the Sanders ads was not due to the usual pressures, but to the decisions made by his national team to foreground identity politics in the weeks after the Iowa primary. As nominees like Elizabeth Warren, Pete Buttigieg and Kamala Harris were likely to drop out of the race, the Sanders campaign engaged in woke virtue signaling in order to appeal to and win over their identity-oriented supporters. Instead of a creating a clear difference from Biden, who could also make good on pandering to diversity while at the same time upholding the fundamentals of the American class system, the Sanders team indexed progressive policy to multiculturalism. Presenting progressivism as a politics of minorities rather than the pluralist façade of the most powerful nation on earth, the campaign failed in two ways: it failed to advance democratic socialism as a vigorous mass movement that represents the will of the majority, and, equally important, it failed to make the case for universalism in political philosophy as well as public policy.

The last chapter makes use of Elisabeth Kübler-Ross's five stages of grieving to discuss five themes related to the period after Sanders suspended his campaign and before the November election: the Bernie or Bust contingent and efforts by 'blue no matter who' advocates to shame Sanders supporters to back Biden; the George Floyd protests and the COVID-19 pandemic; debates about a third party split and the merits of lesser evil voting; the value of culture in the movement; Biden's record as a politician and some after-effects of the attention given to identity and representation in the context of progressive neoliberalism and progressive populism. These themes develop the interaction of class war and culture war issues in specific circumstances, highlighting the difference that a Sanders administration could have made but also some of the lingering problems that were not resolved by the populist left. The question of sectarianism is addressed in terms of the noticeable partisan polarization in the 2020 exit polls as well as in the rival factions of the American left. While some viewed the BLM protests as evidence of the inoperative conditions of the electoral system, the postmodern premises of ultra-left resistance are shown to make for strange overlaps with neoliberal ideology that serve the far right, which can posture as the last bastion of universalism, human rights, reason and objectivity. Building coalitions of the left so as to enrich the political, intellectual and cultural strength of the progressive movement is advocated in terms of socialist politics more generally. As the pragmatism of the populist left fails to reach the level of a mass movement, a more comprehensive approach to radicalism and emancipation is advanced as a means to break with the bipartisan consensus.

The conclusion to the book discusses the immediate consequences of the failure of the 2020 Sanders campaign and more importantly the failure of the Democratic Party to put up any significant challenge to the Republican right. A detailed presentation of Trump's Save America Rally and the attack on the Capitol building demonstrates with perfect clarity the planned election coup by far-right forces inside and outside the U.S. government. A pithy attempt at a second Trump impeachment and a 9/11-style commission were both deflected by elected Republican officials who demonstrated their complicity in sedition. As it became apparent that the first 100 days of the Biden administration would be no better than the first 100 days of Obama, the state embarked on a campaign of disinformation by reviving the fraudulent hypothesis that the COVID-19 pandemic originated in the Wuhan Institute of Virology. These bipartisan diversions from endemic problems were further extended by Republican efforts to erode the freedom of assembly through anti-protest laws and the freedom of speech through efforts to suppress the teaching of critical race theory. While culture wars around woke anti-universalism are opposed by the right, their ideological foundations are by and large anti-left, a situation that further reinforces the bipartisan consensus. After a brief demystification of the concept of reductionism, a program for emancipatory policy is proposed with reference to Henri Lefebvre's study of the ideas of Hegel, Marx and Nietzsche. A more stringent approach for a contemporary left program is needed to go beyond the diversitarian end of ideology.

In previous generations, slogans like 'workers of the world unite' or 'black and white, unite and fight' captured the essence of socialist internationalism. The global left needs to develop new practices, theories, concepts and slogans that can build radical solidarities and that have more integrity than those proposed by identity politics. While we cannot expect that the PMC will support us in this fight, we have no choice but to advance the struggle against the billionaire class and against a petty-bourgeois ideology that after having become hegemonic is now in a phase of decadence.

CHAPTER 1

What Does the Professional-Managerial Class Want?

> The spirit of American capital at its peak in the twentieth century can be summed up in the famous statement: 'What's good for General Motors is good for America.' In the twenty-first century, one might say, rather: 'What's good for Goldman Sachs is none of your fucking business.' The spectacle of disintegration no longer bothers much with keeping up appearances.
> MCKENZIE WARK, *The Spectacle of Disintegration*

∴

The terrain of class struggle is not what it used to be. The call by some on the newly revived American left to engage in class war rather than culture war takes material interests to be ideologically and pragmatically self-evident (Burgis 2020c). One should begin at the start, then, and ask what is a class? In Marxist theory, according to Erik Olin Wright, class analysis distinguishes between class structure, defined as polarized class relations between the proletariat and the bourgeoisie, and class formation, through which workers organize in their interest (Wright 1985: 9). Different modes of production in different historical and geographical contexts give rise to different kinds of class formation. The growth of professional and technical occupations in the twentieth century has led many Marxists to question Marx's belief in the tendency towards polarization. More than a century ago, Marx himself identified the existence of a transitional, petty bourgeois and managerial strata embedded in corporations and state administration. Since class structure exists independently of class struggle, specific people, concrete realities and historical contingencies, class interests can be as variable as class organizations. There is therefore no analysis of material reality without conceptual abstraction, which itself is a product of class struggle. The validity of Marxist concepts is not based on their ability to reflect or describe objective reality, but rather to offer a valid explanation of social phenomena and give an orientation to politics.

In Wright's terms, political ideology is a matter of struggle within rather than between classes. There is no automatic and determinate link between class structure and class formation. Class structure shapes and limits but does not determine class struggle and class consciousness (Wright 1985: 28). As Sanders campaign organizer Jonah Furham once said about the Sanders movement: "The biggest problem right now is the idea of class formation: we don't have a well-formed working class that thinks of itself as a class, that has institutions" (Furham in B. O'Connor 2021). Whereas the question of the peasantry has gradually disappeared from class analysis in developed nations, the problem of new middle classes and their contradictory location in relation to the state, political parties and other realms like law, gender or race, remains a problem for leftist praxis, especially as the study of exploitation is replaced by concerns with 'patriarchal' and 'white supremacist' oppression. One problem for American sociology is the transformation of the middle class from an empirical fact into a scientific concept. It could very well be the case, Wright argues, that variations in petty bourgeois political identification – for example, identification with Hillary Clinton rather than Bernie Sanders – is due to "non-class" structures like race or gender. In any class formation, structural differences and social psychology may be more significant than class mechanisms. Regardless, for Marxist analysis, class structure, which is defined by the capitalist mode and relations of production, defines the organizational dynamics of class consciousness and class struggle, which alone are able to transform class structure. The basic determinant of class antagonism is exploitation, not inequality, oppression or domination. Wright gives the example of domineering parents who have the same class interests as their children. One can also imagine that a racist or sexist worker can have the same class interests as his or her co-workers.

Unlike class exploitation, there is nothing about gender oppression that gives it more structural importance than any other form of oppression. Whereas Marxism seeks the elimination of class society and the destruction of bourgeois rule, feminism cannot be defined as the elimination of gender difference and the destruction of men. While the relations between national, religious, ethnic and gender groups are only arbitrarily conflictual, and need not be, class relations of exploitation are inherently conflictual. That said, reality is inherently contradictory and social difference is fundamental, which makes it such that conflict and alienation are inherent to the world. The point is not only to change reality but to understand it. Contemporary life is confusing because class is only one of the elements of social reality. However, Marxist materialism views capitalist class relations as the basis of historical analysis. A social theory that gives equal explanatory value to all forms of oppression may be considered radical democratic or intersectional but it cannot be considered socialist.

Technically speaking, the petty bourgeoisie, which has also been described as the new petty bourgeoisie, the non-bourgeois middle class and the professional-managerial class, is not a class. Its members are either part of the working class, defined as those who do not own the means of production, or they are part of the executive class, whose wealth and occupation allows them to count among the bourgeoisie. The petty bourgeoisie is therefore divided in terms of class structure and class identification. Individual ownership of the means of production, as is the case with skilled artisans, farmers and small business owners, defines the traditional petty bourgeoisie. Although autonomy is a horizon of socialist democracy, Romantic definitions of independent production are somewhat irrelevant to the politics of collective ownership and socialized production. So is the articulation of proletarian politics with the notion of skilled labor. This contradicts the postulate of André Gorz that the purpose of socialism, mostly due to automation, is for "neo-proletarian" workers to simply free themselves from work and therefore from the traditional movements and organizations of the working class (Gorz 1982: 66–7). Unproductive workers, like artists, intellectuals, teachers, investors, designers, engineers, managers and white-collar workers, have also been considered part of the petty bourgeoisie. Their control of cultural and symbolic capital gives them a privileged role in the reproduction of class relations. Such members of the petty bourgeoisie occupy a contradictory class location. A graduate student, for example, can be considered to be part of both the working class and the petty bourgeoisie, as could an intern working in a high-profile law firm.

One of the contradictions of complex post-Fordist societies, as will be discussed in relation to the theory of the professional-managerial class, is that it is no longer evident that the working class is the class that is the most antagonistic to the bourgeoisie and to capitalism more generally (Wright 1985: 89). For example, according to Alvin Gouldner, the rise of bureaucracy, which is a product of class struggle, has benefitted the petty bourgeoisie rather than the proletariat (Gouldner). Issues like race and gender could also be used to assess the social distribution of assets. However, as Walter Benn Michaels and Adolph Reed have argued, redistribution along race and gender lines can take place without affecting class inequality (Michaels & Reed). Class analysis, Wright argues, benefits from not being extended beyond production and property relations. While it is a common complaint nowadays that Marxian class analysis is class reductionist or class essentialist, the point of socialist politics is not to suggest that class is the only or most important social phenomenon, but rather that it best explains the conditions of social life in capitalist society.

Moreover, while identity, lifestyle, education, career choices and income levels affect people in various ways, a Marxist critique provides a class analysis of these phenomena as well (Wright 2015: 144).

Given that class consciousness in the U.S. is below 16 percent, the petty bourgeois cadres inside and outside government are not likely to use class analysis to understand and explain social phenomena. The growing precarization of the middle and working class is hardly a concern of the plutocratic class whose financial strength defines political objectives. The politicians and union executives who do their bidding have the potential to join the wealthy ten percent. As the ranks of the professional middle-class salariat dwindle and those of the precariously employed, unemployed and underemployed swell, the problems of race and gender oppression are weaponized by the state and by corporations against the working class. In the following, I address the development of neoliberalism in U.S. politics, from the New Deal through to the New Democrats, as a process that has been accompanied by the de-ideologization of the professional-managerial class, which has become an increasingly "mediocratic" instrument of political power. The limits of left populism as an alternative to the technocracy is linked to what the journalist Chris Hedges refers to as the "death of the liberal class" and the resurgence of fascist ideology (Hedges). Or as Chris Maisano suggests, the rise of populism in politics is a "morbid symptom" of the disorganization of the working class (Maisano 2019).

1 From the New Deal to the New Democrats

In the aftermath of the Second World War, a new economy was created based on corporate taxation, government deficits, public spending and consumer demand through higher wages. This led to the so-called 'golden age' of postwar prosperity that lasted through to the 1970s. From 1933 to 1945, the Democratic administration of Franklin D. Roosevelt built a New Deal coalition that included labor unions, farmers, rural white Southerners, intellectuals and various religious and minority groups. The first New Deal mitigated the effects of the economic depression through the establishment of unemployment agencies, minimum wage laws, job creation programs and public works initiatives that gave federal authorities jurisdiction over infrastructure projects. Mortgage relief was provided to millions of people and higher wages were secured through industrial and pro-union legislation. The Glass-Steagall Act cracked down on speculation by separating commercial and investment banks. In 1934, Roosevelt reduced military spending by $1 billion and expanded the New Deal by establishing a program of Social Security assistance for the elderly, the poor and the disabled. His 'Second Bill of Rights' of 1944 made provisions for the right to a job and a living wage, decent housing and health care. Over two terms, the New Deal created 15 million government jobs. Although it is sometimes considered to have been created for the benefit of whites, the New Deal was overwhelmingly supported by blacks and immigrants. It afforded the Democratic Party control of Congress until 1980. The view that New Dealers colluded with Southern racists ignores the fact that three out of every four domestic and agricultural worker who was excluded from Social Security was white. Other mostly white work sectors were also excluded. Blacks who worked in other areas were covered and millions of blacks benefited from various aspects of the New Deal, which was disproportionately beneficial to blacks when compared to the rest of American society. As left radicalism waned in the postwar period, the association of labor politics with the Democratic Party worked to curtail strike activity. Strikes were suppressed by the 1947 Taft-Hartley Act, which altered the New Deal's National Labor Relations Act and placed restrictions on union rights, including solidarity strikes. Although Harry Truman failed to repeal Taft-Hartley, his Fair Deal policy maintained the ideals of the New Deal.

At the close of the Second World War, the largest wave of sit-down strikes in U.S. history led to the Cold War red scare. Eugene McCarthy's anti-communism witch hunts lasted from 1947 to 1953, the same time period in which leaders of the Communist Party were imprisoned and deported. After the 1949–50 expulsion of communist unions, the Congress of Industrial Organizations merged with the American Federation of Labor. Since that time, the employment gap between blacks and whites has progressively worsened. Because the Southern states had few unions, Dixiecrats were able to uphold Jim Crow segregation and class exploitation. Despite the fact that the AFL was hostile to civil rights for blacks, the cause of racial justice was nevertheless supported by the majority of workers. The combination of union activity as well as government policy led in the postwar decades to the gradual desegregation of American life. Presidents Dwight Eisenhower and Truman routinely broke strikes throughout the 1940s. The same Democrat who dropped atomic bombs on Hiroshima and Nagasaki, and who created the policy of Soviet containment through the $12 billion Marshall Plan for European recovery, later inveighed against the military-industrial complex. Corporate power gradually won out against organized labor. In 1948, Truman desegregated the military and in 1954 the landmark Supreme Court ruling on Brown v. Board of Education desegregated schools and made the policy framework of 'separate but equal' unconstitutional. Well before the Civil Rights struggles of the 1960s, the strategy of the state was to use liberal reforms against radical notions of black liberation. Truman's passing of the 1949 Housing Act and the Highway Act of 1956 initiated a process of urban renewal that not only led to patterns of racial segregation but also to class stratification through suburbanization. The relocation of manufacturing to suburbs also contributed to black unemployment and deunionization. Regardless, as much as one third of the labor force remained unionized.

The lynching of Emmett Till in 1955 launched the Civil Rights movement, which was in essence a workers' movement, leading to the 1955 Montgomery Bus Boycott and the leadership of Martin Luther King Jr. in the struggle for racial and social equality. The first Civil Rights bill of 1957 protected voting rights against physical assaults. The Civil Rights movement emerged largely as a result of the support of socialist organizations and the growth of class consciousness among the black steel workers of Alabama. As wages fell in the steel and auto industry, as well as in textiles and meatpacking, manufacturing moved to rural and suburban regions. Investment looked instead towards financial speculation. Black membership in the United Auto Workers and other CIO trade unions caused the ruling class to do two things: on the one hand, block the Civil Rights movement by criminalizing its leaders – with King targeted by the FBI – and on the other, by granting concessions through Civil Rights legislation that could justify American imperialism as a harbinger of freedom and democracy.

By the time that John F. Kennedy became president, the New Deal coalition of labor unions and minorities was challenged by Cold War conservatives who campaigned on tax cuts, small government and inner-city policing. The Democratic administration of Lyndon Johnson pursued government intervention through the Economic Opportunity Act of 1965 and Great Society programs like food stamps, Head Start child and family support, work study, the Job Corps, Medicare and Medicaid. Significant Civil Rights legislation was passed in 1964 and 1965, largely through the efforts of the Student Nonviolent Coordinating Committee (SNCC), the National Association for the Advancement of Colored People (NAACP), the National Urban League (NUL) and African-American churches. The means of pressure that were used included marches, protests, civil disobedience, sit-ins, urban riots, voter registration drives and freedom rides on interstate buses. Much of this effort was maintained in the face of racist backlash, church bombings and murders, including the 1963 assassination of Civil Rights activist Medgar Evers by Byron De La Beckwith, an opponent of integration who was twice acquitted by all-white juries.

The 1963 March on Washington occurred at a time when the division between race issues and class issues was central to the question of political leadership. If the outcome was that Johnson would pass both Civil Rights legislation and inaugurate the War on Poverty through a jobs program, the goal of government was nevertheless to distinguish between the two in the interest of American capitalism. Although the March has come to be seen as an MLK event, it was led by people like A. Philip Randolph and Bayard Rustin, and groups like the Negro American Labor Council, whose social democratic politics and Civil Rights unionism called for government intervention in job creation, job training, union wages, workplace democracy, infrastructure spending and universal health care. This approach contrasted with the Kennedy and Johnson administrations' preference for tax cuts and the incentivization of labor through Community Action Agencies and Model Cities, which attacked job discrimination but ignored the structural unemployment that was caused by the automation that in the 60s destroyed tens of millions of jobs. The ideological solution to the race and class issue was to emphasize the problem of institutional racism rather than institutional capitalism.

The Civil Rights Act of 1964 dismantled Jim Crow segregation in government, public accommodations, employment practices, voting and education. The immediate outcome of the law was the increase of black votes in some counties from below 10 percent up to 60 and 70 percent. The Voting Rights Act of 1965 eliminated discriminatory barriers to political participation, with the number of blacks in government posts increasing from 1500 in 1970 to 8900 by the late 1990s, and the number of black members in Congress from nine in 1969 to 43 in 2013. A 1967 law legalized interracial marriage and a 1978 law defended Indigenous cultural and religious freedoms against the practices of boarding schools. However, all was not well with Civil Rights legislation as Southern Republicans showed more support for the Civil Rights bills than did Southern Democrats. The 1965 Immigration Act replaced race-based discrimination with measures designed to benefit the economy, privileging middle and upper-class immigrants while also making room for low-paying jobs. The Civil Rights laws of the 60s, in other words, were weighted in the interest of American capitalism.

In contrast to today's neoliberal racialists, the Civil Right leaders of the 1960s were closely tied to the labor movement. They fought against poverty, calling for full employment, a guaranteed living wage, housing and health care. Not everything was bad news under Johnson. His Economic Opportunity Act of 1964 and War on Poverty initiative helped to reduce black poverty by 10 percent in only three years and the overall poverty rate by 12 percent. The corporate counter-offensive against social democracy and New Deal interventionism came from LBJ's labor minister, Daniel Patrick Moynihan, whose 1965 report on *The Negro Family* took a conservative approach to the problem of black poverty and unemployment, blaming the matriarchal structure of the black family, racist discrimination and institutional racism rather than the political economy. Stoking fears of anti-white hatred and black criminality, the Moynihan report recommended community programs to solve America's problem of racial poverty. It elucidated the Johnson administration's approach to Civil Rights, which was to facilitate the integration of black Americans in the capitalist attack on socialism, combining group rights with the liberal ideology of individual and property rights. This strategy led to the adoption of policies on multiculturalism by U.S. corporations.

Although the liberal strategy of black, and later, gender capitalism has largely won out, the immediate result was a rift within black politics, with an older generation of black internationalist intellectuals like Richard Wright, Ralph Ellison, James Baldwin, Paul Robeson, Malcolm X, Huey Newton and Bobby Seale creating links with anti-colonial movements abroad. Under pressure from the FBI and J. Edgar Hoover's COINTELPRO, and with the decline of the Civil Rights movement, the Black Power movement emerged in the midst of some of the most momentous riots in American history in Philadelphia and Rochester (1964), Watts (1965), Cleveland and Chicago (1966), Newark and Detroit (1967). Caused by deindustrialization, job losses, unemployment, poverty, malnutrition and housing discrimination, the riots were quelled by an increase in policing and incarceration. The empowerment of black leaders and activists in several cities averted working-class politics in favor of bourgeois class politics. As Touré Reed puts it:

> the Black Power movement ultimately represented a kind of petit bourgeois ethnic-group clientelist politics, which ... identified ethnic group culture as the engine of economic progress and ignored the implications of the transformation of the US economy for African Americans.
> REED 2020a: 125

Making ethnicity the basis of politics in some ways complemented the Johnson administration's attitude towards the distinctiveness of black poverty. Whatever the differences, cultural nationalism, as Rustin had forewarned, would ultimately serve the interests of the aspiring black managerial class.

With his Poor People's Campaign, King advocated a guaranteed income and a living wage. He broke with the Johnson administration, which had prioritized the war in Vietnam over the War on Poverty. His assassination, which happened when he had gone to Memphis in 1968 to organize for better conditions for 13,000 striking black sanitation workers, led to riots in more than 100 cities. This is as much a testament to working-class resistance as it is to the effectiveness of the fascist methods that were used at that time. Under Hoover, the FBI was likely connected to the assassinations of John F. Kennedy in 1963,

Malcolm X in 1965, Martin Luther King and Robert Kennedy in 1968. The riots broke down the increasingly socialist Civil Rights movement and caused it to be replaced with affirmative action and other policies that benefitted the black entrepreneurial class. White and black workers were left out in the cold after budget cuts and plant closures. Capitalist exploitation was replaced with institutional racism as the explanation for inequality and disparity.

The main document on this era is the Kerner Commission that was produced in March 1968 as a government paper on the riots. The 426 page *Report of the Advisory Commission on Civil Disorders*, produced in consultation with politicians, corporate representatives, trade union representatives and Civil Rights organizations, acknowledged that economic problems and class inequality had caused the riots, but that social inequality was not ultimately due to market relations, the profit system, deindustrialization and stagflation, but to racism, police brutality, substandard education and living conditions in the urban ghetto, which was fueled by predatory lending and the practice of red lining that was outlawed by the 1968 Fair Housing Act. The Kerner report argued that if the U.S. was not to move in the direction of two separate societies – a notion that was readily discounted by the exponential growth of interracial marriages – a policy framework against 'white racism' and 'institutional racism' would need to be put in place. The report thereby whitewashed capitalist class interests, from Indochina to the local bank.

The corporate policy framework was further consolidated by the Richard Nixon administration's bipartisan program for a now overtly named 'black capitalism' through the uses of Affirmative Action policies designed to create a black middle class and access to upper income levels. The election of black mayors in dozens of 'chocolate cities,' who campaigned as defenders of minorities and who were supported by corporate philanthropists like the Ford Foundation, allowed the Democrats to replace social reform with the honorifics of a nascent interest-group and identity politics. The politics of the era were confused by a reversal of roles, with the Democratic Party enhancing its relationship with Wall Street and the GOP passing the last wave of entitlement policies, economic regulations and anti-poverty measures like the Family Assistance Plan. Nixon appealed to white workers in the South and the Democrats appealed to blacks, Hispanics, Latinos and immigrants. The federal government increasingly emphasized the importance of policing, linking crime with race riots and launching the War on Drugs. Within the dominant tendencies of American capitalism, the Black Freedom Movement inadvertently contributed to the depoliticization of black politics. Whereas the difference between socialism and liberalism was obvious to the Civil Rights generation, Black Power nationalism emphasized the colonial domination of a generic black community and thereby separated radicalism from political economy. The most immediate result was the ethnic diversification of the ruling class. The benefits of this limited 'black faces in high places' transfer of power was soon curtailed by the federal government's expansion of the carceral state as a means to manage class inequality. The War on Drugs signaled the end of the New Deal coalition and the cooptation of black political leaders through the neoliberal policies of Richard Nixon, Jimmy Carter and Ronald Reagan.

At the time of the last major strike wave in the U.S., from 1969 to 1974, American capitalism had reached the end of the postwar boom, losing its economic advantage to Germany and Japan, and forcing Nixon to finance the economic crisis through social spending on employment and job training programs. This prompted a shift to neoliberal policy, which was spearheaded by the rise of corporate lobbyists and think tanks like the Heritage Foundation and the CATO Institute. Neoliberals called on government to abandon the gold standard and protectionism by deregulating markets, deunionizing labor, offshoring factory production, dismantling welfare, facilitating mergers, lowering taxes and deflating the money supply. After the recession of the mid-1970s, the Democrats under Jimmy Carter led the attack on labor, deregulating industries like transportation and facilitating the financialization of markets. Carter intensified labor market competition, driving down wages and cutting benefits. As the unions buckled under neoliberal directives, the culture of labor all but vanished. According to Sam Gindin, the thrust of globalization was offset by encouraging workers to substitute internationalist class consciousness with individual and family-size solutions: tax cuts to increase consumer spending, working long hours and more than one job, student labor and student loans, household debt, temp work and belt-tightening measures (Gindin). As social programs were eroded and the standard of living declined, workers abandoned the culture of solidarity and began to resent immigrant workers, welfare recipients as well as affirmative action programs for minorities. Identity politics shifted social needs allocations to identitarian, consumer and lifestyle issues that emphasized disparity and difference rather than collective efforts, leaving the majority of the poorest sections of identity groups beyond the remotest potential of assistance by postmodern culture warriors. The universality that was the premise of progressive government intervention – international diplomacy, single-payer health care, free education, full employment, pay equity, living wages, public transit, environmental and consumer protections, immigration rights, reproductive rights, housing rights, child care, elder care and pensions – became a dirty word, reviled and interrogated as an instrument of oppression rather than social equality.

Despite a Democratic majority in Congress and the Senate, the Carter administration's austerity and deregulation agenda strengthened business with payroll taxes and high inflation rates, which provoked another recession. With the Democrats having abandoned the working class, the Republicans under Reagan championed economic growth through trickle-down economics, which resulted in the upward redistribution of wealth through tax cuts for the rich and cuts in federal spending on education, infrastructure and industrial productivity. Reagan encouraged overseas investment and the offshoring of production. He further liberalized financial institutions at home and imposed structural adjustment policies abroad. As wages declined, the result was a predictable increase in poverty, class inequality, unemployment and homelessness. Adding insult to injury, Reagan's War on Welfare created stereotypes of undeserving welfare moms while simultaneously gutting entitlement programs. After his first term, Reagan cut $23 billion in revenue and benefits to low-income families and transferred $35 billion to high-income groups, causing the ranks of the homeless to rise by 1.2 million. Reaganomics drastically reduced spending on Medicaid, food stamps, environmental protection and public housing. Black bureaucrats participated in attacks on low-income housing, rent-intensifying redevelopment and the kind of heritage tourism that propped up a Disneyfied notion of family and community values. Manufacturing wealth was replaced by high tech and banking.

The erosion of urban life gave rise to a fashionable Reagan Noir aesthetic, with television crime shows and films reflecting the bipartisan support for mandatory minimums and tough on crime campaigns that adversely affected black communities. The growth of inequality among blacks was accompanied by the problems of homelessness and attacks on public services. In the years 1980 to 1984, the Republicans won the support of an embattled working class by growing deficits alongside a ballooning military budget and Star Wars trade show extravaganzas. Despite the *détente* with the Soviet bloc, Reagan Noir also spread on a global level as the neocolonial management of global labor markets diverted unemployed working-class youth towards careers in the military. In the first major imperialist conflict since the Vietnam War, George H.W. Bush invaded Iraq in what Saddam Hussein prophesied as the "mother of all battles." Bush's CIA paranoia brought America to perceive terrorism everywhere and in everything, going so far as to manufacture threats when they were lacking.

At the 1983 March on Washington, black leaders like Jesse Jackson and Loretta Scott King had lost sight of what was still imaginable to King. A rainbow coalition was devised to merge the remnants of labor with race, gender and student politics. Nothing came of it. The race and class situation certainly did not improve under the free trade policies of Bill Clinton, who raised taxes and reduced the deficit so as to tackle the Bush recession. Under Clinton, the Democrats pursued a neoconservative agenda of small government and personal responsibility. In keeping with the ideology of individual self-interest, he promoted free enterprise against social democratic alternatives. Pledging to "end welfare as we know it," Clinton brought an end to the New Deal era. Federal safety nets were replaced by block grants, work requirements and lifetime limits on social assistance. He cut federal funding for public housing by more than half. After two terms, the economy grew, but not without the financial deregulation brought on by the repeal of the Glass-Steagall Act. Credit card debt, student loan debt, mortgage debt, as well as asset bubbles in high tech, real estate and money markets boomed as speculation falsified demand. Free trade and the deregulation of financial markets, in part through the repeal of the Glass-Steagall Act, contributed to driving up stock price as well as economic inequality. China replaced Japan as the new Asian tiger, bankrolling the U.S. deficit and the dollar in exchange for the consumption of its low-wage products. Declaring the era of big government to be over, Clinton satisfied the privatization whims of the military and the health care, pharmaceutical and food safety industries. Clinton thus initiated much of the militarism and banking recklessness that George W. Bush would toy around with before handing these problems over to Obama.

Other than his continuation of Reagan's war on the poor with his welfare-to-work programs, one of Clinton's worst policy portfolios was the justice system. In 1987, McClesky v. Kemp had made claims against racism in mass incarceration off-limits as an impediment to the Fourth Amendment. In 1994, Clinton stole the 'tough on crime' platform from the Republicans by worsening conditions in the criminal justice system, escalating bipartisan policies like the War on Drugs, increasing the number of federal capital offenses and upholding racially discriminatory sentences for drug possession. Discriminatory and unconstitutional stop and frisk practices resulted in blacks being 14 times more likely to be searched than whites. The arrest of poor blacks for negligible violations like saggy pants created revenue for cash-strapped municipalities like Ferguson. Meanwhile, Texas governor George W. Bush was opening a new prison every week. Whatever benefits came from Clinton's Race Initiative of 1997–98, it did nothing to alleviate incarceration rates. Similarly, in foreign policy, Clinton spearheaded the NATO bombing of Serbia in 1999, the first post-Cold War intervention in the interest of American and European imperialism, to be followed by the wars in Afghanistan, Iraq, Libya and Syria.

Acquiescing to the right on every conceivable issue, including NAFTA, the Democrats did not prevent the Republicans from taking over Congress. Its evangelical and conservative base made a meal of the Lewinsky affair. Bush gave lavish tax cuts to the wealthy and sat on his hands as New Orleans reeled from the devastation wrought by Hurricane Katrina. Some government spending on entitlements and immigration reform accompanied military Keynesianism, which did little to stem the offshoring of manufacturing jobs to China and elsewhere, dramatically inflating the deficit. Between 2001 and 2012, about 50,000 manufacturing jobs left the U.S. every month. Although Bush increased federal spending on education, he closed good schools. His tax cuts and asset bubbles in subprime mortgages led to the collapse of the banking system.

By the time Barack Obama was elected, the 'hard hats' that Nixon and Reagan had won over, according to Perry Anderson, were replaced by a new demographic, with twice as many whites with college education and twice as many non-whites as well as many women voters joining the electorate (Anderson 2013). The careers of Bill and Hillary Clinton were evidence that the hip baby boom generation had become the new conformists. In 2008, poor whites voted for McCain and wealthy whites voted for Obama. Since Obama was cooler than Hillary, American voters vindicated four decades of black capitalism and neoliberal policy without even knowing it. It felt good and Obama, as Anderson suggests, presented the possibility of a black Camelot. Unfortunately, the romance was ruined by the Lancelot of tax cuts for the rich, the Guinevere of bank bailouts, the Morgan le Faye of privatization and the Mordred of militarism. Obama neglected to prosecute Bush's torturers and close Guantánamo Bay. He pursued Bush's dirty wars in the Middle East, expanding the theater of operations to Syria, Libya and Yemen. His best soldiers killed a defenseless Osama bin Laden, no doubt to prevent the former U.S. ally from further embarrassing anyone at the Pentagon. He let a raft of banksters make off like bandits without so much as a reprimand. After some stimulus spending to weather the recession, much of it bailout money for banks and corporations, Obama went on to charterize schools in a race to the bottom for public education. Although Obama is credited for the Affordable Care Act, even this small achievement was consistent with the neoconservative wish list and kept single-payer at bay. For someone seemingly concerned with health care, his advice to the people of Flint, Michigan, that their poisoned water is fine was typical of the 'post-representational' logic of neoliberal governance. Tuned in to social media, Obama introduced spying on citizens as a matter of technological determinism. The new machines also helped him oversee the largest upward transfer of wealth in American history. His success with the wealthy was not disrupted by Occupy Wall Street, which was displaced by Black Lives Matter, MeToo and a host of campaigns that were then attacked by alt-right trolls as the grievance politics of cultural Marxists. The social media and mass media fanfare created perfect conditions for the Democrats to avoid any self-criticism.

Against this, Donald Trump revived the tradition of anti-communist red-baiting, xenophobia and chauvinism, dumping respectability along with pretenses to democracy. Trump's excesses could easily have allowed the Democrats to carry on with the fiction that they are a progressive party. Instead, they harped on Russiagate for three years until the 2019 Mueller Report made Trump seem honest in comparison. When the British police kidnapped Julian Assange from the Ecuadorian embassy and threw him into a dungeon to await rendition to the U.S., the so-called liberal press exhibited the same colors as brand Obama: nominally progressive. In 2008 the Democratic Party had considerably more support than the Republicans. Obama became the first black president in American history. While this represents an important victory in the struggle against discrimination, over the course of two terms, Obama's neoliberal politics made the majority of African Americans worse off than they were before his presidency. By 2016, support for the Democrats declined to the same low level as support for the GOP. Clinton and Trump tag-teamed in defense of Wall Street, the fossil fuel industry, the health insurance industry, the school-to-prison pipeline, the military-industrial complex and anti-socialism.

Over several decades, the New Democrats did as little as possible to improve the lives of the majority of Americans. Since the 1970s, every administration, Republican and Democrat, has catered to the policy proposals of conservative think tanks and moneyed interests. American unions now represent less than 10 percent of the work force, with less than 6 percent of labor unionization in the private sector – down from approximately 35 percent in 1945. One of the jobs with an increasingly high suicide rate is doctors and nurses, who are caught in a system that no longer allows them to do the work they were trained to perform. The struggle for emancipation in the U.S. is presented as a conflict between progressive and reactionary versions of neoliberal capitalism. The only thing that cuts across this neoliberal consensus are social issues and identity politics. Identity struggles and class struggles, however, are not different versions of the same struggle. Obama's election victory was a momentous historical event. Yet the truth of that event began to crumble the day after his inauguration. When Obama named his cabinet ministers it was obvious that he would not be the candidate of change after all. One would think that his time in office should be enough to have raised some skepticism about the adaptability of identity politics to the worst forms of military imperialism and economic re-feudalization. Be that as it may, Obama campaigned as a post-racial candidate. He never promised a more socialist union. Regardless, it has yet to dawn on millions of Americans how it is that through neoliberal ideology, identity melts into air.

According to Tavis Smiley and Cornel West, it would have been nice to hear Obama use the words 'poor' and 'poverty' once in a while, rather than sound-bite politics that deny reality (Smiley & West 2012: 18). Poverty, they argue, does not discriminate. But the middle class that Obama championed does, especially as the prospect of a comfortable life has been outpaced by a permanent catastrophe that has gradually decimated the middle class. Since the 1970s, they argue, the poor have been blamed for their circumstances. The refusal to implement another New Deal rather than promote the celebrity lifestyles of Kim Kardashian or Sean Combs led to a situation where the top 1 percent of U.S. citizens control about as much wealth as the bottom 50 percent. When Obama came to power, 37 million Americans were living in poverty and 150 million were close to poverty. Today, four fifths of Americans live paycheck to paycheck and one fifth is food insecure. Since Carter, the New Democrats have sat idly by as Hispanic families lost 66 percent of their wealth and African Americans lost 53 percent of theirs. The Obama administration oversaw increases in unemployment, underfunded public schools, home foreclosures, female poverty, malnourishment and homelessness among children. Chains like Target, Costco, Walmart and Family Dollar now serve the poor, Smiley and West remark, while chains like Goldman Sachs, JP Morgan Chase, Citigroup and Bank of America serve the super-rich (Smiley & West 2012: 298). In domestic policy, as in foreign policy, the New Democrat solution to poverty is growing the market in prisons and policing. Under the Biden administration, and despite the fact that the main domestic threat in the U.S. comes from right-wing extremists, the military began to train soldiers to include anarchists and socialists in the same 'political terrorist' category as neo-Nazis.

2   A Stratum without an Ideology

Given the class difference between the artists, intellectuals, politicians and professionals who could potentially lead society in a struggle against establishment forces, and the donor class that funds political campaigns and think tanks, one wonders why so little has been accomplished since the mid-to-late 1990s, when the anti-globalization movement had succeeded in discrediting the neoliberal agenda. The answer to this question has something to do with the contradictory class location of the petty bourgeoisie. In 1977, Barbara and John Ehrenreich provided a useful definition and analysis of the "professional-managerial class," or PMC, that is still used today on the American left. It is worth revisiting their classic essay in order to assess what has changed over time.

"The Professional-Managerial Class" is written from the point of view of the sixties generation of radicals who understood that the postwar left, many of them red diaper babies, was comprised to a great extent of people who were part of and identified as middle-class. In the U.S., the Ehrenreichs argue, the left is middle-class and is not a section of the working class. Even if in orthodox terms this represents a form of revisionism, the PMC can and must be studied as a class in its own right since traditional Marxism lacks the tools to understand it. Without the support of the working class, however, the most that the progressive PMC could ever achieve are marginal reforms. From the outset, then, the PMC is understood, and understands itself, as a non-revolutionary class. Whereas the PMC may express solidarity with the working class, its disposition, as Pierre Bourdieu would say, its *habitus*, is middle-class. Contrary to what Marxists had anticipated, modernization did not cause the petty bourgeoisie to disappear. Instead, a 'salaried mass' of 'white collar' workers, as Siegfried Kracauer and C. Wright Mills had defined it, emerged alongside the industrial proletariat (Kracauer; Mills). By the 1960s, this group that was neither bourgeoisie nor proletariat became necessary for the social reproduction of capitalist class relations, in particular, through occupations in the health and legal sectors, education, the media and the arts, research and engineering, government, management, sales and marketing. In contrast to Nicos Poulantzas, who considered the PMC in orthodox terms as non-productive workers, the Ehrenreichs defined the PMC as a distinct class "because it exists in an objectively antagonistic relationship" to the working class (Barabara & John Ehrenreich 1979: 9). In other words, the advanced stage of monopoly capitalism had created this 'new' and variegated middle class that shared a common position of non-ownership of the means of production and a common set of social and cultural habits, beliefs and lifestyles. Whereas 70 percent of the population is working class, and ten percent is bourgeois, about 20 percent is PMC. In the late 1970s, the American PMC consisted of approximately 50 million workers whose social role was to oversee the reproduction of capitalist class relations and culture.

Although antagonistic to the working class, the PMC shares with it a structural antagonism to the capitalist class. Since the PMC must also sell its (salaried, professional) labor, it understands the contradictions that are inherent in the division of labor. Its social relation to workers, the Ehrenreichs say, mixes contempt with paternalism. If the working class is not to revolt against it, it must reform capitalism in the interest of the relative class of power of the PMC itself. Its most direct means of doing so is the creation and expansion of professional and managerial occupations, organizations and institutions.

The PMC spearheaded the bourgeois reform movement of the early twentieth century through the establishment of settlement houses, welfare, social work, labor statistics, social safety, social housing, home economics, city planning and recreation. It also rationalized the traditional business and trade prerogatives of the bourgeoisie. Inciting philanthropy and social investment, the professionals in the reform movement helped to stave off the threat of revolution and the method of establishing social harmony through the heavy-handed employment of Pinkerton guards. In order to act as the mediators of social conflict, the PMC had to struggle against the bourgeoisie. The autonomy that it gained through education, and the value of its professional advice, could at any time be undermined by capitalist truculence. The task of the PMC has therefore been to save capitalism from itself.

Through the Second World War, the growth of government and the triumph of corporate ideology expanded the ranks of the technocratic PMC and its liberal ideology. Although the top echelons of salaried professionals could potentially join the establishment ruling class, its boards of trustees and country clubs, the majority staked their social power on professional independence and public service, which is the basis of the PMC's culture and means of social reproduction. Anxiety about class reproduction makes the constant revision of social mores one of the preoccupations of the middle-class lifestyle. From second wave feminism and the sexual revolution through various New Left agendas like ecology and the anti-war movement, the PMC was the arbiter of social change. The student radicalism of the sixties is to date its most progressive expression. From 1964 to 1969, Students for a Democratic Society (SDS) articulated the vision of a better world and challenged the capitalists who stood in their way. While also showing contempt for the traditional values of the working class, the countercultural New Left pushed 'the system' about as far as the rest of the PMC was willing to allow it. Pushing back from other side, the university was used to advance militarism and Cold War ideology. In black neighborhoods, the minority PMC switched from Black Liberation and community control to jobs in government and the academy.

The rejection of sixties rebellion enlisted all of the professional help the PMC could muster, from college administration and urban studies to psychiatry and entertainment. If the struggle was to continue, it meant either getting radicals into the professions or creating a new international. The former meant demystifying the conceits of autonomy and politicizing everything, a tactic that capitalism was more than comfortable with. The latter meant insisting on the primacy of class struggle and building vanguard organizations. As this occurred in the late 60s and early 70s, the participatory democracy of old and the lifestyle activism of separatist identity movements were denounced as petty-bourgeois decadence. For the Ehrenreichs, the communist movement that emerged from the ashes of SDS made the mistake of returning to pre-PMC orthodoxy. Rejecting all cultural and intellectual pursuits as just so much 'superstructural' hogwash, it lost sight of entrenched contradictions.

While one might view the Ehrenreichs' theory of the rise and decline of the New Left as itself a PMC view of radicalism, the least one can say is that they never abandoned the centrality of class struggle. The success of their essay led to at least two revisions on their part. In "The Professional-Managerial Class Revisited," Barbara Ehrenreich lamented the fact that by the 1990s, many former Trotskyists had become neoconservatives (Ehrenreich 1990: 185). By the 1990s, feminist radicals had settled for careers. Sympathy for the poor or for radicalism became contemptible. Radical politics was now defined as attentiveness to social and cultural trends. The neocons, who were well versed in New Left ideology critique, turned radicals in the professions against themselves by stereotyping them as an out of touch, affluent and liberal elite. The same PMC that generated the New Left in the 1960s, she wrote, generated the yuppies of the 1980s. Expertise was now marketed for fame and fortune on talk shows and for the sake of admission to a new class of intellectuals who were far removed from labor struggles. With social activism defined in non-class terms, class consciousness was substituted for moral conscience or Oprah-style 'awareness.'

Some three decades after their seminal essay, the Ehrenreichs wrote "Death of a Yuppie Dream," the first obituary of the PMC (Barbara & John Ehrenreich 2013). As they had previously warned, they did not imply with this the irrelevance of the PMC to social theory. What the essay detailed, instead, was the PMC's turn away from public issues and its formerly paternalistic if not dissenting role towards the majority of the population. Abandoning the language of class altogether, the PMC created conditions leading to its own decline. The neoliberal class offensive led by Pinochet, Thatcher and Reagan attacked welfare in favor of free enterprise, free trade, deunionization, deregulation and privatization, a process facilitated by tech innovation and overseen by salaried professionals working for unelected and unaccountable organizations like the Word Trade Organization, the International Monetary Fund and the World Bank. With cuts to professional sectors like public services, health and education, liberal professions began to be managed like for-profit businesses and corporations, creating an exodus of the conscientious into the non-profit sector. Journalism was downgraded by corporate consolidation and the creative class at large was pressured by low pay, long hours and the short-term employment schemes of temp agencies and the gig economy. The PMC lifestyle was now characterized by expensive degrees, lowered expectations and diminishing returns. While consumer prices increased 115 percent between 1986 and 2013, the cost of college education increased 498 percent (Barbara & John Ehrenreich 2013: 9). After 2000, professionalism began to suffer from precarization. Like the working class, the services of the PMC were replaced by cheaper foreign labor. With a new global division of labor created for professional services, the PMC was deregulated, flexibilized and outsourced. Debt leveraging led student debt to outpace mortgage debt and credit card debt. Despite the fact, only 35 percent of graduates were finding full-time employment in their field of work. There are material reasons why the PMC prefers to talk more about identity than class. Fearful of being downgraded into the low-paid workforce, the PMC dropped civic virtue for the sake of a paycheck. This is how professionalism was politicized in the neoliberal era, dragging down the oppositional spirit of the PMC left as well as its dedication to ethical norms and standards.

Two contemporary versions of social decadence define the technocratic PMC in the orbit of the New Democrats: mediocracy and virtue hoarding. Although Obama's post-race rhetoric has done a great deal to champion meritocracy, the best description of Obama's technocratic ideology, as with Clinton before him, is what Alain Deneault describes as "mediocracy" (Deneault). The main skill of a mediocrat is the rejection of the best ideas, when the circumstances demand it, in order to secure power and influence. Mediocrats are neither stupid nor lazy. What characterizes them is their willingness to follow expectations, and in Obama's case those were the standards of the neoliberal technocracy and the corporate class. Their indifference to their own banality creates the kind of subjectivity that does not question a society's ideological foundations and focuses instead on personal advancement. Deneault gives as examples professors who judge student papers to be too theoretical, economists who insist on economic growth and politicians who tell voters that they must obey Wall Street dictates. Their best skill is the ability to dissimulate what they know to be false and damaging to others. Fake wisdom, like that offered by doctors who treat patients for the sake of profit, or journalists who unflinchingly repeat government press releases, do not reveal the rules of the game but assure others that the rules are too complex for people to question them. One finds greed and opportunism where one would expect expertise and service. Strong positions are avoided in favor of power plays and money moves. This is what passes for merit, innovation, creativity and cooperation.

The neoliberal governance that has engineered the transfer of wealth from the majority to the 1 percent and restored an economic aristocracy is euphemistically referred to as 'economic centrism.' Since the 2008 banking crisis and Occupy Wall Street, most people are well aware of economic inequality. The mark of a mediocrat is not to repress the truth but to cynically affirm it by insisting that people do not want to change the system. The Trump election, where a political abomination was chosen over a mediocratic crony, was a measure of the extent to which the neoliberal agenda had created deep resentment against the political establishment. However, disidentification with government is one of the goals of the mediocracy. As a post-political class, the mediocracy ignores the contradictions of free market ideology in favor of the political assault on democracy.

Other than the deflationary perspective of the state of depression, why do people go along with the cynical capitalist realism of the mediocracy? According to Catherine Liu, today's PMC expresses the bourgeois tendencies of its contradictory class location and is now actively fighting a class war against the working class (Liu). The motif of its politics is empowerment through the kind of reified self-transformation that allows it to believe in its cultural superiority. Political correctness and the hoarding of markers of virtue – virtue signaling – prepare it for engagement in moral panics and other pseudo-politics. Hillary Clinton's dismissal of Trump supporters as "deplorables," for example, reflects her elitist attitude towards most blue-collar workers. On the more activist side of things, the culture war convinces the PMC that ordinary things, like reading books, raising children, staying healthy and eating organic food, allows them to make the ordinary into something extra-ordinary. PMC contempt for ordinary people allows reactionary politicians like Trump to fuel resentment and position PMC elites as the enemy of the public. The failure of Elizabeth Warren's appeal to educated suburbanites in the 2020 election is largely due to her having placed her own interests ahead of others. So did her effort to sink the Sanders campaign with pseudo-feminist allegations of something that Sanders may or may not have said reflect the backhanded use of anti-sexism for the sake of career advancement. As with its Romantic, bohemian and countercultural predecessors, the virtue-signaling of the PMC is accompanied by the kind of transgressive 'vice signaling' that serves its bad side as well.

If the only virtue of the PMC is hypocrisy and its willingness to destroy working-class integrity, dashing hopes for universal health care or free college tuition, it manages to stay on top through quasi-religious moral exhortation. Always ready to defend the interests of minorities against those of the working class, which it denounces as racist, sexist, homophobic and xenophobic, today's PMC has revived the conservative culture of prestige, erudition and snobbery of the prewar generations. Downplaying social solidarity, virtue hoarders like Ta-Nehisi Coates, Ibram X. Kendi and Robin DiAngelo call on citizens to vilify history, objectivity and universalism so as to prop up a few careers in neoliberalized academia, the media, government and Hollywood. The PMC problem of virtue hoarding is also found in activist circles, where the fetishization of process and subcultural diversity undermines genuine political opposition. De-platforming left intellectuals like Adolph Reed or Angela Nagle for legitimate criticism of "infinitely demanding" woke politics leaves the working class indifferent to activist politics, or worse, downright hostile, thereby confirming the activist prejudice against the masses and propping up the anti-communist pluralism of the corporate state (Critchley). You were fired for explaining the history and etymology of the n-word? You are living in your car? You skimp on your diabetes medication to save up for food money? Your child's high school was the scene of a mass shooting? Your family was killed by a drone strike? Barack Obama has a playlist for you. Hillary Clinton has advice on how to empower women.

3   The Fall of the Liberal Class and the Rise of the Far Right

In *State and Revolution*, Lenin discusses the notion of the 'withering of the state' as it was debated by Marx and Engels (Lenin 2014). In his "Critique of the Gotha Program," Marx reflected on the problem of premature substitution of the community for state power (Marx). This agency could be referred to as the people, or the masses, but not the proletariat since the concept of the proletariat contains within it an implicit rejection of any organic notion of community. The distinction between community and proletariat raises the problem of the difference between political ideology and political economy. The proletariat is a product of the contradictions of capitalist relations of production and the basis on which a new social order is possible. However, without the control of state power, the proletariat is unable to revolutionize the system of capitalist production and the bourgeois ideology that sustains it. In his critique of the Paris Commune, Marx therefore thought that a state apparatus would be necessary in even a communist society, or at least in the transition from socialism to communism. Still, as Lenin pointed out, Marx did not speculate on what a communist utopia would look like.

Communism, like the proletariat, is a development of the contradictions of capitalism. While capitalism creates the impetus for communism, only an organized and class-conscious proletariat can bring about an overcoming of the relations of antagonism between capital and labor. For this, Lenin developed the theory and practice of the revolutionary communist party (Lenin 1988). Throughout the First World War, workers in different countries were willing to kill millions of workers from other countries for the sake of patriotic nationalism and in the interest of munitions manufacturers. The bourgeois nation-state therefore had to be destroyed and replaced with the party organs of a proletarian International. Against this prospect, fascism misappropriated working-class politics as a means to salvage bourgeois imperialism. Because most wage slaves are not concerned about democracy and the majority are barred from political participation, the bourgeois democracy of capitalist society is a democracy for the rich and powerful. Government institutions and the news media are the managers and publicists of bourgeois political interests. For Lenin, the communist party is the organization of the vanguard of the oppressed classes. Democracy for the poor is not democracy for the "moneybags," whose freedom to oppress must be restricted (Lenin 2014: 126). As opposed to neoliberals, who consider that the market is the best means to guarantee freedom, the communist party and the communist state apparatus is tasked with the restriction of the freedom of those who would oppress the masses in the interest of profit.

In the postwar period, after the defeat of fascism, the role of government has become even more enigmatic. On the basis of international relations of production, the state has become global. Vacillating between liberalism and authoritarianism, global state power absorbs the energies of civil society and social movements into its political monopoly, which is dedicated to economic growth (Lefebvre 1976). The question becomes: Is this politics of economic growth that technocratic politicians propagandize the utopia that social movements want or is it an irrational violence that makes the global state appear like the source of mysterious manipulations? (Jameson). Critical reason and class consciousness chafe at the institutions that stand in the way of a transition away from capitalism. The PMC is one of those institutions.

In the wake of Brexit and the Trump presidency, the PMC set its sights on the working class as the cause of all of social problems. This had less to do with facts than with politics. In 2016, what gave Trump an advantage was the decline in voter turnout, largely due to the fact that Hillary Clinton campaigned on the continuation of Clinton-Bush-Obama policies. Many of the counties in the industrial states of Michigan, Minnesota, Ohio, Pennsylvania, Wisconsin and Iowa who voted Trump had previously voted twice for Obama. Others voted for Green Party leader Jill Stein. In 2016, some 100 million voters abstained or voted for a third party. Working-class Trump voters were not overwhelmingly white, as support for Clinton fell in cities like Detroit, Cleveland, Philadelphia and Milwaukee. Many of the people who had experienced plant closures, layoffs and wage cuts throughout the previous two elections, and who happen to be white, had voted for Sanders in the Democratic Party primaries. No one in the Democratic Party or the corporate media attributed the swing vote for

Trump to the fact that the Democratic National Committee sabotaged these voters' preferred candidate, who had led a New Deal campaign against the establishment and supported activist initiatives to confront corporate power. Those who smeared the working class also liked to boast that Hillary Clinton received overwhelming support from middle and upper-class educated women voters and lost ten percent of union households. Although 37 percent of women voted for Obama, only 30 percent of eligible women voters voted for Clinton. All ethnic groups increased their vote for Trump from 2012 Republican support: whites by an average of one percent, blacks by seven percent, Latinos by eight percent and Asian Americans by 11 percent. If one was to apply the rhetoric of disparity in this case as one does elsewhere, one would be obliged to argue that African Americans, Latinos and Asian Americans are more white-supremacist than whites. But again, that is not the argument that is being made here.[1] While Clinton sought celebrity support in metropolitan counties and promised tax breaks for entrepreneurs, Trump campaigned against elite corruption (Mike Davis 2017). And while Trump increased his support with groups that earn more than $30,000, $50,000 and $100–200,000 annually by ten, six and two percent, Clinton won over from the Republicans affluent voters who make more than $100–200,000, $250,000 and $2–3.5 million by nine, eleven and 60 percent (London 2016).

Since Trump only pretends to represent the interests of working-class Americans, the sum total of the situation is a two-party system that is rigged in favor of the plutocracy. Regardless, the PMC forged ahead with its research on racist concepts like white identity. For instance, Ashley Jardina, the author of *White Identity Politics*, argues that the notion of white identity is taking on increasing importance among Americans, who sometimes link identity to their sense of political resentment (Jardina). While none of her research is conclusive with regard to the association between white identification and racism, there is no question that Trump played on the status anxieties of whites (Chotiner). Another researcher in this field, Joan C. Williams, uses the construct of the white working class to explain the Trump election victory (Williams). That the center-right PMC elite is now using working-class resentment to explain everything, David Roediger argues, is but one example of how race issues are used to blunt class issues (Roediger 2017b). Not surprisingly, Williams' book ignores the role of the wealthy. According to Gurminder K. Bhambra, most Trump supporters were middle-class whites. Those working-class people who did elect Trump – about 1/3 of his supporters – included minority voters. Similarly, the

---

[1] For a critique of disparity research, see Reed & Chowkwanyun.

typical Leave voters were older middle-class voters from Southern England. The media commentary on those left behind by deindustrialization, automation, outsourcing and immigrant labor can be charged with "methodological whiteness," she argues, which confuses questions of class and identity (Bhambra). These observations confirm Walden Bello's argument that modern far right movements have middle-class origins – Italy in the 1920s, Indonesia in 1965, Chile in 1973, Thailand in 2001–14, India in 2014 and the Philippines in 2016 (Wray). Although described as populist, the counter-revolutionary thrust of far-right movements prevents grassroot insurgencies among the lower classes. Rejecting liberal democracy for its failings, right-wing movements erode Enlightenment values of due process, minority rights and secularism. In such situations, the middle class is more active than the working class in the promotion of anti-socialist politics, charismatic demagogues and nationalism.

Liberals typically define socialists and fascists as two sides of the same totalitarianism. Yet liberalism can be no less extreme. Since the collapse of the Soviet Union in 1989, triumphant capitalism has turned against its own legacy, developing a politics of what Tariq Ali refers to as the "extreme center" (Ali). Unable to make good on progressive platforms, social democratic parties were replaced in the early 2000s by conflict-averse 'third way' politics beyond left and right partisanship. The capitulation to deregulated capitalism and imperialist war has delivered liberalism to authoritarian sycophants who are more concerned to reproduce themselves than they are with the concerns of people whose lives they destroy. With Blair's New Labour as with Clinton's New Democrats, the encouragement of entrepreneurial individualism and privatization brought about an ideological counter-revolution. While markets are susceptible to risks, powerful nations and wealthy individuals can weather disasters. This "dictatorship of capital," Ali argues, is the result of bipartisan collusion.

In *Death of the Liberal Class*, Chris Hedges describes the abandonment of political liberalism. According to Hedges, classical liberalism emphasized the equality of individual moral status and the use of reason for the sake of human progress. This logic was extended through the redistribution programs of the welfare state, labor rights and civil rights. Liberal ideology declined after WWI as corporate culture began to use permanent war as a propaganda tool to manipulate the mass culture that was otherwise pacified through consumerism and the cult of the self. Roosevelt's New Deal was the last phase of classical liberalism in the U.S. and was followed by Cold War anti-communist liberalism, which was at odds with the workers' movement and with the state regulation of capital. A new form of neoliberal capitalism embraced militarized imperialist expansion through the globalization of production and trade relations.

Just as transnational corporations dominate other nations, they enforce social inequality in domestic policy by staging elections that they otherwise control. The 'boutique activism' of identity politics allows neoliberals to harken back to a classical liberalism that is no longer effective at the level of the corporate state (Hedges 2010: 39). Hedges argues that the Democratic Party is worse than the GOP when it comes to peddling platitudes about individual moral vocation. By preventing progressive forces from influencing policy and effecting reforms, the establishment creates a power vacuum that is filled by corrupt politicians who are more than willing to do the bidding of the billionaire oligarchy. Those civil servants, journalists, educators and intellectuals who fight for the common good are denounced as parasitic elitists. Government offices, universities and media institutions are consequently stacked with neoliberal conformists.

One of Hedges' influences is the political philosopher Sheldon Wolin. In *Democracy Incorporated*, Wolin argued that the current form of government in the U.S. is an "inverted totalitarianism" where democracy and populations are managed in the interest of corporate domination (Wolin 2008). Through the military mobilization of social existence in the interest of corporate profit, constitutional freedoms are constrained by the fear of death. This fear is channeled towards targets like communists, terrorists or some other specter that threatens the political imaginary, which is defined in terms of power rather than principles. From the outset, all talk of electability is not only a losing proposition but is beside the point if the U.S. is to maintain its role as the mafia enforcer of the world market. Unlike classic fascism, inverted totalitarianism does not advance the claims of a master race, but rather the interests of shareholders. Rather than destroy liberal institutions, inverted totalitarianism guts them out from the inside, turning them into empty receptacles that are refilled with contents that have nothing to do with their original purpose. For example, when one thinks of election campaigns, voters are not asked to choose a leader who will implement the policies that the people desire, but rather a representative who fits the myth of American exceptionalism.

One of the indications that we are coming to terms with the death of the liberal class and the inversion of its classic principles is the raft of debates that educational institutions have been hosting on the merits of socialism versus capitalism. Such debates are phony to the extent that they are construed in advance from the point of view of liberalism. Socialists do not consider liberals to be a loyal opposition. Rather, socialism understands itself as a stage beyond liberalism. Socialism does not fight against liberalism per se. Socialism mitigates the worst aspects of liberalism by subsuming its contradictions at a higher developmental stage. This has caused postmodernists to reject socialism as an ideology that is inherently tied to bourgeois modernity.

As it emerged in the late 1800s, the fascist movement learned from socialism the theory of historical materialism based on successive modes of production, from slave societies to feudalism and capitalism (Sternhell). After World War I, fascists determined that working-class people had more in common with the bourgeoisie of their respective nations than they did with workers from other countries. The Great War taught them that workers would rather die for nationalism than for internationalism. Fascists therefore took from socialism its theory of history but rejected Enlightenment principles. Postmodernism and so-called 'cultural Marxism' has inadvertently reproduced many of the ideological foundations of fascism: the rejection of Enlightenment universalism; the rejection of bourgeois materialism and scientific objectivity in favor of subjectivism and the will to power; identity politics that ignore class conflict within specific groups; the aestheticization of politics and the spectacularization of transgression. In contrast to identity politics, socialism is not premised on identity as the material foundation for politics. If identity was accepted as the basis of politics, there would be nothing to distinguish socialism from fascism. Socialism, in contrast to both fascism and postmodernism, does not reject Enlightenment universalism but rather seeks to resolve its contradictions in a progressive direction. Stalinism and the theory of 'socialism in one country' is an aberration of communist politics. Regardless, the horrors of Stalinism have served capitalist propaganda since the 1930s. The Holocaust, as well as similar experiences like the bombing of Hiroshima and Nagasaki, gave rise to new forms of capitalist regulation. As anti-racism and anti-sexism became part of corporate liberal ideology in the postwar era, only the Soviet Union stood in the way of what, after its collapse, became the neoliberal decimation of political rights in favor of the economic incentivization of everything from new technologies to new subjectivities and lifestyles.

In the mid-1930s, Herbert Marcuse described how it is that fascist state regimes struggle against liberal values, bourgeois materialism and Marxist offshoots (Marcuse 2009). Fascist totalitarianism heightens the importance of a 'heroic-volkish realism' based on blood, race, honor and organic social bonds. It does so against knowledge, reason, individual freedom, bourgeois security and political society. To the extent that fascism accepts the Marxist notion of social totality, it replaces this with the concept of organic totality. The romanticization of valor links the heroic individuals of organic community to the 'dark forces' that nourish them. Against intellectuals, the powers that he or she draws upon are life, nature and anything that does not require reasoned justification. This force that is 'beyond good and evil' is thought by fascists to make history. Just as today's racialists and corporate feminists want to see politicians and celebrities that 'look like me,' the charismatic totalitarian leader is defined by the naturalness of their embodiment rather than their arguments. Such political existentialism and phenomenological reduction ostensibly liberate life from the economic and social forces that drive historical transformation.

Fascist irrationality, Marcuse argues, is situated at the level of the contradiction between the social relations of production and the level of productive forces. Any transformation in the technical development of capitalist production – as is now the case with digitization and social media – can stimulate totalitarian fantasies of indestructability. As this totality of identity is programmatically mystified, Marcuse says, social criticism is foreclosed. The organic totality of identitarian unity is thus presented as the opposite of social class or universal justice. Instead, universalism is made into naturalism. Even liberals come around to attacking the achievements of the bourgeois revolutions of 1776 and 1789 as nationalist demands replace ideals of liberty with the authoritarian function of the state, in particular, against challenge by socialist enemies. With property as the guarantee of economic progress as the guarantee of social progress, the only enemy of the resulting nationalism and identity politics is Marxist socialism. In other words, and as Marcuse puts it, fascism is accepted insofar as it can save culture from socialism. Totalitarianism never abandons liberalism entirely since it accepts economic liberalism, private enterprise and entrepreneurialism. The capitalism that the petty bourgeoisie rejects is only the capitalism that blocks its ideology of irrational heroism and self-interest. This particularism, however, is not universally extended to all humans, but is reserved for the exceptional group, whose historical becoming is associated with divine providence.

As Marcuse notes, the irrationalism of volk nationalism relies on and parasitizes the rationalist view of society, which seeks to discern and comprehend what is good, true and right. To the extent that postmodern theory rejects the rational cognition of reality, its own version of identitarianism is without even the naturalist justifications of fascists. This allows conservative critics to then champion liberal reason while at the same time ignoring the problem of totality. It is correct to defend objectivity to the extent that a rational theory of society is critical, but it is incorrect to the extent that it rejects the transformation of social relations. The conservative critique of woke identitarianism, defined as social justice activism, thereby colludes in the irrationalism that Marcuse identifies. Identitarianism does not reject reason but binds reason to hierarchy and domination. It enslaves humans to predatory instincts. The irrationality of identity, as championed even by today's activist progressives, annihilates reason by making naturalized pre-givens into the normative grounds of politics.

For Marcuse, the anti-liberalism of fascist nationalism is simply a crass version of liberalism proper, which adheres to an ahistorical understanding of the laws of social life. Domination by capital and the blockage of social progress is rationalized as communitarian interest. This version of organic totality has no concrete social theory and acquires its meaning only in terms of the status quo. The capitalist basis of classless national unity, Marcuse argues, underwrites a "hard, cynical realism" and rejection of intellectual efforts in favor of an "archetypal" overcoming of social contradictions (Marcuse 2009: 19). Morality and ethical values are made to hinge on the metaphysical certainties of identity, even the fluidity of identity, if need be, which is another dimension of the same tautology. Rebellious opposition to falling standards of living is channeled into the spirit of sacrifice, distorting courage into a means to justify what cannot be justified. Instead of social norms, an existential state of exception defines everyday life as a non-ideological struggle against the enemy. Trump-style discrimination is not only an attack on minorities but is also a confirmation of their importance in contemporary ideology. Since there can be no challenge to the state monopoly on violence, the pluralism of class interests is reduced to the pluralism of identity groups. The mere existence of multicultural plurality thereby confirms and validates the power of the state.

4 Left Populism as Compromise Formation

The progressive populism that the Sanders campaign developed to fight progressive neoliberalism and authoritarian populism was egalitarian and universalist. However, as a form of left populism, it also evinced certain structural and ideological limitations. The left populism that has developed in the wake of communist internationalism is, as Gregory Meyerson says of post-Marxism, a "compromise formation" (Meyerson 2009). The various forms of post-Marxism, from the New Left to new social movements and radical democracy, are premised on the abandonment of revolutionary class struggle and its replacement by various other means for people to define political struggle. According to Ellen Meiksins Wood, the Eurocommunist tendency that developed in the 1960s accepts capitalism and advocates popular alliances between classes. Since the working class is assumed to be non-revolutionary, the agent of change shifts to surrogates like students, academics, women, subcultures, lumpen elements, Third World peasants, immigrants, causes like ecology and anti-militarism, or social engineering through technology and alternative economies (Wood 1998: 15). Replacing the analysis of the mode and relations of production with the question of social oppression, analysis resorts to metaphysics and radicalism devolves into voluntarism. The goal of the left becomes the reform and management of capitalism rather than its overthrow. As politics is increasingly made independent of the political economy, economism is replaced with ideas that do not interfere with the capitalist system. Political parties cease to be working-class organizations and instead represent PMC and ruling-class interests.

Among the intellectual changes that have facilitated this shift towards left populism was the acceptance of discourse theory by Ernesto Laclau in *Politics and Ideology in Marxist Theory* and later by Laclau with Chantal Mouffe in *Hegemony and Socialist Strategy* (Laclau; Laclau & Mouffe). Accepting nationalism and popular democracy within labor politics, Laclau and Mouffe redefined socialism along non-ideological and class neutral lines. Seeking to win the middle-class support of the petty bourgeoisie, radical democracy shifted the definition of the contradictory location of the PMC from a class contradiction to an ideological contradiction (Wood 1998: 50). Politics became a matter of building popular alliances against the corporate state. This bypassing of the question of relations and mode of production, combined with the autonomization of political ideology from class relations, was linked to a pseudo-Gramscian use of the concept of hegemony that replaced the capitalist totality (the concrete universal) with abstract notions of power-resistance (the empty seat of power). In addition, the application of Foucauldian discourse theory allowed materialism to be recombined with a host of non-Marxist methods, from linguistics and semiotics to phenomenology, analytic theory, cybernetics, deconstruction and standpoint epistemology. As ideology was relativized, so were truth claims and politics remade into matters of social construction.

Dissolving ideology into discourse allowed radical democracy to disown Marxist class struggle in favor of multiple sites of power and disparate forms of resistance. Since discursive power is not specific to capitalism but refers more generally to social norms, labor becomes only one of many forms of social practice. Having rejected the theory of capitalist exploitation, radical democracy detaches politics from material interests. Workers are deemed to be no more alienated by capitalism than anyone else and so have no objective interest in socialism. Creating a people out of a pluralistic society in constant flux becomes the goal of popular democracy. The working class is deemed to be no more revolutionary than any other social force, whether based on race, gender, sexuality, or any other constituency seeking social change. New social movements and the politics of identity, Wood argues, legitimize liberalism, social fragmentation, consumerism, technological determinism, intellectual self-promotion and political voluntarism (Wood 1995). In response to such charges, new social movements attack Marxism as reductionist. For Marxists, the fact that class is not the only principle of stratification adds no further insight into the logic of capital. The centrality of class, on the other hand, tells us a great deal about how race, gender and other categories and issues, like ecology, are shaped by capitalist social relations.

The fact that left populism, or democratic socialism for that matter, is not a distinct ideology from socialism, liberalism and fascism allows it to act as a comprise formation, providing ideological cover for systemic problems that are avoided in the interest of pragmatic compromise. Thomas Frank champions populism as an alternative to the two-party system as well as a homegrown tradition based on the ideals of Thomas Jefferson and Thomas Paine, that is, rather than Karl Marx (Frank 2020: 53). As it happens, on the suggestion of Eric Foner, Sanders altered his George Washington University speech, "Where We Go From Here," to limit his examples of social democracy to the American tradition. In any case, if the Sanders campaign resonated with American youth as successfully as it did, this likely had less to do with their familiarity with the nineteenth-century People's Party than with the shift from global protests against neoliberalism to renewed grassroots involvement in political party organizations, as was also the case with Syriza in Greece, Podemos in Spain and Corbyn in the U.K. According to Paulo Gerbaudo, the more recent form of populism is linked to distrust of neoliberal institutions and draws on the anarchist thrust of anti-globalization (Gerbaudo). Today's progressive populism is more libertarian and individualist than predecessors, he argues, more participatory and less focused on labor issues.

In *For a Left Populism*, Chantal Mouffe adds to left politics the radical democratic rejection of 'class essentialism' and its replacement with an intersectional equivalence between issues (Mouffe 2018). In her view, the traditional parties of the left were unable to take into account the new social movements that emerged in the late 1960s – second-wave feminism, the gay movement, anti-racist struggles and ecology. Radical democracy's anti-essentialist approach to multiple struggles and the articulation of plural demands must now, she claims, establish a political frontier between the technocratic, oligarchic elite and the people. "The populist moment," she adds, "is the expression of a set of heterogeneous demands, which cannot be formulated merely in terms of interests linked to determinate social categories" (Mouffe 2018: 18). Class is no longer central, but is now peripheral to the struggle between left-wing and right-wing populism! In keeping with Laclau's definition of populism as a discursive strategy of construction that is without programmatic content, Mouffe's left populism rejects "abstract" universalism in favor of a continuous process of negotiation. She argues that the left must learn from Margaret Thatcher by creating a new hegemony, using populism for progressive objectives. For this to be possible, the left must cease to be a socialist left and must focus on relations of power instead of relations of production. Rather than a break with liberal democracy, what left populism envisages is a 'radicalization' of liberal-democratic ideals of freedom and equality.

One obvious problem with left populism, as was the case with radical democracy, is that even if it succeeded in everything it wants – in particular, through a change in government – it would not solve the problems that are specific to capitalism. Insofar as the populist struggle can be defined against white workers, or any other majority or normative group, left populism has the same ideological limitations as all populisms do, which is the organization of politics along the lines of a struggle between two social groups, usually the people and elites, which is a logic that has nothing to do with genuine socialism (Žižek 2006a). For Marxists, capitalism does not malfunction because of the greed of the neoliberal elite. Crisis is endemic to capitalism in even the best of circumstances. One reason why the PMC has become mediocratic is due to what Mark Fisher defined as capitalist realism: "the widespread sense that not only is capitalism the only viable political and economic system, but also that it is now impossible to imagine an alternative to it" (Fisher 2009: 2). After culture, politics, science and even identity have been reduced to economic imperatives, there is nothing left to believe in and so people's healthy skepticism regarding political manipulation, Michael Hardt and Antonio Negri argue, has become an autoimmune disorder (Hardt & Negri 2017: 6).

5 The Wages of Wokeness

Just as activists are overly wary of political parties and organizations, woke elements are by and large clueless when it comes to legitimate critiques of identity politics. This is a problem of both ideology and politics that cannot be assuaged by liberal guilt or resolved through tactical alliances. The class critique of identity politics is more complicated that the either/or, and/or rhetoric that dismisses class politics as essentialist, economistic, determinist and reductionist (Frase; Singh & Clover). With regard to the latter, Adolph Reed writes:

> Class reductionism is a myth. But like other myths, it reveals a great deal about our deeper systems of belief. Even if it tells us nothing about the people who are accused of it, it tells us a great deal about the accusers – the professional-managerial guardians of elite discourse. Most of all, the class reductionist myth gives powerful expression to the class-bound

desire to address the supposed interests of women, racial minorities, and other marginalized populations at the expense of broad, downward economic redistribution. Nothing declares one's own class allegiances more eloquently, after all, than the accusation that one's opponents care only about class.

REED 2019

A figurehead of this PMC agenda within the racialist camp is the writer Ta-Nehisi Coates, who argued that the class-first politics of the Sanders campaign, which did not advocate for reparations, was a "white agenda" that would reinforce white supremacy (Coates 2017: 114, 540). Leftist intellectuals like Reed, who have denounced the identitarian agenda as a class politics of the PMC, expose unresolved problems between the old and new left. In 2020, the NYC Democratic Socialists of America steering committee called on the Afro-Socialist Caucus to cancel an event with Reed on the basis of his alleged class reductionism. The Marxist faction in the DSA, sometimes known as Class Unity, says that the liberal wing of the DSA leaves them unable to defend Marxism against accusations of reductionism (Nogales C.). Not one to take prisoners, Reed criticizes the black activist class that panders liberal anti-racism, critical race theory and intersectionality, including the activists around Occupy Wall Street and the DSA (Reed 2016b).

Reed's colleague, Walter Benn Michaels, views the obsession with diversity as an ideological diversion from class issues (Michaels 2006). Michaels' book, *The Shape of the Signifier: 1967 to the End of History*, compares the contemporary focus on identity and ontology to the emphasis on the so-called materiality of language in postmodern cultural theory (Michaels 2004). A cultural mindset that emphasizes the notion that bodies matter, race matters, and so on, has led to a situation in which questions of meaning, belief, politics and aesthetics are systematically evaded in favor of the materiality of objects. As Paul Gilroy has observed, the capitalist fetishization of the black body makes it difficult to liberate humanity from race thinking (Gilroy 2002: 12). For Michaels, this capitalist materialism has everything to do with the 'post-historicist' shift away from questions like socialism vis-à-vis liberalism, towards material, affective, consumerist, linguistic, subjective, technical, cultural, etc., problems that transcend political and ideological disagreement. Postmodern appeals to who and what you are rather than what you believe, Michaels argues, avoid historical meaning in favor of experience, going so far as to stake contemporary struggles on the experiences of the past, like slavery and the Holocaust. Such experiences, however, are part of human history and are not the possession of select identity groups and their would-be representatives.

The cringeworthy spectacle of Michelle Obama demanding a vote for Joe Biden as a means to bear witness to the tragedy of slavery is only one such effrontery (Biden).

In post-structuralist circles, the post-historicist emphasis on identity and experience has given an inordinate importance to the 1977 "Black Feminist Statement" of the Combahee River Collective, a small group of black lesbian activists who argued that struggle must begin from a subjective perspective and that from there, struggle can intersect with the struggles of others. The CRC is commonly viewed as one of the foundational texts of the theory of intersectionality that has been advanced by the feminist legal scholar Kimberlé Crenshaw (Crenshaw). In books like Asad Haider's *Mistaken Identity*, the CRC is touted as the model for political organizing that is best able to move the left forward since it asserts that revolutionary socialism was mired by racism and sexism (Haider). That this assertion makes short shrift of the history of the left is partly what makes it attractive to thinkers whose materialism is more informed by postmodern discourse theory than the radical tradition. On the face of it, *Mistaken Identity* is a critique of the kind of progressive neoliberalism one finds with politicians like Obama or ideologues like Coates. However, its purpose is to find a way for young activists from different backgrounds and with different agendas to get along. The radical left, though, is not bereft of legitimate critiques of identity politics, with, for example, the late Bruce Dixon characterizing the intersectionality of race, gender and sexuality as "brood parasites" that kill its class politics host (Dixon). Such "class-splaining," as Roediger describes the work of David Harvey, Adolph Reed, Walter Benn Michaels, Paul Street, Cedric Johnson and Ellen Meiksins Wood, is, he says, nothing more than a "conspiracy theory" about how neoliberal elites have shifted the terms of social struggle from class to identity (Roediger 2017a: 34). The post-Marxist compromise formation here takes the form of political dysphoria since the overall argument that is made by these leftist intellectuals is that identity issues obscure class issues and therefore play a role in the reproduction of class society. As leftists, class-splainers cannot be accused of ignoring questions of identity, difference, oppression, discrimination and structural inequality. That is why they more than others come under attack by identity brokers and race managers. The rationale for compromise with identitarianism has more to do with winning elections or pursuing PMC careers than with building a movement around an authentic left ideology and anti-capitalist program. It is for this reason that Reed and Johnson have not only made valid criticisms of the CRC as a model for left politics, but have also pointed out the limits of a distinctly black politics in the age of New Democrat neoliberalism (Reed 2018; Johnson 2017).

The stereotype of workers as regressive straight white males inflames the reactionary woke politics of the PMC. People on the left should learn to not take the bait. As Nancy Fraser and Liza Featherstone have stated,

> feminists have a special duty to oppose the progressive neoliberals among our number: those happy to hobnob with plutocrats who enthuse about "leaning in" and "cracking the ceiling," while abandoning the vast majority of women to corporate predation. We should also oppose those who instrumentalize gender grievances, deploying them not to benefit women, but to undermine Sanders, divide the Left, and bolster the centrist and conservative cabals that have repeatedly and callously failed us.
> FRASER & FEATHERSTONE

They go on to suggest that the Sanders campaign has identified unions, anti-racists, immigrants and environmentalists as the left's most likely allies. However, as Jodi Dean has discussed in her book *Comrade*, there is a difference between an ally and a comrade (Dean 2019). It is not only party hacks like Nancy Pelosi and John Lewis who lean in, the process goes all the way down.

As for neoliberal conspiracy, we are now familiar with the ploy used by politicians to dodge accountability by accusing their critics of sexism, racism, anti-Semitism, or what have you. In October 2020, for example, after Democratic House Speaker Nancy Pelosi rejected Trump's $1.8 trillion fiscal stimulus offer, Democratic presidential nominee Andrew Yang told CNN that he thought Pelosi should have accepted the deal, since, in the midst of the COVID-19 crisis, a lower amount than what was desired by the Democrats would be better than no deal at all. Pelosi's spokesperson, Jorge Aguilar, then re-tweeted Christine Pelosi's tweet to the effect that Yang should not refer to Pelosi in a familiar way as Nancy and that his disagreement with her is an indication of "everyday sexism" (The Hill 2020d). When in June 2021, Minnesota representative Ilhan Omar criticized the U.S. for its complicity with the atrocities committed by Israel against the Palestinians, she was rebuked by Pelosi, her House leadership team and other House Democrats for defending terrorists and harboring "deep seated" anti-Semitic sentiments (Pengelly).

The class function of identity politics in neoliberal times is hardly limited to the U.S. In 2018, the members of Canada's left-of-center New Democratic Party chose Jagmeet Singh as its leader. Of the four candidates for the NDP leadership, Singh was the weakest on policy. However, his ethnicity as a Sikh Canadian was viewed as a diversity asset. The main criterion that one can assume got him elected was the fact that the NDP wanted someone with media charisma in order to compete against Justin Trudeau. The same can be said about the election of political centrist Annamie Paul to the leadership of the Green Party of Canada in 2020. A black and Jewish lawyer, who equivocated during her campaign on almost all issues, Paul attacked her socialist opponent Dimitri Laskaris on the basis of identity, accusing him of anti-Semitism due to his support for Palestinian rights. In such instances, identity acts as the inherent transgression of colorblindness. Race is not the only ploy in these political charades. When in April 2021, allies of the former Green Party leader Elizabeth May were criticized by the Paul administration of systemic racism, the May loyalists circulated an open letter denouncing the scapegoating of women (Hepburn). Neoliberal reverse colorblindness was also in evidence when Karen Wang, the Liberal candidate from Burnaby South, ran on the basis that her Chinese ethnicity made her a better choice for her riding, given its Asian demographic. Having expressed the unofficial function of identity in today's equal opportunity neoliberalism, which is to appeal to people on the basis of identity rather than policy, Wang was obliged to quit the byelection race and apologize to her opponent, Singh (Zussman).

Progressive neoliberalism operates most effectively when it functions like an open secret. The cabinet of the Liberal Party that was formed in October 2015 was celebrated for its diversity and gender balance. It included an indigenous minister, an Indian-born Sikh minister, a former Somali refugee minister, a gay minister and a quadriplegic minister. With Chrystia Freeland as Minister of Foreign Affairs, Trudeau declared that Canada would be pursuing a feminist foreign policy and prioritizing female power on the world stage. After doubling its military investments to satisfy NATO dictates, this same cabinet, as well as the NDP under Singh, seconded Trump's support of Juan Guaidó as the self-declared leader of Venezuela, a move that bolstered the right-wing regime of Jair Bolsonaro, who was good friends with neo-fascist leaders Benjamin Netanyahu and Viktor Orbán. In the Throne Speech of September 2020, which came during a spike in COVID-19 infections, the Trudeau government assured Canadians that its back-to-work and back-to-school herd immunity policy would be feminist and intersectional (Maclean's Editors).

Neoliberal policies like human rights imperialism are now going through a form of postmodern rebranding. In Spring 2021, the C.I.A. released several advertisements that seek to recruit millennials through celebrations of intersectionality (CIA). One might excuse an imperialist institution for pandering diversity but academia is no less to blame. Around the same time that these C.I.A. ads were being criticized for their promotion of 'woke imperialism,' an essay by Cara Daggett published in the *Internationalist Feminist Journal of Politics* was frequently mentioned in left news media. Titled "Drone Disorientations," the article abstract reads:

> Killing with drones produces queer moments of disorientation. Drawing on queer phenomenology, I show how militarized masculinities function as spatiotemporal landmarks that give killing in war its "orientation" and make it morally intelligible. These bearings no longer make sense for drone warfare, which radically deviates from two of its main axes: the home-combat and distance-intimacy binaries. Through a narrative methodology, I show how descriptions of drone warfare are rife with symptoms of an unresolved disorientation, often expressed as gender anxiety over the failure of the distance-intimacy and home-combat axes to orient killing with drones.
>
> DAGGETT

With this sort of thinking, the destruction of Gaza by the Israeli government is not so much a matter of ethnic cleansing as it is a problem of heteronormativity. The only problem with the essay is that it was not written as a 'grievance studies' hoax.

The function of identity in today's neoliberal world is like the concept of *jouissance* in Lacanian psychoanalysis. In *The Wages of Whiteness*, Roediger develops W.E.B. Du Bois's theory that the reason why Southern white workers did not ally themselves with oppressed black workers was because racism gave them a "psychological wage" through which poor whites could consider themselves superior to poor blacks (Roediger 1991). One can no longer presume such a wage, only a negative insistence that intervenes most forcefully in social discourse because it serves no purpose. Ideology does not simply refer to material reality in a direct way but is interpassive. I enjoy identity because others do or because others tell me that I should. Further still, the Lacanian Real has no immediate support in material reality but is virtual. This is why *jouissance* irrupts through subjectivity in ways that are unconscious, uncontrolled and even unwanted. Identity politics is one of the ways that ideology attempts to cope with the void of social difference. That is why identity politics is not the most effective when it exerts its force directly, as might be the case for example with Black Power militancy, but when it acts as an agent of superego guilt, shaming 'normal' subjects for something that they themselves are no more accountable for than anyone else. The more normal you are, the less you are allowed to enjoy your identity. While one might think that European white men are disadvantaged by this the opposite is true since anti-normativity allows them to more easily occupy the normative position. Although everyone knows that nothing about race or sexuality automatically makes someone a better or more competent person than anyone else, this logic can remain ideologically operative so long as the big Other does not know it. One might say in this regard that Black Lives Matter has it backwards. From the perspective of neoliberal post-politics, Black Lives are Virtual. Reality is sustained by fictions. Without these fictions, reality disintegrates. The function of the professional-middle class is to understand, manage and motivate this unconscious ideological surplus in the social order. It may be the case, though it is hardly necessary, that black individuals, or any other social group, be given a privileged role in this endeavor.

CHAPTER 2

Bernie Beats Trump, Clinton and Obama Beat Bernie

> Since the 1970s there has been a tendency to see the left essentially as a coalition of minority groups and interests ... This is understandable enough, but it is dangerous, not least because winning majorities is not the same as adding up minorities.
>
> ERIC HOBSBAWM, "Identity Politics and the Left"

∴

Although the Trump administration is said to have caused a dramatic rift within the Republican Party, his plutocratic politics have only broken with tradition insofar as he has added the element of far-right fanaticism. The attitudes that Trump's alt-right supporters propagate are designed to inflame culture wars, not solve them. They do this because culture wars obscure the processes of capitalist exploitation and weaken worker solidarity. During the 2016 Clinton campaign, so-called progressives were encouraged by the prospect that a fiscal conservative and war hawk would become the first woman president. In that context, Sanders took a great deal of flak for stating to the media that he did not think a candidate should be elected on the basis of their race or gender but rather on the basis of their politics. In doing this, Sanders advocated the kind of emancipatory universalism that several decades of New Democrat centrism and postmodern 'difference politics' had worked to discredit. In 2016, Sanders had the support of only 9 out of 187 congressional Democrats (Gautney 2018: 99). Hillary Clinton denounced his campaign as outrage unproductively directed against the billionaire class. In *What Happened*, she argues that Sanders helped to pave the way for Trump by dividing the Democratic Party (Clinton 2016: 445–6). Clinton attacked Sanders from the right, saying that his impractical policies would have increased taxes on middle-class families. So is WikiLeaks publisher Julian Assange, then holed up in the Ecuadorian Embassy in London, blamed for plotting with Putin and Trump the release of her emails along with stolen files from the Democratic National Committee.[1]

---

1 WikiLeaks claims that the hack of the Democratic National Committee computers took place before most of the 20,000 stolen emails had been written. Since the DNC email system

Clinton attributes resentment to Trump voters, who are represented as anti-immigrant and anti-minority white men without college degrees. Economic anxiety, she argues, caused voters to make the wrong choice. After the Republican victory, Clinton Democrats avoided any consideration of their party's policy blunders, which have accumulated imperiously since the 1980s. As Žižek remarked in January 2016:

> One has to repeat again and again that Clinton's defeat was the price she had to pay for neutralizing Bernie Sanders. She did not lose because she moved too much to the Left but precisely because she was too centrist and in this way failed to capture the anti-establishment revolt that sustained both Trump and Sanders. Trump reminded some of his voters of the half-forgotten reality of class struggle, although, of course, he did it in a distorted populist way. Trump's anti-establishment rage was a kind of return of what was repressed in the moderate liberal Left's politics focusing on cultural and PC issues.
>
> ŽIŽEK 2019a

After the election, the Democrats spent the next three years spinning a story about Russian interference in the elections. Ahead of the 2020 primaries, the two-year Mueller investigation determined that there was no conclusive forensic evidence that it was Russian hackers who stole Democratic Party documents in 2016. Even if Russian attribution was proven, the motives would remain to be explained. The true scandal around Russiagate is the fact that the DNC colluded with the Clinton campaign against Sanders as well as the fact that Clinton played lapdog to Wall Street interests. The leaks did not win the election for Trump, however, who was no more popular than Clinton. The Mueller report did reveal that someone in Russia spent $75,000 on Facebook ads, emails and texts. In comparison, the two main parties spent $5 billion on election campaigning. A Clinton Super PAC called Correct the Record is known to have spent more than $1 million hiring online trolls to spread disinformation about the Sanders movement. The right-wing head of CTR, David Brock, was exposed on several occasions for providing false information to the media to smear Sanders. Trump supporters and alt-right trolls also posed as Bernie Bros to smear the Sanders movement (Weaver 2018: 190–216). Noam Chomsky argued that Russiagate was so farcical as to be unworthy of discussion. Beyond

---

was easily compromised, hacking by someone in Russia or anywhere else could have been expected. Sanders towed the party line on the unproven allegation that the DNC emails were stolen by hackers working for a Russian intelligence agency. See Sanders 2018: 31, 139, 331.

those aspects of the hack that are undetectable, Chomsky noted that neither party was concerned that the Israeli Prime Minister gave a speech to the U.S. Congress criticizing American foreign policy – a rare breach of sovereignty that went unreported by the corporate media. The U.S. proudly interferes in Russian elections and goes well beyond this when it overthrows governments. Since the late 1800s, the U.S. has participated in the overthrow and replacement of no fewer than 84 foreign governments. The real issue, according to Chomsky, is the interference in U.S. elections by the corporate sector that pays for campaigns and buys elections. Lobbying in Washington D.C. and campaign funding since Citizens United are unacknowledged aspects of political manipulation that far surpass anything that can be attributed to WikiLeaks.

The biggest news from the Mueller report was not that Trump did not collude with Putin in the supposed Russian manipulation of the 2016 election, but that Trump threw his weight around by illegally interfering with the investigation. Why Trump would do this if there was nothing to find is simply more evidence that he suffers from the kind of pathology that made him unfit for office. Trump otherwise increased military pressure on Russia and pulled out of the INF nuclear treaty with Iran, which distracted from the international cooperation required to tackle climate change. After the Mueller investigation floundered, the Democrats failed to impeach Trump for obstruction of justice.

In his "Where We Go From Here" speech of 2018, which is the title of one of his books, Sanders advised Democrats to take stock of the 2016 fiasco by building a stronger progressive platform and bringing fundamental reforms to the party itself (Politics and Prose). For too long the party's business model has failed, he argued, causing the loss of legislative seats. Sanders did not mention how it is that after the Trump election, the Democratic Party and the mainstream press complemented Trump's anti-Muslim and anti-immigrant policies with anti-Russia and anti-China xenophobia. He repeated his oft-stated claim that the job of the progressive movement is to bring people together around an agenda that speaks to the needs of working families and working people of all races.

Establishment Democrats almost unanimously defend identity politics but do not defend class politics. The 2016 Sanders campaign was focused on challenging the control of government policy by the corporate and billionaire class. For this reason, Sanders' first presidential campaign received 16 negative articles in only one day in the Jeff Bezos-owned *Washington Post*. In 2016, none of the major news dailies supported Sanders except for the *Seattle Times*. The *New York Times* advocates for identity politics with as much ferocity as it advocates for imperialist regime change wars. It is true that Sanders supporters are found among civil rights activists, the women's movement, the environmental movement, the trade union movement and young people more generally. The overlap with some identitarian groups does not change the fact that those who supported Sanders did so because he was attacking big money politics. Sanders asked Americans to consider whether it is appropriate that three people own more wealth than the bottom half of the American people. Unlike Clinton, Sanders did not put his faith in the Democratic Party but in the American people, arguing that when they are given options, they are far more progressive than the media and the establishment presume. Most Americans support progressive policies that work for the majority and not just the wealthy.

Sanders approached politics on the basis of civil and political rights. He attacked social inequality, militarism and environmental degradation through the kind of progressive policies that link universalism to emancipation. He did not critique universalism as an ideology whose function it is to mask dominant interests. The people in the Clinton campaign who invented the Bernie Bro meme understood this. By defining Sanders supporters in this way, they attempted to deny Sanders the cause of emancipatory universalism and force him into a defensive mode as either a victim of the neoliberal establishment or as a victimizer of minorities. Since Sanders is a white male, this shallow attack had a spontaneous basis in empirical reality. Radical politics, however, is not reducible to empiricism. If this was the case, there would be no defensible argument to be made in favor of socialism. There would be no such thing as social progress, only an eternal present under the sign of capital.

Sanders supporters did their best to ironize the Bernie Bro and Bernie Broad appellation. This minimum of ideological passivity may have helped to maintain morale, but it was not by itself a significant political statement. The maximum of passivity, you could say, was produced within the two Sanders campaigns as it gradually oscillated from class politics to identity politics. Much of this had to do with the populist trend. Populists are anti-elitist on the whole, which shores up the 99 percent against the oligarchy, but does not gainsay the communist critique of massism. Populism may have been good enough to counter the right's exploitation of popular discontent to nefarious ends, but without challenging capitalism as such, it was susceptible to radical democratic compromise. And American workers have had enough of compromise. In the following I examine Sanders' two campaigns to win the Democratic Party nomination. Any observer of American elections has to be awestruck by the onerous convolution of the primary process. Despite all of the intricacies of this process, I focus specifically on the gradual 'wokification' of the 2016 and 2020 Sanders campaigns. If this attention to identity issues appears to distort the purpose and overall agenda of the Sanders movement, one can only seek to explain why it played the extensive role that it did in 2020.

1   Millennials Feel the Bern

No fewer than three books were authored by Bernie Sanders in the lead up to the 2020 Democratic Party nomination race. These documents, which function as means to communicate and propagate Sanders' political agenda, provide the best description of his political philosophy, including his views on identity politics. Source material also includes a 2018 book by Jeff Weaver, Sanders' campaign manager and former chief of staff, and a 2018 book by Heather Gautney, a staffer in the 2016 campaign. The first of the Sanders' books, *Our Revolution: A Future to Believe In*, was written in advance of the 2016 nomination race (Sanders 2016). It goes into detail on Sanders' policy positions and also provides a glimpse into his personal background. The following are his main policy platform positions across the two campaigns:
- redress wealth inequality: the top 10 percent of the 1 percent own more wealth than the bottom 90 percent; 99 percent of new wealth goes to the top 1 percent; the top 10 percent owns 76 percent of total wealth; 540 U.S. billionaires are worth c.$2.4 trillion; 43 million Americans live in poverty; 20 percent of children live in poverty; 1.4 million school children are homeless
- end income disparity: pay equity for women; women comprise 66 percent of minimum wage workers and earn 80 cents on the dollar compared to men; pay equity for minorities; half of blacks and Latinos earn less than $15/hr; women of color earn 63 cents on the dollar, Hispanics 54 cents and Native Americans 58 cents; raise wages rather than subsidize corporations
- raise wages: raise the federal minimum wage of $7.25 to a living wage of $15-an-hour minimum; the minimum wage has lost 30 percent of its purchasing power since 1968; had the minimum wage kept up with inflation it would be $28/hr; 70 percent of job growth is in the low-wage sector; higher wages reduce poverty, reduce crime and contribute to job growth; higher wages are better for the economy, better for people's health and reduce job turnover; low wages increase welfare outputs and thereby subsidize the corporate preference for low wages
- unionization: make it easier for workers to join unions (11 percent of public sector workers and 7 percent of private sector workers are unionized); improve work conditions and encourage employee-controlled enterprises to make business local; make workers into owners
- improve employment benefits: improve paid family leave and medical leave; provide paid sick leave for all; extend the length of paid vacations, with a guaranteed 10 days of paid vacations; Americans work 419 more hours annually than Germans and 84 more than Canadians

- employment policy: create millions of new jobs through a $1 trillion federal jobs program rebuilding infrastructure projects; job creation as an alternative to Universal Basic Income or Reparations; real unemployment is close to 11 percent, or 20 million Americans; build and improve the electricity grid, dams, water infrastructure, bridges, roads, public transit, high-speed rail, affordable housing, news schools, child care centers, a universal broadband Internet system
- trade policy: trade agreements should have binding labor, environmental and human rights standards; reject trade agreements like NAFTA and TPP that benefit the wealthy; eliminate the investor-state dispute settlement system that allows foreign corporations to steal from taxpayers; impose social tariffs on imported goods
- health care: create a single-payer Medicare for All (M4A) health care program paid for with $1.38 trillion based on employer and household premiums as well a progressive taxation; universal health care as a human right, as opposed to a government option within a private health care system; after the Affordable Care Act, c.30 million Americans remain without health insurance and as many are underinsured; eliminate the complicated health insurance system; the U.S. has the most expensive health care system and the lowest performance results among industrialized countries; lower the cost of prescription drugs
- social welfare policy: strengthen and extend Social Security, Medicare, Medicaid and nutritional programs; the Social Security trust fund has $2 trillion in surplus and adds nothing to the deficit; provide better care for elders and better work conditions for care workers; improve access to public housing and reduce gentrification schemes
- taxation: implement progressive taxation to rebuild the middle class and raise the median family income; billionaires do not spend, invest or create jobs; the U.S. is the richest country in the world, with $88 trillion in total wealth; make large corporations pay their share of taxes; 90 percent of taxes are paid by working families; reform the personal income tax system and establish a progressive estate tax; crack down on tax avoidance, tax loopholes and tax havens, which amount to $700 billion in annual tax avoidance; collect unpaid tax revenue by large corporations
- banking and financial reform: reform Wall Street speculation and corruption; cap the size of the largest institutions; 10 financial institutions control $10 trillion in assets; reduce system risks like bribery, conspiracy, rate tampering, collusion and fraud; change the policies that created a revolving door between Wall Street and the federal government; tax Wall Street speculation; reform credit rating agencies; re-establish the Glass-Steagall

Act to break up big banks and separate investment banks and insurance companies from commercial banks; limit predatory lending on mortgages and credit cards; control ATM fees and payday lending; allow the Postal Service to provide bank services, especially in rural areas; reform the Federal Reserve to focus investment on social spending
- ecology: implement a Green New Deal; reverse global warming by transitioning away from fossil fuels towards energy efficient, sustainable energy like wind, solar, geothermal and biomass; put a tax on carbon to cut carbon pollution by 40 percent by 2030 and 80 percent by 2050; oppose new pipeline projects; ban fracking; leave it in the ground policy
- criminal justice: abolish the death penalty; end private prisons; reform the criminal justice system; the U.S. spends $80 billion annually to keep 2.2 million people in prison; reform policing to stop police brutality; address the problem of structural and institutional racism in policing and in economic inequality more generally; decriminalize mental illness; demilitarize the police; end the war on drugs and jailing of people for nonviolent crimes; legalize marijuana; between 2001 and 2010, there were 7 million marijuana possession arrests, which disproportionately affect blacks who are seven times more likely to be arrested for possession and face more serious consequences for the same crimes; decriminalize drug addiction
- immigration: comprehensive immigration reform; provide a pathway to citizenship for undocumented immigrants and offer permanent residency to people born in the U.S.; extend labor protections to undocumented workers; prevent trade deals from undermining labor rights abroad and forcing emigration; protect the rights of detained immigrants and refugees; end family detention; end privately run immigration detention facilities; crack down on unscrupulous employers
- decolonization: protect the rights of 2.5 million Native Americans; indigenous people are more likely to be impacted by mining, dumping and development; indigenous people experience high levels of inequality, unemployment, police murder, poverty, suicide and alcoholism
- democracy: election and campaign finance reform; make it easier (not harder) for people to vote; overturn Citizens United to limit campaign costs and contributions by vested interests; strengthen the Voting Rights Act; 63 percent of Americans did not vote in the 2014 midterm elections
- education: improve school funding and invest in k-12 early education, with a focus on early 0–4 education; implement the Sanders College for All Act to make public colleges and universities tuition-free; cover 100 percent of the cost of books and room & board for low-income students; 70 percent of undergraduate students have debt; 43 million owe more

than $1.3 million in student loans; student loan debt is larger than the combined household and credit card debt; 25 percent of borrowers are delinquent or in default; improve state contributions to higher education and reduce government profiteering from student debt; de-commoditize the education sector
- communications: reform and democratize media; the corporate media suppress criticism that is in the national interest; 6 corporations control 90 percent of media (Comcast, News Corp, Disney, Viacom, Time Warner, CBS); 15 billionaires own these 6 companies
- foreign policy: reduce military spending and improve Veteran services

When the race for the nomination began in April 2015, the Sanders campaign understood that it was taking on the Democratic Party establishment and that Sanders would be viewed as a fringe, outsider candidate. When all was said and done, the 2016 Sanders campaign won 13 million votes, 22 states and 46 percent of the pledged delegates. Overwhelming support among millennials was one of the campaign's most significant assets, indicating the desire among youth for a systemic change to how politics is conceived in the U.S. Large rallies also indicated that Sanders-style democratic socialism was downright popular. In addition, the other main feature of the 2016 campaign was the revelation that you could run a presidential candidacy on small donations, without billionaire contributions and without super PACs. Some 2.5 million Americans from low and moderate-income backgrounds made 8 million contributions to the Sanders campaign in the amount of around $27, almost all of it collected online. Sanders raised a total of $232 million in small donations, a few dollars short of the $1 billion that is now required to run a presidential campaign. This represented more individual donations than any previous candidate in presidential election history. A less well-publicized fact was Sanders' choice to not work with the usual cast of political operatives and consulting firms that are needed to run a presidential campaign. Sanders had to create a lean but progressive staff that could manage federal and state campaign teams, campaign strategy, research, speeches, communications, technology, fundraising, security, legal matters and travel logistics. Since in 2016 there was no one willing to go up against the Clinton political machine, Sanders decided to run a race that he was unlikely to win. His purpose was less to become president than to force issues onto the agenda that are a continuation of the struggles of the labor movement, the Civil Rights movement, the women's movement, the gay rights movement and the environmental movement. When Sanders launched his campaign, he asserted the fact that it was not about him, but about the needs of the American people and the policies that can address those needs.

If *Our Revolution* argues for the centrality of class analysis in socialist politics, it should be said that where identity is concerned, the main motif of Sanders' speeches was the concept of social solidarity. "They know, and I know," he writes, "that we are stronger when we stand together and do not allow demagogues to divide us up by race, gender, sexual orientation, or where we were born" (Sanders 2016: 13). Sanders emphasizes the diverse backgrounds of the people at his rallies: "blacks, whites, Latinos, Native Americans, Asian-Americans, young and old, gay and straight, people who immigrated here and those born here" (Sanders 2016: 187). However, as soon as Sanders says this, he shifts from identity to the embeddedness of social justice issues in the fight against the oligarchy and for economic and environmental justice. In other words, at no point in his campaigning, either in 2016 or 2020, did he problematize the difference between the class war and culture wars, opting instead for an inclusive universalism against unchecked capitalism.

Sanders' discussion of his family background in *Our Revolution* is brief. He mentions growing up poor in a crowded Brooklyn apartment. His Jewish father's family had been killed in Poland during the Nazi assault. His first understanding of the deficiencies of capitalism, he relays only half-jokingly, came when the owners of the Dodgers moved the team from Brooklyn to Los Angeles. While a student at the University of Chicago, Sanders was a member of the Young People's Socialist League and the Student Peace Union. He also became the campus vice president of the Congress of Racial Equality (CORE), whose activities focused on desegregating Chicago housing. Sanders was photographed during a demonstration to desegregate the public school system, a striking difference from Biden, who at that time opposed the use of busing to desegregate schools. Sanders demonstrated during the famed 1968 Democratic Convention and also participated in the 1963 March on Washington. He spent time in a kibbutz, worked for a Head Start program in New York City and in 1968 moved to Vermont, where he had various occupations, including a small company he started that made documentary filmstrips for schools.

In his earliest attempts to get elected, Sanders campaigned with grassroots organizations against the Vietnam war and for women's rights and economic justice. In 1981 he won the mayorship of Burlington as an independent and campaigned against downtown business in favor of working-class neighborhoods and low-income groups. As the only socialist mayor in the U.S., Sanders made Burlington a leader in low unemployment, quality public schools, energy efficiency, tech innovation and social issues like gay rights and immigration. In 1990 he was elected as an independent to Congress, where he campaigned against the first Gulf War. One year later he formed the House Progressive Caucus, spearheading the resistance to NAFTA and the pharmaceutical industry. Sanders was elected as an independent to the Senate in 2007, where he helped to pass the Affordable Care Act and protect Social Security. He opposed the extension of the Bush tax cuts under Obama with the at that time longest recorded filibuster.

As a democratic socialist, foreign policy is one of Sanders' weakest policy areas. Throughout his life and career in politics, Sanders opposed the war in Vietnam and the U.S. coups in Chile, Guatemala, Nicaragua, Congo, Brazil, Iran and elsewhere. He voted in favor of the unconstitutional bombing of Serbia. In 2001 he voted for the Authorization for Use of Military Force (AUMF), supported sanctions and regime change in Iraq, justified the war in Afghanistan and Obama's drone assassination program. In 2003, he opposed the invasion of Iraq. He supported Obama and Clinton's regime change operation in Libya. His thinking on Syria is inconsistent with his stance on diplomacy. Sanders opposed the Netanyahu regime in Israel while at the same time criticizing Hamas for its use of terrorist violence. He has also ignored the persecution of Julian Assange, Chelsea Manning and Edward Snowden.

On the whole, Sanders sought to shift American politics away from subservience to Wall Street and corporations by campaigning in states and counties that had been abandoned by the Democrats to the GOP. Not satisfied to raise money from billionaires to pay for advertisements, he campaigned 'on the ground' by holding rallies and town hall meetings with low-income and working-class communities across the country that have been devastated by decades of hardship. While voting was viewed by Sanders as essential to change this situation, white racism was used by Republicans to divide the working class and compel them to vote against their best interests. Minorities in states like Georgia, who typically vote Democrat, have been deliberately thrown off of voter rolls. Greg Palast notes that in 2016, 1.3 million out of 8.6 million votes were not counted in California, where Clinton beat Sanders by only a slim margin. Had Sanders not lost California, according to Palast, he might have gone on to win the 2016 nomination race (Palast). An unfair political process makes it difficult to implement measures that would benefit the majority of people. For this reason, Sanders defined his campaign as more than an election race. Telling the truth about what is going on in American politics meant involving millions of people in a grassroots challenge to the economic status quo. In order to facilitate this process, rallies and town hall meetings were live-streamed and then re-edited into short videos that were viewed by millions. The 2016 campaign garnered millions of Facebook and

Twitter followers. Surrogates drawn from government, the labor movement, the activist milieu, academia and the world of celebrity were enlisted to encourage organizational support. Paid volunteer coordinators were hired for all 50 states.

Setting off on the campaign trail, the Sanders team focused all of its energy on the first two states voting in the primaries: Iowa and New Hampshire. While Clinton hosted lavish fundraisers for wealthy donors, Sanders held two to three events per day, drawing large crowds and, as he says, doing what expert political consultants tell you not to do: discussing the major problems facing the country. Party insiders were reluctant to join the state-based staff, fearing retribution from those who supported Clinton, who was viewed as the incumbent. Obama dissuaded Biden from running and promoted Clinton as the strongest candidate. Weaver suggests that Obama did this in order to prevent Biden from splitting Clinton's votes and also to preserve his dubious legacy (Weaver 2018: 241). Things changed quickly after Sanders announced his run. More than 100,000 people joined the Sanders campaign in fewer that 24 hours. In this campaign, as throughout his entire career, Sanders determined to not use an attack strategy or negative ads. As a senator, he is known to have passed a record number of amendments and most of those would not have been possible without securing Republican support. Sanders chose to focus on policy rather than personality, favoring social activism over connections to powerful donors.

One of the goals of the Sanders campaign was to shatter the myth that constituency groups are monolithic. In July 2015, only one month after announcing his candidacy, Martin O'Malley, the former governor of Maryland who was also in the leadership race, was protested by Black Lives Matter activists at the annual Netroots Nation Conference. O'Malley's assertion that all lives matter was jeered by the crowd. When Sanders spoke after O'Malley, he agreed that black lives matter, discussed his history as a Civil Rights activist and his policies on economic justice, unemployment disparities and criminal justice reform. He was disrupted by BLM a second time a few weeks later in Seattle, where this time the crowd turned against the activists. While many leftists viewed the attack as a pointless provocation, the Clinton camp used the incident to pit neoliberal identity politics against social solidarity. The BLM provocations did not harm the Sanders campaign, however, and even led to the hashtag #BernieSoBlack. In response to the #SayHerName slogan, Sanders added the name of Sandra Bland and other victims of police violence to his speeches. Similarly, Sanders' reply to Remaz Abdelgader at a National Student Town Hall, and on the subject of Islamophobia, earned him support among

Muslim voters. According to Gautney, the campaign responded to BLM in three ways: 1) by meeting with anti-racist activists, working with high-profile black and Latino surrogates, and hiring staff to do more outreach to minority voters; 2) modifying Sanders' stump speech to emphasize his Civil Rights activism; 3) modifying the campaign platform to address racial disparities in wealth, employment, the criminal justice system, voting rights and other areas. Sanders also adjusted his tour schedule to make more stops in underserved communities (Gautney 2018: 144–5). Sanders therefore adjusted his campaign in response to criticism and to deter from PMC race and gender shaming. Weaver mentions that Sanders' first speeches emphasized the commonality of the problems facing people but that over time he changed his presentations in order to articulate the ways in which people of color are particularly disadvantaged (Weaver 2018: 123).

The leaked DNC emails have shown that Tom Perez, who would go on to be the chairman of the 2020 DNC, advised Clinton to make use of identity politics to present Sanders as tone deaf on the needs of minorities. Prominent women activists like Gloria Steinem and Dolores Huerta, and groups like NOW, Planned Parenthood, Emily's List and the pro-choice group NARAL, exploited gender difference to advocate for a first American woman president and to paint Bernie as a brocialist. According to Weaver, the narrative that the Clinton campaign wanted to spin was that Bernie was only concerned about economic issues and was indifferent to women and minorities (Weaver 2018: 139). The Bernie Bro attack meme was created by Robinson Meyer for an article published in *The Atlantic* in October 2015. The article is less about Sanders than it is about his supporters, who are described as educated but idealistic young men. As the meme spread, Bernie Bros were depicted as zealous, rude, racist and misogynistic. The meme ignored the fact that Sanders was as popular with young women, blacks and Latinos as he was with white men. As Gautney argues, Sanders' policies were more pro-woman and pro-minority than Clinton's corporate agenda. The pro-Clinton statement made by Madeleine Albright to the effect that "there's a special place in hell for women who don't help each other" did not need to be altered one iota to make the case for Sanders against Clinton. Gautney is also correct to say that all politics in a capitalist society is class politics (Gautney 2018: 175).

In September 2015, polls showed Clinton leading with 44 percent of voters, Sanders with a close 30 percent and Biden with 18 percent. The polls that followed the first televised debate revealed the generational divide in the electorate. Clinton did better with seniors who had lived through the Cold War, who have a negative impression of the word socialism and who do not use social media as their main source of information. By November, polls indicated that Sanders was viewed as the strongest candidate to run against the Republicans, thereby repudiating the centrist view that Sanders was unelectable. Throughout the campaign, Sanders was shown to beat Trump in 28 out of 30 national polls, far better than Clinton and often by double digits (Sanders 2016: 337). The Clinton campaign fought back with massive ad buys. Although Sanders considered ads to be secondary to on-the-ground campaigning, expensive ads on national television have an inordinate influence. The results of the February primary in Iowa was a 50/50 tie. Sanders won more votes but Clinton won 701 delegates to Sanders' 679. The primary caucus system that is in place in some but not all states is geared, precinct by precinct, to winning delegates rather than votes, a complicated and drawn-out process that requires strategic planning through realignment stages. There are no fewer than 1700 precincts in Iowa. Since Sanders had 84 percent favorability with people under 29 years of age and 58 percent favorability among those under 44, it was important to get them to register, caucus and vote in New Hampshire and elsewhere, especially Nevada, which is one of the most diverse states. That meant doing better, Sanders says, to make the candidate known to Latino and black voters. Sanders won New Hampshire 60 percent to Clinton's 38 percent, and lost Nevada with 47 percent to Clinton's 52 percent. Getting independent Latino and young black voters to register as Democrats in states with closed primaries – a convention that should be eradicated, along with primaries and the super/delegate system – is important to fighting voter suppression. However, since registering with a party is a voluntary action, it can leave millions of voters disenfranchised. Although this is matter of voting access, it is also presented as a question of identity politics. Much of the support for Sanders in Nevada was no doubt thanks to Latino and black outreach, which belied the narrative that his campaign was not popular with minority voters. There is nevertheless more to this process than meets the eye.

The February primary in South Carolina was a long shot. Despite the support of black leaders and celebrities like Ben Jealous, Nina Turner, Erica Garner, Spike Lee and Danny Glover, and surveys which showed that Sanders had 73 percent favorability ratings with black voters, Clinton had the support of centrist African-American politicians like John Lewis and Christale Spain. Sanders did more campaigning in South Carolina than Clinton, but the Clintons were well-known in the South and were readily associated with Obama. Congressman James Clyburn claimed that Sanders' plans for free college tuition would harm HBCUs. Sanders did better with Arab voters in Michigan than with middle-aged and senior black voters in the South. Clinton won the state 86 percent to Sanders' 14 percent, despite outreach efforts with the black community. Clinton won 90 percent of the black vote, mostly due to the perception that she was a sure bet against the Trump Republicans.[2] With 54 percent favorability among blacks under age 30, 72 percent support among Asian-American millennials, 60 percent with Latino youth and 45 percent among white millennials, and going on to win 80 percent of Asian-American youth voters, 79 percent of white millennials, 75 percent of Latino youth and 57 percent of black youth, Briahna Joy Gray later commented that Sanders did not have a race problem but rather a pundit problem (Gray 2017a). In the end, it was age and not race that determined the outcome. On Super Tuesday, and in the states that follow almost immediately afterwards, the Sanders campaign lost all 6 Southern states, but did well in Vermont, Massachusetts, Colorado, Minnesota, Oklahoma, Kansas, Maine, Nebraska, Michigan, Idaho, Utah, Alaska, Hawaii, Washington, Wisconsin, Wyoming, New York, Rhode Island, Kentucky, Indiana, West Virginia, Oregon and California, either winning these states or losing by only a narrow margin. His campaign did well with unionized nurses, postal workers, media workers, transit workers and the rank and file in SEIU and AFL-CIO affiliates.

Although Sanders could have dropped out of the race sooner, his campaign decided to stay on through to the Convention so as to influence the Democratic Party platform in the oncoming race against Trump. With the help of Cornel West, Keith Ellison, Deborah Parker, Bill McKibben, Jim Zogby and Warren Gunnels, Sanders says that he helped to draft "the most progressive political platform in the history of the country" (Sanders 2016: 365). The platform committee met in early June and many of its policies were included in the platform. At the outset, the Clinton team opposed Medicare for All, a ban on fracking and efforts to stop the Trans-Pacific Partnership that was being promoted by Obama. The Sanders team succeeded in including the expansion of public health insurance for middle-aged adults, the expansion of Social Security, a $15 minimum wage, the renewal of Glass-Steagall, postal banking, a tax on fossil fuels, lower costs for drugs, abolition of the death penalty as well as for-profit prisons and detention centers, the legalization of marijuana, the closing of tax haven loopholes, an end to deportation raids, automatic voter registration, public financing for elections, the improvement of Native American rights and easier access to unionization.

On July 12, Sanders endorsed Hillary Clinton for president. From July 25 to 28, the Democratic National Convention was held in Philadelphia. It

---

2 On why black voters did not support Sanders in the South Carolina primaries, a conservative anti-union state, see Johnson, 2016.

included 1,846 Sanders delegates from every state. Sanders says he was proud of them: "Black, white, Latino, Asian American, Native American, gay, and straight – they embodied what must become the future of American politics ... the face of the political revolution" (Sanders 2018: 30). These Sanders delegates were very angry about the WikiLeaks revelations from a few days earlier, which revealed DNC collusion with the Clinton campaign, a process that had begun as early as 2014. Under the direction of Debbie Wasserman Schultz, an Obama appointee, the DNC had plotted to attack Sanders' atheism and to manufacture misinformation. In order to avoid financing regulations, the DNC re-routed money that was meant for state Democratic parties to the Clinton campaign. It allowed the Clinton campaign, Hillary for America, to launder millions in donations beyond the allowed limit. This joint fundraising scam between the Clinton campaign and the DNC starved state parties and down-ballot candidates of needed funds. DNC rules were changed to benefit Clinton by limiting the number, schedule and parameters of debates, going so far as to give her the debate questions ahead of time. Schultz also concocted an overblown narrative about a negligible breach in the DNC voter databases, suspending VAN access by the Sanders campaign at a critical moment before the Iowa primary. Whereas the Sanders campaign was denied access to expensive information it had paid for, the Clinton campaign was given free access to expensive VAN donor lists. The DNC then fed the media false information about what became known as the VANghazi incident. Schultz also attacked Sanders in the media ahead of the Nevada primary, around the same time that the state Democratic Party was clearly meddling in favor of Clinton. While Clinton blamed the DNC for her failings, the Sanders campaign managed to raise nine times more money for down-ballot candidates than the greedy and self-interested Clinton campaign. To save face, the vice president of the DNC, Donna Brazile, made a public apology to the Sanders movement and let go several incriminated staffers, including Schultz. Just as soon as that was done, Perez was appointed as chair of the DNC, which he went on to purge of progressives.

Against the threat of a Trump presidency, Sanders pleaded with his comrades to support Clinton and to honor the Obama legacy. Instead of admonishing the Democrats for turning away from ordinary Americans and drifting further to the right, Sanders could have joined the Green Party ticket, as St. Clair points out. Jill Stein had graciously offered Sanders the leadership of the party. The reason that people talked about lesser evil voting, St. Clair says, is because Clinton is evil (St. Clair 2016: 4). The deals she struck with Sanders on the DP platform would be rejected as soon as she was elected. The important difference between the right-wing populists and the left-wing populists, according to St. Clair, is reflected in the fact that Trump was prepared to burn down the old Republican party, feeding off of people's rage. Gautney counters that Sanders did not want to crash the party but reform it. Sanders nevertheless delivered his followers to a candidate and to a party that does not represent their interests. St. Clair disagrees with the view that Sanders delegates were black and Hispanic outcasts. Rather, he argues, they were mostly middle-class suburbanites who wanted to make the American Dream real again through the memory of the New Deal and the Great Society. Sanders avoided running a negative campaign against Clinton. At the Democratic National Convention he subdued the ire of those who have been screwed over by bad trade deals, Wall Street, the military-industrial complex and the pharmaceutical industry – all those interests that the Sandernistas were called upon to have the guts to go up against. Whether supporting a war criminal who received more than half a million dollars from Goldman Sachs for three lousy speeches was worth the chance to run again in 2020 is a question that tends to be decided by what one thinks about one of the oldest parties of the ruling class. For all of the Bro-baiting, black voters and white women did not save Clinton from defeat. Low voter turnout, voter suppression, wall-to-wall Trump coverage and pandering to people on the basis of their identity rather than doing anything to help them led to a loss for the Democrats. Undaunted, they geared up to do it all over again in 2020.

Sanders' next book, the *Bernie Sanders Guide to Political Revolution*, was published in 2017 as a ready reference for understanding his policy positions. It is dedicated to the young people of America, which Sanders defines as "the most progressive generation in the history of our country" on account of the fact that it opposes racism, sexism, homophobia, xenophobia and oligarchy (Sanders 2017: 5). This book reflects the impact of the criticism made of his first campaign as well as his enhanced focus on identity issues as a means to distinguish himself from Trump while also appealing to Democratic voters. In 2016, Sanders won more youth votes than Clinton and Trump combined. He congratulates this generation for rejecting the values of the Trump right wing. If in this book, Sanders maintains his stance that the majority of Americans support a progressive agenda, he emphasizes the fact that the progressive movement "must move aggressively to combat racism, sexism and homophobia" (Sanders 2017: 11). The purpose of the book is to encourage young and working people to revitalize American democracy by reforming government. Sanders is more insistent in this case that health care and environmental justice must be connected to women's rights and racial equality. What the book ignores is the fact that the right has more than just economic policy with which to move the left further to the center. Identity politics and culture wars have been one of these methods. What was gained and what was lost by enhancing this electoral strategy is not something that can be assessed by listening only to Sanders speeches.

The heightening of the anti-oppression politics of the PMC in the *Bernie Sanders Guide to Political Revolution* and in Sanders' 2018 book, *Where We Go From Here*, should be conceived as strategic not only vis-à-vis Trump, but also against the numerous Democratic Party nominees that would be used to block his chances of leading the Sanders movement to the presidency in 2020. Here too, Sanders opens his text by combining the left populist struggle against the oligarchy with appeals to identity, writing:

> We're making progress when millions of people, in every state in the country, take to the streets for the Women's March in opposition to Trump's reactionary agenda. We're making progress when an unprecedented grassroots movement elects a young African American as mayor of Birmingham, Alabama. [...] The good news is that the American people are far more united than the media would like us to believe. [...] It was not an immigrant picking strawberries at $8 an hour who destroyed the economy in 2008. It was the greed and illegal behavior of Wall Street. It was not transgender people who threw millions of workers out on the street as factories were shut down all across the country. It was profitable national corporations in search of cheap labor abroad.
> SANDERS 2018: 8–9

Designed in part to make the case against Trump, *Where We Go From Here* describes Sanders' activities as a senator from the moment he lost the nomination in 2016 through to August 2018, when he launched the Our Revolution organization, which, like the group Justice Democrats, seeks to close the gap between social movements and electoral politics by promoting progressive candidates to Congress. "People who a few years ago would never have given a moment's thought to becoming involved in electoral politics," he writes, "are now running for office – and winning. Political barriers are being opened that will not be closed" (Sanders 2018: 371). Some of these people are Alexandria Ocasio-Cortez, Rashida Tlaib, Ilhan Omar, Ro Khanna, Ayanna Pressley, Jamaal Bowman, Pramilla Jayapal and Cori Bush. It should be said that none of these politicians are socialists and that despite their progressive credentials have shown themselves to be susceptible to centrist pressure as well as liberal identitarianism.

Sanders' book mentions the Women's March, about which he tweeted to Trump: "President Trump, you made a big mistake. By trying to divide us up by race, religion, gender and nationality you actually brought us closer" (Sanders

2018: 100). He links American imperialism to the re-appearance in the U.S. of fascism and xenophobia, criticizing Trump for equivocating about the two sides who confronted one another at the Unite the Right rally in Charlottesville in August 2017, which led to the murder of Heather Heyer by a self-identified white supremacist. Sanders then ties American foreign policy to mostly economic objectives, himself equivocating on Cold War politics and the independence of countries like North Korea, Cuba and Venezuela. He makes a rather bad case for democratic socialism, stating: "I strongly agree with Winston Churchill, who believed that 'democracy is the worst form of government, except for all the others forms'" (Sanders 2018: 138). Upholding American-style democracy and the international order established by the U.S. since the postwar period, defined as the use of diplomacy instead of force, he denounces the War on Terror as a failed strategy but concedes to the Great Power Conflict policy of the Pentagon by singling out the Russians. The common humanity that Sanders appeals to is emphasized at every turn in the book as black and white, male and female, gay and straight. His frustration with the Democrats is not on the question of diversity, however, but on the avoidance of progressive policies. His claim is that the two together are what makes American democracy work. With regard to William Barber's National Action Network, which he defines as the closest thing today to MLK's Poor People's Campaign, Sanders says that in the tradition of King, people must fight racial injustice at the same time as economic injustice. He namechecks BLM co-founder Patrice Cullors and activist Shaun King as heroes. A government that is representative, he argues, is not extreme, unrealistic or even radical.

The political revolution Sanders advocated in advance of the 2020 nomination race would be based on a common humanity and progressive policy. The political scientist Jodi Dean once said to localist anarchists that "Goldman Sachs doesn't care if you raise chickens." One should bring this up to date for the Bernie Sanders left with the motto that Goldman Sachs doesn't care if you're black or white, male or female, gay or straight. Neither does Donald Trump. Neither did Obama and neither does Biden. And for that matter, neither does a genuine leftist. Negotiating the fault lines between universalism, inclusivity, diversity and woke identitianism is easy enough when you are up against a reactionary like Trump. But against twenty Democratic candidates who are progressive on social issues but neoliberal on policy, there is no room to muck about. Sanders should have hit his opponents with a left-wing agenda and forget about triangulating on social issues. That his campaign failed to do so is less a weakness of Bernie Sanders and more a predicament of the contemporary American left.

2   Whose Revolution? Whose Party?

In *The Once and Future Liberal*, Mark Lilla warns that if American liberals do not look past the Trump Republicans and reject the drift of the Democratic Party away from the "Roosevelt Dispensation" and towards the "Reagan Dispensation," they will continue to lose elections (Lilla). One of the reasons why this shift to the right has occurred, he argues, is because educated urban elites have retreated from universalist political consciousness. Instead, they perceive all issues through the lens of identity, which prevents people from thinking in ways that would allow them to achieve what they say they want. His evidence of this overemphasis on "identity liberalism" is the Democratic Party homepage. In contrast to the Republican Party homepage, which presents a unified vision of conservative principles and values, the Democratic Party website provides no mission statement regarding where the party wants to go and instead directs the browser to a link titled 'People' that then takes the browser to a menu of seventeen distinct identity groups, including women, Hispanics, LGBT, Native Americans, African Americans, Asian Americans and Pacific Islanders.

Beyond the issue of how it is that multiculturalism, identity politics, radical democracy, privilege theory, intersectionality, micro-politics and difference politics interact with various strands of the left – social democratic, socialist, communist and anarchist – there are at least two ways of interpreting the reorientation of the Democratic Party around identity groups. One is that identity is in fact a politics rather than simply an issue that can be viewed from different political perspectives. Intellectual variants like standpoint epistemology and discourse theory might lead someone to argue that identity issues have to be reckoned with in their own terms and cannot be subordinated to macropolitical ideology. While this understanding of identity is not compatible with Marxist materialism, it is compatible with the post-politics of progressive neoliberalism as well as the metaphysical materialism of today's postmodernized anarchist left. In fact, identity politics is one of the means through which the ultra-left and the social democratic left distinguish themselves from and marginalize the radical left. The pluralism that is celebrated by the Democratic Party website would therefore be consistent with the political expectations of establishment centrists as well as the NGO-type academic activists in the Sanders movement. Left populists tend to be divided on this issue, with some of them rejecting political correctness, and others, like the rebranded radical democrats, rejecting so-called class essentialism. Leftists who readily confront issues of race, gender, sexuality, religion and nationality under global capitalism but who do not concede to identity politics, standpoint epistemology, intersectionality, the infrapolitics of resistance or the diversity agenda of corporate capitalism more typically reject the PMC politics of identity. However, to say that identity politics is a class politics does not prevent this sentiment from being confirmed by Democratic Party centrists, as is the case for example with Seth Masket, who argues that identity and ideology are two sides of the same coin. What he is no less reluctant to say is that this coin is a neoliberal politics that replaces policy issues and ideological debate with the demands of electability and narratives that define equality along identitarian lines only (Masket).

The second approach is less principled in its understanding of the relation between identity and politics and is more pragmatic with regard to the realities of human variance, defined in terms of demographics, and the need for political parties to address different identitarian constituencies in their election platforms and campaign outreach. An advocate of this second approach is the civil rights lawyer Steve Phillips. In *Brown Is the New Black*, Phillips argues that the Democratic Party would be making a mistake if it avoided a variegated constituency approach (Phillips). Demographic analysis, he argues, allows us to appreciate the growing reality of a "new American majority" and the fact that Democrats who want to win elections will need to solidify a coalition comprised of progressive people of color (now 23 percent of eligible voters) and progressive whites (about 40 percent of white voters and 28 percent of the electorate). Since this new majority is growing among immigrant groups, with a dependable black base that consistently votes Democrat, Phillips recommends appealing to Latinos especially. How one goes about this will vary among candidates, but Phillips recommends the popular policy priorities of economic justice, immigration reform, election reform, criminal justice reform, environmental justice and universal health care. The fact that neoliberal Democrats have no intention of making any reforms on these issues is beyond the scope of his analysis. As long as Democrats, who are presumed to be progressive, appeal to people on the basis of identity they will fare well with voters. Failure to plan for race-specific outreach, Phillips contends, will allow Republicans to target minority groups and promote conservative candidates of color. Partisan preference must therefore be articulated with what he refers to as cultural competence.

A specialist on the use of cultural competence for electoral outreach is Chuck Rocha, the self-defined "Mexican Redneck" who was hired by the 2020 Sanders campaign for its Latino outreach. Rocha's book, *Tío Bernie: The Inside Story of How Bernie Sanders Brought Latinos to the Political Revolution*, is both a chronicle of the campaign and an advertisement for the specialized services that his consultancy firm, Solidarity Strategies, can provide for prospective political and corporate clients (Rocha). Rising through the ranks of the union movement in Texas and then across the U.S., Rocha had been active in Democratic Party politics for 30 years before Weaver signed him on in 2015 as someone who could help Sanders win the strategic Nevada vote ahead of South Carolina and Super Tuesday. Rocha mentions the impact of the BLM Netroots intervention on Weaver's strategy. Having helped the 2016 campaign in various ways, including the selection of black and Latino staff, Rocha was hired for the 2020 campaign as one of the main national team leaders, where he made sure that people of color were given prominent roles at every level. This included Nina Turner as campaign co-chair and Briahna Joy Gray as national press secretary. Both of the latter helped to write policy and advertisements, and helped to conduct HBCU tours in South Carolina. Faiz Shakir was selected as campaign manager, Ari Rabin-Havt as chief of staff and Ro Khanna, Carmen Yulín-Cruz and Ben Cohen as national co-chairs. More than 200 Latino organizers were hired on to Sanders' national campaign, in large part to win Texas by flipping the Latino turnout from 40 to 50 percent (Davis, 2020). Rocha suggests that in 2020, as in 2016, Americans needed to be "made uncomfortable" about racial inequity (Rocha 2020: 58). He helped Sanders change the way that he talks about immigration issues especially and gave him production ideas for TV ads that would highlight his family history and the deficiencies of Trump as the divider-in-chief. One of Rocha's tasks was to identify places where people of color make up a substantial part of the district and communicate with them through direct mail, digital, radio and Spanish-language ads. Although Spanish-language communications tend to disadvantage Latino voters by reinforcing personal and cultural appeals rather than knowledge about policy differences, a candidate cannot affect policy if they do not get Hispanic voters to the polls (Abrajano). One might also consider that appeals to demographics, as with other minority preferred positions, like anti-Castro sentiment, anti-abortion groups or the gun lobby, have their own distorting effects, especially if your goal is to advance progressive universalist policies (Bishin).

The racialist deconstruction of politics helps to reconstruct it along the lines of markets and issues. These distinct issues, like immigration reform, health care or abortion rights, are then packaged as sold piecemeal to different demographics as political products. Tulsi Gabbard, for example, campaigned almost exclusively on foreign policy and Andrew Yang distinguished himself by promoting UBI. This can also be done negatively. Kamala Harris nearly blocked Biden's ascent on the basis of his reactionary stance on busing and desegregation, while Elizabeth Warren succeeded in emasculating Michael Bloomberg for his sexism. One of the reasons why Sanders was as successful as he was is because he himself does not approach politics as a set of piecemeal issues that can be pitched randomly but views them through an integral, ideological and partisan lens that is simultaneously universalist and progressive. The same can be said about Biden, even if his politics are conservative. For people of this generation, political competence is more fundamental than cultural competence. However, as the chosen leader of a new generation of pro-socialism millennials, whose campaign slogan was 'Not Me, Us,' Sanders accepted that his legitimacy came from his ability to represent his constituency. The Bernie Bro narrative could not be wielded against him, Rocha argues, if opportunities were given to young black and brown people, most of them women, in all of the top staff positions (Rocha 2020: 81). As could be expected, this was not discussed by the press. Further, hires were not selected among well-connected Ivy Leaguers, but through activist networks.

Kicking off the campaign in his hometown of Brooklyn allowed Sanders to connect his family's immigration story to that of other Americans. After he suffered a heart attack in October 2019, Alexandria Ocasio-Cortez was among the first politicians to call him in the hospital and to endorse his campaign, which rebounded, along with his health, at a rally in Queens that was attended by 26,000 enthusiastic supporters. Sanders turned the tables on progressive neoliberalism by stating in his speech: "Take a look around you and find someone you don't know – maybe somebody who doesn't look like you. Are you willing to fight for that person as much as you're willing to fight for yourself?" His words cut across the 'multicultural faces in high places,' 'people who look like me' and 'seat at the table' empowerment rhetoric that defined even his campaign. With this, Sanders marked a crucial difference between the professionals whose job it is to count the number of black and Latino voters in every county, and the actual leadership. It was a Maoist gesture, which asserts that the contradiction is within the people themselves, that flew under the radar of even people like Rocha who define and market themselves first and foremost as Latinos. As Rocha acknowledges, Sanders did not change his message when talking to Latinos, African Americans or any other group. And Sanders ran in 2020 with essentially the same platform as in 2016: universal health care, Wall Street reform, the taxation of billionaire wealth, free post-secondary education, student debt forgiveness, workplace democracy, housing as a human right, a $15 minimum wage, abolition of private prisons, comprehensive immigration reform, an end to fossil fuel subsidies, international diplomacy and a Green New Deal.

Sanders and Ocasio-Cortez understood what they were up against. In his State of the Union address on Tuesday, February 5, 2019, Trump declared his support for a right-wing regime change operation against the Maduro government in Venezuela. In reference to the rising popularity of Sanders and AOC,

Trump asserted that "America will never be a socialist country" (Glasser). In a speech in Florida on February 18, delivered a few days after he declared a state of emergency in order to push through his plans for a U.S.-Mexico border wall, Trump inveighed against communism and socialism, arguing that communism is imperialist in essence and that its twilight hour in the Western hemisphere had arrived. Of course, the U.S. has a history of right-wing anti-communism and its governments have always assisted authoritarian regimes against left-wing movements. Trump's red baiting was not only consistent with his oligarchic politics and the role of Washington in the regulation and enforcement of global capitalism, but was an opening salvo in the 2020 presidential race. Democratic politicians responded in various ways, with Ocasio-Cortez retorting "I think he's scared" (cited in Re). With the wave of teacher strikes in 2018, there was reason to think that Trump was in fact scared of losing to a socialist candidate.

Well before the nomination race got underway, Trump baited Sanders and the social movement left in order to create a situation that would help the right wing of the Democratic Party nip a Sanders government in the bud (Tumulty). Peter D. Hart, a Democratic Party strategist, reported to *The Los Angeles Times* that the Democrats do not want to run on labels: "What they want to run on are programs, ideas and directions for the country ... If the label is 'capitalism vs socialism,' capitalism wins and socialism loses" (Barabak & Mason). One day after Trump's Florida speech, Sanders announced that he would be running for the Democratic Party nomination in the 2020 presidential election. Sanders avoided the capitalism versus socialism setup and instead denounced Trump as a "pathological liar" as well as "a racist, a sexist, a homophobe [and] a xenophobe," calling on grassroots movements to fight back (Meyer).

In 2019, it was possible that Trump's antics and demagoguery would win him yet another election, especially if the Democratic Party pitched him against a neoliberal centrist. In the previous election, polls indicated that only the Sanders campaign could compete against Trump's economic nationalism. Trump's anti-socialism tactic was designed to help elect a right-of-center Democratic Party candidate, which would help him run as the populist anti-establishment candidate. All of the twenty or more candidates, excepting Sanders, would fit the bill for the kind of culture war that Trump specialized in. For this not to happen, Sanders would have had to come on strong with his social democratic agenda. Outside of the two-party monopoly, the Sanders presidency was the only hope for any improvement in domestic and foreign policy in the years ahead. When campaign strategist Stephen Bannon was fired by Trump in 2017, he revealed his alt-right strategy with a statement to the effect: "We want the Democrats to talk about racism and sexism all of the time. If they talk about identity, we can beat them with economic issues" (Lopez). The exit polls of 2016 indicated that around 1 percent of the electorate was concerned with identity issues while about 50 percent of voters were worried about economic issues (Andrea Fraser). Trump had no way to attack Sanders except with Cold War rhetoric, which would nevertheless bring life and death issues like health care, militarism and ecology to the foreground.

Trump was not the only person involved in red baiting. As early as March 2019, Obama responded to the Sanders campaign with a speech in Berlin where he denounced criticism of the Democratic Party. Obama pledged to work with Nancy Pelosi to prevent a drive towards the left within the party that could lead to a replay of the Clinton defeat in 2016. When Perez was chosen as DNC chair, Bill Clinton admonished him: "This is not going to be the party of Bernie" (Allen & Parnes 2021: 22). John Kerry also wanted Sanders stopped. Sadly, Michael Moore, who later went on to become a Sanders surrogate, suggested in the summer months that Michelle Obama should run for president since she would not put up with Trump's bullying (Michallon). Moore was expressing early signs of the strategic voting hang-up, which is also known as insincere voting. It seemed out of place for the director of the 2009 documentary *Capitalism: A Love Story*. Carl Beijer argued that widespread knowledge about Sanders and his campaign for social and economic justice was out of the bottle and it would be cynical for neoliberals to think that they could continue to dominate politics without people rising up against them (Beijer). Moore was not so naïve, however, as to think that the Democratic establishment would help Sanders win the presidency. A television commercial by New Faces GOP candidate Elizabeth Heng juxtaposed an image of Ocasio-Cortez and images of mass killings by the Khmer Rouge, with the statement: "this is the face of socialism." The irony would likely be lost on audiences that the U.S.-backed Khmer Rouge was but one of the nefarious outcomes of the American imperialism that is defended by not only by the likes of John Bolton and Lindsey Graham, but also by the two dozen presidential candidates that would be lined up against Sanders, including Joe Biden, Elizabeth Warren, Beto O'Rourke, Kamala Harris, Kirsten Gillibrand, Cory Booker, Tom Steyer, Deval Patrick, John Delaney, Michael Bloomberg, Amy Klobuchar and Pete Buttigieg.

Having supported most of the above candidates for the Democratic Party leadership, Obama called for moderation in political ideology as the best means to beat Trump. A November article by Ryan Lizza in *Politico* made it known that Obama and the majority of party factotums were more opposed to a Sanders nomination than a second Trump term (Lizza; Savage). Obama offered the media a few mea culpas about the failures of his bipartisan strategy so that he could then demand more sacrifices: financial deregulation, the deunionization of labor, school closures, protection of the health insurance industry, environmental free-for-alls, trillion-dollar regime change interventions and the continued militarization of police. As if Americans had not had enough of this lackey of Wall Street and the Pentagon, Obama told an audience of financial donors at the Democracy Alliance in Washington D.C.:

> This is still a country that is less revolutionary than it is interested in improvement. They like seeing things improved. But the average American doesn't think we have to completely tear down the system and remake it. [...] There are a lot of persuadable voters and there are a lot of Democrats out there who just want to see things make sense. They just don't want to see crazy stuff. [...] Even as we push the envelope and we are bold in our vision, we also have to be rooted in reality and the fact that voters, including the Democratic voters and certainly persuadable independents or even moderate Republicans are not driven by the same views that are reflected on certain, you know, left-leaning Twitter feeds. Or the activist wing of our party.
> SEGERS; GUARDIAN STAFF; RELMAN

As Neil Young says about climate change deniers in the song 'Shut It Down,' blindness to problems makes people "as cool as they can be." Obama understood that his version of moderate is the reactionary radicalism of the extreme center and its willingness to carry on with a program of social inequality, austerity, war and ecological destruction. Although the media reported that Obama's comments referred to the left-leaning candidates Sanders and Warren, it is more accurate to say that they directly targeted the Sanders campaign, which called for the kind of "political revolution" in American politics that was certainly feasible and not more radical than what had hitherto been achieved through the New Deal and other examples of government support of working people. Sanders replied to Obama's attacks with the argument that his policies would not tear down the system and are popular objectives that could have and should have been implemented decades ago (Guardian staff). Media outlets nevertheless depicted Sanders as a reclusive curmudgeon who wants to tear down the system (Girigharadas; Dovere).

As Obama no longer had to contend with the demands of the office of the presidency, he more clearly showed what his politics had been all along. Obama voiced his opposition to Warren's criticism of Wall Street and stated his intention to intervene in the 2020 primaries if Sanders got anywhere near the Democratic nomination. Like the rest of the donor class, Obama benefited from Trump's policies. As for Trump, his decision to attack China with trade war measures sidestepped the Democrats' plans to build a military offensive against Russia by supporting the fascist regime in Ukraine. Despite his signing of the United States-Mexico-Canada Trade Agreement, Trump's ratings were climbing. Michael Bloomberg promised to defeat Trump through lavish advertisement spending. Given that the billionaire was not polling so well, the Warren campaign issued an advertisement in November titled "Elizabeth Warren Stands Up to the Billionaires" (Warren). The ad identifies the net worth of the billionaire pundits who had spoken out against her in the mainstream media. Her cast of white male billionaires is contrasted to a mostly teenage and twenty-something audience of ebullient young women, which gives the impression that capitalist exploitation is based on age, race and gender oppression. The ad indirectly attacks Sanders, who had been defamed in the media as too old to be president. Warren had more in common with Obama and Bloomberg than her anti-billionaire advertisement let on. With favorable profiles in the mainstream press and among right-wing factions of the Democratic Party, Warren's ability to "inflict pain" on corruption in the financial industry, symbolized in the advertisement by her flailing hands, was complemented by indications that she was prepared to defeat Sanders and his un-American ideas about socialism. Bloomberg News, hardly a neutral source in these matters since it is owned by Michael Bloomberg, reported in July that Warren was gaining the support of wealthy bankers. For many on Wall Street who supported Obama, one article said, "Warren is an acceptable alternative to candidates who trigger their most visceral objections: Republican President Donald Trump on the right and Senator Bernie Sanders, a self-described democratic socialist, on the left" (Nguyen & Pager).

No doubt the billionaire class preferred Biden or Buttigieg, but if they could not get their backscratcher of choice, Warren's acceptance of Wall Street campaign financing implied that some regulation would be preferable to the industry than an ideological offensive that mobilized the grassroots. A corporate lawyer, Warren began her political career as a conservative and was a registered Republican through the Reagan era until 1996. Her favorite president is Teddy Roosevelt and her conservative critique of the state of economic crisis ultimately places trust in the fairness of capitalist social relations. Warren came to prominence when she was chosen to lead a panel overseeing the 2008–2009 bank bailout and was later noted for proposing and establishing the Consumer Financial Protection Bureau. Her Plan for Economic Patriotism was premised on economic security doctrines that have been devised in coordination with the military and intelligence apparatus. Like other right-wing Democrats, she perceives Great Power Competition from

China and Russia as the leading challenge to American supremacy. Although she criticized America's 'forever wars' in the Middle East, she has no record of opposition to imperialism. In 2016, she campaigned for the hawkish Clinton rather than Sanders. She has also sought to build her security credentials by serving on the Senate Armed Services Committee and traveled to the Middle East with John McCain and Lindsay Graham. In 2019 she voted in favor of Trump's 4.7 percent increase to military spending, which was already larger than the next 14 biggest military spenders combined, including Russia, China, Britain, France and Japan. Her stated defense of American workers and industry on the basis of security and patriotism, which did not address immigration issues, was closer to Trump's agenda than her "feminist" attack on white male billionaires suggests. She did not oppose the privatization of education through charters and instead called for accountability in the process, posing on American Federation of Teachers picket lines in Chicago and offering band-aid remedies to school defunding and closures. Her support of corrupt unions like the United Auto Workers is only as significant as the outcome of the major strikes of 2019, which led to concessionary contracts, plant closures and "good American jobs" for lower-tier, part-time and contract workers who are being nickel and dimed into early "retirement." Although Warren claimed that in the 2020 Democratic nomination race she would not accept super PAC money, she changed her mind after the Iowa and New Hampshire primaries, in which she placed fourth and third, on the argument that the male candidates have super PACs. The truth of the matter is not gender but the fact that in the lead-up to Super Tuesday, Warren had run out of campaign financing and needed to revise her stance. None of her pandering of identity politics and denunciation of discrimination would have improved the lives of the majority of young women shown in her advertisement. The current system of global capitalism is, as Ralph Nader once said about the Chevrolet Corvair, "unsafe at any speed." If the Sanders campaign had tire pressure that was manufactured for greater safety, Warren's slogan of 'Dream Big' and 'Fight Hard' to rebuild the middle class was designed for greater comfort but was likely to "tuck under."

Not to be outperformed, Pete Buttigieg, who was beating Biden in the New Hampshire polls in November 2019, released a television ad called "Big Ideas," in which he attacked the tuition-free public college proposals of both Sanders and Warren (Buttigieg). Buttigieg's objection was that this universal policy would also benefit the children of millionaires. In contrast, his proposal would make college education free for only those households that earn less than $100,000 per year. Buttigieg's defense of means-testing was criticized for the threat it posed to primary and secondary education, Social Security, Medicare and other public services like libraries, parks and fire stations. Such regressive tax measures were criticized by progressives as disingenuous since they privilege privatization and the profit motive for public services at the same time that they shift Democratic policy further towards Republican objectives. The subtext of the ad tells a different story, however. Buttigieg says that he only wants to make promises he can keep and does not want to "turn off" half of the country before getting into office. As he dismisses people like Sanders who would want college education to be "free for even the kids of millionaires," he jerks his arm and clenched hand as though he is milking a cow. The gesture could also be thought to be demonstrating a handjob. In this sense, the word "kids" alludes to LGBTQ constituencies and "millionaires" refers to people who are celibate, straight and monogamous. This interpretation of the ad is underscored by the fact that some of the audience in the small, rustic setting, are nodding in agreement as though some of them are giving blowjobs. Three of the men shown in the space of a few seconds are bald. The act of making agreement seem like someone is giving a blowjob has been a commonplace of gay public performativity for several years already. The difference is that here the so-called margins are not only being mainstreamed but are being used to advance a neoliberal agenda. The combined effect is that Mayor Pete is "representing" the gay community at the same time that he is undermining political representation. While such democratic agonism has been developed by the postmodern left, it is here deployed as neoliberal camp, which brings to light two considerations: the fact that such so-called agonism is based in petty transgressions that do as much to privatize and gangsterize public deliberation as anything else – a topic that is as stale as the Foucault-Habermas debates – and also the fact that such hipster subtext and pride signaling actually does very little for the LGBTQ constituencies who would be impacted by Buttigieg's policies.

A candidate from South Bend, Indiana, Buttigieg raised considerable campaign funds from Wall Street and Silicon Valley. He is known for his work helping McKinsey clients invest in war zones. After Biden declined in the polls, Buttigieg came out as the next in line to lead the right wing of the party. His profile as an openly gay candidate appealed to progressives, as did his Harvard and Oxford education. However, Buttigieg's role in the U.S. Army organizing death squads in Afghanistan, which is difficult to account for in terms of his professed Episcopalian beliefs, made for worrisome foreign policy. As another pawn in the 'national security' agenda, Buttigieg's gayness was as relevant to progressive politics as Obama's blackness and Clinton's womanhood. Like his mediocratic colleagues, he defended the neoliberal consensus and not the interests of the majority. His only advantage was that like the former president, he was relatively unknown, young, sophisticated and willing to compromise with power.

Kamala Harris, for her part, ran a very weak campaign. Her advisers suggested that she needed to attack Biden to prove her mettle when going against Trump. Since Biden was known to have opposed desegregation through school busing, on the view that such social engineering was unpopular with white and black parents, Harris claimed that the success of his position at that time would have prevented a person of color like herself to be in the race with him. Her campaign immediately marketed t-shirts with the slogan 'That Little Girl Was Me.' On the basis of this attack, Harris polled in second place for two weeks. Regardless, her record as a conservative prosecutor and her overall smarminess failed to secure the confidence of voters.

Candidates like Warren, Buttigieg and Harris appealed to a disingenuous version of Antonio Gramsci's notion of the war of position, where the left must use identity to win the popular support that will give it political power. However, because it is tied to neoliberalism, this use of identity does not take part in the greater and ultimately more important war of maneuver. The issue for the left is not that minority politicians like Obama, Clinton and Buttigieg can more easily appeal to demographic groups and their progressive allies, but that politics is being redefined by the post-Fordist knowledge and culture industries that assert PMC prerogatives and the empowerment of a generation of precarious workers whose chances of gainful employment decreases in inverse proportion to the demand that they instrumentalize identity. The least one can say about the 2020 Sanders campaign is that it attacked progressive neoliberalism by associating racial and gender signifiers with progressive policy initiatives. An August 2019 interview between Sanders and the celebrity rapper Cardi B captures the Sanders campaign's effort to reach the masses by combining Brechtian instruction and pleasure. The artist opens a YouTube video with the somewhat incomprehensible statement:

> See ... professional, bitch all motherfuckers coming after me on my last video, so now I'm about to get ignorant. First and first, I'm not tellin people to get edecated when it comes to these candidates with no fuckin clout. Every two days, I'm getting a hundred thousand followers. My engagement is crazy. My music is sellin, my shows are sellin. I'm good. And I been doin dis shit for a hot minute. I been preachin about politics since I had crooked teeth. Every other day I'm on live, talkin about dis shit.
>
> All Urban Central

Instead of complaining about Trump, who is "put on blast" she says by Twitter, people should have listened to the stripper, who is trying to make change happen by paying millions of dollars in taxes. The video closes with a picture of the interview in which she and Sanders discuss the issues of police violence, unemployment, immigration reform, universal health care, $15 minimum wage, FDR's New Deal, free post-secondary tuition and political participation (Sanders Channel 2019b). The rapper Killer Mike, who is known for his political activism, also filmed an interview with Sanders in 2019, comparing his agenda to MLK's Poor People's Campaign (Sanders Channel 2019c).

By February 2020, establishment Democrats showed that they would not give an inch on the possibility of transforming the party from the inside. The white electorate, however, was trending hard left (Allen & Parnes 2021: 237). While Hillary Clinton crowed to Ellen DeGeneres that Bernie was promising the moon, Buttigieg was busy rigging the Iowa caucus and Biden was ordering debate audiences to stand to attention in favor of the kind of hawkish politics associated with Dick Cheney and Donald Rumsfeld. For primary candidates, winning in Iowa is often decisive. Buttigieg had spent more than $2 million on campaign ads already and focused all of his efforts on that state. Meanwhile, the Trump impeachment had not done as much damage to Biden's reputation as might have been expected. Since the CNN-sponsored *Des Moines Register* poll showed that Biden was losing his lead to Sanders, Buttigieg's communications director, Liz Smith, used a single error to cast doubt on this trusted poll, thereby denying Sanders two crucial days of positive media coverage. The official results from Iowa were suppressed indefinitely due to glitches with the app that precinct workers were supposed to use to report results. The app, it turned out, was developed by Shadow Inc., a company headed by the wife of Buttigieg's senior advisor, and Acronym, a company connected to Clinton associates.

Through this and other DP and DNC manipulations, the Iowa caucus was intentionally botched. Despite Buttigieg rushing to declare himself the winner, Rocha's Latino strategy had paid off and workers defied union directives to hand Sanders his first win. Biden's name-calling of citizens dog-faced pony soldiers and cockroaches had not failed to be noticed. Centrist Democrats desperately began to consider Bloomberg their man. Something had to be done. At the CBS-hosted Democratic Party primaries debate on February 7, George Stephanopoulos led the attack against Sanders by asking the nominees to debate whether or not democratic socialism is appropriate for the party. He did not ask whether neoliberalism is better for America since that would entail asking whether people prefer a better life and a future for humanity to drone strikes and money grabs in the Middle East. It was obviously the term socialism and not identity politics that was perceived as a threat to the over-inflated military behemoth that is dragging the entire world down its ignominious path.

By late February, most of the candidates, excepting Biden and Bloomberg, were effectively out of the way of a Sanders nomination. His campaign was set to absorb many of the middle-of-the-road liberals who favored Harris, Yang, Booker, Klobuchar, Buttigieg and Warren for identitarian reasons. His campaign began to make something of the fact that Sanders would be the first Jewish president. More importantly, his supporters reported furiously that Sanders could knock out Trump with a strong left hook of working-class proposals and a right hook of inclusiveness. With 2016 still in the shadows, and with polls indicating that Trump would likely win against a Biden or Bloomberg nomination, Sanders could have criticized identitarianism as a feature of neoliberal centrism and go all out with progressive universalism. However, tagging different demographics is part of the game of winning election victories in different states and at different moments of a campaign. With the odds in his favor, Sanders was hard-pressed to break with the universalism that had served him throughout his lifetime. Echoing MLK's words on the fact that one should judge someone on the basis of their character rather than their race, Sanders added to this Buttigieg and the Iowa Democratic Party chairman's efforts to rig the vote: "If you cannot win an election based on your ideas and your character," he said in his speeches at that time, "then you should get the hell out of politics and get another job." Having won New Hampshire and with Rocha's Latino strategy kicking into gear in Nevada – with rank and file workers defying union misdirection there a well – Sanders became the first presidential candidate to win the first three primaries.

At the February 25 Democratic Party presidential debate, CBS host Gail King introduced the last segment by asking Sanders and the other nominees to discuss the biggest misconception about them and what motto best represents them. Having told his interviewers at the *New York Times* that he is the kind of candidate who will fight for working people, but that he is not the kind of politician who will send people a birthday card on their birthday, it was no surprise when Sanders replied that the biggest misunderstanding about him is that his ideas are radical. His favorite motto, he said, is Nelson Mandela's slogan: 'It always seems impossible until it is done.' Sanders, we might think, avoided talking about himself in his reply, for example, in comparison with Biden joking about losing his hair and Bloomberg half-heartedly joking about his height. In the context of the most important election in recent history, the easiest thing to do was to babble on about personal hang-ups rather than about public policy. Being 'big enough' to admit that one has personal anxieties might demonstrate humility to voters, but it could also demonstrate that one is not so political as to challenge the power structure. Sanders' personal touch was to avoid self-serving narcissism and say that progressive policies, because they have been enacted by governments worldwide, are nothing to get tied up in knots about.

Corporate pundits like Chris Matthews and Rachel Maddow attempted at every stage of the campaign to avoid policy issues by propagating misinformation. This included the assertion that Sanders was not popular with black voters and that his own supporters were brown shirts, which led to criticism which obliged Matthews to take his retirement from news showbiz (Dugyala). Neo-Nazis were hardly typical Sanders supporters and he himself denounced anyone in his movement who resorted to sexism or racism. However, none of that sort of thing actually matters when the criteria of political knowledge are reduced to identity. Michael Eric Dyson acknowledges the half of this when he says: "Barack Obama's presidency … has hardly put a dent in the forces that pulverize black life … That does not mean that Obama's presidency bears little symbolic value" (Dyson 2016: 49). The effort to alter beliefs and value systems by tinkering with media signifiers comes around to the issue of the personal in the political. Does someone use their identity to wokewash postmodern nihilism or do they stand for something that is socially significant? Matthews' open admission that the Democratic Party would likely prefer a second Trump term to a Sanders administration is nothing that the left had not been saying for several months already. The difference is that Matthews' stance was a form of pretense misrecognition. The slightest amount of research easily disproved the disinfotainment trotted out by people like Matthews and Maddow.

One of the first lines of attack by media pundits against Sanders was his age, a point that was never raised about Biden or Trump. After his stent operation, which actually improved his condition, the question of his age was transferred to the question of his health. Around that time, the Sanders campaign used the senator's age to his advantage by emphasizing his long record of progressive activism as a mark of authenticity. Bernie Sanders, unlike the world of news, memes and advertisements, was not changing on a daily basis. Warren tried to spin his constancy to suggest that the same record could be construed as a long series of failures to (single-handedly) change American society. Both Warren and Clinton misinformed reporters about his views on the role of delegates with respect to his insistence on the primacy of the popular vote. Warren's disinfotainment was no more convincing than Clinton's pandering to shock jock Howard Stern. Clinton told Stern that Sanders had not shown enough support for her in 2016, despite the fact that he gave 40 rally speeches on hers and the Democratic Party's behalf to defeat Trump, while Clinton herself only gave 10 speeches for Obama after she lost to him in 2008 (Marcetic 2019b).

An attack meme works best when it is true. Crooked Hillary, Pete the Rat and Warren the Snake have more veracity than Crazy Bernie. Warren earned the enmity of the Sanders movement when during the 2020 primaries she twice accused him of suggesting that a woman could not be president. Sanders met privately with Warren on December 12, 2018, mostly to know if she would be running. Warren wanted to know why Sanders would be running against her in 2020. He discussed with her his belief that he did not think that she or Biden could beat Trump. Sanders argued that Trump, who referred to Warren as Pocahontas, would weaponize identity to attack her. As well, in contrast to Warren, Sanders had not publicly attacked Obama and the Clintons. Both agreed that they would not attack one another during the nomination race, a pledge that Warren rescinded ahead of the Iowa caucus. It cost both of them the nomination.

After winning the popular vote in the first three primaries, Sanders was expected to win either a majority or a plurality of delegates at the national convention. With only one week remaining until Super Tuesday, the Democratic Party establishment scrambled to block his path. In the South Carolina primary, the influential congressman James Clyburn, a member of the Congressional Black Caucus, encouraged a Biden vote. Winning South Carolina had been Biden's strategy to win the nomination. This was the same strategy used by Obama and Hillary Clinton, with whom Biden was associated by black voters. Leaders in the Congressional Black Caucus directed poor and working-class blacks to oppose Sanders and emphasized Biden's association with Obama. Biden obliged Clyburn by promising to name a black woman to the Supreme Court and as Vice President. As early as summer 2019, nearly three quarters of black voters and a sizeable portion of conservative whites favored Biden. The belief that Biden was the best choice to defeat Trump is the main reason for his appeal among black Democrats. Biden won 61 percent of the black vote in South Carolina and 49 percent of the total black vote, with 20 percent of the total black vote going to Sanders and single-digit percentages for the other nominees.

After the South Carolina primary, according to Allen and Parnes, panic had set in with party heavyweights. Warren, Buttigieg, Klobuchar and Bloomberg were effectively out of the running but were still set to siphon votes from Biden. Sanders was expected to win a large number of delegates in Texas, California and elsewhere. A small lead in state delegates would allow him to reap the whirlwind. Biden had made no effort in any other state. "For the anti-Sanders wing of the party," write Allen and Parnes, "the best move was to coalesce behind a single candidate who could easily defeat him. But through four states, no candidate had won a majority of the vote" (Allen & Parnes

2021: 435). Obama was now prepared to support Biden. Buttigieg was advised to drop out of the race by his staff and by Jimmy Carter. Obama also called on him to drop out. Senate Majority Leader Harry Reid called Amy Klobuchar to do the same. Both of them understood that they had a brighter future if they did not alienate the party brass. Their supporters were now encouraged by Obama to vote for Biden. Without any ground game and with no path to victory, Warren, who had campaigned against Sanders and other nominees on gender politics, decided to remain in the race. While Buttigieg and Klobuchar endorsed Biden, Warren stayed in the race to prevent her supporters from going over to Sanders. Obama also called on party donors to support the candidate from MBNA. In record time, a party coup had been orchestrated. As Trump stated during the October 6 debate with Biden: "If Pocahontas would have left two days earlier, you would have lost every primary." More accurately, Biden would have won the South Carolina primary but would likely have fallen out of the race.

With Obama's support, an establishment fixture scored large majorities with African-American voters, especially in Alabama. In contrast, Sanders did well among Latino voters. Sanders won only 23 percent of the vote among educated women. As for his popularity with millennials, these fickle supporters turned out in even smaller numbers in 2020 than in 2016. Biden performed particularly well with black voters and non-college educated whites. Despite the Sanders campaign going to great lengths to emphasize solidarity across identity groups, the neoliberal Biden, who has a history of discriminatory policies, did best among blacks who consider race issues to be more important than economic inequality. As Keeanga-Yamahtta Taylor argued, Biden's success on Super Tuesday "reflects the fact that we haven't fully interrogated Barack Obama's tenure" (Taylor 2020a). In the end, the electorate chose a white male capitalist to go up against another white male capitalist.

3   Malarkey

The lesson of the 2016 and 2020 elections is the problematic nature of a left politics that is based on appeals to identity and demographics rather than universalist policies and class opposition to neoliberal ideology. Biden's authoritarian demeanor improved his likeability among voters. Now *that* is something to consider, other than white working-class racism, as a factor in the 2016 Trump election victory. The lesson of Super Tuesday is that woke politics interfere with political reform. Sanders declared on that evening that the debate going forward will be a contest of ideas.[3] The advantage Sanders had against Trump was his opposition to bad trade deals, cuts to Social Security and military misadventures overseas. Issues like tackling climate change appeal to people across identity categories. On the whole it was neoliberals like Buttigieg, Harris, Klobuchar and Warren who privileged diversity as a selling point. However, in order to avoid being baited on the issue of diversity, the Sanders team made the mistake of caring too much about the fact that it could walk and chew gum at the same time. Whether this skill would impress voters remained to be determined. In any case the establishment had more than cast its lot. The only thing it had left to use against Sanders was the prospect that his success would lead to a replay of the Trump victory. What they wanted was Biden as usual, which, when translated into policy, meant millions without health care, the continuation of wars in the Middle East, increased billionaire wealth, corporate profits and ecological doomsday scenarios.

If American progressives had not yet interrogated Obama's tenure, the same could be said about Biden. In 2012, after having rejected the possibility of further government investment and turning towards austerity, Obama campaigned with attack ads against his opponents and with appeals to identity politics. Beyond election victories, the failure of that successful strategy was brought home, first, with the indifference of the Obama administration towards the plight of working people in the U.S. and abroad, and secondly, with the inability of the Democratic Party to self-correct after the defeat of Hillary Clinton to an alt-right charlatan. It is one thing to find woke rhetoric among neoliberals, or in the intellectual swamp of postmodern academia, but it is another thing to find it among people who describe themselves as socialists. For the most part the class function of identity politics is unknown to people who should know better and are afraid to ask. Media messages and incidents in the Sanders campaign bring to mind the flawed logic of woke identitarianism. Yet the progressive movement simply does not want to face its end of ideology problem. The Sanders campaign team generously allowed surrogates and supporters to come to the movement as they are and without expecting doctrinal uniformity. As long as people were generally in favor of progressive policy changes and were able to mount a critique of the establishment, they were welcomed to the revolution. This made some sense and had some advantages as a kind of ad hoc social movement strategy. It also had disadvantages insofar as it prevented the movement behind Sanders from leading the ideological

---

3 For a discussion of the African-American vote on Super Tuesday as an anti-Trump vote based on the perception of Biden's greater electability, and despite African-American support for socialist policies, see Ford; Jacobin Magazine 2020a.

struggle. It certainly avoided the necessary task of elucidating the ways in which identity politics obscure class politics.

The limitation of the 'big tent' aspect of the Sanders campaign is that it is suited to left struggle as much as liberal pluralism. There is a case to be made for solidarity across struggles, but how one goes about this makes democratic *socialism* essentially different from the kinds of politics that are based on nationalism, identity politics and micro-politics, especially in their postmodern and neoliberal versions. The point is not the obvious one that the Sanders campaign dared to speak about the working class, but the fact that the Sanders campaign and the movement that supported it did not have the courage to address the problems that intersectional identity politics pose to radicalism. That is why, at the penultimate moment, and after the successful Democratic Party coup, talk about a 'rainbow coalition' was too little too late.

The reason that class struggle is not about asserting an identity, Žižek argues, is because class struggle is not about inclusion. Recognizing differences has more to do with managing social antagonisms within the already existing and dominant forms of capitalist universality. The left has only itself to blame when it substitutes left-liberal identitarian inclusion for radical social change. Without even worrying about conservatives, it is fair to say that the blacks who voted for Biden reflect the social realities that are masked by boutique activism. Although the rhetoric of post-blackness that Obama is known for is little more than a pretext for capitalist values, its universalism is correct. However, one can also locate this universalism on the side of blackness, as the work and activism of Cornel West demonstrates. And West is correct that only Sanders had a sense of the *emancipatory* universality that does not depend on identity, but that targets the capitalist relations through which people's identities are made both meaningful and meaningless. While older African Americans placed their hope in the American Creed and played by the rules of the capitalist world, the younger generation of blacks has replaced the mass politics of patriotism with the difference politics of identity. That this racial turn is a product of the retreat of the left since the 1960s is difficult to impart to a generation that has been weaned on austerity, privatization and policing.

Playing by the rules of intersectionality is the way to get along in academia, in activist politics and in the cultural sector. It means that one does not have to take the risk of being a revolutionary socialist, which for the most part is inoperative in PMC circles. Diversity is social grease geared for the networks that are already in place. If the left is to be anything more than a mouthpiece that comes in all shapes and sizes, it needs to reimagine revolutionary praxis. By the same token, socialists must support all of the above social justice issues by emphasizing the fact that capitalism cannot and will never deliver on these – not because of sexism, white supremacy, homophobia and xenophobia, but because capitalism is founded on social inequality and exploitation. In these terms, Sanders is the only presidential candidate who showed the remotest sense of what needs to be done. In the Sanders-Biden debate of March 15, Biden did not hesitate to attack Sanders for his socialist views. This was not something that Sanders was ashamed of since it was the basis of his very legitimate support. As a pre-postmodern octogenarian, Sanders understood this better than the millennials who are hooked on left populism and virtue signaling. Before Super Tuesday, the journalist Zaid Jilani was reporting favorably on what looked like an eventual Sanders majority vote. After the media-backed coup that was staged by establishment Democrats, Jilani criticized Sanders for over-emphasizing the socialist aspects of his platform, now being used to explain the sudden change in voter behavior (The Hill 2020g). In only a few hours, the socialist veneer of idealistic youth had cracked.

What low youth voter turnout had not accomplished in ending Sanders' bid for the nomination, COVID-19 finished off. The blooper-prone Biden quarantined himself in his basement for the remainder of the presidential race, allowing Trump to fumble the pandemic while at the same time defending lawless anti-mask fascists against George Floyd protesters. The less Biden said about the problems facing the country, the more his approval ratings increased. With a Vice President as unappealing as Kamala Harris, whom even the Congressional Black Congress was not impressed with, the mantra of party unity rallied all of the usual suspects around a status quo rejection of Trump craziness. The August convention featured several Republicans in addition to a speech by Obama that linked the imperfections of the Constitution to a racialist understanding of police reform. The theme of the event was a reworking of the late 60s anthem by Buffalo Springfield 'For What It's Worth,' performed by *Kinki Boots* star Billy Porter against a gay-themed afro-nationalist backdrop. The first six months of the Biden administration demonstrated what the Democrats' mediocratic virtue hoarding was actually worth: the failure to impeach or prosecute the leader and the Republican party supporters of a fascist coup attempt on the U.S. Capitol; federal neglect of the state of Texas after winter storm Uri knocked out the power grid; the appointment of an advocate of Ukrainian fascism, Victoria Nuland, as Undersecretary of State for Political Affairs; the appointment of Obama-Clinton crony, union-buster and enemy of Social Security, Neera Tanden, as director of the Office of Management and Budget; trade war against China, promotion of the Wuhan lab leak conspiracy theory, false allegations of Uyghur genocide and support for Hong Kong separatists; failure to reform immigration and the reopening of Trump's child detention centers; the anti-worker and pro-union boss PRO Act;

failure to deliver on student debt relief, except for streamlining the elimination of debt for permanently disabled students; joint border control with Latin American demagogues; support for Department of Justice surveillance of journalists and continued persecution of Julian Assange; defense of illegal military surveillance of citizens and tracking of anti-capitalist extremists; defense of Israeli apartheid and war crimes like the continued bombing of Syria, Iraq and Somalia; billion-dollar arms deals with the arab emirates; defense of the Israeli bombing of Gaza; a record military budget and an additional $2 billion for Capitol police; a lackluster bipartisan infrastructure bill based on raising gas prices; reversal of promises to end the death penalty; the rejection of a public option for health care and refusal to raise taxes on the rich. Although widely criticized by the media, Biden did the right thing when he followed through on Trump's plan to withdraw from Afghanistan. However, having spent $2 trillion on an unjustified and two decades-long foreign occupation that killed 150,000 Afghanis, one third of them innocent citizens, the U.S. can hardly be credited for a job well done.

CHAPTER 3

Elective Affinities

> You can probably make them do anything for you: sell people things they don't need; make women who don't know you fall in love with you.
>
> VANCE PACKARD, *The Hidden Persuaders*

⁂

Enthusiasm around the Bernie Sanders campaigns has given rise to a new generation of activists and media personalities. In 2018 it seemed as though the leftist solidarity that had built up around the Arab Spring, the Wisconsin uprising, Occupy Wall Street and the Quebec student strike had all but abated and been defused by fragmentation. Black Lives Matter, MeToo, March for Our Lives, the Women's March, Extinction Rebellion and similar activist campaigns had taken the focus off of the political economy of neoliberal globalization. It was as though you could not attack the problem at the root but could only approach it indirectly. Since most people accept capitalism but do not accept police violence, sexual assault, mass shootings and ecological catastrophe, single issues seem like a safer bet for activists and professionals of various sorts.

The diversification of politics along identitarian lines defined the 2020 Sanders campaign far more than the 2016 campaign. The people who conceptualized and created the advertisements for the 2020 campaign deserve criticism for wokewashing progressive politics. Even though the 2020 Sanders team did not do any negative campaigning against the other party nominees, it did do negative campaigning against people who do not identify with the postmodern ideology that has come to be accepted by the professional-managerial class. This is problematic since there was no need for the Sanders team to buttress its democratic socialist program with the anti-oppression discourse of progressive neoliberals. Without question, the social justice agenda of new social movements activists is popular with the educated cadres of the social base, who not only enjoy but demand to be interpellated on the basis of their identity. These contradictions must be elucidated rather than concealed.

The use of woke signals in Sanders advertisements and during Sanders events is due to an ideological demand that comes from the realm of what

Lacanians refer to as the big Other. This demand is as ideological as it is unconscious. Beyond the need to counter Trump's discriminatory demagoguery, woke politics has run an ideological deficit as a tool of the neoliberal class. To date, the rejection of woke politics has come mostly from conservatives and liberals, who defend Enlightenment universalism along with capitalist social relations (Murray; McWhorter). On the whole, the anarchist left and postmodern academia are supportive of identity politics and tend to situate it beyond the question of 'modernist' macro-politics. When it comes to identity politics, much academic 'left' discourse merits the epithet 'cultural Marxism,' with the added caveat, as Žižek argued in his 2019 debate with Jordan Peterson on the subject of Happiness: Capitalism vs. Marxism: "they're not Marxists" (Peterson). Woke identitarianism does not make for the most radical expression of left politics. Far from it. The following examines specific advertisements and town hall events from the 2020 Sanders campaign. I preface this with some general remarks on the sociological analysis of advertising, with some more specific reflections on political campaign advertising and celebrity endorsement.

1   Your Candidate Here

The sociology of advertising is mostly concerned with consumer behavior. Political advertising can be extrapolated to imply concern with voter behavior. Advertising has more in common with practical disciplines like anthropology and psychology than it does with critical disciplines like political philosophy and psychoanalysis. While advertisers never promise their clients that advertising works, they will tell them that failing to advertise will concede the market to your competitors. In the realm of political advertising, research-driven ads and creative ads allow campaigns to inform audiences and shape their perception of the candidate. One can go further to suggest that political ads also shape politics. For example, the "bourgeoisification" of the working class in the U.K. in the 1970s caused the Labour Party to make itself more inclusive and appealing to "new social classes" beyond industrial blue-collar workers. They were not only prompted to do so by Thatcherism but also by the influence of the advertising firm of Charles and Maurice Saatchi (Delaney 2015: 43).

While consumer and voter choice cannot be predicted, producers need consumers and candidates need voters. Advertising competition is a means to stabilize consumer and voter anxiety (Lury & Warde). For this reason, advertisers sell their services to anxious politicians, whose views of the electorate are shaped by the demographic and psychographic measurement methods of advertising and polling agencies. Assumptions and expectations concerning voter behavior are built into advertising messages that tautologically mirror, replicate and confirm research findings. Advertising therefore has a propensity towards what Roland Barthes referred to in *Mythologies* as doxa: the transformation of meaning into form (Barthes 1972: 131). All advertising is therefore, from the perspective of the producer or politician, a kind of Faustian bargain. As consumer segmentation multiplies the number of target markets, specialized knowledge becomes unverifiable and gains a more comforting than scientific function. It is fitting then that the main advertising platform of the Sanders campaign was 'Bernie's Yearning,' a Ben & Jerry's Ice Cream flavor developed by the national Sanders campaign co-chair Ben Cohen.

As early as the turn of the last century, Thorstein Veblen recognized that consumerism created an abstract relationship between producers and customers (Veblen). The rise of advertising was related to efforts on the part of producers to penetrate resistant markets and to create new desires. The abstract notion of consumer choice mystified conspicuous consumption beyond the level of need towards that of lifestyle, which emphasized visibility, display and status buying. According to Stewart Ewen, twentieth-century captains of industry mobilized Madison Avenue firms to reorient consumer practices around the needs of capitalist producers through the promotion of uniformity (Ewen 2001: 41). Despite its diversity, the American market could be nationalized by associating consumerism with the struggle against communism. Class struggle was remade into a mass culture version of individualism: the commodity self. According to the world of advertising, anxiety about worthlessness could be alleviated with toothpaste or a new car. This was only slightly different from the emerging night life that construed cinema, jazz clubs, alcoholism and anonymous sex as the lodestar of alienated life in the lonely metropolis. The only truth in advertising was the mission to overcome the traditional values of puritanism, thrift and self-sufficiency. Associating consumerism with social change, advertising replaced class antagonism with the 'marginal utility' of this product instead of that one. The creator of the public relations industry, Edward Bernays, viewed the manipulation of hearts and minds as a propaganda battle against anyone who refused the directives of corporate America. As wages stagnated, the sense of helplessness tied workers to the authority of business. The privileging of youth was later related to the capitalist need to control labor. Rejecting mature citizens, advertisers idealized pleasure-seeking young adults as an ideological weapon against labor rebellion. Lifestyle change, loose morals, leisure and what Bourdieu refers to as the "fun ethic" were motivated through advertising as a paradoxical escape from capitalist society (Ewen 2001: 200; Bourdieu 1984: 318–71).

Much like bourgeois art, and to extrapolate from the writings of Herbert Marcuse, advertising reproduces the reality principle and the terms of the given society. Its realism is therefore only partial and affirmative. It does not struggle against the intensification of "administered unification," but denies the dread of political desublimation that is pursued through advertising (Marcuse 1977). Irony, detachment, narcissism and hedonism are the traits that link emotional shallowness to aggression. As these become ways of knowing among cliquey cognoscenti, countercultural attitudes are opposed to the perceived hypocrisy of straight society. According to Pountain and Robins, the positivistic laziness of cool culture defines the "medio-cracy" of those who control the youth market and its ostensibly oppositional politics (Pountain & Robins 2000: 45). Status struggle with a petty-bourgeois accent elevates moral ambivalence through the affirmation of vitality, the body, life, love, sensuality, movement and hope.

The reaction to the neoconservative cooptation of countercultural attitudes for the sake of laissez-faire economics and yuppie entrepreneurialism led in the 1980s to a cultural politics of consumption. This Cultural Studies approach tends to be more structuralist than materialist. Market forces are separated from political economy and redefined as flexible and culturally encoded processes (Jackson). Using the base and superstructure model against Marxism, class issues are said to be replaced by questions of gender, sexuality, environment, ethnicity and embodiment. However, as these "enabling" theories of culture became increasingly "banal" and anti-radical, so did awareness of complicity with commodification and the catastrophes of everyday life (Morris). If the tribalism of consumption replaced the mass logic of shared symbolic codes, as Rob Shields has argued, then identities also became more disconnected and less autonomous (Shields). Postmodernism not only privileged the decentered consumer, it made the product secondary. According to Andrew Wernick, promotion is dynamic (Wernick 1991: 189–90). In the process of exchange, promotion becomes reflexively implicated in what it promotes. Whereas such commodity aesthetics is linked to mystification, there is nevertheless no possibility of paring away the original object from the symbolic currency that promotion brings into circulation.

Among the various ways in which different countries regulate paid political advertising, the U.S. is unique in its laissez-faire approach (Holtz-Bacha & Kaid 2006: 12). Television advertising is provided through the private and commercial system and ad time is purchased by campaigns, parties and PACs rather than provided for free by the state – with the exception of some public funding for the Public Broadcasting Service and National Public Radio. Due to the candidate orientation of the American presidential system, the personalities of politicians are given more importance than is the case in other countries, where party affiliation plays a stronger role (Kaid). Broadcasters in the U.S. are prohibited from censoring or altering the content of political ads and sponsorship identification is required. Personal candidate identification increases personal responsibility and reduces the likelihood of negative ads. Political ads are made for radio and television broadcast, print media and social media. Unlike debates and interviews, ads allow campaigns to control the message that is broadcast. As the most costly aspect of most campaigns, advertising increases the dependence on financing. Insofar as Sanders relied on small donations to finance his campaigns, his team limited the influence of wealthy donors on his uses of promotional material. By extension, he also mitigated the redefinition of citizenship into political patronage. Since the U.S. has lengthy and drawn-out elections, exposure to TV advertising is more likely to increase voter turnout and voter knowledge of the positions of different candidates. In addition, and due to the dire state of TV news in the U.S., voters are more likely to be informed by TV ads than by news networks, especially low-involvement voters and late deciders. However, ads are not always effective in the way they were intended. For this reason, positive ads tend to reduce the chances of backlash and negative evaluation.

As TV news becomes more oriented towards entertainment than education, elections and politics are drawn into the vortex. After Ronald Reagan made the transition from Hollywood to government, the idea that politicians are little more than paid actors brought with it the expectation that politicians should entertain. Donald Trump has extended this downward spiral from Reality TV through to White House disinfotainment. Not only does neoliberal government and its press services sell soft news, it also leads the lifestyle page. According to Ellis Cashmore, the Monica Lewinsky affair was the biggest news story of 1998 and Lewinsky was the most famous female celebrity of the 90s (Cashmore 2006: 209). Blurring the lines between politics and celebrity sells newspapers as well as government. If this leads to a loss of credibility, Cashmore argues, it also leads to a political system that supplies politicians "who are ideologically indistinguishable and who are projected as much as entertainers as political leaders" (Cashmore 2006: 211).

Celebrity culture obliges politicians to use marketing and advertising techniques to brand themselves and to find people who will endorse their brand. Obama, Cashmore says, branded himself as a post-racial president. In doing so, Obama was pursuing a path already established by black celebrities like Oprah, Naomi Campbell, Denzel Washington, Beyoncé and Tiger Woods, who, according to Jacqueline Jones, find nothing incongruous about being paid millions of dollars while most African Americans languish in poverty (Cashmore 2012).

The point about post-race is that it makes this incongruity disappear. As Chris Hedges puts it: "Brand Obama offers us an image that appears radically individualistic and new: It inoculates us from seeing that the old engines of corporate power and the vast military-industrial complex continue to plunder the country" (cited in Cashmore 2012: 33). Brand Obama distracted Americans from the actuality of neoliberalism by offering them a simple means to discharge the history of slavery and Jim Crow segregation. As a celebrity politician, and not unlike a Lacoste golf shirt, his candidacy turned voting into a form of compensatory consumption – a high-end consumable offered to poor and low-income groups.

The respectable style of male blackness performed by Obama contrasted with his predecessor, the 'celebrity' son of a former president, whose Texas manner was marketed as 'Dubya.' According to Jeremy Hockett, brand 'W' communicated an emotional rather than rational political meaning (Hockett 2005: 72). Reducing politics to a war of images rather than ideas, branding allows almost anyone to become president. By reflexively reclaiming the stereotype of the ignorant Southerner, Bush Jr. could potentially appeal to media savvy liberals. In addition to marketing the concept of 'compassionate conservatism,' Bush's down-home charm allowed partisanship to be combined with brand loyalty. Since Southerners are often stereotyped as intolerant, and thereby made into a national scapegoat, 'W' recontextualized this prejudice in an affirmative mode. Much in the same way as Obama, the surplus of symbolic meaning that Bush manipulated provided cultural refuge for his policies of militarism and tax cuts for the rich. Having conquered anti-Southern chauvinism and vindicated the Great State of Texas, Bush went on to streamline politics and policy through personified simplification. The marketing of the literal representation of 'W' as a brand impressed with a red-hot iron on the hide of the USA further established the obscene side of Bush's image as a member of the shady Skull and Bones society.

The repetition of a brand image over time creates 'message discipline' and allows a new candidate to associate themselves with either the citizens they claim they will represent, the program they are advancing, the party they seek to lead or the country they wish to govern. A brand image may be more successful with one of these tasks than another. For this reason, political campaigns rarely rely on only the candidate themselves in their promotional efforts and seek celebrity endorsements to supplement the candidate's image. Endorsements can come from the field of politics but can also be drawn from society at large. The inability to win an endorsement, as for example Biden's failure in 2019 to win the support of Al Sharpton, can contribute negatively to a candidate's image. At the same time, the failure to endorse a popular candidate can also reflect negatively on the trustworthiness of the prospective endorser.

According to Malik and Sudhakar, celebrity endorsements bring almost automatic attractiveness and expertise to a product (Malik & Sudhakar 2014: 260). Through repeat exposure, stimulus creates conditioned response, allowing positive feelings to be transferred from the celebrity to the product.

The 2020 Sanders campaign slogan, 'Not Me, Us,' and the accompanying logo, which shows an anonymous crowd of multicolored supporters framed inside the silhouette of Sanders with his fist raised, made U.S. citizens into his ultimate endorsers. More important than any celebrity and more important than even Sanders himself, 'the American people' and not Democratic Party insiders or the billionaire class were made into the *raison d'être* of the Sanders campaign. This exercise in populist de-branding, de-commodification and de-celebritization asserted the idea that it is 'the people' who are attractive and trustworthy. However, as with all populism, an enemy, identified as 'the elite,' must be singled out and distinguished from the public. In addition to the donor class, Sanders consistently targeted Trump in his stump speeches. He criticized over and again Trump's racism, sexism, homophobia and xenophobia. When one then considers the use of identity politics in Sanders 2020 advertisements, the critique of Trump could be thought to spill over to identify Trump supporters as racist, sexist, homophobic and xenophobic Americans. While everyday Trump supporters could not be directly denounced as part of the plutocracy, the specter of American fascism was implicit as a looming threat.

2   I'm Bernie Sanders and I Approve This Message

In *Our Revolution*, Sanders asserts the fact that the media shape our lives, tell us what our needs are and manipulate our political consciousness by deciding what is realistic and what is not. What the mainstream media do not do, he argues, is describe human suffering. When as a senator Sanders called a press conference against proposed cuts to Social Security – an event that was attended by national groups that represent some 50 million citizens – he was stunned that it did not receive any coverage. He writes:

> What I learned from that experience was that, as a general rule of thumb, the more important the issue is to large numbers of working people, the less interesting it is to corporate media. The less significant it is to ordinary people, the more attention the media pays. Further, issues being pushed by the 1 percent get a lot of attention. Issues advocated by representatives of working families, not so much.
> SANDERS 2016: 839

When Sanders launched his presidential campaign in 2015, the announcement was buried on page 19 of the *New York Times*. As his campaigned gained traction, he was eventually covered by the main for-profit national networks, news shows, morning shows and magazines. Still, with even these opportunities, corporate media want short answers that keep the news entertaining and that do not criticize corporations. In most cases, the mainstream media prefer to focus on candidates' personalities, gossip, scandals or screwups than they do covering social issues, policy positions or a politician's qualifications.

According to Weaver, campaigns and the media do not have the same objectives. While media want access to candidates, information, breaking stories and anything relevant to voters, campaigns want positive stories about the candidate and their platform. Since Sanders never resorts to personal attacks or runs negative ads, he was at a disadvantage compared to Trump, whose ratio of 'earned' media was exponentially greater. If marketing seeks to impose message discipline, Sanders says he was faulted by the media for spending too much time discussing and explaining issues to audiences. Consequently, ABC News dedicated 81 minutes to Trump in 2015 and 20 seconds to Sanders. By March 2016, Trump had received $2 billion in free coverage compared to $321 million for Sanders and $750 million for Clinton. Across the networks, Trump received more coverage during the 2016 elections than all of the Democratic Party candidates and Republican Party competitors combined. More than any previous politician, Trump gave the media what the media itself did not know it wanted: money.

Although Sanders managed to bring some issues like class inequality to news shows, corporate platforms are not the best vehicle for political messaging. This makes campaign advertising for TV and radio a political tool that Sanders says his 2016 team could not afford to ignore (Sanders 2016: 227). While his 2016 advertisements were produced by Revolution Messaging as well as the media consulting firm DML (Devine, Mulvey and Longabaugh), his 2020 ads were produced by Rocha's political consulting firm Solidarity Strategies. In 2016, the Sanders campaign produced no fewer than 1,185 digital ads, which were distributed through social media. Videos posted on YouTube were viewed 30 million times and on Facebook 43 million times. Paid advertisements made for television and radio began to be aired in November 2015. Different types of ads 1) informed people about the candidate, his background, his accomplishments and his effectiveness, 2) let people know that the system and the economy are rigged in favor of the wealthy and powerful, and 3) presented testimonials by workers whose concerns would be addressed by Sanders' policy program. Among the more popular, the ad titled "America" featured the music of Simon and Garfunkel and established the candidate's popularity with ordinary Americans (Sanders Channel 2016a). "Sons of New York" drew a parallel between Sanders and FDR, and "It's Not Over" included testimony by Erica Garner, who says she is for Bernie because he is not afraid to go up against the criminal justice system (Sanders Channel 2016c; Sanders Channel 2016b).

Many of the 2016 Sanders campaign ads were made by Revolution Messaging. Founded in 2009 by Scott Goodstein, who had worked for the Obama campaign in 2008, RM has specialized in demographic information systems that allow campaigns to contact voters through mobile devices as well as direct calls. The same system can be used for online fundraising and online advertising. By creating the website BernieSanders.com, RM signed up 185,000 people who donated $3 million in the first four days of the campaign. Spreading the word about small donations allowed the Sanders team to delay traditional broadcast advertising until the primaries. The essence of social media, Goodstein argues, is constant messaging in different formats for different kinds of people.

Arun Chaudhury, a partner at RM and former Obama White House videographer, echoes Wernick's theory when he contends that for winning U.S. elections, political ads are more important than the rest of the campaign. A lecture he gave in 2020 explains to clients how to run campaigns in an era of distrust and fake news (BKB | HC). Building the popularity of the candidate, he says, is more important than the content of campaign messages. Since there is no one size that fits all in politics, the goal is to combine political messaging with compelling narratives that people will seek out by themselves. As with movement building, part of the strategy has to be to reflect where people are at rather than forcing something alien on them. What matters to voters is not the campaign team but the conditions where they live. The message should therefore appear to already exist in the world of the voter. Chaudhury's creative approach rejects the use of scientific data and privileges imaginative guesswork. As far as multiculturalism is concerned, his view of the famous United Colors of Benetton ad campaigns is that even though they show diversity, what they are actually doing is showing multiple versions of the same type of person. This was the case with Obama ads, where working-class voters were being addressed but without showing working people. Chaudhury's theory is that pride and dignity are more common than self-interestedness. In other words, you cannot tell people that they are wrong about their political views, but you can tell them that they are special. Whereas print media is suited to learning, visual advertising is geared towards feeling. Ads communicate politics by allowing viewers to feel safe as they watch other people identify with or learn from a candidate. Controversial subject matter, like strike activity or protests, is not necessarily a bad thing, he says, since it can allow a campaign to attract new people. However, the more established an incumbent, the more they can afford to avoid controversy and not go into details about a given issue. Popular politicians like Bill Clinton, Obama and Trump can avoid describing serious problems. Since their views match those of the establishment, they easily blend into the 24/7 news cycle of the corporate media. Popular front movements like the Sanders campaign must instead balance different ideas so that people with a similar sensibility can feel like they are moving in the same direction. The goal is to make noise and let others worry about explaining things. With these thoughts in mind, the following addresses some of the problems with the 2020 United Colors of Sanders strategy.

Heading into the primaries, the Sanders campaign issued an advertisement (Figure 1) as well as an episode of its *Hear the Bern* social media program on the subject of intersectional identity politics (Sanders Channel 2020c; Sanders Channel 2020e). Both of these feature Barbara Smith, one of the founding members of the Combahee River Collective, who had worked with the Sanders team in 2016 and endorsed him in 2020. In previous weeks, Sanders' national press secretary, Briahna Joy Gray, had been emphasizing intersectionality as an important concept for the Bernie campaign. It is not clear if the purpose here was to promote Sanders or identity politics and the theory of intersectionality. Deflecting criticism from the left, Gray suggests in this *Hear the Bern* episode that 'identity politics' is one of the most vilified terms on the right. Smith is credited with having coined the term in the late 1970s, a fact that by itself should not make someone favorable towards it.

FIGURE 1   Barbara Smith endorsement ad for Bernie Sanders, February 3, 2020
SOURCE: BERNIE SANDERS/YOUTUBE/SCREENSHOT

It is assumed by the CRC that different groups face challenges that are entirely unique to them. This suggests that experience and standpoint are satisfactory as epistemological frameworks. Not only is this claim disingenuous, but it could also be used to dismisses socialist radicalism. As Adolph Reed puts it: "Whatever the Combahee River Collective may have been in its brief and generally unnoticed existence, it never demonstrated aspirations to building a mass political movement" (Reed 2018). Reed adds further that the race reductionist perspective, even when it is intersectionally combined with class considerations, is not only vulnerable to anti-left tendencies, but is often intentionally so. Regardless of Smith's personal credibility as a leftist activist, which is not in question, the CRC's definition of a politics based of race, gender or sexuality has less to do with movement building than with ontology. The tendency of the PMC to celebrate non-white, female or gender non-conforming candidates on the basis of their identity allows subjective and group motives to replace political concerns. It also allows unprincipled political actions to be justified on the basis of identity, past experiences or historical traumas. Reed writes:

> This politics is open to the worst forms of opportunism, and it promises to be a major front on which neoliberal Democrats will attack the left, directly and indirectly, and these lines of attack stand out in combining red-baiting and race-baiting into a new, ostensibly progressive form of invective. Hillary Clinton's infamous 2016 campaign swipe at Sanders that his call for breaking up big banks wouldn't end racism was only one harbinger of things to come. Indeed, we should recall that it was followed hard upon by even more blunt attacks from prominent members of the black political class.
> REED 2018

If the CRC was critical of black nationalist and radical separatist movements, it is less clear how intersectionality has contributed to the left by displacing theories that are based on universalism. In pseudo-Gramscian mode, intersectionality, according to Kimberlé Crenshaw, rejects universality as the position of the white male who masquerades as non-racial and non-gendered objectivity. Objectivity is thereby downgraded as "reified white male thought" (Crenshaw 1989: 154). Similarly, objectively feminist critiques of patriarchy are downgraded as white. Capitalism, which like objectivity cannot be thought to have a race or gender, is downgraded as racial capitalism. This, in essence, is the opposite of the notion of black capitalism, which preserves the objectivity and desirability of capitalist relations, then adds to it a positivist sense of particularism.

The extent to which the theory of intersectionality can be separated from postmodernism and post-structuralism is an issue that can be debated at length. (Science & Society Editors). A long-time advocate of race and gender considerations within Marxist class analysis, Angela Davis cites the work of Cedric Robinson and his concept of 'racial capitalism' as essential to the work of new formations like BLM. No one theory can possess a total theory of freedom, she argues, especially if it does not account for the multiplicity of possibilities. (Davis 2017: 590.) Without a doubt, the work of contemporary materialist scholars like Lise Vogel, Vivek Chibber and Holly Lewis can and have contributed insights about the ways that the totality is differently and contradictorily structured (Vogel 1983; Chibber 2013; Lewis 2016). However, in contrast to their work, postmodern theories that reductively prioritize identity, sometimes veering into metaphysics, phenomenology or structuralism, are de- and anti-totalizing in nature, displacing Marxism and making class structure one of many forms of oppression. Marxism has never been oblivious to oppression, as noticed for example in Marx's discussion of the conflicts between English and Irish workers, or Engels' writings on the bourgeois family. Marxism is not and has never been limited to economic class relations. Whether or not gender and race issues have been adequately addressed by various political regimes in the last two centuries, the socialist tendency is rarely less advanced than the rest. That is not the point. To appreciate the conflicts that animate contemporary debates, one has to not only offer a historical and political analysis, one has to decide whether or not, and to what extent if at all, postmodern theories displace and dislodge Marxist theory.

While Marxism avoids reductionism, it also avoids nihilistic relativism. Radical left theory need not stake everything on political economy either, as evidenced by Alain Badiou's meta-political critique of the "democratic (capitalist) materialism" of languages and bodies, which merely recognizes the infinite multiplicity of ontology. Badiou's theory of the event argues instead that all aesthetic, political and scientific truths are generic and universal (Badiou 2005; Badiou 2013). Interestingly enough, Badiou's work, which has some investments in Lacanian psychoanalysis, concords with Frantz Fanon's 'working through' of particularism is his championing of universalism (Fanon). In this regard, identity politics that are not part of the anti-universalist 'ultra-politics' of the reactionary right are either oriented towards the 'archi-politics' of communitarian thinking, which adapts easily enough to the 'para-politics' of neoliberal capitalism, or they follow a leftist 'meta-political' tendency that is focused on universal policies that advance the public interest (Rancière).

These distinctions, according to Žižek, do not capture the distinct problems of contemporary post-politics, where political parties that are led by enlightened technocrats are also guided by liberal multiculturalists. Their foreclosure of revolutionary left politics results in a return of the Real in the form of "postmodern racism," where competing interests are regulated by police logics and the needs of the market (Žižek 2004: 72.) Instead of the working class demanding their universal rights, he argues, we have particular social strata who insist on their particularity. This is fine as far as human rights are concerned but it leaves capitalism in place. With the hegemony of the corporate state, there is no one to whom one can demand that truly universal rights are respected. While there are laws against discrimination, there are no laws against economic inequality. Beyond technological development, most of it oriented towards capital investment, post-politics has no sense of progress beyond the recognition of difference, as with Justin Trudeau's statement that the marginal 2 percent difference between the way in which women have suffered economically from the COVID-19 crisis, in comparison to men, makes his plans for economic recovery into a "she-covery" from the "she-cession" (CBC). Improving the social status of the black middle class in Canada, while the overall fortunes of the middle-class are shrinking, will not improve the lives of men and women working in factories in Shenzhen and Dhaka. In fact, moral exhortation about so-called equity will not improve the lives of anyone anywhere. The working class is not the universal class because it is the most oppressed, but because of its place in the production process (Tietze). This alone explains the crucial difference between class reduction and class politics. The left can be anti-racist and anti-sexist without at the same time abandoning revolutionary anti-capitalism. However, new social movement advocacy that is focused on non-class social change and the different forms of oppression is less valuable as an explanatory framework, even where racism and sexism is concerned (Foley). In essence, intersectionality fragments society into identity groups, which is an odd procedure for categories like race and sexuality, as many ostensibly revolutionary identity groups have discovered. Intersectionality tends to make the lived experiences of the most disadvantaged groups the focus of politics. This procedure is alien to Marxist theory, which is not premised on the objective reality of marginal social groups but on the analysis and critique of capitalist ideology. And as Marie Moran has demonstrated, the ways in which the concept of identity is deployed today is specific to the age of postwar consumer culture (Moran). In addition, conservatives and liberals can be sympathetic to oppressed groups without being socialists.

Although the purpose of the *Hear the Bern* episode was to establish Sanders' trustworthiness when it comes to identity issues, the episode promoted Smith and the CRC as models for the contemporary left, a subject that was never broached by Sanders himself, most likely because the intricacies of postmodern academia are not something he is concerned with. His deferral to the activists around him has been more patronizing than principled. Sanders in fact is not oriented towards identity politics but rather towards emancipatory universalism. Barbara Smith indicated that she herself does not understand this distinction very well when she emphasizes how it is that Sanders has shown throughout his life, for example with his activism in CORE and in his opposition to the Vietnam War, that he is able to work with and for people whose struggles are ostensibly not his own. This implied that even a white Jewish American male can be progressive. Such activism as Sanders has participated in is not a matter of intersectionality, but is attributable to the fact that a universalist politics is irreducible to ontology and cuts across all of society. When Sanders talked about fighting for someone who does not look like you, he never suggested that struggles are wholly independent. Without universalism and the co-implication of struggles, the word solidarity has no meaning.

A few days after the Barbara Smith episode, *Hear the Bern* posted another show on how it is that LGBTQ+ issues cannot be separated from the need for universal programs like Medicare for All. Titled "Big Tents & Iowa," the episode is framed around the kind of both/and, identity and class, discussions that have been debated in the DSA, in the pages of *Jacobin* and on the *Verso Blog* (Sanders Channel 2020f). From a socialist perspective, class and identity are not interchangeable as equivalent concepts, though this is the case with the radical democracy and left populism articulated by Laclau and Mouffe. Not only is class analysis a distinct form of analysis, but one problem with the both/and formula is that it sometimes presupposes a class subject who is not part of a minority constituency and thereby reinscribes the liberal association of labor with prejudiced white men. The correct solution to this is the assertion of left internationalism. The false solution, which one is more likely to encounter on the populist left, is the assertion that the working class is diverse and multiracial. Another false solution is the specification of a 'black' left or 'feminist' socialism. However important these designations may be for heuristic reasons and have been in specific historical struggles, the subject of the socialist left is humanity. Without the universal dimension, there is no left politics. The fault line of American politics is not the color line but the prospects of emancipatory universalism.

Barbara Smith later appeared on the news show *Democracy Now* in a segment titled "How Bernie Sanders changed his views on identity politics." The show's host, Amy Goodman, asks her: "In 2016, Bernie Sanders said identity politics distracts from what he considered real issues, like economic inequality and the decline of organized labor. Has he changed his view of identity politics?" Smith replies:

> I think he's obviously changed. And that's manifested in the kind of campaign that he's running. There's such a commitment to having a diverse, multiracial, multiethnic, various religions – I mean, I loved the coverage of the mosque, where people voted in Iowa, and how 99 percent of the people there, many of whom were immigrants, how they voted and supported Bernie Sanders. But that took outreach from the campaign. That did not just magically happen. I think that he has changed.
> Democracy Now 2020b; see also Democracy Now 2020a

Goodman's use of the words "real issues" does a great deal to skew the question in Smith's direction and just as much to evade the fact that problems that are specific to various constituencies have never been ignored by the socialist movement, which predates the CRC by at least one century in its negotiation of questions of nationalism, race, gender and sexuality. The crucial difference is that socialism is not grounded in notions of individual and group experience. Goodman's question altogether ignores the fact that there are valid arguments to be made against identity politics, none of which are addressed by Smith. Given the overall retreat of the left in the postwar period, the rise of identity as a concept that has structured much political thought since then leads to the false assumption that the prewar 'old left' was not progressive on identity issues, and secondly, that the development of identity politics in the postwar period, while the left was in retreat, implies that the contemporary 'new left' can do without socialism and the radical legacy.

How is it that identity politics could appear to be an adequate substitute for the socialist left? Intellectuals associated with 'New Times' Cultural Studies argued that since capitalism is inevitable, the goal of the left, as represented by the Labour Party in the U.K. and the Democratic Party in the U.S., should be to emancipate capital from labor through technology, new social movements, personal politics, consumer politics and ideological-cultural struggle (Hall). The result was the development of a plurality of sectional interests and movements that essentially corrupted socialism. Ignoring macro-political issues allowed conservatives to define the common culture, leaving to the 'loony left' the task of generating hip content for consumer capitalism. According to Ambalavaner Sivanandan, Thatcherism appealed to working people by replacing the politics of class war and labor struggle with authoritarian populism. On the left, the focus in the 1980s on civil society issues brought about the pluralist politics of difference as a new kind of socialism that was detached from class relations and economic analysis. At the same time, neoconservatives waged a relentless assault on labor rights and the gains that workers had achieved over decades of struggle. Instead of Fordist standardization and unionization, the new economy would be built on globalized and flexibilized labor, deregulation, marketing, design, diversification, lifelong learning, job retraining, mobility and opportunities to reinvent oneself. Instead of collective solidarities, the new high-tech economy of rugged individualism maximized consumer choice and signifiers of cultural identity within relations of competition. As Sivanandan puts it:

> By personalizing power, 'the personal is the political' personalises the enemy: the enemy of the black is the white as the enemy of the woman is the man. And all whites are racist like all men are sexist. Thus racism is the combination of power plus prejudice; change the person and you change the office. Hence the fight against racism became reduced to a fight against prejudice, the fight against institutions and practices to a fight against individuals and attitudes.
> SIVANANDAN; see also SMITH

As wages declined and job security eroded, the culturalization of politics made the war of maneuver into a lost referent and a floating signifier suited to pop culture and historicist kitsch. People like Clinton, Blair and Obama replaced industrial policy with a hegemonic strategy that combined diversity with the interests of shareholders and investors. The new image of caring grifters, the willing executioners of a state apparatus that replaced doctors with soldiers, was the end result of four decades of Thatcherism and Reaganism. Beyond the usual realpolitik, identity groups came to view their oppression in sectarian and oppositional terms, abandoning the claims to universality that could embed their struggles within international socialist solidarities. Victim politics found their grounds of redress within the actually existing neoliberal relations of exploitation. This is the case even as concepts like racism shifted from matters of individual prejudice to institutional and structural conditions. Through grievance politics, references to socialism were used to confirm and validate capitalism rather than fight against it.

Another bid was made for the Combahee River Collective at a pro-Sanders event that was not directly connected to his campaign. In the symposium "Class Warfare: The Future of Left Politics" that was hosted by Harvard for Bernie students on January 28, Sanders surrogate and co-founder of Dream Defenders Philip Agnew emphasized the importance for him of the CRC and its intersectional approach to identity and class (Harvard). Agnew was the conductor of a proto-evangelical moment at the Iowa City Sanders rally with Alexandria Ocasio-Cortex on January 24. The sort of bland leftism that is represented by surrogates like Agnew give the false impression that there are two versions of identity politics: a correct leftist version and a more compromised version that is suited to the state-corporate diversity agenda. One could also add rightist versions.

The history of the socialist movement, not to mention the history of Enlightenment politics, is premised on the philosophical distinction between universalism and particularisms of various sorts. In its Hegelian version, there can be no particular group who stands in for the universal as such, only groups whose exclusion from the universal allows them to make claims to it, as for example Marx's view of the proletariat as the universal class. Particular groups can only make claims to the universal as a claim on political principles like a common humanity, equality and human rights that should be available to all. Socialism is a critique of the concrete universality of capitalism and not the false universality of white European men. While these two universalisms overlap in terms of historical emergence, they should not be conflated. Black and Hispanic capitalists are equally subject to socialist criticism. To be a universal subject implies, paradoxically, to be able to stand outside of one's particularity and view oneself and others critically, as it were, to not be reduced or reduce oneself to one's racial or gender identity, which is the gesture of all discriminatory thinking. On account of this, it is easy enough to understand, since we all have particular selves, that some form of discrimination is inevitable. No amount of good intentions can alter this fact, which cannot be resolved through ever-greater levels of vigilance, as with for example the Nation of Islam under the leadership of Louis Farrakhan. Most contemporary advocates of identity politics have come to their understanding through the postmodern critique of universalism and meta-narratives. It is only since the turn of the millennium, however, that leftists have begun to reckon with the failures of postmodernism, which is now in evidence as the alt-right attacks postmodernism as the offspring of the Frankfurt School (Lütticken). What all of this has to do with civil rights struggles is grist for the academic mill and the chattering classes. For the broader polity, politics tend to be decided by big money.

To the left of Cornel West at the "Class Warfare" panel, Agnew came across as what Hegel referred to as "the beautiful soul," which is a stage in the dialectic of self-consciousness in which the individual projects their own disorder onto the world and attempts to cure this by imposing the law of the heart on everyone else. To West's right was the late Michael Brooks, a left streamer who, going in the opposite direction, was punching his palm while insisting that the U.S. is in the midst of a civil war. This active part of the dialectic of consciousness, in contrast, does whatever it thinks is right because it is certain of itself. By summer 2019, after the shooting spree of Kyle Rittenhouse at a George Floyd protest and the Trump-authorized execution of the antifa protester Michael Reinoehl, his comment became more palpably real. They continue as anti-protesters drive their cars into crowds and people are assaulted or killed for demanding that others respect COVID mask-wearing directives.

After Gray and Smith informally launched the Sanders campaign into the realm of identity politics, the woke floodgates opened onto what was previously a long series of rallies and town hall meetings where Sanders focused on social problems and policy solutions that were for the most part defined independently of identity markers. On February 14, the Sanders campaign posted an advertisement on the Bernie Sanders YouTube channel featuring an endorsement by the actor and activist Matt McGorry (Figure 2) (Sanders Channel 2020k). McGorry is known for his television roles on soap operas like *One Life to Live* and drama series like *Orange Is the New Black*. According to Wikipedia, he identifies as a feminist. The McGorry ad, which was posted one week after the *Hear the Bern* episode with Smith, deviates from the usual and begins with the statement: "I'm a heterosexual white man who is committed to racial, gender and economic justice." McGorry is shown at a BLM rally holding a placard that reads: Show Up For Racial Justice. The rest of the ad advocates racial, gender, economic and climate justice, endorsing Sanders for his record of standing up for all of the above progressive issues.

On an immediate level, there is nothing problematic about the ad or the good intentions of the intersectional approach to issues. Since most Americans have no idea what intersectionality means, it might even come across as something progressive that is being developed in the universities. People go along with it the same way they follow other trends. On a theoretical level, however, which is to say, on a political level, intersectionality is a problematic orientation for the left. One of the more incisive statements that Andrew Yang made at the February 7 Democratic debate was that the Democrats have to stop talking as though Trump is the cause of all of their problems. Trump is a symptom of more fundamental contradictions. The same is true for someone who is compelled to introduce himself through politically correct self-positioning: "I'm a heterosexual white male." This, for a white male, is less a matter of self-affirmation than a confessional incantation of what one is not: I'm not sexist, racist, homophobic, etc. It is an identification of guilt structures that is designed to bring an invisible social norm into the open, or at least to share the condition of visibility that minority subjects often do not have the luxury of avoiding. Such admissions of guilt, however, take ontology for granted and thereby fail even the most rudimentary test of criticality. They have less to do

FIGURE 2   Matt McGorry endorsement ad for Bernie Sanders, February 14, 2020
            SOURCE: BERNIE SANDERS/YOUTUBE/SCREENSHOT

with politics and more to do with social capital. No one fighting in anarchist and communist organizations during the Popular Front would have said such a thing, though they might have said: I joined the International Brigades to fight fascism. The question for the left is whether the shift from internationalism to intersectionality represents progress or whether the trendiness of the latter is due to the withering of radicalism.

Diversity virtue signaling has become standard in the neoliberal academy, in corporate board rooms, in government and in the culture industry. Against the usual post-structuralist and social constructionist hermeneutics of suspicion, which incite minorities to assert their identities and attack the privileges of the invisible norm, confessional self-positioning is better understood as a feature of the contradictions of global capitalism. If the fascist solution to the contradiction of labor and capital is to identify an enemy who threatens the unity of the body politic – Jews, communists, homosexuals, blacks, Muslims, immigrants, etc. – global, neoliberal, multicultural capitalism does the opposite, solving the inherent contradiction, or more exactly obscuring it, by emphasizing diversity. An example of this is provided by the black public intellectual Henry Louis Gates Jr., who boasted during the primaries that Michael Bloomberg's vast fortune was the only thing that could save the world (Marchese). As with commodity fetishism, the point of ideology critique is not simply to demystify the phantasmagoria of wokeness and lay bare the specific interests that lie behind the surface phenomena. The fetishistic surface is part of the material foundation. In a world of flexibilized entrepreneurial individualism, subjectivity becomes part of biocapitalist regulation and integration. Narcissistic assertions of identity come to stand in for and replace the kind of leftist organization that links proletarianization and labor redundancy to the value-added cost of merchandise. Since at least the 1960s, the Democratic Party establishment has defended civil rights agendas within the terms of corporate capitalism. Since the 1990s, neoliberal racialism and corporate feminism have been used to attack the vestiges of the welfare state, leading not only to the decline of unionized labor and contribution of corporations to the tax base, but to the attack on universal rights and freedoms. The solidarity of struggles recognizes the diversity of humanity but it does not do this on the basis of identity. There are historical, economic, philosophical, theoretical, political and even cultural reasons why this is so. Unfortunately, the majority of artists and intellectuals are not up to the task of elaborating these issues, leaving activists and concerned citizens with little more that feel-good and feel-bad formulas with which to fight the rightward drift of politics.

On February 16, the Sanders campaign released two new advertisements on the Bernie Sanders YouTube channel. These ads were likely made to be viewed on cell phones and tablets and they do not include a Sanders approval message. The impression is that they were targeted to young people who support progressive issues. Both commercials repeat what we already know, and which no progressive would disagree with, which is that radical politics does not tolerate discrimination, which is something that Sanders said at every one of his campaign rallies. However, both commercials promote identity politics in ways that are ideologically centrist. Instead of catering to dubious politics, more could have been done by the Sanders campaign to educate people about the kinds of identitarianism that are now more part of the problem than the solution. This is not to deny constituencies the ability to demand redress for issues that are specific to them or that are in the process of being formulated for the first time, but it is to reject the ways in which gender and race politics have served capitalism better than socialism, especially since civil rights discourse has by and large shifted towards postmodern difference politics.

The first of these two advertisements, titled "We're Building the Coalition to Beat Trump," shows Washington state congresswoman Pramila Jayapal debunking the Bernie Bro meme on the Bill Maher television talk show (Figure 3) (Sanders Channel 2020s). Jayapal does not effectively debunk the Bro myth but rather, and very problematically, confirms it. Maher asks: "Bernie does worse with white men than anybody. And it's more women who are for him, more Latinos. How did we get it wrong?" It is not clear who the 'we' is in this sentence, whether the media, centrists or the Democrats in general. Maher

FIGURE 3   Pramila Jayapal on *Real Time with Bill Maher* in a Bernie Sanders post, February 16, 2020
SOURCE: BERNIE SANDERS/YOUTUBE/SCREENSHOT

suggests that Twitter is to blame. Jayapal replies that Twitter is a big part of it but then gets to her more important point. She says:

> Bernie Sanders has assembled the most diverse coalition there is. He is energizing young people. He's got tons of women of color. He's got tons of people of color more broadly. But he is also playing to a forgotten group of blue-collar workers who really believe he's going to fight for them. And that combination of this very diverse coalition of voters that have not turned out before, that frankly any other candidate would have been thrilled to have this kind of coalition – he's got them, but he is also speaking to a lot of people that really feel like he will fight for them. I mean, just – in 2016, we lost Michigan for the first time in 28 years – Democrats lost Michigan. We lost Wisconsin for the first time in 32 years. Guess who won 71 of 72 counties in Wisconsin? It was Bernie Sanders. So when you look at the appeal of Bernie Sanders, I think it is really unusual to have somebody who can do both things – really build that broader base, but also play to these – some of them Trump supporters.

Of course, Sanders had to unite progressives of all stripes. The question here is what is meant and understood when people use the word workers. The way that Jayapal describes the situation seeks to reverse-engineer the 2016 debacle. If one was to agree that Trump is the symptom and not the cause of systemic social problems, one would see that Jayapal is not addressing the issue on a more fundamental basis, which has to do with problems created by neoliberal globalization. Maher would not likely go along with that, so instead she focuses on how voter disaffection is reflected in the decline of support for the Democratic Party. A few words drawn randomly from a television interview does not tell us anything much about Jayapal's politics overall. Nevertheless, the way that issues are framed by the media is indicative of the ways that ideology shapes politics.

Capitalism is unique among historical modes of production insofar as discrimination is not essential to its functioning. What capitalism depends on is production and consumption for the sake of surplus. Today's biocapitalism encourages people to sell themselves and to market their identity as stakes in a game of competitive self-promotion. As workerists put it, identity markers are capitalist capture devices. Although there are no societies in which you do not have problems of discrimination, capitalism exists everywhere in the world and reproduces the same relations of exploitation. Global humanity is therefore confronted with the problems of capital accumulation in ways that are distinct from the racism and patriarchy that we find in pre-capitalist societies. On the other hand, capitalism and bourgeois ideology have created new kinds of race and gender relations that did not pre-exist capitalism. The obvious example is the creation of scientific racism in the eighteenth and nineteenth centuries in order to justify modern forms of slavery, which, as Ellen Meiksins Wood has demonstrated, is distinct from ancient slavery. Although theories of race have been debunked by science, they continue to shape the way we talk about the ethnic groups that are mentioned by Jayapal. By the same token, when she speaks of Trump supporters, one presumes that by this she means the thousands of 'white male workers' in the rust belt states who switched from the Democratic Party to the GOP. The myth that is reaffirmed by the Jayapal ad is that white workers are the group that is responsible for the turn towards Trump and that needs to be brought back into the Democratic Party fold. These are the workers who switched parties in the late 1970s and 80s when politicians were promoting deindustrialization and offshoring. The socialist counterpoint to that is the fact that workers form a class of people who can be found everywhere in the world and whose exploitation is structurally necessary to capitalism. The further point to be made is that identity politics is also a class politics, but a politics of the global petty bourgeoisie that is now being wielded across the spectrum by the agonistic left, the neoliberal establishment and the political right.

Whether workers voted for Trump because he promised to bring back jobs or because they are racist matters a great deal. It is the rejection of neoliberal centrism that was revealed in 2016 and not a significant spike in racism. The further presupposition is that racial and gender groups share common political beliefs and values. They do not. In the video, Jayapal presents Sanders supporters as if they form two separate groups. On the one side, you have a diverse coalition of young people, women and people of color. On the other side, you have white blue-collar workers. This is a false dichotomy. If white workers appear as a group it is because they are more numerous. The white working class is a statistical phantom and not a political constituency. If a person of color is not necessarily feminist or socialist, the same can be said about white workers. Not enough Democratic Party operatives and supporters acknowledge how it is that neoliberal centrism actively organizes the pauperization of the population for the sake of billionaire wealth.

Although the Sanders campaigns did a great deal to demystify class and labor issues, members of the Democratic establishment considered it advantageous to continue blaming the white working class. In November 2019, the super PAC known as American Bridge 21st Century ran three advertisements against Trump and with no clear policy objective except for its representation of working-class Americans who admit that they were mistaken in their support for Trump in 2016. Lori Malburg, a resident of Romeo, Michigan, where Ford had announced plans to close an automobile factory, states in one ad that she is angry that Trump broke his promises. She is now embarrassed that she voted for him (Bridge Project). Mark Graham from Pennsylvania thought that Trump would bring change but now considers him to be a bully who does not understand life in a blue-collar town like Erie (American Bridge 2019a). David Soborowicz, a plumber from Wisconsin who likes to race snowmobiles across water, says that the fact that Trump did not look like a politician "made him look like me" (American Bridge 2019b). One is led to think that the fun he says people have when snowmobiles sometimes sink in the river is ostensibly the same logic that people like him applied to the 2016 elections. These American Bridge ads contrast with the directness of a Sanders television ad from November 2019 (Figure 4). Titled "Big Us," it shows Tom Blanchard, a farmer from Iowa who likes Bernie, he says, because he is honest and fights for the average Joe rather than Wall Street, Hollywood, big oil, big pharma or big anyone else. Bernie, he says, is just big us (Sanders Channel 2019d).

As the 2020 campaign was heading towards the end of the primaries and Super Tuesday, many more misguided advertisements were posted on the Bernie Sanders YouTube channel. One of these, titled "Let's Elect the First Jewish President," shows Jamie Margolin, a founder of the international youth

FIGURE 4   Tom Blanchard, a farmer from Clinton, Iowa, in a Bernie Sanders ad, November 26, 2020
SOURCE: BERNIE SANDERS/YOUTUBE/SCREENSHOT

climate justice movement called Zero Hour, which endorsed Sanders in early February (Figure 5) (Sanders Channel 2020i). Margolin says: "If Bernie Sanders was elected, he would be our first Jewish American president. As a Jewish American, that would be a huge step forward in this country and blowback against the rise of anti-Semitism in this country." The ad shows the far-right demonstrations in Charlottesville, with people chanting "Jews will not replace us." Margolin says: "And then having a Jew literally replace them, would be like – that would be so satisfying." Trump infamously defended the neo-Nazi marchers, saying that there were fine people on both sides of the protests, fascists and anti-fascists. The ad asserts that anti-Semitism continues to fester in America, that hate crimes have increased in major cities and that Jews suffer the most persecution. Sanders is shown saying: "I know about what crazy and radical and extremist politics mean." Images of concentration camps are shown, with people entering a gate with the German word *arbeit* (worker) on it. Sanders says that he is proud to be Jewish and that his identity is an essential part of who he is as a human being.

Although it might seem insensitive to say this, tragic experiences of suffering and hateful discrimination do not necessarily make people more progressive and do not prevent people from later advocating the same kinds of hatred against other groups. One should not index pride to experiences of

FIGURE 5   Jamie Margolin in a Bernie Sanders campaign ad, February 24, 2020
SOURCE: BERNIE SANDERS/YOUTUBE/SCREENSHOT

discrimination. Although one would not know it from this advertisement, what makes Sanders progressive is his universalism and not his ethnic pride. After Iowa and New Hampshire, Sanders was not leading with voters because he is Jewish. He was leading because he is a comrade, a brother who happens to be Jewish. If after a first term as president Sanders had turned out to be like Obama, what good would his Jewish pride have served anyone? As for anti-Semitism, the late David Graeber made the observation that accusations of Labour Party anti-Semitism in the British press were wielded almost exclusively by the conservative right. In 2015, there was 1 charge of Labour anti-Semitism and zero charges of Tory/Conservative anti-Semitism. In 2016, there were 2,530 charges of Labour anti-Semitism and zero charges of Tory/Conservative anti-Semitism. In 2017, there were 93 charges of Labour anti-Semitism and zero charges of Tory/Conservatism anti-Semitism. In 2018, there were 6,790 charges of Labour anti-Semitism and zero charges of Tory/Conservative anti-Semitism. In 2019, there were 3,820 charges of Labour anti-Semitism and one charge of Tory/Conservative anti-Semitism (Graeber).

There is an important difference between actual neo-fascist hate crimes and false charges of anti-Semitism. In the Margolin ad, Sanders says that he looks forward to being the first Jewish president in American history. A voter could have looked forward to that day, but the reason is because the morning after his election victory Sanders would have set to work making the U.S. and the rest of the world a better place. The Sanders campaign was not a campaign organized to replace a skinhead with a Jew. Sanders was not reclaiming what rightfully belongs to Jews, but claiming what belongs to every American citizen. This could be done in the name of a persecuted people, but there is no question that Sanders understood how it is that global capitalist restructuring, as Karl Polanyi argued in *The Great Transformation*, could lead to reactionary movements (Polanyi). As standardized by bourgeois ideology, nationalism has not been the best source of progress in Third World countries. Where socialist movements have made some gains, they have been attacked mercilessly by imperialist countries like the U.S. in favor of right-wing regimes. American politics should therefore be defined in relation to global capitalism. In February 2020, progressive identitarians did not have a viable candidate other than Sanders. With the Warren campaign dwindling, the Sanders campaign attempted to win over her supporters. Despite the adverts, it is doubtful that Sanders had changed his views about identity politics and it is more likely, as Chaudhury suggests, that election advertising strategy is approached somewhat independently of program. Still, one must wonder why any socialist would want to pander to the kind of postmodern nihilists who reject universalism as a weak appeal to the Kantian notion of perpetual peace, a cynical view that is nothing more than a defense of perpetual capitalism.

On February 18, the Sanders team released another problematic advertisement. Titled "Trump Is a Fraud and a Liar," it features Shaun King, a civil rights activist and Sanders surrogate (Figure 6) (Sanders Channel 2020p). In this ad, King propagates the skewed notion that the white working class is the natural home of racism. Since 2016, this scapegoat has served in many journalistic accounts of the Trump victory. In more serious reporting, the issue focuses on those people in the rust belt states that first supported Sanders but later voted for Trump. King says:

> Bernie resonates in places where Trump won. Here's the thing. To win this election you have to win the electoral college. Trump won 30 states in 2016 and he won in places where Bernie actually crushed it in the Democratic primaries. Bernie won 71 of 72 counties in Wisconsin. Trump won there. Bernie won every single county in West Virginia. Trump won there. Donald Trump exploited real pain and problems in this country and began to scapegoat African Americans, immigrants, other marginalized communities, LGBTQ folk, as demagogues always do. And Donald Trump, as a con man, began making promises that he never intended to keep. And Bernie said the Democratic and Republican establishment has

failed people all over the country and people feel that failure and take it personally.

As this point, when King is talking about people who are suffering, the ad shows Sanders comforting middle-aged white women who are visibly distressed. There have been countless Sanders town hall meetings where scenes like this demonstrate the senator's understanding of the problems that people face and the policy issues that would alleviate them. King then says:

> Donald Trump understood that and exploited it for his own gain. People were so agitated and frustrated and felt that this guy actually believed in them, when in reality it was just a con. And so you have millions and millions of white folk in this country who voted against their own self-interest. They need an elimination of medical debt. They need equal access to health care.

This section of the ad shows what looks like alt-right supporters with a flag that says 'Trump: Make America Great Again' as well as a black and white 'Liberty or Death – Don't Tread on Me' flag. King ends with the assertion:

> There are rural communities all over this country where hospitals are closing down. There are counties all over the state of Tennessee where there's nowhere to deliver a baby. When Bernie wins this nomination, Bernie is going to take this fight to Trump in all 50 states and fight to win the hearts, the minds, and votes of everyday people all over the country.

This last section shows Tom Blanchard, the farmer from Fairfield, Iowa, who was featured in the "Big Us" advertisement from November 26. Whether intended or not, the ad establishes a structural dichotomy between minority groups on one side and potentially racist white workers on the other. Millions of white people, we are told, voted against their own interests in 2016. Nowhere in this is there any assessment of the fact that Trump support was greatest among affluent whites with lower levels of education. Less education might mean that people are less likely to respond to being criticized by what they perceive to be educated liberals. This advertisement is probably not addressed to them, but rather to audiences who will be reassured by the stereotypes that are evoked. As for educated middle-class voters, many of them are decidedly against socialism even though they unwittingly prefer socialist policies.

The fact that Trump won in places that had supported Sanders tells you more than one thing. Yes, Trump lied to people, but what is missing from this

FIGURE 6   Activist Shaun King in a Bernie Sanders advertisement, February 18, 2010
SOURCE: BERNIE SANDERS/YOUTUBE/SCREENSHOT

account is any reference to Hillary Clinton and Barack Obama. Decades of neoliberal policy have caused people to understand that both parties are responsible for their problems. In a sense, the New Democrats are doubly responsible because they were supposed to be more progressive. Many people who voted for Trump likely did so as a protest vote, directing their anger at the Democrats rather than abstaining or scrapping their ballots. They did the wrong thing, but their reasons may be valid. These people were not likely to be impressed one more time by someone like Obama who assured them that he feels their pain and understands their frustration. After three years of Russiagate and a phony impeachment trial, they wanted to know who is going to do something about the corruption that the mainstream media and the Democratic establishment had done little more than enable. The point of neoliberal politics is not to reduce the size of government, but to chip away at the belief that the system can work for ordinary people. Those who accept the premise reject politics and look out for themselves, buying into the same system that turned them away. It is therefore unfortunate that video footage of Blanchard was wrenched from the original "Big Us" advertisement and reused as a stand-in for this type of know-nothing working-class worker who needs health care but stupidly votes for Trump.

As the Sanders campaign was in the process of winning support away from a half-dozen nominees, his team began to focus on winning the election at the expense of championing universal policies. Trading on readymade assumptions about the electorate in kneejerk Internet fodder is one way to keep up with the 24-hour news circus. In the end, however, and despite the intentions of the people involved, the campaign compromised the principled stance that Sanders had taken most of his life. It was a risk that should have been avoided. With the decline of postmodern pessimism and the decadence of petty-bourgeois hegemony, the left needs to rebuild and renew not only its social base but also its intellectual and cultural credibility. A genuine left does not build its politics on the kind of prideful superiority that merely redoubles the ignorance of bigots. That is the significant difference between a revolutionary movement and a loyal opposition.

On the same day that this unofficial ad with Shaun King was released, another 30-second ad was posted. Titled "Dalhi | Bernie Sanders," it includes a tag line which indicates that it was approved by Sanders (Sanders Channel 2020d). The ad shows Dalhi Myers, a councilwoman from Richland County, South Carolina, who switched from Biden to Sanders. Myers says she believes that nothing is more important than defeating Trump. As she says that she wants the movement to have the same momentum it had in 2008, the ad shows Sanders walking alongside Obama. The imagery implies that Obama endorses Sanders though this was never the case. The ad also shows two close-ups of black men, leaving it up the viewer to decide whether they think that Obama did everything he could to help African Americans. Through the intermediary of the speaker and the image of Obama, the ad acknowledges the fact that most African Americans vote Democrat. After Obama and Trump have done the bidding of the oligarchy, the shift towards social democratic policies is especially important for people of color who are disproportionately disadvantaged. The ad is not particularly identitarian and is simply descriptive of the fact that Sanders needed the support of black voters in South Carolina.

On the day of the South Carolina primary, the campaign released an ad titled "Investing in HBCUs" that shows Briahna Joy Gray meeting with activists and students who are discussing the pressure they face and the importance of historically black colleges and universities (Figure 7). The ad begins with Sanders talking about higher education. It includes a clip with Sanders surrogate Phillip Agnew, who talks about making sure that the state legislature "looks different" (Sanders Channel 2020g). The phrase is an allusion to the 'looks like me' rhetoric of African Americans and other minority groups who, in the manner of #OscarsSoWhite, emphasize the importance of black faces in high places. The politics of positive stereotypes and middle-class respectability was meant to appeal to the conservative tendency of black South Carolina voters. Like Biden, Sanders promised at one of his contemporaneous rallies that he would

FIGURE 7   Bernie Sanders campaign advertisement promoting HBCUs, February 28, 2020
SOURCE: BERNIE SANDERS/YOUTUBE/SCREENSHOT

nominate a cabinet that "looks like you." Of course, coming from Sanders this promise made a significant difference from the same promise coming from Biden. However, there is little in that promise that demonstrates any criticism of the way that the bourgeoisies of all constituencies have been bought off by corporate capitalism. In the ad, Bernie surrogate, activist and entrepreneur Ja'mal Green mentions the problem of student debt and says: "We're here to talk about any policies that are important to you." Its promotional display of aspiring black youth may have geographic and demographic relevance but seems disjointed from what Shaun King was discussing only one week earlier.

On Super Tuesday, an ad titled "With These Hands" was released on the Bernie Channel (Sanders Channel 2020t). It features Sanders surrogate Nina Turner and focuses on her 'With These Hands' slogan as images flash by with people whose left and right hands show written statements that read: Justice/For All, Protect/LGBTQ, End/Racism, Value/Care Work, Free/Child Care, End/Wars, Medicare/For All, Green/New Deal, Equal/Pay, Disability/Rights, College/For All and Palestinian/Human Rights. The ad calls for an end to the vestiges of classism, racism, homophobia and xenophobia. We see the left and right sides of the faces of people of different genders and ethnicities mixing and matching. The wonky guitar music used for this ad makes it far less interesting than the excellent "Trump's Worst Nightmare" ad from February 2, and only slightly more woke than the "Pramilla | Bernie Sanders" ad of February

26, in which Jayapal says that the system is corrupted by big corporations who think that they can buy elections (Sanders Channel 2020q; Sanders Channel 2020m). In comparison, the ad titled "A Different Kind of Campaign," which was released on March 3, shows the multiracial character of Sanders supporters but without making identity or diversity the essence of the stated message (Sanders Channel 2020a).

One might think that woke constituencies can motivate radicalism through virtue signaling. Unfortunately, this is as much a part of the system as its critique. The problem was not with Sanders. The problem was with the woke elements around him, who are informed by some version or other of postmodernism, whether that is progressive neoliberalism, radical democracy, micro-politics, privilege theory or some other form of identity politics. None of Turner's wild gesticulating on the Bernie stage has more to say about the issues than Sanders' calm demeanor. In other words, the force of matter is not more politically salient than the force of ideology. Using a collage format, the Turner ad transforms revolutionary art into petty-bourgeois activism. Agitation takes place within a market society that is integrated by capital flows. The use of the hand motif could be thought to reference the labor process. A "hand," in traditional terms, is an employee rather than a property-owning capitalist. However, in the Marxist analysis of capital, the notion of individual labor is displaced by the concept of socially necessary labor time, which means that no particular hand is essential to the process of valorization. It is not only that one hand is interchangeable with any other, but that no individual pair of hands escapes capitalist abstraction.

Capitalism devalues labor in favor of mechanization, work speed-ups and other forms of management that are implemented to increase profits. The exchangeability of specific issues within macro-political processes is what makes the important difference between capitalism and socialism. Regardless of the unique qualities of the multicultural array of faces and hands on display in the "With These Hands" commercial, none of what is called for in terms of higher education or criminal justice reform can be achieved by placing the emphasis on cultural difference. The smiling faces of the individuals reflect the kind of 'folk politics' that displaces rather than radicalizes the relations of labor. Being the change you want to see has to mean more than the narcissistic satisfaction of seeing people who 'look like me' in media representation.

In his discussion of Alfred Soth-Rethel's *Intellectual and Manual Labour*, Žižek suggests how it is that pathological phenomena like the commodity form can help to solve the riddle of autonomy, subjectivity and knowledge (Žižek 1989: 16). The busyness of all the hands on the planet do nothing to alter the abstraction that takes place through the capitalization of global markets. The materialism that is typically discussed in postmodern cultural theory implies bourgeois materialism and bourgeois ideology. Would a petty-bourgeois materialism be any different from this or just a reflexive diversion? Beyond the question of discrimination, we presume that the fact of being black and brown, gay and straight, male and female is the key to transforming exchange relations. The reality is that diversity and multiculturalism are not a challenge to the objectivity of capitalism but are rather one of its supports. The question of exploitation therefore appears in these commercials despite the fact that no workplaces and no productive labor is shown. The images 'think' despite the fact that the subjective experience that is demonstrated through affect and the body has no direct connection with the reality of work life. These products of the political creative industry are polyphonic in the sense that histories of class struggle speak through them *despite* their silence regarding the everyday reality of people everywhere whose undervalued and misappropriated labor makes these ads possible. They are, as such, indices of an ideological field in which socialism is proscribed.

On March 8, an ad called "Arab Americans in Michigan Are All in for Bernie" was posted on the Bernie Sanders YouTube channel (Figure 8) (Sanders Channel 2020b). It features Michigan representative Abdullah Hammoud, who asserts that Sanders' values coincide with those of Arab Americans, which, he adds, are those of all Americans. He says: "Although Trump is in the White House, the divisiveness that's been plaguing our country has been happening far before Trump ever assumed office. And unfortunately, I believe will be here after Trump leaves office." What Sanders' values are and what the plague is that divides the country is addressed in terms of the candidate's "equitable platform across the board," meaning, "the injustices and the systemic racism that has been built and baked into the system." Hammoud says that Sanders is more than an individual, he is an "idea" that can be defined as "this community aspect of lifting all of us to ensure that we all have that equal and equitable opportunity." He then mentions that two of his Arab sisters, Rashida Tlaib and Ilhan Omar, have endorsed the senator from Vermont. Sanders, he says, understands that the Muslim vote is not to be taken for granted, concluding: "I have a strong sense that Michigan will overwhelmingly go for Bernie Sanders, and one of the reasons is that the Arab American population and the Muslim American population are going to be that swing vote that deliver[s] strong results for Bernie Sanders." In other words, Sanders has a progressive agenda and a class politics that includes anti-racism and anti-xenophobia.

Hammoud turned out to be correct and Michigan Muslims, who constitute about three percent of the state population, voted overwhelmingly for Amo (uncle) Bernie. At a rally in Dearborn, Sanders was joined on stage by dabke

FIGURE 8   Bernie Sanders campaign ad featuring Adbullah Hammoud, March 8, 2020
SOURCE: BERNIE SANDERS/YOUTUBE/SCREENSHOT

dancers along with the Palestinian-American comedian Amer Zahr. Sanders asserted: "Our job is to bring people together, whether they are Muslims, whether they are Jews, whether they are Christians, no matter who they may be." On the same day that Sanders rallied in Dearborn, the Israeli-American businessman Hannan Lis campaigned for Biden with Jewish leaders and the local American Israel Public Affairs Committee. When Israeli police attacked Jerusalem's al-Aqsa Mosque in May 2021 and went on to shell Gaza citizens, Biden gave the Israeli state the usual American consent and military support. Sanders for his part wrote an op-ed for the *New York Times* that was critical of the equivocation on the conflict, affirming that Palestinian lives matter (Sanders 2010).

There are pressures involved for candidates who seek to push the status quo in a more progressive direction. Immigrant communities in the U.S. have traditionally been associated with left-wing radicalism but these days new arrivals are often more concerned to conform to the American Creed. Democratic inclusivity has been official ideology in Western democracies since the postwar period. Although there is no doubt that Sanders is a man of principle, the rhetoric of democratic values is vague enough to be inclusive of the best international diplomacy as well as the worst military and economic imperialism. The same democratic rhetoric can be used to attack Venezuela or support Saudi Arabia. One of the most direct ads to emerge from the Sanders campaign team, posted on YouTube on March 9, was an endorsement by Jackson, Mississippi Mayor Chokwe Antar Lumumba (Sanders Channel 2020l). Lumumba argues that the problems that the world faces require radical solutions. In contradistinction to campaign rhetoric that Sanders' New Deal policies are not radical, Lumumba embraces the term and argues that a radical is someone who seeks change and is not satisfied with the status quo. He lists Sanders in a group of people that includes Ida B. Wells, Fannie Lou Hamer and Medgar Evers. The ad makes the connection between political vision and the realities of people's daily struggles. It is unfortunate that there were not more ads like this one shown before Super Tuesday.

3 The Difference That Universalism Makes

A standard if hackneyed criticism of any social theory that does not prioritize identity is that it suppresses difference. As with the Christian injunction to love the sinner but not the sin, the postmodern critique of universalism presumes that Enlightenment theories abjure those things that make people who and what they are. One accepts black people, for instance, but not their blackness. Postmodernism, in comparison, fetishizes difference but fails to say what makes something or someone socially, political and culturally relevant or correct. In this way, it absolutizes difference and defends incommensurability. Attacking the modern presuppositions of objective truth and historical progress, postmodernism in the arts and post-structuralism in philosophy, according to Richard Wolin, take part in the tradition of counter-Enlightenment, undermining morality and inviting social chaos (Wolin 2004). One is thus at a loss to discover that nihilism is at the core of contemporary demands for social justice. The obsession with power, language and discourse among activists, according to Helen Pluckrose and James Lindsay, is due to the direct application – or rather, misapplication – of postmodern philosophy to social practice (Pluckrose & Lindsay). Dividing the world into dominant and marginal identities, 'social justice warriors' dismantle knowledge and seek to impose radical relativism, skepticism, pessimism, cynicism, irony, perversion, subjectivism and ambiguity, all the while presuming to be advancing the cause of justice. In Adolph Reed's estimation, this leads to a "flight from concreteness," on the one hand, and an apocalyptic rhetoric that then justifies the slightest gestures of "resistance" and "transgression" as a challenge to entrenched inequalities (Reed 2000: vii, xiv). The fact that positionality soon becomes intellectually and politically regressive makes no difference when marginality is valued as a bargaining chip in forms of "elite brokerage" and "interest-group" activism. For

Mitchell Dean and Daniel Zamora, what appears as populist social movement activism is simply neoliberal governance:

> Neoliberalism as a thought collective and path dependency has largely succeeded in the economic 'neutralization' of the political left in the first two decades of the twenty-first century. The search for a left governmentality, or the making of the welfare state a 'vast experimental field' by centre-left parties, together with a widespread intellectual anti-statism and rejection of formal politics in favour of local social movements and the vitality of civil society, has undermined labour and social democratic parties' organic concerns with the conditions of the working and precarious populations, leaving little effective voice of discontent other than anti-globalist appeals to a 'walled sovereignty.' Instead, as exemplified by the Hillary Clinton campaign in 2016, the centre-left has become – or at least can readily be portrayed by its opponents as – the party of diversity and 'politically correct' identity politics disconnected from fundamental concerns around economic exploitation, widening inequality, narrowing life chances and falling life expectancy for a sizable segment of its traditional constituency.
> DEAN & ZAMORA 2021: 400–1

As conditions worsen for marginalized communities, the organic leaders and intellectuals that emerge from those milieux are less likely to have concrete solutions to concrete problems, as Reed would say, and more likely to 'represent' the human 'possibility' that different sensibilities embody. Instead of concerted action, bearing witness and cultural hipness spiritualize resistance in the form of vicarious pride (Reed 2000: 77–100).

As the 2020 Sanders campaign wound down, one of the last town halls he held revealed the difficulty of advancing a class agenda in the context of social justice activism. On March 7, the Sanders campaign convened a town hall on racial and economic justice in Flint, Michigan (Figures 9 and 10) (Sanders Channel 2020o). The meeting did not address the problems of neoliberal postmodernism, but they were evident to anyone who is impractical enough to have studied critical theory. Sanders prefaced the event with his usual speech. This was followed by presentations given by four local activists and Cornel West. The presenters demonstrated different understandings of how it is that the struggle for racial equality intersects with the struggle for class equality. At the outset, the discussion was ideologically biased against both of these struggles. To begin with, if democratic socialism is not a struggle against capitalism, but accepts capitalism as the best means to secure democracy, then there is no possibility for equality except in the freedom to exploit and be exploited. Socialism does not seek equity within class hierarchy. Socialism seeks equality by first establishing how capitalism works and based on this understanding moving towards a political system that changes social relations by enhancing democratic control of the means of production as well as social control of the surplus wealth that is created through the division of labor. This may be a tall order for a town hall dealing with immediate problems but one had to wonder if any of the presenters shared this basic understanding of class politics.

The first presenter, Nayyirah Shariff, is the director of Flint Rising. The group was formed in the aftermath of the Flint water crisis. Shariff discussed the inability of state and federal governments to handle public health disasters. She argued against the privatization of water and addressed the fact that countless communities across the country are now dealing with the same problems encountered by residents of Flint. Her call for justice includes health care for all, educational resources as well as the repeal of the "fascist and anti-democratic" Emergency Manager laws that were still active in her city. Shariff said that the people of Flint are tired of broken promises and the way that the city is a campaign stop for politicians who are indifferent to the plight of people who experience water shut-offs, high water rates and evictions. Her presentation

FIGURE 9   Victoria Dooley, Jennifer Epps-Addison and Nayyirah Shariff at Sanders Town Hall on Racial and Economic Justice, Flint, Michigan, March 7, 2020
SOURCE: BERNIE SANDERS/YOUTUBE/SCREENSHOT

was straightforward as a community organization endeavor focused on rights issues.

On the question of virtue signaling, the next presenter was the most woke. Jennifer Epps-Addison is the Network President and Co-Executive Director of the Center for Popular Democracy. She began her presentation with bilingual hellos, a salute to the "beautiful people" in the room, and a reminder to the assembled that the movement is connected through "joy, love and community." Epps-Addison exuded a mix of positive thinking and petty-bourgeois militancy. She is typical of the new class of activist leaders who make their careers by connecting people involved in social movement organizing. As discussed by the Endnotes collective, this new wave tends to be comprised of college-educated and middle-class leaders who make activism into a profession through the NGO sector (Endnotes 2015). As is the case with Black Lives Matter, the groups that these leaders represent often receive their funding from philanthropic foundations with ties to corporations and the political establishment. Part of what they do is redirect political energies that have splintered off from official political channels back in the direction of representative institutions through appeals to identity. "Our movement is all about community," Epps-Addison said, "and you cannot let anybody else define who we are and what we're about." From the start of her speech, movement politics was defined by identity rather than, as Hammoud had it, values and principles. She argued:

> We cannot let the pundits tell us who we are, because if they see this room, they see the resilience and spirit that the people of Flint have, they see the energy for transformation and for a new world – only that can define who we are. So we are beautiful, family, so when I say good evening, family, I just need y'all to say: good evening, family!

Like a pop musician addressing a new crowd, the singer flattered the locals. She then presented herself as the president of a national network of grassroots community organizing groups. Having spoken about "family," she then said that she does not want to code or sugar-coat her words, and so she explained that we not only have to take on the corporations and the billionaires, but that if we want to transform the world, we must take on white supremacy, "for real." She continued:

> We have to understand that capitalism and white supremacy are two sides of the same coin. They're not disconnected or disjointed. We have to understand that, you know, I love the spirit of this campaign – Not Me, Us – because Senator Sanders understands that we don't need – and

> I love my white brother – but we don't need white politicians to tell us black people what we need for liberation. Our movements have been telling this country what our liberation looks like for generations. We just haven't had politicians who listen. Please understand, when they call us radical, that in 1964 at the march for jobs and freedom, Dr. Martin Luther King already called for the living wage. He said $2 an hour then, so guess what, that's 17 plus today. So this $15 an hour minimum wage is a compromise. It is not radical. Understand that. Now, I am a queer, black woman from the Midwest. ... And so, I need folks to understand something about the movement traditions that I come from. Of course, I come from a black movement tradition. That's a tradition that the Black Panthers had a Ten-Point Plan for how we liberate this country. ... But I want you to also know that we in the Midwest come from a beautiful tradition. They tell us that progressivism can't win in the Midwest. Someone needs to inform them that the Midwest is the birthplace of progressivism.

Epps-Addison went on to emphasize the fact that criminal justice reform and mass incarceration are not the only black issues, that "our" liberation is linked to a system that exploits, extracts and profits from the criminalization of "our" bodies. It has done so since slavery, she said. This has always been the plan, she argued, reiterating the trope of racial capitalism that has otherwise been subject to critique (Meyerson 2000). The system is not broken, she says, it is doing what it has been tasked to do. The most pivotal moment in her lifetime was the Crime Bill of 1994, which put billions of dollars into the mass incarceration machine. The tanks in Ferguson were funded by the Crime Bill, which was authored by Joe Biden. She stated that the M4BL and BLM did not change the consciousness of the U.S. in order to return to the status quo, but for the liberation of the People. Sanders, she concluded, understands that the Crime Bill was wrong and will repeal it as a commitment to "our" communities.

Nothing that Epps-Addison said would be disputed by most liberals. The reality, again, is not only that racism and capitalism are two sides of the same coin, but that anti-racism and capitalism are also two sides of the same but different coin. The claim that Bernie's $15 minimum wage is lower than MLK's $17 is more a matter of one-upmanship than labor theory. Since race managers and race brokers always emphasize identity issues as equally if not more important than class issues, with the usual criticism of Marx and whoever it may be as Eurocentric or not race and gender conscious enough, one can readily demonstrate one's identitarian distance from "white" politicians, intellectuals or historical figures without making even the most rudimentary argument. Wearing large earrings with images of the continent of Africa, Epps-Addison was much clearer on who she is than why it is that Sanders is losing African-American votes to Biden.

The next presenter, Dr. Victoria Dooley, is an advocate of Medicare for All. Dooley was equally militant-seeming but demonstrated more bluster than political acumen. Dooley mentioned MLK's assertion that injustice in health care is the most inhuman form of inequality. African Americans, she said, have been fighting for the right to not die from illnesses that are too expensive to treat since the days they were freed from slavery. Segregated hospitals were underfunded and this, she said, has been used as an excuse to argue that blacks are a weaker race:

> We died because they killed us. Fast forward to today. With every effort we have made in this nation to insure more people, whether through Medicaid or Medicare or the Affordable Care Act, every single time, there is still a disproportionate amount of poor people of all colors – black and brown people – who are left behind, who are left uninsured.

After the Affordable Care Act, she said, black people are still twice as likely to be uninsured or under-insured when compared to white people. "Call me a conspiracy theorist, but I don't think that is a coincidence." The only way to be certain that "people who look like me" are insured, she added, is to bring in Medicare for All. "Everyone is included – nobody who looks like me is excluded." Medicare for All is not only health insurance for all. It is health care justice for all. Dooley said that she has delivered babies that have been poisoned by lead water and who are given Medicaid, which restricts people's ability to go to any doctor, pharmacy or hospital they choose.

At this moment in the presentation, Epps-Addison rose from her chair to encourage others in the room to stand and applaud. Dooley concluded her presentation with the following:

> If black lives matter, doesn't our student debt matter? If black lives matter, doesn't our health care matter? If black lives matter, doesn't our ability to afford college matter? Senator Sanders is not here to pander. He's here to provide answers to the problems that we are suffering in this community. He's here to cancel student debt. He's here to cancel medical debt. He's here to make public colleges, universities and HBCUs tuition free. They are public. You don't pay to walk down the public sidewalk. You don't pay to go to the public library. You shouldn't have to pay to go to the public college.

The problems that Dooley identifies are serious and need redress, but the pertinent questions are how and why things have gotten this way, and what can be done to change the system. The problem cannot be adduced to a white conspiracy and the solution cannot be reduced to the existing neoliberal policy orientation. Plenty of whites have no health care and many wealthy blacks have perfectly adequate health care plans. Dooley also alluded to the fact that receiving Medicaid is embarrassing to poor blacks whose class status is therewith revealed to doctors. Medicare for All, however, is not a solution to embarrassment about one's class status but to delivering affordable, efficient and effective health care. In saying this, Dooley revealed how it is that her politics has more in common with the bourgeois values of the black middle class than with democratic socialism.

The third local presenter was former Michigan congressman and senator Don Riegle. Floyd McCree, he said, was the first African-American mayor to be elected in a big American city that was majority white. We crossed many barriers, he said, because we care about each other. This diverse community has established union rights with the UAW and struggled for workers until bad trade deals took jobs to other countries. Riegle did not mention the series of sellout contracts and UAW corruption that is also accountable for the loss of jobs. He addressed the problem of low minimum wages and the problem of upward distribution of wealth, where three families own more wealth than the bottom half of the country. "So it's time to figure out who is on your side," he said, "and who's side you're on." Regarding racial justice, Riegle promised that Sanders would put a cabinet together with people that look like those in the room. "I want to see all these racial groups, and I want to see all these ethnic groups around that table and bringing the truth around that cabinet table and getting rid of those people that are there today, who are working against the common good of the country." The problem of course is that Biden could, and did, put together a cabinet of people who have the same gender and ethnicity as those in the room. After Super Tuesday, Kamala Harris and Cory Booker came out with a Biden endorsement, no doubt hoping to secure jobs in his administration.

The last local presenter was Brandon Snyder, the Director of Detroit Action, which is a community-based group dedicated to building power for working-class black and brown people in the Michigan area. A young activist, Snyder's politics are as basic as fighting for good jobs, good schools, safe neighborhoods and ending mass incarceration. His grandparents had moved to Michigan from Georgia and Alabama in order to escape "white" terror and with the hope to live the American Dream by working an honest day's work for an honest day's pay. His family worked in the automobile industry in Detroit, which has been devastated by economic blight, lack of access to health care, closed schools, austerity and the emergency management of billionaires like Mike Ilitch and Dan Gilbert, who have influenced policy by buying up the downtown. Development is happening, he argued, for the rich predators who benefit through white supremacist policies like red lining, predatory lending and the extraction of wealth. Detroit Action is fighting back, he said, by giving black and brown people a voice in the political process. Snyder ended his short talk with a question: "Senator Sanders, how does your housing justice plan correct the generations of white supremacist policies that we've seen in our housing? What will you do to make sure that black folks will have access to opportunities here in Michigan and throughout this country?"

The insistence on white supremacy does not demonstrate a great deal of awareness of the history of left radicalism. There was no analysis of capitalism involved, no mention of the history of class struggle and internationalism, little awareness of cross-racial alliances on the left and no sense that there might be something to lose by emphasizing theories that are based on race reductionism. Sanders replied to Snyder but he also turned the question around by putting a question to the final speaker, Cornel West. He said:

> The headline 'Biden sees advantage with Michigan black voters' suggests Biden will do well with black voters. In terms of what's going on with the African-American community, where 1/3 of children live in poverty, have lower life expectancy, where workers make 76 cents on the dollar compared to whites, where million are uninsured, where black women are 3.5 times more likely to die from pregnancy than whites, where the home ownership gap between blacks and whites is wider than it was in 1900, where the education system is crumbling, where students are leaving schools in debt, etcetera. Do you think ... given the reality, the condition of the African-American community right now, that supporting the same old type of politician is going to address these issues?

West responded with the kind of fighting spirit that comes from the sense that learning, rather than posturing, enhances political radicalism. He replied that the question has a profiling dimension and that he would not allow anyone to ride his back in that way. West did not immediately allow for the possibility that Sanders was listening rather than lecturing, as suggested by Epps-Addison. And that precisely is the problem with the damned if you do, damned if you don't blackmail of race metaphysics. Accordingly, West said, when you see him you see both his tradition and his community as well as white people

FIGURE 10   Cornel West at Sanders Town Hall on Racial and Economic Justice, Flint, Michigan, March 7, 2020
SOURCE: BERNIE SANDERS/YOUTUBE/SCREENSHOT

like Michael Moore. Moral and spiritual formation is not determined by skin pigmentation, West said:

> You gotta decide who you are. And the reason why I'm with this brother … is because we are experiencing a massive moral and spiritual collapse of integrity, honesty and decency in the country. And I don't care what color you are; I don't care your gender; I don't care your sexual orientation; it is a moral and spiritual crisis. And Sanders exemplifies honesty, integrity and decency. Do you know how rare that is in the political class, when most of them are up for sale?

West's universalist stance cut across the kind of racialist rhetoric that submerges politics behind the obsession with white supremacy as the nation's original and eternal sin. Despite the dreadful realities of racist terror, the ascription of human cruelty to the mere fact of race is neither accurate or helpful. It belongs to the ideologies that created racism as a belief in the inherent difference between people and which has been used to justify inequality. West made the important point that Sanders, unlike the lackey competition, is not for sale. What matters about Sanders, he said, is his intellectual and political commitment.

West argued that going forward, voters will have three choices: 1) vote for the fascist gangster in the White House who defends big money and the military, disregards the rule of law and demonizes the weak; 2) vote for a neoliberal centrist who is also tied to big money and the military, who brags about the invasion of Iraq and who, like Milly Vanilly, is a fake; or 3) vote for the real thing. Bernie, he said, is part of the legacy of those who focus on the least of these. We do not, he said, get caught in the "isms" of socialism and communism; likewise, we do not get caught on the chocolate side of everything. Although blacks have been the most progressive community in the U.S., black leadership has been corrupted by money and status. Since the 1940s, the black middle class has made access to opportunity the measure of progress and has ignored the problems that affect the poorest among them. Blacks have avoided the best and have accepted the mediocre and the middling. "I'm going with the best of America," he asserted, "I'm going with Bernie Sanders."

On September 20, 2019, at a town hall meeting at Bennett College, Adolph Reed met on stage with Phillip Agnew, Nina Turner, Cornel West, Danny Glover and Killer Mike (Sanders Channel 2019a). He said that the voting age in 1964 was 21, which meant that he could not cast a ballot for Lyndon Johnson and his Great Society platform. When he was 21 he participated in an anti-election rally. The issues of labor rights, environmental justice, gender rights and civil rights received more support from Richard Nixon at that time than from any of the Democrats. The reason any gains were achieved at all was because social movements were strong enough that Nixon had no alternative. Reed said that in 2015 he was expecting to vote Democrat by default but was excited when he heard about the Sanders campaign. For the first time, he said, we had the chance to fight for what we want and need instead of what we think we can get:

> We have to take it now. We have been going through this 'lesser evilism' thing now for so long ... and one of the takeaways from the 2016 election that nobody wants to talk about ... is that between 6.5 and 9 million people who voted for Trump had voted for Sanders and for Obama at least once. So what that means is that it's not a simple straightforward story of white supremacy. It's the fact that the Democrats have not offered working people of any color, age, race, gender ... anything, for so long. But here's the downside of this moment. What makes this election so important is, on the one side, the possibility that we have to win what we want, and on the other side, the reality that another four years of Trump will be followed by a version of Bolsonaro or Orbán. We're at a moment in American society now ... when the class contradictions in American society are greater than they have ever been in the history of the Republic,

but nobody wants to talk about it. The fact that nobody wants to talk about it is a function of the fact that the contradictions are so sharp.

In contrast to what Lumumba says in his video, we cannot simply be as radical as possible "until we see a society beyond contradiction." This false notion of Hegelian synthesis has long been rejected by Marxist analysis, which emphasizes alienation – alienation in global capitalism as well as alienation in identity.

On March 8, 2020, after the town hall meeting on racial and economic justice discussed above, Jesse Jackson gave a talk in Grand Rapids in support of Sanders. In response, Sanders compared his campaign to Jackson's 'rainbow coalition' strategy of the 1980s. In *The Parallax View*, in a section titled "Over the Coalition Rainbow," Žižek mentions Thomas Frank's discussion in *What's the Matter with Kansas?* about how it is that conservative populists have transformed the meaning of what West refers to as the "moral and spiritual bankruptcy" that is at the heart of American politics (Žižek 2006c; Frank 2004). By focusing on morality, West takes a stand against any system of power that denies people's humanity. However, he avoids to some extent a more explicit class analysis. This is why both West and Sanders define themselves as democratic socialists and not socialists. The re-emergence of the fascist right complicates the critique of moral and spiritual corruption since fascists have also used the appeal to morality and spirituality against capitalism and bourgeois materialism. Conservatives in the U.S. and elsewhere have come to perceive progressive neoliberals as a decadent class that undermines individualism, patriotism and the virtues of hard work. The problem is that what they want – more individual freedom, lower taxes, deregulation, traditional values – justifies the corporate state power that undermines their ability, as citizens, to influence government in the interest of working people.

In May of 2021, in an open letter that was similar to those that were penned by retired generals in Spain and in France, dozens of retired U.S. officers questioned whether Biden won the election and cast doubt on his fitness to rule the nation. The generals and admirals argued that the country's constitutional freedoms and liberty were threatened by Marxism and socialism. Not that these fascist officers actually need to believe what they say, but one would have difficulty finding much evidence to support their worry. The lie that Biden stole the election is what was used to justify the botched effort by Trump supporters and far-right militias to stop the ratification of the vote count on January 6. Whether or not such outright fascism helps to promote 1776 against 1619 makes little sense without the slightest understanding of 1776, let alone 1848, 1871, 1917, 1949 or 1968.

CHAPTER 4

Less than Bernie

> I kept the faith and I kept voting / Not for the iron fist but for the helping hand / For theirs is a land with a wall around it / And mine is a faith in my fellow man.
> BILLY BRAGG, 'Between the Wars'

•••

> The big Other is a virtual order which exists only through subjects 'believing' in it; if, however, a subject were to suspend its belief in the big Other, the subject itself, its 'reality,' would disappear.
> SLAVOJ ŽIŽEK, *Less than Nothing*

•••

The psychologist Elisabeth Kübler-Ross is famous for explaining how it is that people who experience loss or receive bad news go through five stages of grief. As discussed by Žižek, the first stage is *denial* and incredulity regarding what is happening; this is followed by the *anger* that erupts when one can no longer deny what has happened; next is a *bargaining* stage to delay or diminish the impact of the bad news; whatever happened in the bargaining process, the subject eventually goes through a *depression* stage of libidinal disinvestment from the lost object; lastly, a stage of *acceptance* allows someone to live with the new reality or to be prepared were it to happen again (Žižek 2010: xi-xii). Those who campaigned for Sanders and who placed their hopes in his candidacy were more than slightly disturbed or annoyed by the upset that was orchestrated behind the scenes by the Democratic Party establishment to block the Sanders nomination and the much-needed shift of policy in a more democratic direction. Sandernistas were flummoxed, discombobulated, crestfallen, dispirited. Not that they never expected the worst, but they had allowed themselves to fight for and hope for something better by going through established channels. As Žižek says elsewhere, they followed Sanders on a course that is neither pragmatic opportunism – the hegemonic strategy where the left functions as the good conscience of the ruling class – nor principled opportunism, where the maintenance of ideological purity leaves the left ineffective (Žižek 2021). Cynics might think of this as 'third way' triangulation, but the lesson of dialectics is not the difference between two positions, but rather the difference between the difference within a position and a non-position.

The following charts five stages and five themes of mourning after the Sanders campaign got blindsided in the lead-up to Super Tuesday. The first stage, denial, describes the glib reaction of centrist Democrats and the role they expected a compliant left wing of the party to play. The next stage, anger, addresses the George Floyd protests as well as the COVID-19 pandemic, both of which were mishandled by the same centrist powers that everyone was expected to support. Bargaining took place as progressives debated the merits of lesser evil voting and the prospect of a third party. If there was no possibility of moving the 'Overton window' just one inch to the left, then why waste more time propping up a neoliberal husk? While culture is not typically associated with depression, criticism of the Sanders campaign 'going woke' was met with the kind of anti-intellectual and anti-cultural bombast which recommends that voters leave political strategy to the apparatchiks in and around the DSA. Lastly, acceptance describes the record and policies of the man who would be king – the candidate anointed by party insiders who had assured wealthy donors that "nothing will fundamentally change" (Derysh).

1 I Know There Is No Democracy, but I Choose to Ignore

In 2016, the 'Bernie or Bust' attitude among Sanders supporters with no sympathy for the wisdom of pragmatic compromise did not get very far. Sanders rejected Jill Stein's offer to lead the Green Party ticket and proceeded, as he had promised, to support the Democratic Party nominee. This decision allowed him to run again for the party nomination in 2020, but it also made those who reject arguments about lesser evil voting somewhat more adamant than the first time around. The difference now was the threat of a second Trump administration, which played dramatically to Biden's advantage. And so once again Sanders threw his lot in with the party.

On March 11, the Sanders campaign team released an ad featuring the comedian Sarah Silverman saying that Sanders is her kind of Jew because he cares more about his fellow man than about his hair or his outfit (Sanders Channel 2020n). Bernie is a mensch, she says: "I've always loved Bernie. When he asked me to speak at the [2016] DNC, it was bittersweet for all of us. But I did it because it was important to come together to defeat Donald Trump. I'm gonna vote for whoever the f**k is the nominee with gusto, but I believe Bernie is the right one." Silverman advocates for people over profits and the need for a movement that is willing to fight power. If the coronavirus is what voters require to understand the need for Medicare for All, then such phenomena are like elections in which it can never be predicted who will win. "So, yeah," she says, "maybe no one's predicting it, but it's happening. There's only one candidate that has a movement behind him, and that's Bernie." Silverman was correct about the fact that Sanders was the only rebellious candidate. She was incorrect, however, about the idea that one should vote for whoever is the nominee. One could not vote for Biden with gusto. Although the election of Obama was an important victory for civil rights, the first black president joined a growing list of war criminals and commandeered an administration that was worse on most crucial issues than the previous government of George W. Bush. Whether Biden would be an improvement on Trump or a continuation of Trump policies, save for the replacement of discrimination with anti-discrimination, is the crux of the matter for the nominal left around the Democratic Party. If Sanders lost to Biden, anyone who planned to vote Democrat right or wrong would be cursing all the way to the polling booth. What was the purpose of the Silverman advertisement?

In the postwar period, as the golden age of economic prosperity absorbed the class struggle into the consumer culture and the anti-communist conformity of the Cold War, big ideological debates were replaced by systems analysis and bureaucratic technique. In an increasingly complicated world, people began to trust experts and liberal capitalism promised the surest avenue to prosperity. Once the postwar economic boom came to an end, economic growth declined, wages stagnated and workers' demands increased. This was also the time of post-colonial independence movements, the Chinese Cultural Revolution, the rise of student protests and new left social movements. Wary of socialist politics, the ruling class reintroduced nineteenth-century free-market ideology in order to secure gains for the economic elite at the expense of those gains achieved by workers through the welfare state. By the 2000s the Democratic Party establishment elicited such a low level of confidence that it was engineering its own version of the Boris Johnson administration. The term 'status quo' is perhaps too moderate for a system that can no longer even pretend to be concerned with social reproduction, let alone human survival. Despite the fact that all polls indicated that Sanders had the policies that resonated with the majority of voters and with which the Democrats would easily have beat Trump, the party establishment and the corporate-owned media did everything they could to prevent a Sanders nomination.

In September 2016, Silverman appeared on *Real Time with Bill Maher* to discuss how Sanders had been sidelined and how she subsequently became an enthusiastic supporter of Hillary Clinton. Silverman expressed her dismay about the Bernie or Bust people: "I don't know what their long game is. I don't know what their perfect, dream scenario is. I earnestly am asking, or am I being obtuse?" (cited in Miller) No wonder that four years later Silverman stated at a Sanders rally in Los Angeles that democratic socialism has nothing in common with socialism, which she said is the same thing as communism (Los Angeles Times). The difference between socialism and communism is the fact that one term sounds more congenial and less communist than the other. Regardless, it is the term socialism in democratic socialism that defines people's "perfect dream scenario," with the caveat that the ends do not justify the use of any means necessary. For neoliberals, any kind of socialism, even a moderate FDR social democratic reformism, cannot be perfect and so cannot be part of the political process. Because countless Sanders supporters actually believe in one version of socialism or another, the Democratic Party machine promotes militarism rather than reform. It fears that the slightest bit of welfarism will shatter the myth that only privatization and the upward distribution of wealth is possible. Silverman alluded to such neoliberal hysteria when she stated in L.A.: "Bernie is a democratic socialist. The only way we will become Russia is if we get four more years of this lunatic wannabe dictator, and his corrupted, enabling Senate of henchmen." To Silverman, Biden's connections to the American and Ukrainian oligarchy smelled better than Putin and Xi Jinping. Tragedy, as Woody Allen says, is the essence of comedy.

In 2016, the comedian and talk show host Bill Maher supported Sanders over Hillary Clinton. In 2020, he supported Amy Klobuchar. How can someone with an adult understanding of politics shift their support from a democratic socialist to an establishment neoliberal? On *Real Time with Bill Maher*, the champion of political incorrectness came out to support the same corporate elite that had pushed Russiagate and pseudo-impeachment rather than worry itself about the electorate. Resuming the neoconservative business mantra that gangsters do it best, Maher stated that democratic candidates – now down to Sanders and Biden – need to stop telling him who they will not take money from. "Money from *baaad* people," he spewed on an episode in March:

> I don't care if they're bad. I just want to know if their money is good. Democrats – always living in the world that ought to be, rather than the one that is. "My campaign is funded by the people." Well great, but I've got some bad news for you: the people are broke. Bernie Sanders does the best among Democrats, raising $46 million in February, but in the same

period the Republicans raised $86 million – some of it from Americans! Because Trump will take money from anyone: super PACs, corporate lobbyists, drug dealers, Russian mobsters, foreign dictators. He will, and has, stolen money from his own charities. Meanwhile, Democrats are competing to see not who can attract the most donors, but to see who can refuse the most. Because they're pure. Pure losers. Bernie Sanders brags that he accepts no money from corporate PACs, super PACs, fossil fuels, insurance, drug companies. No siree! If you want to give Sanders money, you had better be able to prove you don't have any. ... This isn't purity, it's vanity. It's unilateral disarmament. It's bringing a hug to a gun fight. In 2008, no one took more money from Wall Street than Obama, and then he got elected and passed the biggest Wall Street reform in generations. ... He made Elizabeth Warren's plan – the Consumer Financial Protection Bureau – a reality. So, when he ran for re-election, Wall Street was pissed. They didn't give him nearly as much, but he took what they gave, and then he fucked them again! This is how you play the game. Call him impure, a corporatist, a moderate – fact is he did more to reign in Wall Street than all the peacocking comment-board socialists combined. And I don't care which old white guy we wheel into the Oval Office, if Trump can take money from criminals and governments, you can take it from Etna. And here's a little secret about economics [he says with his pinky in the air]: when you take money from bad people, it's money that they, the bad people, don't have. It's not a donation at all, it's a fine. ... For fuck's sake it's money, not kale. ... None of it is pure. ... So, you say, some of the people donating to Democrats are bad? I say, here's how we know they're good: because they're giving you money to beat this guy: [picture of Trump].

Real Time with Bill Maher

For all of his bluster, the long and the short of it is that Maher is a liar. Obama did not punish Wall Street. Obama bailed out Wall Street, which handed working Americans their ass on a plate. Obama is doing fine giving hundred-thousand-dollar speeches to bank executives. And Maher is fine being a mouthpiece for oligarchs like Michael Bloomberg who want to own the country. Bloomberg has supported CIA Democrats as well as Republicans.

What Silverman and Maher have in common is the situation that we all confront when the labor movement and socialism have been so weakened that fascism is emerging as the only alternative to the neoliberal consensus. Their respective approach to this issue corresponds to the difference that Žižek identifies between a fool and a knave. "The fool," Žižek writes, is a simpleton, a court jester who is allowed to tell the truth precisely because the "performative power" (the sociopolitical efficiency) of his speech is suspended; the knave is the cynic who openly states the truth, a crook who tries to sell the open admission of his crookedness as honesty, a scoundrel who admits the need for illegitimate repression in order to maintain social stability.

Žižek adds to this a reference to contemporary politics:

> Following the fall of Socialism, the knave is a neo-conservative advocate of the free market, who cruelly rejects all forms of social solidarity as counterproductive sentimentalism; while the fool is a multiculturalist "radical" social critic who, by means of his ludic procedures destined to "subvert" the existing order, actually serves as its supplement.
> ŽIŽEK 1999: 206

In 2016, the Bernie or Bust movement reacted angrily to the scandal that the DNC had rigged the nomination race in favor of Clinton. The Democratic establishment attempted to lie their way out of it by shifting the blame onto WikiLeaks and the Russians, eventually projecting Russian connivance onto Trump and even Sanders (Gabbard). None of the Democratic Party's empty posturing throughout the course of the Trump administration did the slightest amount of good for people who do not respond favorably to the deceptions of hack journalists and policy experts whose mouths are tied to their paychecks. Clinton was not significantly better than Trump and neither was Biden. There is good reason to believe that both of them are as bad as Trump if not worse on some issues. Since Democrats are supposed to be the progressive party, their skullduggery makes them more reprehensible than Republicans, who more honestly display their contempt for democracy.

What Sanders supporters wanted was progressive change. This is the kind of change that does not frighten them away from words like radical and socialist. On this score they are not purists. Purists understand that the Democratic Party is a dead end and so do not vote for either of the two establishment parties. Purists are radical in the sense that they understand that only a shift to the left can secure popular participation and conscious struggle for a better world, which means challenging capitalist domination and securing gains for the working majority. And capitalists never tire of pointing out the contradictions of socialism. Rhetoric about purity and impurity is simply a diversion from open admission of fundamentally different political commitments. The courageous Sanders movement consists of vanguard social formations that are at the forefront of ideological struggle. They are the leadership that Sanders supported as a politician who has always participated in social movement struggles. Sanders refused to link their fate to the kleptocracy that denies climate change and perpetuates criminal wars. All that a lazy-faire establishment needs to do to undermine this leftist leadership is accurately portray its politics while at the same time suggesting in conspiratorial ways that this is wrong. Take for instance this statement in an article in *The Atlantic* on the 2016 Bernie or Bust phenomenon:

> In reality, like any political gathering at which participants insist on the need for a revolution that radically upends the existing order, those present did not represent a majority of Americans, let alone 99 percent, whether they are right or wrong. They did not even represent a majority of Democrats. ... That isn't, however, how the Bernie-or-Bust folks see it. They represent themselves as democratic revolutionaries who represent the repressed voice of a supermajority-in-waiting. Those who disagree with them are, by extension, treated as illegitimate – they are presumed to be oligarchs, or tools of billionaire donors like the Koch brothers, or allies of the Democratic establishment and Hillary Clinton who, in the telling of Bernie-or-Bust, stole the election.
> FRIEDERSDORF

In fact, Clinton and the DNC did work to steal the nomination in 2016. No amount of Purell hand sanitizer is going to make a difference to a virus known as the truth. In 2020, the crew of crony nominees who supported a lame Biden campaign staged a media-backed coup against Sanders. They could not and cannot, however, stage a coup against his supporters. Even if the DNC got the result that it wanted, it would not get the majority of Sanders supporters to tow the line, and for this reason, it risked losing to Trump. Like Maher, however, they could care less. If they did, they would have been focused on economic justice all along. If they were focused on electability, as they pretended, they would have backed the one candidate who beat Trump in 95 percent of polls rather than the candidate who was showing signs of cognitive decline. This reality is not merely a matter of partisanship, with reports from as far afield as India stating the obvious: "So if President Trump is rubbing his hands in glee, Establishment Democrats have no right to complain. They brought this upon themselves" (Shali).

Generations that have been weaned on end-of-ideology nihilism no longer believe that we can know the difference between virtue and vice, good and evil, which are terms that belong to the worlds of religion and metaphysics. What matters are the relations of power that are delineated within mechanisms of social control. The drama of Joe Biden announcing cabinet nominations that would include Michael Bloomberg, Jamie Dimon, Pete Buttigieg, Kamala Harris, Amy Klobuchar, and other servants of power, indicated that once the likes of Maher and Silverman had convinced Sanders supporters to sell themselves to the devil, there would be no Democratic Party to rescue them from oblivion (VandeHei and Allen).

The difference between Sanders supporters and the Democratic establishment is that the wealthy elite seemingly have very little to lose and workers have certainly been losing for several decades already. What Maher was actually saying is: "You are the losers, and we, the wealthy, are the winners. We can't lose because we're rich." That is why Silverman said that she would fuck any old Democratic candidate, because she is part of the same class of people who can afford to pretend that everything is fine in Jerkwater USA. The complement to this mendacity are the banal platitudes that are pumped out by NGOs, new social movements and activist groups. Filling the ideological vacuum that has been created by the absence of a strong labor movement and radical political parties, these groups give lip service to oppressed identities – some of whom can hardly be considered oppressed – but not to the possibility of a radical change to the profit system. This much is acknowledged by even a neoliberal ideologue like Francis Fukuyama, who wonders why the left has focused more on promoting the interests of groups that are perceived to be marginal than on economic equality (Fukuyama 2018: 23).

In an ad posted on March 17, the actress Laura Gómez endorsed Sanders on the basis of his generosity, arguing that he sees only the best in people and not the worst (Sanders Channel 2020h). Against this piece of fake wisdom, we should apply the Žižek test and ask the question: Would Sanders see the best in Adolph Hitler and not the worst? Sanders opened most of his speeches with the claim that Trump is the most dangerous president in American history. He stated that Trump is a racist, a sexist, a homophobe and a xenophobe – as though these traits are matters of ontology rather than politics. Would Sanders also say that Trump is funny? One could go on to find other qualities. Perhaps Trump's toupee hair style and orange skin are not so strange after all. In another ad, posted on the same day, Ezra Koenig and Chris Tomson of the band Vampire Weekend endorsed Sanders on the basis that whereas most political candidates are self-contradictory, Sanders has been consistent and on the right side of history for the past four decades (Sanders Channel 2020r). Putting these two ads together, one might reasonably ask that Sanders not only criticize Trump as a pathological liar, but, if he is to be consistent, denounce Biden as a pathological liar as well. A few weeks before the South Carolina vote, Biden had falsely claimed that thirty years previously he was arrested in Soweto for trying to meet with Nelson Mandela. There was nothing to stop Sanders from attacking Biden on his record of sexism, racism, homophobia and xenophobia. To keep with the campaign slogan 'Not Me, Us,' Sanders' supporters could have reminded him that his friend was not their friend. Or had the Sanders movement entered the same state of denial as Sanders himself?

When it became clear that Sanders was out of the election race, the spectacle of pseudo-politics began in earnest. This was what many Americans had wanted all along and is what the media would undoubtedly be supplying for the next several years. Among the first to come out of hiding was P. Diddy, a.k.a. Puff Daddy, a.k.a. Sean Combs, who shocked the universe with his message to Biden that he needed to do something to win his vote (The Hill 2020c). On April 27, on the television show *No Filter With Naomi*, hosted by supermodel Naomi Campbell, Brother Love told viewers:

> The Black vote is not gon' be free. We're gonna have to see some promises. We're gonna have to understand what kind of deal we're getting out of – what are we getting in return for our vote? Nothing has changed in America for Black America. And, in order for us to vote for Biden we can't be taken for granted like we always are because we're supposed to be Democrats. Or because people are afraid of Trump. (...) It's whoever is going to take care of our community, whoever wants to make a deal, it's business at this point. We can't trust politicians. So we want to know very clearly, just like Trump made it clear that he wanna build a wall, Biden needs to make it clear that he's going to change the lives and quality of life of Black and brown people. (...) I will hold the vote hostage.
>
> cited in FRAZER

In the early 2000s, Diddy's Citizen Change initiative launched the Vote Or Die campaign to encourage young voters to exercise their citizenship rights. According to Charise Frazer, Diddy first criticized the Democratic Party in 2016 for shortchanging the black vote, saying at that time that blacks need to "revolutionize" the voting game by withholding the vote for whoever is making the best offer (Frazer). The scandal *du jour* in April 2020 was the fact that Diddy deleted a Twitter comment by Kenny Burns, who accused him of being irresponsible by not focusing on the need to vote Donald Trump out of office. Diddy replied: "To whom it may concern it's called BLACK LEVERAGE. THIS IS NOT FOR ANY OF YOU SCARED TO DEATH TOM NEGROES! Love. This is #SMOKE" (Ivey). For Frazer, another Trump presidency would ensure disparities between black and white Americans and so privileged black Americans like Diddy and Kanye West should be criticized for encouraging blacks to disenfranchise themselves. Fair enough, but what about poor folk?

On the question of electability, there is an important difference between debates among leftists and arguments put forward by identitarians. P. Diddy was not heard from when Sanders, the candidate whose platform had the most to offer poor black and white Americans alike, was still in the running. He only came out when the election game was safely nestled between the two factions of American capitalism. His gangsta rhetoric that he is holding his vote for ransom merely added a touch of menace to his phoneyness. As it turns out, the media stunts of black celebrities are not so different from woke academia, as described in Roger Lancaster's critique of a blog post by Judith Butler that inveighed against Trump's America First jingoism (Lancaster). According to Lancaster, avoidance of socialism has the effect of redefining and pacifying the critique of capitalism. Although we cannot say that Diddy is concerned to avoid the charge of economic reductionism so as to maintain academic respectability, we might imagine that ranking among black millionaires makes for different kinds of demands and expectations. For Lancaster, the essentialist thinking that emphasizes disparities among ethnic groups ignores the question of who shares what risks. What progressive neoliberals want to avoid are conversations that lead back to class politics.

Socialism does not ask people to show their ID papers, Lancaster argues, but rather channels politics away from philanthropy and interest groups, and in Diddy's case, we could add business rationality. In the realm of woke politics, everyone's individual responsibility for social structural problems is so microthin that guilt relations demand pointless self-culpabilization. Are today's Gillette advertisements against toxic masculinity really the best that socialism can get? Projected inward as well as outward, the guilt and suffering Olympics get faster, stronger and higher ever year. In the process, the categories of the unemployed, poor, food-insecure, homeless and destitute are depoliticized and resemanticized as those whose condition evokes pity and maybe even empathy, but nothing so alien or demanding as class solidarity. Obama avoided being associated with Biden until 20 days before the November 4 election. By that time, Trump had only a 13 percent chance of winning. When interviewed about his vision for 2021 and beyond, Obama shamed voters for the failures of his administration, suggesting that if progressives had wanted progressive legislation, they would have had to "get out there" and work harder (Pod Save America. See also Secular Talk). Holding Biden's feet to the fire is what now justified voting for anyone but Trump. However, by November, progressives had been through two additional phases of grieving. If the George Floyd protests had captured the anger of the progressive movement, they also undermined the 'bargaining process' and deliberation of a third-party split. The moment for deciding 'what is to be done' was averted by movement leaders. A weak political subjectivity chose to let the Democrats off the hook and instead challenged the Republicans on the terrain of culture wars. Trump goons proceeded to attack conscientious citizens as far-left antifa terrorists and denounce face masks as threats to personal safety and liberty.

2   I Can't Breathe

The advent and rapid spread of the COVID-19 pandemic was another occasion to take seriously Naomi Klein's theory of the shock doctrine (Klein 2007). The idea is that neoliberal market policies have risen to prominence as part of a deliberate effort to exploit crises in such a way as to impose unpopular policies that disadvantage workers and support the ruling class. Citizens who were too economically crippled to organize effectively in their own interest could have expected that corporations would try to profit from the pandemic, least of all by privatizing vaccines and their application. The Canadian government, for instance, used the crisis to ram through the US-Mexico-Canada Trade Agreement and strengthen military ties with the U.S. (Jordan 2020a; Jordan 2020b). Given that the U.S. government had embarked on a disastrous 'herd immunity' policy that placed profits ahead of public safety, the spread of the virus in a country that does not guarantee free health care for all of its citizens was projected to affect some 200 million people. It was estimated that by the time the virus was under control, as many as 21 million Americans could require hospitalization and as many as 1.7 million could die from the disease. The economic impact of the coronavirus pandemic was expected to destroy not only millions of lives, but also $2.7 trillion of global GDP in 2020. In early March, the stock market had seen its worst sell-off since Black Monday in 1987, and the global stock exchanges saw their worst sell-off since 2008. Appearing in the company of health care and retail industry executives, Trump announced that private sector players like Walmart and Labcorp would be given the onerous duty of testing and therefore profiting from the disaster. In addition to these quick fixes, Trump also announced $1.5 trillion in Federal Reserve money for the financial system, an amount that was double the initial 2008 bank bailout. It amounted to 1000 times more money than the World Health Organization had requested to manage the virus emergency. In other words, amidst a pandemic that threatened to take millions of lives, the billionaire class took extensive measures to protect its investments first and foremost (Lantier & Damon). And these measures worked. According to the Institute for

Policy Studies, global billionaire wealth increased $5.5 trillion during the first 17 months of the pandemic (Collins). As for the rest of the population, Trump used culture war tactics to make the rejection of face masks as important to his supporters as red MAGA hats (Parton).

The wealthy have access to the best health care facilities and equipment. At worst, COVID-19 would cause them to die with dignity, and not as the result of a triage between people with a better or worse chance of dying. After Trump announced the CARES Act, the stock markets responded with the largest run-up in human history. Not that these measures were a zero-sum game entirely, but Washington's personal best in this instance was overall the worst that the American public had seen. In the context of the government's bailout measures, the $1200 stimulus checks that some Americans were to receive, which was counter-balanced by the trillions of dollars of liquidity handed to corporations, would in the long run cost each U.S. citizen $18,000 (Not Bill Murray). As Sanders tweeted: "When we say it's time to provide health care to all of our people, we're told we can't afford it. But if the stock market is in trouble, no problem! The government can just hand out $1.5 trillion to calm bankers on Wall Street" (cited in Lowrey). As the coronavirus pandemic spread across the globe, it mutated according to political ideologies. Rob Urie writes:

> Through the virus, a new light is being shone on four decades of neoliberal reorganization of political economy. The combination of widespread economic marginalization and a lack of paid time off means that sick and highly contagious workers will have little economic choice but to spread the virus. And the insurance company pricing mechanisms intended to dissuade people from overusing health care ('skin in the game') means that only very sick people will 'buy' health care they can't afford. ... The most fiscally responsible route, in the sense of assuring the rich don't pay taxes, is to let those who can't afford health care die.
>
> URIE

If this sounds unproductive for capitalism, think again. Neoliberal outsourcing, deskilling and deunionization were engineered to provide capitalists with a younger, cheaper and more flexible labor force. From Clinton to Obama, health care has been indexed to pricing mechanisms that discourage the purchase of overpriced health services and that incentivize superior service provision for those who can afford it. This two-tier system corresponds to the notion of health care as a luxury commodity. If someone chooses to purchase health care, they do so as part of a business strategy that takes a risk on the best way to promote oneself on the social market. Do I buy insulin for my diabetes, or do I buy food?

By May 2020, an estimated 27 million Americans – about one third of the workforce – were unemployed and 40 percent of small businesses were likely to go bankrupt in the next few months. Some 33 million filed for unemployment claims and 11 million were working part time. Rather than introduce a Universal Basic Income or a similar form of living wage income insurance, neoliberals opted for the entrepreneurialization of the self. People were obliged to quit their jobs or go on strike for the right to self-quarantine and save themselves. Just as corporations downsize after automating and offshoring labor, governments welcomed the pandemic's Malthusian solution to the political challenge that was being mounted by strikes and demands for reform. Nevermind that Sanders was the only legitimate candidate in the race whose policies were according to every measure the policies that are the most popular with voters, when people saw the disaster coming, they had to decide what frightens them the most: death from the neoliberal plague or democratic socialism (Žižek 2020a).

Sensing that economic crises had not only brought an end to the golden age of postwar prosperity but also to the long neoliberal consensus of the last four decades, the bourgeoisie geared up for a full-on assault (People's Forum NYC). In the 2020 Democratic presidential debates, candidates were asked to determine what is the biggest threat facing the nation. By the summer of 2020, the nation was now experiencing three simultaneous threats: mass deaths from lack of preparedness for dealing with the coronavirus pandemic, government bailouts to banks and corporations at the expense of everyday people, and a climate crisis that would be ignored for months if not years. Everything was done that could be done to respond to these crises in a piecemeal way rather than through a gradual dismantling of the profit system (Mealy).

While the immediate task of new social movements was to make the case to the masses that the days of neoliberalism have come to an end, most people were preoccupied with paying the rent. Progressive centrists had been successfully inoculated against the demand for maximum safety nets and investment in public services to build a green economy (Brown). Instead, the democratic socialist agenda was replaced by Biden's efforts to leverage the affect of "suburban Facebook empathy moms" and rebuild the reputation of George W. Bush. "We are not partisan combatants," Bush said to the public in his COVID video message, "We're human beings, equally vulnerable and equally wonderful in the sight of God" (KETKnbc). Empathy and kindness, Bush said, are the tools that will ensure a national recovery. Former national security advisor Susan Rice tweeted: "There is no one kinder, more empathetic and caring than

@joebiden. He will lead America with ... compassion and decency" (Rice). One got the impression that conservatives were reading Žižek's *Pandemic!*: "So there is a hope that corporeal distancing will even strengthen the intensity of our link with others" (Žižek 2020b: 3).

In the summer of 2020, Trump and Biden had more than just the coronavirus to be worried about. On May 26, protests erupted in Minneapolis in response to the police murder of George Floyd. The protests, which are associated with BLM and M4BL, took place in more than 2000 cities and involved approximately 20 million people, constituting the largest wave of mass protests in American history. In addition, more than 8,700 solidarity demonstrations took place across 74 countries. Although most of the protests had been peaceful, rioting in some cities led to severe repression, with the National Guard and military called in to impose curfews. Over the summer months, as many as 19 protesters were killed and 14,000 arrested. All of this occurred against the prospect that Trump would refuse to concede to his political opponent if he lost the November election. With this in mind, Trump increased funding for local police departments and ordered the Department of Justice to implement Operation Legend, a deployment of federal agents to suppress protests.

The Black Lives Matter movement emerged in 2013 to protest racial profiling, police brutality and racial inequality in the criminal justice system. For BLM activists, the disproportionate number of black deaths caused every year by police is evidence of systemic racism and so BLM activism ties in more generally with racialism and anti-oppression activism. BLM has close ties to the Ford Foundation, the George Soros-backed Open Society foundation and the Borealis Foundation, which are connected to the Democratic Party establishment. On the whole, BLM avoids criticism of the corporate oligarchy and focuses on race-specific demands like reparations and symbolic victories like name changes and monument removals. The outlook of BLM is consistent with the Democratic Party's shift from labor rights and civil rights to the kind of identity politics that supports the profit system and the interests of the black middle class. The BLM 10-Point Manifesto has brought needed attention to police reform, with valuable suggestions on how to improve police accountability and reduce the likelihood of profiling and excessive force. However, the focus on racism and white supremacy rather than capitalism as the explanation for disparities in police violence and other issues reduces black politics to the logic of equal opportunity exploitation.

Even where racism exits, there is no reason to assume, as do most BLM activists, that anti-racism rather than universalism is the best solution. Anti-racism tends to reduce politics to questions of ontology rather than social, political and ideological processes. Since BLM integrates readily with neoliberalism, it does very little to challenge market forces. In addition, the promotion of black unity by the black PMC has problems of its own. For instance, the co-founder of the Black Lives Matter Global Network Foundation, Patrisse Khan-Cullors, now socializes with affluent celebrities and owns several properties worth millions of dollars. It is suspected that some of this money was misappropriated from BLM activities. The families of Tamir Rice and Richard Risher, who were murdered by police, have accused Cullors of profiting from the murder of black people, raising millions while doing nothing for the people impacted by police violence. Other activist leaders who have come under criticism include Shaun King, Lee Merritt and Melina Abdullah.

The overwhelming support of BLM by corporations and the Democratic Party establishment has led to criticism of its PMC political orientation and the limits of identity politics. As a tool of the ruling class to divide workers, anti-racism and anti-oppression discourse have produced strange bedfellows, like for example Chuck Schumer and Nancy Pelosi sporting Kente cloth and bending the knee at a contemptible ceremony for BLM in June 2020. Republican senator Mitt Romney joined a BLM protest in Washington, D.C. on account of the random fact that his father, George Romney, was the governor of Michigan during the Detroit riots of 1967 (Coppins). There is no doubting the legitimacy of the outrage of the hundreds of thousands of people who have demonstrated against the police murder of George Floyd, who is one of about 1000 people who are killed every year by police in the U.S. And there is no doubting the legitimacy of the protests against Trump's draconian response, which included denunciations by his Attorney General of antifa as a "domestic terrorist organization" (Bray). One may disagree with the call to use violence against hate groups, but antifa is not on the same order as groups that make race hatred the basis of their ideology. The point though is that Trump and the establishment made extensive use of the shock doctrine to increase the wealth of the oligarchy and create state of exception legislation that gave government authorities like the FBI the authority to persecute leftist opposition. Since antifa is not an organization but a social movement tactic, any leftist protester, even Mitt Romney, could be subjected to COINTELPRO-style criminalization. Trump's warning to the protesters that "when the looting starts, the shooting starts" was as politically reactionary as former Obama security advisor Susan Rice's suggestion that the uses of protest to contend that there is something wrong with American capitalism are "right out of the Russian playbook" (Sprunt; Schwartz 2020).

Trump's speeches against socialism, which are echoed by Democrats like Obama, Clinton and Biden, are not empty posturing. While these people can be trusted about this, they cannot be believed about concern for those who are 'represented' by unaccountable social movements like BLM, MeToo, March for Our Lives, Women's March or Extinction Rebellion. Worldwide solidarity marches create a potential for political mobilization. However, insofar as protests do not have a clear political agenda, they are mired in the kind of victim politics that have latched onto identity issues and populism. Such protest movements mobilize citizen indignation but channel it back into pseudo-conflicts like Biden versus Trump. It seemed for a while that the millennial left had understood the problems with neoliberal policy. Some correctly responded to the establishment effort to block the Sanders movement with a #NeverBiden refusal to go back to the terms of 2016. Yet, after Trump flexed a little military muscle, erstwhile radicals fell in line, demonstrating that their leftism is more democratic agonism than class consciousness. This is the kind of left you have when you ignore the critique of political economy and resort to morality as your main criterion of political change. Once you have done that you soon resort to the kind of sentimentality that replaces socialism with woke indignation and activist preening.

After the collapse of the Sanders campaign there was a chance for the left to regroup around a third party. For this to have happened leftists of various stripes would have had to direct their animus against neoliberals, the corporate kleptocracy and postmodernists alike. Instead, discussion was reduced to warnings against Bolshevik takeovers and complaining about Karens (Jacobin Magazine 2020b; Reed 2020b). Kimberlé Crenshaw made the revanchist argument that the resurgence of BLM activism in June 2020 was evidence of the failed universalism of the Sanders 2020 campaign (Crenshaw cited in Ember 2020a; see also Jacobin Magazine 2020c). You would be hard pressed to find very many people who approve of police murders, whether they are racially motivated or not, which is why the number of people supporting BLM protests is overwhelming. However, as Ralph Nader argued, when in 2018 the Reverend William Barber and Liz Theoharis started a country-wide Poor People's Campaign, they received almost no press coverage and poor people did not come out to support this effort at coordinated action (Ralph Nader Radio Hour 2020). By the end of 2020, BLM and related groups had received some $5 billion from corporate America for anti-racism initiatives. Regardless, for some commentators, criticism of BLM was proof enough that the left has a class reductionism problem (Cozzarelli).

Inasmuch as BLM activists interpret problems of global capitalism in terms of race determinism and pseudo-religious notions like racism as America's original and eternal sin, as promoted for example by the *New York Times* 1619 Project, there is nothing getting in the way of angry demonstrators except more policing (North & Mackaman). Against racialist iconoclasm, Trump threatened heavy penalties for anyone smashing statues and burning flags. In a postmodern universe, there is less demand for heroes than there is for empowerment at the local and micro-political level. Big ideas, like freedom, justice and progress, are desublimated in favor of the nitty gritty of who benefits and who decides, often too granular to have any impact on the broader polity, as with for example the breakdown of the Women's March and various Pride marches. Unfortunately, it is sometimes enough that decisions be made by the right kind of person. When a number of officials quit the neoliberal administration of Chicago Mayor Lori Lightfoot in Fall 2021, the beleaguered leader said that she would only give interviews to black and brown journalists. Not surprisingly, when questioned about her Chicago Monuments Project initiative, through which statues of George Washington and Abraham Lincoln were threatened with removal on racialist grounds, Lightfoot said that such men never anticipated that a black woman would become the mayor of a major American city. In this context, there is not much sense talking about the neoconservative attack on the professions, or the twilight of Enlightenment. If cities, like museums, are civilizing rituals, as Carol Duncan once argued, city fathers inevitably turn out to be corrupt, either as sexists, racists or homophobes, or as people whose wealth is the result of disreputable investment in property, labor exploitation, militarism and imperialist machinations. When socialism is out of the question, the game of power belongs to whoever is ambitious enough to join the ranks of the mediocracy. If there is something slightly inept and narcissistic in all of the COVID-1619 iconoclasm, as Michael Eric Dyson has referred to it, it is in relation to the defects of those personalities that are somehow, amazingly, still high up on their plinths: Barack Obama, Joe Biden, Donald Trump, Nancy Pelosi, Stacey Abrams, John Bolton, James Clyburn, Lindsey Graham, Mitch McConnell or Mike Pence (IntelligenceSquared). If the American public manages to replace Confederate statues with something nicer than graffiti scrawls and fake blood splatter, one would hope that they are not replaced with today's neoliberal leadership, which is exactly what has been proposed for the Illinois state Capitol, where representatives have suggested that a statue of a founding Illinois senator who owned slaves, Stephen A. Douglas, could be replaced with a statue of Obama, a noted war criminal. Ironically, these are the kinds of politicians who are interested in their own kinds of iconoclasm, for example, replacing the elected Venezuelan president Nicolás Maduro with the fascist coup plotter Juan Guaidó.

The crisis of the American left after the close of the Bernie 2020 campaign led to the re-emergence of woke culture wars as the means through which the struggle was to move forward in the midst of a bogus election contest between two factions of the same capitalist agenda. With 5 percent of the global population, the U.S. now had 25 percent of COVID-19 cases and deaths. By the end of summer 2020, as many as 300,000 Americans had died from the virus. The unemployment rate was close to 20 percent. Against the prospect of a left insurgency, neoliberals across the left-right spectrum advocated more woke messaging. In June, contributing editor at *Jacobin* and DSA member Chris Maisano rejected the conservative postulates of Ross Douthat, who argued in the *New York Times* that the wave of protests against police violence were an indication that the Sanders campaign, if not the Sanders movement, has lost the battle for the left (Maisano 2020). Douthat took the hundreds of millions of dollars that corporate America invested in anti-racism initiatives as evidence that class politics lost out to a milquetoast left that is subservient to the oligarchy. Maisano suggested instead that the "political revolution" that was galvanized by Sanders continued to have momentum. Maisano's article reiterates the views of some leftists who argue that the universalist left and universalist right are similar in their opposition to postmodernism and so-called cultural Marxism. His rebuttal to Douthat is that "cynicism" regarding "woke capitalism" is bait that should not be taken. Maisano denounces Douthat for taking advantage of ongoing struggles between class-oriented radicals and the intersectionalists who have hung on to the accusation of "class reductionism," a term that is tautologically used to wield Marxist theory against Marxists. Such conservatives, according to Maisano, want to drive a wedge through the Sanders movement and win over the "class-oriented left." Slightly more progressive spirits attempt to divide the Bernie left inside the DSA from the opposite, pro-intersectionality angle, but to the same effect, by denouncing so-called class reductionism. Unfortunately, Maisano's rainbow coalition orientation tends to undermine the materialist understanding of oppression. Though he does not say so, he implies that to advocate for class struggle as the best solution to various forms of oppression makes the work of the right easier by accepting the way that conservatives oppose class politics and racial justice. Yet conservatives do not advocate struggle against the ruling class and the profit system. What Maisano's stance does not allow for is the fact that today's capitalism benefits from both racism and anti-racism efforts, a situation that calls for the critique of facile 'both/and' formulas and their replacement with socialist thinking based on principles and strategies that look beyond the bipartisan setup and beyond the power/resistance logic of the postmodern left.

According to Maisano, for Douthat's argument that the Sanders left lost out to woke politics to be credible, Douthat would have to acknowledge everything that was done by Sanders campaign organizers, and not only the "cultural liberalism" aspects. Douthat would also have to recognize that the politics of the BLM protesters are not as limited as the politics of the politicians and corporate

CEOs who would like to channel mass outrage into a few police reforms and public murals, like for example Washington D.C. mayor Muriel E. Bowser's painting of the words 'BLACK LIVES MATTER' on the thoroughfare between 16th and K Street NW. Maisano adds to this the usual postmodern relativism. If BLM is vulnerable to co-optation, so are labor struggles. True, but this statement points to the difference between the DSA and an organization like, say, the IWW. Concerning the acceptability of BLM to the establishment, Maisano writes: "The threat of corporate 'blackwashing,' as Cedric Johnson has called it, is very real. But this is not sufficient grounds on which to reject the protest movement as hopelessly liberal or incompatible with working-class politics" (Maisano 2020). Johnson, for his part, is quite right to denounce middle-class intellectuals for feigning a "post-traumatic slavery disorder" and for correctly identifying their woke anti-racist rhetoric for what it is: liberal racialism (Johnson 2020a; see also Johnson 2020b and Jacobin 2021b).

The problem, as presented by Maisano, is posed from a racialist and identitarian perspective. Intersectionality is not a politics, however. It is a means to manage political conflict by fragmenting and multiplying the number of axes against which the social antagonism between labor and capitalism can be redistributed. The politics of recognition and dignity are by and large irrelevant to the politics of redistribution. Efforts to undermine awareness of the fact that police violence in the U.S. is inherently a matter of class warfare do not contribute to class consciousness and left strategy. This is true despite the potentially racist motivations of killer cops and despite racial disparities in the prison and justice system.[1]

Liberal interpretations of political unity have dominated American politics throughout the twentieth and early twenty-first centuries. Since the rise of American socialism in the late nineteenth century, the pressure placed on leftist organizations and coalitions has typically come from the ruling capitalist class, which has made use of racism to divide workers against one another. As Richard Hofstadter has argued, violence in the U.S. is typically wielded by various segments of the working masses – nationalities, religious groups, ethnic groups – against one another rather than against the dominant capitalist class (Hofstadter). This makes anti-racism strategically important to the left. Leftist solidarity across struggles is not, however, what race managers and race

---

[1] Racialism is the main problem with the otherwise well-intended research of Michelle Alexander in *The New Jim Crow: Mass Incarceration in the Age of Colorblindness* (Alexander). The same could be said for the articulation of a distinctly 'black' left in Keeanga-Yamahtta Taylor in *From #BlackLivesMatter to Black Liberation* (Taylor 2016). For an analysis of the incongruities of racial disparity in police violence, see Parenti 2020.

brokers expect of people today. What is desired is more along the lines of moral conversion, replacing universal human rights and left solidarity with practices and theories that derive from the kinds of nihilism, relativism and eclecticism that are the foundations of neoliberal post-politics. Social critics like Maisano believe that no one should have the luxury of abstaining from struggles against injustice. However, not so long ago, a black radical like James Baldwin never lost sight of the universality that made the notion of equality operative. The postmodern suspicion of universalism has become particularly entrenched with intersectionality, which many Marxist feminists and black Marxists argue belongs to the postmodern, neoliberal camp.

Intersectionality theory allows for the more bourgeois sectors of academia to seem more radical by aligning with the new social movement ultra-left at the expense of the organizational and institutional 'old left.' Intersectionalists relativize capitalist exploitation as one among many forms of inequality. Rather than decommodifying social relations, intersectionalists like Nancy Folbre seek to expand the spheres of life that are dominated by capital (Folbre). This tends to coincide with contemporary anarchists' acceptance of capitalism as the immanent state of things and a nascent organizational communism at the level of mode of production (Hardt & Negri 2000). Unlike anarchism, however, intersectionality is not a politics and is described by its own adherents as, first, a critique of the supposed universalism of liberal feminism, and second, a wide range of projects that are enabled by the application of the concept to various fields of study (Salem). For some, intersectionality is nothing more politically committed than a metaphor. It is less a method than it is an orientation towards identity, diversity, inclusiveness and multiple forms of marginalization, all of which confuse critical concepts and categories of thought. Territorial disputes around who has the right to discuss intersectional theory creates blackmail scenarios that undermine universalism, leading some, like Eve Mitchell and Sharon Smith, to reject intersectionality as a neoliberal means to redress problems of social inequality. As a seemingly Marxist approach that accepts the methods of post-colonialism, post-structuralism and critical race theory, not to mention the problematic reification of identity categories like race, gender and sexuality, intersectionality is rather a product of discourse theory, which substitutes the abstract notion of power for the critique of capital. Ashley Bohrer describes intersectionality as "Marxish," a statement that should be accepted since, unlike the work of Bourdieu, this eclectic method presumes that values and dispositions are unrelated to social class (Bohrer). That this fashionable approach has been institutionalized in many gender and women's studies departments is sometimes ascribed to the corporate university agenda of liberal multiculturalism (Nash 2014: 45). "In a capitalist society," writes Hester Eisenstein, "class is not at all the same kind of difference as race or gender" (Eisenstein 2018: 259). Giving equal weight to each of the race, class, gender and sexuality 'vectors' through the use of the intersection metaphor, she argues, leads to a superficial analysis of social forces and cannot substitute for class analysis.

Whatever their intentions, most racialists are hardly aware of their affinities with the anti-Enlightenment conservativism that informs postmodern theory. Knowledge of this reactionary legacy has not been a significant part of the postmodern and Culture Studies curriculum. It re-emerges in even black Marxism when atavisms like the cult of ancestors or strategies of maronage are used to self-segregate from anything that could be associated with European modernity. This has nothing to do with socialism, but it is compatible with alternatives like left populism, counterculture and reactionary conservatism.

According to Žižek, the crisis of the new populism is due to a mistrust of representation. When no politician adequately represents the people, representation itself is suspect. Rather than abolishing formal democracy altogether, populism cobbles together an inconsistent mix of measures to bribe identification with various, often unaccountable, sources of authority. Through aesthetics, populists can appeal to obscenity while at the same time maintaining the self-deception of innocence. If right populists oppose the liberal establishment, so do politically correct left populists, who hope that the system will collapse under the pressure of its own contradictions. The purpose of left populism is not to win power, but to disclose the illusion of neutrality and bring out the dominant order's racial, cultural, gender and other biases (Žižek 2020c). Its stylistic form is anger about the fact that liberal equality has not been actualized. For Žižek, there is a problem with this stance as well. The excessive moralism of political correctness is fake, he writes,

> because it covers up opportunist calculus, hypocrisy, and self-righteousness. It is full of its own unwritten rules: minorities that count more than others; subtly different criteria for what is prohibited and what is allowed, criteria which change quickly like fashions; anti-racism based on hidden racist arrogance (a white guy who asks others to assert their identity renounces his identity and thereby reserves for himself the position of universality); and, especially, the awareness of which questions are NOT to be raised (radical social change, etc.).
> ŽIŽEK 2020C

Left populism remains within the liberal framework insofar as its solution to structural inequality is focused on individual moral responsibility, attitudes and behavior. Its privileged realm of analysis is not economic and political change but social identity. The woke left operates through a kind of analytic blackmail based on the simplest agency-structure paradigm of sociology. People are either subjectively problematic or they are structurally guilty. This double extortion allows postmodern leftists to avoid genuine sociology and to 'socially construct' the world as they see fit, usually based on their personal identity and experience rather than on a set of universal, collective principles. The affinity with simulation theory is apparent as postmodern intellectuals begin to imagine that they can hack and reprogram reality according to their personal whims or subcultural trends. It is easy enough to see why, when they inevitably fail to have a macro-political impact, they become all the more resigned, moribund, cynical and nihilistic in their pessimism. The development of Afro-pessimism is an unfortunate outgrowth of this sort of postmodern nihilism and making Afro-pessimism more intersectional will hardly improve the situation of oppressed people.

Pluralist and multicultural politics fit comfortably with the ideology of the Democratic Party. This is why the left-liberal politics of the PMC asserts that the Democratic Party needs to be reformed rather than rejected (Guastella 2020a). Just as we are asked to think of ourselves as the victims of statues of people who are as inoffensive as Voltaire, or the victims of images of a white-looking hippie Jesus, we are also asked to bend the knee for Joe Biden (Carr; Palma). Is all of this humble pie not odd for a culture that prevents performers from wearing blackface? Not really. It is what you get when you have lost the perspective of universality and reduced it to crude materialism, which, when ground down to a fine powder, gets shifted about like semiotic sand in a digital desert. If history has never ceased to be written by the victors, as Walter Benjamin argued in his "Theses on the Philosophy of History," does postmodernism offer us nothing more than the status of victim, which today is treated as a historical norm (Benjamin). The flipside to all the statues of historical figures who do not embody contemporary values are those newly created monuments that do (Di Liscia). The underside, however, is the undercurrents of resentment that are allowed to fester, like those that are depicted in Kara Walker's *Fons Americanus* (2019), a commission by the Hyundai automobile manufacturer that was more generous towards Walker than it is towards its employees in the U.S. and South Korea. According to Michael Glover, such works that deconstruct racist stereotypes do not collectivize society according to high-minded ideals, but rather along the lines of darkness, blame, negligence, cruelty, indifference, guilt, misery and other terrible things (Glover). You've come a long way, motherfucker.

Marxism is a critique of liberalism. It identifies contradictions in bourgeois ideology and bourgeois political economy and on this basis seeks to advance the cause of human progress. When socialism is conceived without the universal and emancipatory aspects of Enlightenment, the result is fascism. When capitalism is conceived without the universal and emancipatory aspects of Enlightenment, the result is fascism also. If one is to be a socialist it is necessary to understand Hegel and dialectical materialism. When dialectical and historical materialism became the official ideology of the state parties of the communist International, 'diamat' became orthodoxy. In the postwar period, intellectuals and the petty-bourgeois counterculture decided they had had enough of party discipline as well as the centralized bureaucratic systems that guided industrial production. The era of affluence and consumer capitalism created a funhouse of new possibilities. Even though living 'off the grid' was a dream that was increasingly made possible by the exploitation of Third World labor, the general conditions of affluence made good on the idea that mechanization and scientific management could be used to bring people more leisure time and free them from unnecessary toil. Since the petty-bourgeois class did not own the means of production, the next best thing was to live a life that anticipated new social relations. Manners and lifestyles that were liberated from the status quo suggested that living on the cheap and outside the usual standards of the nuclear family could disturb and awaken social consciousness. Such lifestyles were more or less reserved for the children of middle-class parents, who themselves became part of the system after they had done LSD, slept around and returned from their trip to India or their stint in a kibbutz. Some retained their idealism and understood that if you want to be taken seriously as a leftist, it is better to think of Marxism in terms of an open-ended rather than orthodox materialism. Phenomenology, existentialism, cybernetics, structuralism and what became known as postmodernism provided alternative concepts without which it is almost impossible to appreciate the social, political, cultural and intellectual context in which today's new social movements function.

Beyond the simplistic opposition of race reductionism and so-called class reductionism, a more complex debate between dialectical materialism (the old left) and eclectic materialism (the postmodern left) animates leftists around the Sanders movement. According to the literary theorist Joshua Clover, the year 2020 witnessed two politics, which he defines as "the election" and "the riot." Although both forms of politics took place against the unfolding of the coronavirus pandemic, this is not, he argues, the main cause of the distinction. He writes:

> From January to April, official politics was dominated to the exclusion of all other stories by the presidential election, which means for the most

> part the Democratic primary and then the responses to it by President Reply Guy. It is a commonplace to note that, in the U.S. especially, presidential elections have the power to draw all other politics into them and perhaps have this as their essential purpose, absorbing the power of social movements with the to-date unmet promise to organize their energy and magnify their capacity. There was, in effect, nothing else to talk about ... [T]he election's domination of political space grew even more total, as it remained while absolutely everything else was squeezed out. Nothing else was happening and nothing else *could* happen.
>
> CLOVER 2020

This is fairly accurate for those who considered the 2020 election to be the most important election in their lifetime. Some of these people are leftists who were never convinced by the ultra-left stance that rejects elections as nothing more than a deception. Moreover, many social movement anarchists and even communists found reason to take interest in the Sanders campaign – more than the election as such. The Sanders campaign became a litmus test on whether or not anything can displace neoliberal hegemony. Regardless, Clover asks leftists to presume that there are social movements on one side and electoral politics on the other. He continues:

> And then came the uprising following the police murder of George Floyd, itself happening in the wake of police or police-deputized murders of Breonna Taylor, Ahmaud Arbery, and so many others. Unfolding against and in the penumbra of the pandemic, the national riot displaced the election coverage swiftly and utterly. It happened within days, maybe hours, as the nation pivoted from one politics to another. At the end of May and into June one could watch national news for days, a week, and encounter no mention of Joe Biden, much less Bernie Sanders or Liz Warren (one would hear periodically from Amy Klobuchar, but only because of her unfortunate record as the former attorney for Hennepin County where Floyd was killed). How to name these two politics, if not the election and the riot?
>
> CLOVER 2020

Pursuing the insights of his 2016 book, *Riot. Strike. Riot*, Clover was even before 2020 convinced that in a world of post-Fordist biopower, it is mostly riots that are available to the left as a strategy of resistance (Clover 2016).

The mainstream condemnation of violent protests is subject to movement critique since it creates a dichotomy between rational debate and peaceful demonstration, on the one hand, versus the use of power and direct action on the other. For postmodernists the question of tactics is further displaced by the argument that the mainstream media and politicians are logocentric, or some similarly impractical shibboleth. Just as Marxist intellectuals once looked to Third World liberation movements and the so-called margins as the place from which revolution was still possible, with for example Jean-Paul Sartre writing the preface for Frantz Fanon's *The Wretched of the Earth*, Clover and likeminded people on the postmodern ultra-new left find that black American grassroots activism is a particularly if not uniquely catalytic agent of change (Fanon 1963). All of this leads Clover to suggest that the protests are fluid and rhizomatic, breaking down the dichotomy between words and matter into recombinant forms. It is the mainstream that polices words and matter, keeping them apart so that nothing will change. An intellectual movement which assumes that we are always already involved in language games, if not in the prison-house of language, is not surprised when its relativistic nihilism proves to have no meaningful bearing on reality. For this reason, it can provide an endless supply of fascinating and perverse commentary, but it cannot be thought to constitute a political leadership.

Although countless intellectuals have made valid critiques of postmodern theory from the left, social justice activists tend to take these for granted as much as they do the legal equality of citizens. Take for example the decision by the authoritarian government in Turkey to convert the Hagia Sophia back into a fully operating mosque. A rather sorry article published in *Hyperallergic* attacks appeals to the concept of "universal heritage" that marks the medieval building's protected UNESCO status (Press). The Hagia Sophia does not belong to "all of us," the author suggests, or to an abstraction like "humanity," but rather belongs to the residents of the city, who are mostly Muslim. Since the notion of universality has been used by European and American powers for purposes of conquest over the last 200 years, he argues, why should we carry on with this failed project? The author ignores the fact that both Christianity and Islam have been used as pretexts for conquests of various sorts. The real question is whether, like many racialist critics of Marxism, we really want to make the pre-Enlightenment era and religion the model for government.

Another example of postmodern anti-Enlightenment anti-universalism is the campaign by Meena Harris, the niece of Kamala Harris, to change the name of the George Washington High School in San Francisco to the name of Maya Angelou, who studied there as a youth. Harris is the founder and CEO of Phenomenal Woman Action Campaign, a company that for the most part sells BLM t-shirts and that is self-described as "a female-powered lifestyle brand that brings awareness to social causes." In an article written for *Glamour* magazine,

Harris says that she collected 22,000 signatures to name the school after the legendary poet and activist, who is known to many for her performance at the inauguration of Bill Clinton (Harris). Harris presents this proposed name change in the context of the toppling of Confederate statues. It is not entirely incidental that Harris launched her petition at the same time as the Board of the San Francisco United School District held meetings to discuss changing the names of those schools in its district that commemorate former slave owners, including George Washington, Thomas Jefferson and Ulysses Grant. One is led to speculate that Harris is assisting the neoliberal racialist technocrats who instigated a nation-wide debacle by proposing to destroy the New Deal murals created by Victor Arnautoff for the GWHS. If the name of the school was changed, there would be no reason why the murals should be preserved. Harris' petition ignores the fact that the building was designed in the 1930s by the leading architect in San Francisco and in the context of the Popular Front against fascism. Over the course of 2019, the murals were defended by dozens of associations that represent the highest level of professional, intellectual and artistic opinion. This was matched by overwhelming community support for the murals by the students of the school, the school alumni and the general public. Even the activist grandson of Maya Angelou defended the murals against the name change proposition (Jones). Harris' petition misinformed the public about the GWHS and leeched off of an already-existing controversy in order to gain attention for her woke brand. None of this has anything to do with social justice, but members of the public are none the wiser when neoliberalism blends seamlessly with academia. While this may not reflect the ideas of someone like Clover, it is part of the context in which postmodern academia and postmodern activism create conditions that reinforce neoliberal governance. And what about Sanders? No one in the Democratic Party presidential nomination race weighed in on the GWHS controversy. When in 2019 a copycat campaign to destroy two Sam Kerson murals depicting the history of Vermont and the Underground Railroad was begun by two racialist "activists" at the Vermont Law School, on the disingenuous view that a progressive left depiction of slavery and abolition was offensive to black students, a tractable administration voted to have them removed and thereby destroyed (Fawbush). When asked to intervene, senator Sanders deferred to BLM and to the decisions taken by the school administration.

Another writer whose discounted Marxism creates a simplistic opposition between the election and the protests is Asad Haider, the author of the widely discussed book *Mistaken Identity* (Haider). In an interview with Rafael Khachaturian, Haider dismisses the notion that the Trump presidency was caused by the resentment of the white working class, which he correctly says is a fantasy of the liberal intelligentsia (Haider cited in Khachaturian). The cause of Trump, he argues, is structural rather than conscious. Our task today, according to Haider, is to "make antiracist politics integral to class politics, and class politics integral to an antiracist politics" (Khachaturian). However, rather than discussing the paramount contribution of the labor movement to antiracism and to the Civil Rights struggle, Haider focuses on the racism of the labor movement.

Like any left scholar who wants to be taken seriously, to survive if not thrive in his field and be effective in politics, Haider must demonstrate that he is not merely repeating Marxist dogma, providing "predetermined answers" to "questions that may come up in the course of political practice" (Haider cited in Khachaturian). This is true to some extent, since politics is conjunctural, but not all aspects of Marxism need to be revised at every moment of political struggle. Are the minor practices of social movement actors enough to bankrupt the entire history of the organized left, so as to undermine "objective analysis" and "the idea of class as a pre-given" (Haider cited in Khachaturian). Even more fantastically, how likely is it that someone who is as Foucauldian in his Marxist scholarship as Haider will build a theory of emancipatory politics from scratch? If such a theory is being attempted, one would like to see the results. If Marxism has failed at being projective, as Haider argues, it nevertheless provided an unprecedented analysis of class society. What made Marx prophetic was the depth of his understanding, on which he built his criticism of capitalist society, and not his ability to predict the future. Why would a Marxist fault the originator of the method of dialectical materialism for not being a magical wizard? The race and class debates among Marxists that Haider mentions are more accurately debates between Marxists and postmodernists.[2]

It is obviously true that Marxism does not exist in isolation but is part of a longer history of modern emancipatory movements. Haider considers that it is impossible to formulate universality at the level of abstractions like human rights, human nature or a particular set of political principles. It is not only political liberalism that is abstract, however. So is the flawed understanding of universalism that motivates identity politics. The experience of oppression confirms and reinforces abstraction by reifying identity. Haider contradicts himself when he says that he rejects abstract principles as the basis of universality. He argues that the name communism is only useful today if it preserves

---

2 The publisher Verso is now so divided on these issues that its editors published a disclaimer of sorts with the presentation of Dean and Zamora's *The Last Man Takes LSD* in order to satisfy both camps (Bugden). A key text in this discussion is the invaluable book by Zamora & Behrent.

the "absolutely egalitarian principle of the emancipation of all" (Haider cited in Khachaturian). He then says:

> The pandemic, first of all, completely validated the program for universal healthcare that had been at the center of the Bernie Sanders campaign. It showed the rationality and necessity of this program ... Nevertheless, the way that the establishment, with Sanders's support, coalesced around Joe Biden, showed the limits of trying to work within the state. ... The rise of autonomous movements against state racism and state repression is extraordinarily significant in this sense, because in many respects these movements are more politically advanced than elements of the Sanders campaign. They have entered into direct confrontation with the state and also capital, responding not only to the systematic impoverishment which targets Black people, but also the mass unemployment and impoverishment which has only been exacerbated by the pandemic.
> Haider cited in KHACHATURIAN

There is political truth in both the Sanders campaign and in the protests against police violence. There is nothing, however, to suggest that one expression is more advanced than the other. In fact, a good case can be made that the establishment is much more comfortable with riots and protests, which allows it to use military force, than it is with a democratic socialist in the White House. On the whole, the results of the 1968 riots led to more poverty for African Americans. What matters in such social explosions is the balance of class power and not the identitarian composition of social movements.

Events in Kenosha and Portland, where armed protesters shot and killed counter-protesters, or vice versa, give us a sense of just how desperate and dangerous the culture wars have become. In August, more than 1000 National Guard military police were sent to Kenosha to suppress BLM protests. Kyle Rittenhouse-Lewis, a 17-year-old from Illinois, traveled to Wisconsin to join the Kenosha Guard, a group of self-appointed community guardians. Angered by the riots, he shot and killed two white BLM protesters. The Kenosha police were supporting these armed militiamen. Sadly, but not surprisingly, Trump argued that Rittenhouse was defending himself from attackers (Lock). The self-styled avenger later became a celebrity of the fascist right. Visiting Kenosha, Biden added little more than moral support for back identity politics while making no promises to improve anything either in terms of economic justice or police reform. The victims, Joseph Rosenbaum and Anthony Huber, did not fit Biden's campaign strategy because they were working-class whites.

Biden is no more supportive of protesters than Trump. Although the two presidential candidates blamed one another for the clashes in the streets, both of them supported the same law and order policies that defend the interests of the plutocracy. Meanwhile, a BLM march from Wisconsin to Washington D.C. was organized and supported by establishment figures like Al Sharpton and Kamala Harris, who restricted the problem of police violence to race issues. Harris played a similar role when in April 2021 she was sent to Mexico and Guatemala to investigate the 'root causes' of immigration to the U.S. Citing poverty, political corruption, extreme weather as well as racial, gender and sexual violence, Harris, who is the daughter of immigrants, made deals with the security forces of an extreme-right politician, Alejandro Giammattei, to secure access to cheap labor and suppress the flow of migrants, saying to the people of Guatemala who are thinking of migrating to the U.S.: "Do not come" (Taylor & Keith). She provided a politically correct cover to the mission by contributing a well-publicized $40 million to empower indigenous women and girls, as though the inequality of American and Latin American societies was not being enforced. The Biden administration carried on with Trump policies on the U.S.-Mexico border, reopening detention centers to break up migrant families and dumping illegal immigrants in Mexico without any concern for their health and safety (Treene & Kight; Beauchamp 2021).

A reverse parallel case of Rittenhouse is the fate of Michael Forest Reinoehl, an antifa protester who shot Patriot Prayer supporter Aaron Danielson in Portland, Oregon. Reinoehl told reporters that he had acted in self-defense against a would-be assailant brandishing a knife against him and another protester (VICE News). Later taking his family into hiding, Reinoehl feared turning himself in to the police who were collaborating with right-wing counter-protesters. After Trump demanded his arrest, Reinoehl was summarily killed by a special task force led by U.S. Marshals (Wilson & Freda). Attorney General Barr applauded the execution as a "significant accomplishment in the ongoing effort to restore law and order to Portland and other cities" (Gentzler).

Citizens with different political views killing one another will do nothing to change the existing state of affairs. In fact, pointless violence reinforces the status quo. There are class issues at stake, but they are obscured when they take the form of petty-bourgeois excess. Quite often, progressive culture warriors make use of normative tropes as both real and imagined bogeymen (Heath & Potter). From the work ethic to patriotic fervor, the bugbear of the counterculture was conformity. The obsession with fighting 'the system' created the paranoid conditions in which any form of political commitment was viewed with suspicion. At the same time, the counterculture contained reactionary elements, which today have come to the foreground through the postmodern nihilism of the alt-right.

The rejection of normativity now exists on both sides of the culture war. For example, a September 2020 issue of *Time* magazine, titled "The New American Revolution," profiled prominent African-American activists, artists, athletes and businesspeople. In between the lines of her interview for the issue, Angela Davis endorsed Biden as an imperfect but acceptable candidate. Such content dovetails easily with the main function of the issue, which is to hype the latest music video by Pharrell Williams and Jay-Z called 'Entrepreneur,' which fist-bumps a set of successful black business people, including the owners of one of Obama's favorite soul food restaurants. These are said to be visions of a black future that fulfil a nation's promise. Much the same can be said about the celebrity grievance of Breonna Taylor, the emergency medical technician who was killed by Louisville police officers on March 13, 2020. Taylor became one of the more prominent figures of BLM vigils and demonstrations. Protests in Louisville persisted from May through September, leading the Democratic Governor of Kentucky, Andy Beshear, to declare a state of emergency, impose lockdowns and set up barricades manned by National Guardsmen. The state Attorney General, Daniel Cameron, an African-American Republican who was elected on a law and order platform, denounced the outrage expressed by "celebrities and influencers" and dismissed the protests as "mob justice" (Ceron). In June, Alicia Keys, Jada Pinkett Smith, Queen Latifah, Tracee Ellis Ross, Solange, Selena Gomez, Tessa Thompson, Janelle Monáe, Rihanna, Beyoncé, Cardi B and Oprah called for justice for Breonna Taylor. It is no secret that today's celebrity politicians, athletes, musicians, entertainers and pundits are involved in wokewashing their diversified business portfolios. The grafting of identity politics onto neoliberal capitalism is now official Democratic Party strategy. For this, the Democrats increasingly rely on celebrity support to channel outrage about social inequality back into democratic-sounding platitudes. As identity-driven movement politics like BLM and MeToo take precedent over issues like single-payer health care, ecology, demilitarization, immigration reform, a living wage *and* police reform, the fashionable issues that appeal to middle-class suburbanites leave the interests of the vast majority of the working class out of the picture. Once identity has become your brand, it seemingly no longer matters what politics you uphold, what you are willing to do to please those in power or even the crimes you commit.

The notion that 'race matters' is now a kind of folk wisdom that places movements like BLM in the same league as neoliberal government. As class politics is now almost automatically rejected, the so-called left has given up on struggle and solidarity for the sake of a system in which politics is less a matter of principles and beliefs than it is a form of pragmatism that blackmails people into submission. The recent turn to organizational politics is a practical consequence of the failure to build emancipatory politics on the basis of horizontalist new social movements. After a phase of summit hopping and encampments, the millennial generation of anti-capitalist leftists realized that they could not advance their causes without attacking the power of the moneyed elite. The dissipation of OWS into BLM, MeToo, March for Our Lives, Women's March and other hashtags movements was reassembled for a while around the Sanders campaign. What is still missing from much of this opposition is the glimpse of a third party that made its necessity felt for only a short while before celebrities began their anti-Trump harangues in favor of Biden. The George Floyd protests and the attacks on symbols of the Confederacy re-energized the BLM movement that from the start had been appended to the Democratic Party establishment. As the failed response to the economic and social crisis created by the coronavirus pandemic set in, the need for a universally emancipatory left could not be ignored.

3 Sectarians, Splitters and Fellow Travelers

After Sanders lost the nomination, there was plenty of cognitive dissonance on the social democratic left. The party insiders who had conspired against him began to show some concern about how to win over his supporters. As early as April 2020, according to the *New York Times*, the Democratic establishment was now said to love Bernie, even if he was not a lifelong Democrat like Biden. Obama also came out with a few kind words for Sanders: "Bernie is an American original, a man who has devoted his life to working people's hopes, dreams and frustrations" (Moreno). Never has a politician cherished the frustrations of the electorate more than Obama. In what the *Times* author refers to as the "rush to show appreciation," Biden also had good things to say insofar as people like Sanders are "willing to sacrifice their ideals in the interest of beating Mr. Trump" (Ember 2020b). The neoliberals had no choice but to be nice since Sanders was so dutifully compliant. Sanders supporters were slower to come around. Keeanga-Yamahtta Taylor voiced the common sentiment that Sanders had won the ideological battle. Even if he had not won the majority of delegates, he showed that progressive policies were popular with the American public and that he was the best candidate (Taylor 2020b). Cardi B, for her part, got in on the spectacle of defeat, accepting Biden as the inevitable Number 46 (The Hill 2020b). Others, like journalist Krystal Ball, warned that Blue MAGA supporters cannot shame the left into propping up the people who manufactured the Orange Menace (The Hill 2020f). Briahna Joy Gray suggested that government officials like Kamala Harris seem to think that it is not okay for people to die of coronavirus but that it is okay for poor people without health care to die of cancer. Harris and her supporters reacted promptly to the insensitivity of the statement, not because the poor are without health care, but because Harris' mother died from cancer (Wright 2020). Establishment centrists also used their 'bad cop' angle, blaming Sanders in advance for a potential loss to Trump and as a way to pre-empt criticism for the reality that they had chosen Biden (Sullivan, Scherer & Weigel; The Hill 2020e). Others still, like Kyle Kulinski and Glenn Greenwald, debated whether after Super Tuesday Sanders should have disguised himself as a moderate rather than a populist outsider (The Intercept 2020b).

The overall problem, if Trump was to win again in 2020, was that those who accepted the Biden nomination would inevitably look for someone to blame rather than obsess over election strategy mistakes. Those who would never vote for Biden could more readily remind leftists that Sanders had encouraged Americans to think in ideological terms. Glen Ford, the late editor of the *Black Agenda Report*, was concerned about Biden's success among black voters (Ford). Biden did not win the black Democratic contest because blacks are anti-socialist, he argued, but because blacks feared losing the election to Trump and his "White Amerikaner Party." Rather than voting on the basis of their political convictions, the strategy of most black voters was to avoid losing catastrophically, which meant accepting the decadence of moderate "crackers" and the "Black Misleadership Class." Seeing that the powers that be and the corporate media would not concede an inch to the Sanders campaign, the African-American electorate accepted the dictates of the party brass. Moving on, Ford placed his hope in mass organization outside the party:

> Even if a fraction of the tens of millions of Sanders supporters reject their leader's expected call to go all-in for a nominee and party that is determined to suppress them, a mighty and independent mass movement can be built in a relatively short space of time. Indeed, that was always the best outcome of the decade's resurgence in anti-capitalist, anti-racist politics. The Democrats were always a dead end, but folks had to get their asses kicked TWICE to learn that you can't turn a ruling class party against the ruling class. … It is certainly clear that progress depends on mass action in the street that changes popular assumptions of what is possible.
>   FORD

In the difference between leftists who believe in anti-institutional and anti-systemic strategies, and those who seek change by occupying state institutions, Ford placed his hopes with new social movements rather than official organizations.

Seattle councilwoman and Socialist Alternative member Kshama Sawant, who made for one of the most exciting Sanders surrogates, wrote a somewhat more orthodox response to the Sanders defeat, reiterating her 2016 conclusion that we need to win every vote to build the largest possible base of support for the kinds of ideas that the Sanders campaign represented (Sawant 2020). This movement must also build a new party that is of, by and for working people and not the billionaire class. The relentless opposition of the Democratic Party establishment to radical social change requires, she argued, that we distinguish between the friends of the working class and fake progressives like Elizabeth Warren. This effort should include mass demonstrations. Since Sanders was likely to support Biden, Sawant insisted that the political revolution must remain the priority of the left. Biden is not our friend, she said, and his corruption is good reason to take the first decisive steps beyond the "rotten, corporate Democratic Party" (Sawant 2020).

Sawant's use of the #DemExit hashtag is consistent with the views of the party that she is a member of, Socialist Alternative, which is a revolutionary Marxist-Trotskyist organization and a member of the International Socialist Alternative. In social democratic and democratic socialist circles, such groups are often referred to as sectarian. The word sectarian means different things to different people, even if it is more generally used as a pejorative. In mainstream American discourse, sectarianism refers to polarization within the two-party system. For example, a 2020 article in *Science* magazine argues that whereas liberals and conservatives used to vote for both parties, support for either the Democratic Party or the GOP is now polarized along several axes: political, racial, religious, educational and geographic (Finkel et al). As politics becomes a form of identity, sectarians become more openly hostile and uncooperative, making it impossible for the government to pass legislation on important issues like climate change. Among the causes of polarization, the article identifies the deregulation of broadcast news, social media echo chambers and the mobilization of outrage by politicians who adopt anti-democratic tactics to stimulate activism. It recommends public debate and the protection of democratic rights as means to reduce sectarianism.

The thought that shoring up consensus between the two parties of the ruling class will enhance democracy is laughable. This leads to the more common understanding of sectarianism. On the American left, sectarianism means splitting the Democratic Party through reformism or abandoning the party altogether. Sectarian groups in the U.S. have pursued both paths through what we could refer to as First, Second, Third and Fourth International strategies.

Nineteenth-century Lassalleans in the Socialist Labor Party of North America sought to make use of the state to advance the interests of trade union workers. In response, trade unionists assembled in the American Federation of Labor and their more militant comrades joined the Industrial Workers of the World. Anarchists formed the Revolutionary Socialist Party and followers of Eugene Debs formed the Social Democratic Party of America. In the twentieth century, two main tendencies were split between the Socialist Party of America (SPA), who ran officials for government office, and the Communist Party (CPUSA), which at its height in 1939 included 100,000 members. Both parties were undermined by government repression during and after the Second World War. Those who split from the Stalinist USSR followed the Trotskyist tendency, starting with the League of America (1928), the Workers Party (1934), the Socialist Workers Party (1938), the Workers Party/Independent Socialist League (1940), Workers World Party (1959), Socialist Equality Party (1964), Freedom Socialist Party (1966), Spartacist League (1966), Socialist Action (1983), Solidarity (1986) and the International Marxist Tendency (2002). The socialists, for their party, split from the SPA to form the social democratic American Labor Party (ALP, 1936), which was supported by the Congress of Industrial Organizations (CIO).

In the postwar period, Civil Rights leaders like A. Philip Randolph and Bayard Rustin played an active role in the socialist movement, as did New Left tendencies, which ranged the entire left spectrum. Michael Harrington, a political theorist and professor of political science, led the student movement through Students for a Democratic Society (SDS) and into what has become the Democratic Socialists of America (DSA), which is not a party but rather a socialist non-profit organization that in the 2000s increased its membership to over 90,000 members. This latter-day SDS has been co-chaired by Barbara Ehrenreich and includes notable members like Cornel West, Alexandria Ocasio-Cortez, Rashida Tlaib, Jamaal Bowman and India Walton. The DSA seeks to reform the Democratic Party and supports progressive candidates for public office.

On the more socialist-communist side of the spectrum, it is nearly impossible to keep track of all of the splits and tendencies that occurred since the 1960s. The Progressive Labor Party (PLP, 1962), which split from the CPUSA, is typical of the anti-revisionist Marxist-Leninist line. This tendency had to negotiate whether they stayed connected to Third World revolutions in China, Cuba, Vietnam, Albania and elsewhere, leading to the multiplication of factions. In 1972, the reformist Randolph-Rustin and AFL-CIO tendency formed around the Social Democrats (SDUSA) and radical New Left SPA members formed into the Socialist Party USA (SPUSA). Many groups existed only for a short while in the 1960s and 70s, including the Black Panther Party, the Yippies, the Revolutionary Communist League and the Weather Underground. Among those groups that are still active today, in addition to some of those mentioned previously, there is the Revolutionary Communist Party USA (RCP, 1975), the Communist Party (Marxist-Leninist) (1977), the Freedom Road Socialist Organization (FRSO, 1985), the Party for Socialism and Liberation (2004) and the American Party of Labor (2008). Leftists are also organized through trade unions and state-level groups like the Vermont Progressive Party have had a notable influence. The Green Party, which ran Ralph Nader as a third-party candidate in 1996 and 2000, has been active in California especially and in 2021 had 245,000 members. It is difficult to know what the combined strength of all of these left sectarian organizations might be, but if one was to include unionized workers, the American left consists of approximately 15 million people. Given the popularity of socialism, anarchism and social democracy among millennials, that number is likely to increase in the years ahead. Despite the fact that the membership of left-wing organizations is under one million, these groups, as well as radical intellectuals, artists and activists in the U.S. and internationally, are the vanguard of the American left.

From a radical perspective, the word sectarian has four meanings: opposition to the Republican party, factional opposition to centrist Democrats, opposition to the Democratic Party and/or opposition to other sectarian groups. Negotiating a third party split from the Democratic Party is difficult enough but in the midst of a class war that is in full force, a climate catastrophe, forever wars, a deadly pandemic and a racialized protest movement that is focused almost entirely on police violence, the chances that leftists could rally together to create a unified front presents unfavorable obstacles. This is not to suggest that these different strategies are opposed to one another. What the Sanders campaign showed was that it was possible to move beyond anti-globalization activism towards building organizational power. In Quebec, after the 2012 student strike first mobilized hundreds of thousands of students and then almost the entire population, the student organizations that led the strike, which became a social strike against neoliberalism, have been dismantled. The province is now governed by a Trump-style conservative party. The important question for the left is how to build and maintain organizational power.

For some socialists, the Sanders defeat was something of a 'told you so' moment. Reporting on the *World Socialist Web Site*, Eric London not only reiterated the Socialist Equality Party position that the Sanders movement was a deception all along, since the Democratic Party cannot be reformed, but also that the DSA has played a cynical role as its instrument (London 2020a). The article illuminates the kind of squabbling that both weakens the left and strengthens it. Referring to an online discussion moderated by *Jacobin* editor

Bhaskar Sunkara on the subject of what to do after the Sanders campaign, and that featured Meagan Day, Matt Karp, Amber Frost and Michael Brooks, London mentions several points that the SEP could never go along with: rejection of the idea of forming a socialist party, keeping the Democratic Party in mind as an option, and relying on some measure of good luck (Jacobin Magazine 2020d). London retorts: "If Sanders merely suffered from 'bad luck' in 2016 and 2020, why not try again in 2024? And what about the past century of failed efforts at reforming the Democratic Party?" (London 2020a) Against the rejection of sectarianism by would-be socialists who denounce Trotskyists as "armchair revolutionaries," London reminded his readers of the fact that reformists have always fought against the radical left.

The problem with this April 2020 debate comes around to questions of strategy and leadership. On this score, Sunkara came across as a radical bourgeois ideologue. He was not thinking from the perspective of the workers' movement, but from the perspective of the class of people who seek to lead workers in the fight for social progress. The difference is subtle but it marks a distinction between radicals and pragmatists. One might think that Sanders agrees with him when in July 2021 he rebranded his Our Revolution advocacy group to Pragmatic Progressives. Sunkara argued that sectarian socialists are satisfied to stay small. He defined the base of the movement that he would like to build as "not just the socialist left," but "people who are more attracted to anti-establishment left populism," who are "non-ideological" but believe in egalitarian politics. For socialist politics, in contrast to what Sunkara thinks, the 'base' of our movement is not only the working class, but the political economy: the mode of production and social relations of production. On that basis, it is impossible for people to be 'non-ideological.' It is for this reason that Marx invented the term *proletariat*, which, unlike forms of ultra-politics, does not allow politics to be remade into matters of ontology. This means that the revolutionary movement can include people from the middle and upper classes. Socialists make class rather than people the basis of analysis and struggle. Anti-establishment populism has roots in the American revolutionary tradition, but it has a more immediate grounding in postwar counterculture. The countercultural politics of anti-normativity are today essential features of corporate ideology across the political spectrum. What makes populism appealing to Americans is the fact that it conveniently eclipses the rest of the world from political consciousness. Insofar as populism proscribes socialist politics, it has greater affinity with the right than the left. In the context of neoliberal globalization, American populism acts as a modification rather than a replacement of corporate liberalism. American populism is thus a feature of American exceptionalism.

Sunkara argued that we need a new institution but not a socialist party. This is an odd thing to say for someone who has published a book titled *The Socialist Manifesto* (Sunkara). Here is another instance of decaffeinated politics, or what Žižek refers to as the ideology of postmodern consumerism, which offers you a product deprived of its harmful substance, like diet cola or non-alcoholic beer. Another example is the fiasco around Nathan Robinson, the author of a book titled *Why You Should Be a Socialist*, who fired most of his staff at the journal *Current Affairs* when they petitioned him to make his organization into a cooperative (Robinson 2019; Ellefson). Like Robinson, Sunkara reduces socialist politics to improved material conditions within the existing capitalist arrangements. This pragmatic tendency on the left is typically inept in its understanding of dialectical materialism and its reductionist description of materialism, which it opposes to a non-Marxist understanding of idealism. The anti-dialectical and anti-sectarian cues that Sunkara gave to his compliant cast of young radicals led to a tawdry discussion, which plays well as YouTube chatter but leaves to be desired as far as radical praxis is concerned. For the worker with some time to spare, any of the classic texts in the revolutionary tradition is more formative. Even Stalin's primer on historical and dialectical materialism would do one better than the processed leftism that today's streamers pander for the sake of followers and clicks.

Michael Brooks, who was host at that time of the online Michael Brooks Show, made several good points in this discussion. Emphasizing the importance of organized labor, he very correctly suggested that those who want to play a part in left politics need to let go of subcultural practices that create woke in-groups that are based on insular ways of being. This is the kind of politics that propped up Warren's attacks against Sanders. He questioned the limits of Sanders' bold rhetoric when compared with the importance of campaigning. That is true but those who volunteered for Sanders I am sure did so because they were energized by his bold rhetoric, which was mentioned by his surrogates at almost all of his rallies. Brooks suggested that we are sick of competing over the destiny of the professional-managerial class. The fact of the matter is that in a post-Fordist economy, the petty bourgeoisie defines the dominant class ideology. This makes the sociological concept if not the support of segments of the PMC indispensable.

Playing on the theme of imagination versus materiality, *Jacobin* staff writer Matt Karp argued for a "synthetic" middle ground. What the Sanders movement inspired, he says, is a "material imagination" that did not exist in 2014 and 2015. He defined this material imagination as "bread and butter social democratic issues." Unfortunately for Karp, this is what Lenin in *What Is to Be Done?* denounced as 'economism' and trade union consciousness, meaning: the reduction to politics to better work conditions, shorter hours and better wages. If only radicals had thought of bread and butter issues before! Meagan Day, another staff writer at *Jacobin*, appealed to "non-sectarian socialists" inspired by the Sanders campaign. She argued that "materialists" do not believe that the world changes as a result of ideas. She then immediately contradicted herself by adding that when people's expectations are changed they fight differently. Day suggested that expanding people's imagination to believe in things like single-payer health care is important to left strategy. Too bad that people could not be brought to believe that it is neoliberal ideology and government that prevents them from having health care and other social benefits. That would save us a lot of trouble. Amber Frost, who is one of the hosts of Chapo Trap House, home of the so-called dirtbag left, was sober enough to say that she would not be voting for Biden and does not plan on withdrawing into local feel-good projects that have more to do with charity and volunteerism than socialism. The Bernie phenomenon, she argued, was not actual socialism but had more to do with raising people's sense of optimism.

Organized socialists like the Trotskyist SEP were derided during the *Jacobin* discussion as sectarian, while disorganized socialists like members of the DSA were safe for inclusion in the space of social media commentary. On the other hand, members of Socialist Alternative joined the DSA in 2021 for the sake of possible collaboration in the creation of a mass party of the working class and the advancement of Marxist ideas (Sawant 2021). In "Dialectical Gymnastics? No Thanks!" Žižek discusses one of his countless versions of Lacan's theory of *jouissance* (Žižek 2012: 54–9). He asks how it is that we can avoid nihilism once the cracks have been revealed in the big Other of the symbolic order. The big Other can be many things, but in this case it could be the Sanders campaign or the Democratic Party. The lack of the Sanders signifier remains part of the political symbolic order, even if it is barred. Sanders is now the unsayable element that is inherent in the sayable. This explains why it is that there were so many Sanders memes that recycled the iconic symbols of the communist left – hammers and sickles, red stars, etc. From the perspective of communism, the big ideas that motivated the Sanders campaign are the material elements that allowed voters to intervene in U.S. politics (BTV SB College). Once people have decided that they have had enough of neoliberalism, or once they decide that they have listened enough to the chatter of pundits, they will act.

A third party on the American left would need to function as an umbrella for actually existing left parties as well as progressives more generally. While encouraging intellectual freedom and autonomy, a meta-party would acknowledge the limits if not the outmodedness of postmodern identity politics. It would rehabilitate the Frankfurt School, the best work within Cultural Studies and other strands on the international left that advance the class struggle. Alternative media channels should be encouraged so that leftists can develop a common strategy based on shared principles. This would mean paying less attention to corporate media. Far too much energy is wasted responding to the stupidity of the extreme center and right. Because the intellectual, cultural and political acumen of the left is being reduced to watered-down, consumer-friendly versions, we co-opt ourselves in advance. We do not need to worry about attracting supporters. We need to be the left, which, on the basis of its energy, veracity and integrity, can lead the necessary struggles that people will support with enthusiasm and dedication. If such a third party is not possible and differences on the left are not insurmountable, then the Democratic Party will likely continue to serve its purpose as the graveyard of social movements.

By mid-April, Sanders was busy shaming his supporters who refused to vote for Biden with the accusation that they are being irresponsible (Walters & Gambino). This sentiment came from anarchist quarters as well when Noam Chomsky was called upon by Mehdi Hasan to repeat the same statements that the activist scholar made in 2016 – and which Chomsky has been making for decades already – that a vote that is not cast is a vote for Trump (The Intercept 2020a). Similar warnings came from the former leaders of Students for a Democratic Society in an open letter published in *The Nation*, whose editors had supported Warren for the nomination (SDS; Finn). In 2016, Žižek provocatively stated that he was correct to say that voting for Hillary Clinton would have been worse than voting for Trump since only the radicalization of the Democratic Party can avoid the dangers that are in the making: border walls, ecological catastrophe, nuclear war, unchecked executive power (Žižek 2019c; Žižek 2016; Al Jazeera 2016a; Al Jazeera 2016b; Dabashi).[3] Žižek was not endorsing Trump. He was seeking to undermine the stupefaction that results from the kind of false choices that reinforce capitalist domination. As Trump destabilized the status quo from the extreme right and Sanders did the same from the universalist left, the asymmetry of the two ruptures made it apparent that only the left struggle disturbs global capitalism. Although he did not believe that a right-wing victory would create the conditions for the emergence of an authentic left, Žižek argued nevertheless that the Trump victory created the conditions for class struggle to emerge within the Democratic Party. He never called for alliances to be made with Trump supporters, though he does believe that the working class must be won over to the left. His argument was

---

3   For a correct analysis and further discussion of Žižek's provocation, see Ettinger; Hamilton & McManus.

that the neoliberal consensus that sabotages leftist solidarity produces Trump supporters. Despite all evidence to the contrary, Sanders supporters and people like Žižek are blamed for Trump. Given the negative reaction of the left to Žižek's provocation in 2016, Žižek avoided making any pronouncements on the Biden vote until after the election, when he collegially conceded to Chomsky's point. An article by Žižek was published in *Jacobin* in December 2020, indicating that for some the unofficial social movement prohibition against him, as represented for instance by an attack article in *Current Affairs*, had been lifted (Moller-Nielsen). Žižek has otherwise been banned from mainstream news media.

Only the radicalization of the left can avert catastrophe. However, as soon radical leftists are heard from, they are accused by pragmatists of idealism. Discussing third-party politics after Sanders, Adolph Reed and Michael Brooks discussed some of the common views on the matter: the danger of the left project being turned into moralistic advocacy through foundations and NGO-style politics; the NGO left emphasizes process over goals; people who are serious militants must not expect to win Democratic Party nominations; the Sanders campaign was an ideological victory, especially due to the popularity of M4A, which is the kind of campaign issue around which the left can build a movement; the left needs to connect in a genuinely popular way with working people and broaden support through their networks; the fact that young people now identify as socialist is disingenuous insofar as the term functions as an empty signifier – a living wage, for example, does not need to be referred to as socialism but could be referred to as a demand for economic justice; third parties like those led by Jesse Jackson and Ralph Nader are little more than fanciful means for people to vent their frustrations; left politics must be built around substantive issues like labor power and environmentalism; the left needs to move beyond woke correctness and acknowledge ordinary people; leftists need to connect with people and broaden their base of support (Michael Brooks Show 2020b). Their discussion did not address sectarianism until Brooks argued that having a party named after 'workers' is a romantic fantasy when compared to building power through movements. Reed replied that one of the dangers to be avoided is "the Trotskyist thing" of pamphleteering at strikes in the hope of hooking unsuspecting workers who are desperate for support. Brooks mentioned that politicians like Al Gore do not listen to Trotskyists or Maoists, and that these kinds of people are not the ones who organize AFL-CIO demonstrations. Sectarians, Brooks argued, pretend that other people's organizational work is part of their teleology about revolution. Sectarians therefore cannot recognize labor activity for what it is. Reed replied that Internet platforms have made it easier to do this sort of thing and "sell yourself the bill of goods," transforming the simple factuality of events into ideological doxa. He then suggested that people who are not respected understandably take aggressive and extra-ordinary action. Reed rejected vanguard groups who infuse labor activism with revolutionary content.

This discussion leads one to think that socialists are to blame for the problems of capitalism. If they are not to be offensive to ordinary workers, socialists should act like fellow travelers to trade unions. According to Reed, talking to leftists with party ties is somehow more dubious than being misrepresented by union bosses, the mainstream press or an influencer with a Patreon page.[4] Although the *World Socialist Web Site* is the most widely read socialist daily online, represents one century of radical praxis and has an international presence, Brooks did not hesitate to tout his inexperience as "helpful and important" to labor power. And if nothing comes of it, he said, "we'll just do Pocahontas jokes and at least people can laugh" (Michael Brooks Show 2020b). For Reed, abstract visions belong to the distant future. He welcomed the collapse of the Soviet Union since it disabused the American left of communism. The Sanders campaign did not need socialism, he argued, and Americans understand that the choice is between authoritarianism and social democracy. Controversies among academic and nominal leftists, he concluded, are meaningless. While fully appreciating Reed's scholarship, activism and dedication to the left, and even his sardonic humor, one can only regret the way that he moralizes his comrades. In-fighting is nevertheless endemic on the left and is a matter of course in politics.

The discussion between Reed and Brooks exhibited a contradictory stance towards the postmodern notion of the end of history. On the one hand, they both accept the macro-political framework of politics and support the notion of emancipatory universalism. On the other hand, the notion that workers will spontaneously organize without either the leadership of a radical movement or support from political insiders and organizations is somewhat deluded. After four decades of neoliberalization, organized labor in the U.S. has dwindled. The better part of the agonist left has not only abandoned party politics but organized labor along with it. Where left politics has not devolved into horizontalist constituent and destituent power, with a few public intellectuals and collectives reaping the whirlwind, class consciousness among the masses has been replaced by postwar petty-bourgeois anti-authoritarianism. In terms of vanguardism, the evasion of the leadership question, however you define

---

4 On the problems of trying to build a left movement through online streaming, see Kuznetsov & Ismangil.

it, places the left on the reactive side of capitalist structural transformation. If social democracy remains the means and the ends of left politics, one will inevitably remain within the end of history paradigm, which is clearly inoperative. As Žižek said on the occasion of his reception of the Holberg Prize: "Are you still a Fukuyamaist in the sense of we just make the system function a little bit better? I'm skeptical here" (Holberg). When socialist parties have millions of members, as some do in countries like India, all organizational means function as vehicles of class consciousness. There is no good reason why meeting workers on the front lines of the class struggle should be satirized as predatory behavior. The assault of DSA activists by United Mine Workers of America officials in May 2021, on the suspicion that they were SEP members, is a small reminder of the need for solidarity.

Given the above, it was interesting to hear Reed discuss these issues with David North, the chairman of the SEP, in an October encounter moderated by the Political Science department at the State University of San Diego (Political Science SDSU). North argued that there is not much left of American democracy now that both parties conspire to remove all restraints on the exploitation of the working class. Reed concurred, warning also against populism on the right and left. Populism is rather a sign that neoliberalism, as a nominally democratic order, can no longer maintain its legitimacy. Although they concurred on most issues, Reed and North did disagree about whether or not leftists should vote for Biden. North argued that nothing is more destructive than telling workers to vote for bourgeois parties, and then, as Chomsky says, "fight like hell" once Biden is in office. The broader question is, why is there no socialist movement in the U.S.? Reed countered that voting for the lesser of two evils must be seen as an unpleasant but necessary act of promiscuity. As Reed put it in 2016 about Hillary Clinton: "vote for the lying neoliberal warmonger: it's important" (Reed 2016c). Against his more recent suggestion that sometimes one has to clean the toilet – meaning, vote for Biden while holding one's nose – the problem is that the left has been cleaning the toilet on a full-time basis for quite some time now. Reed and North also differed on how you go about building the left. Although this debate mostly reiterated what is already known about the differences between Trotskyists and democratic socialists, it did raise a problem that is normally attributed to the petty-bourgeois character of the identitarian left. The ideology that has sustained revolutionary communism for almost one century has become inoperative among those who accept the bipartisan framework as a practical reality, if not as the 'discursive' context of today's conjuncture.

Who is going to lead the movement and how is perhaps less important than building organizational strength. The fact that the pragmatic left is willing to entertain conversations with the radical left is a step in the right direction. It goes some distance from Chomsky's attitude that when it comes to voting for Biden, there is no debate (Halper 2020b). That there is in fact discussion on the matter is evidence, to Chomsky, of the collapse of the left. It could be thought, instead, that these debates are evidence of the rise of left militancy. The disappearance of communism on the world stage has made not only the Republicans immune to pressure, but the Democrats as well. In addition, the loss of union jobs makes mass protests less effective than they were when they had union support. The corporate media have also adapted to the spectacle of demonstrations by inoculating viewers to socialism through the twaddle of idiotic pundits. This situation caused journalist Chris Hedges to warn against despair (Mediasanctuary). Biden and the Democratic Party, he argued, will not save us from the rise of the fascist right for one simple reason: the two parties are in agreement on all of the major, substantive issues, including militarism, policing, free trade, deregulation, the control of elections, ecocide and the limitless exploitation of labor. Voting for Biden will do nothing to cripple the power elite. What it will do, Hedges argued, is manufacture consent for endless wars, bloated military budgets, the apartheid state of Israel, mass surveillance, the abolition of due process and habeas corpus, austerity, cuts to Social Security, low wages, unemployment, offshoring, the assault on education and health care through privatization, police impunity, fracking, student debt, the elimination of abortion rights, the purchase of election victories and the corporate plundering of the commons.

The Democratic Party, in Hedges' view, is an arm of the corporate state that uses government as an instrument of pillage. Jeff Bezos, who is one of the richest men in the world, added $72 billion to his wealth during the year 2020. His personal worth is $200 billion and the company he founded, Amazon, is worth $1.58 trillion in market capitalization. Amazon paid zero taxes in 2019. Meanwhile, Amazon workers are paid minimum wage to work over-hired part-time jobs in factories with little to no coronavirus hygiene. Employees, some of whom should be enjoying their golden years, had to self-administer nasal tests and there were no bonuses for working in Amazon's hazardous work environments. Breaks are practically non-existent and employees are constantly expected to reach their work quotas at faster rates. Managers walk around to ensure that workers scan something every five minutes. Failure to do so is registered by computers that then oblige workers to see a manager. Employees bring items to scan with them to the bathroom so that is does not seem like they are slacking. As if that is not bad enough, they have to ask a manager for permission to go the bathroom. Most of these Bezos minions are rude and mistreat his modern-day serfs. Bezos is not alone. In 2020, while 3.8 million people died from government herd immunity policies, the total combined wealth of the world's billionaire class rose from $5 trillion to $13 trillion. Due to rising stock prices, private financial assets rose by 8 percent to $250 trillion, with the ranks of those whose earnings are above $100 million growing by 10 percent to count 60,000 individuals. That same year, according to the World Bank, an additional 124 million people sunk below the international poverty line, bringing the total number to 750 million. Keeping up the appearance that the Democratic Party can be reformed and that Biden is not as bad as Trump, Hedges says, appeals to people's best impulses for the sake of greed and crime.

It is worth noting that much of what the far right has done in the last few decades is organize its own law schools, colleges, lobby groups and media platforms. That is good enough reason to credit our sectarian comrades. When reform is no longer possible, the solution is either fascist tyranny or socialist revolution. Insofar as the Democratic Party establishment and its hangers on continue to reject the negativity of revolutionary politics and instead prop up the fantasies of bourgeois democracy, the rejection of global capitalism will continue to propagate (Dean 2009). Even if this struggle is interminable, with new dark ages ahead, it is better to face the horror with a sense of purpose than to allow the resources of the radical left to decay.

Although the Democratic Socialists of America voted at the 2019 convention to not campaign for any Democratic Party candidate other than Sanders, they eventually reversed course by mobilizing to get the vote out for Biden and against Trump (Leigh). The dilemma of damned if you do, damned if you don't, was rejected by only two prominent left intellectuals, Chris Hedges and Richard Wolff (Halper 2020a; AcTVism Munich). Hedges and Cornel West went on to endorse the Movement for a People's Party, which mixes Sanders-style populism with libertarianism and social democracy. This diffident effort to create a third party based on policies that duplicate the goals of progressive Democrats ignores the difficulty of advancing a social welfare agenda under the current circumstances.

People who reject the prospect of building a left movement outside the Democratic Party have replaced Marxism with a fake form of objective fatalism: there is no alternative. A third party already exists wherever people reject the two parties of the right. The question is: How do you organize the working class? Perhaps we should ask this other question: What kind of left asks us to reject the prospect of building a movement outside the Democratic Party? Let us be clear also that it is the elite establishment that is 'outside' the system. They are the outlaws. We are the ones who, even despite ourselves, make the system work. What then is the class perspective on the PMC that asks us to vote dishonestly? Whenever people who call themselves socialists are confronted with the prospect of radicalism, 1001 excuses are made as to why this is impractical. The logic of activism shifts to academicism and back, avoiding the possibility of a radical communist movement organized around parties and workers' organizations. Given its support of socialism, the younger generation is desperate for leadership (Fitzgerald & Black). Most Americans, close to 90 percent, feel that their country is off-track. Having politicians and intellectuals reassure them about Biden was a dangerous illusion.

4   When I Hear the Word Culture, I Reach for the Political Economy

In the summer of 2020, Angela Nagle and Michael Tracey co-authored an article that offers several explanations of why it is that the Sanders campaign failed (Nagle & Tracey). The article is titled "First as Tragedy, Then as Farce" in order to distinguish the 2016 and 2020 Sanders campaigns. It introduces the notion of a "fusionist" left as the main reason given for the Sanders defeat. Their thesis is similar to the arguments presented here. The authors argue that Sanders had a considerable advantage when entering the 2020 race, thanks in part to a smart campaign team and considerable campaign donations. Despite the hostility of the Democratic establishment, his loss was not a foregone conclusion. The reality, they argue, is that Sanders was defeated by popular vote and so the result of the election reflects the failure of the entire American left. The authors downplay several possible factors contributing to his defeat: the role of the corporate media, the large number of Democratic Party nominees, the supposed threat Sanders posed to the Democratic establishment, and the notion that Biden was the favored candidate.

After these explanations are elaborated, the article focuses more closely on the possibility that the Sanders campaign did not understand the electorate. The Sanders team operated in the intellectual firmament of the activist and media left, they argue. The influence of the campaigners on the candidate was noticeable in the difference between how he ran in 2016 and in 2020. Due to the Trump presidency, American liberals have had a perfect excuse to ignore their own failings. This made the populist Sanders movement a potential threat to the Democratic Party status quo. It was an opening that the Sanders campaign understood but avoided as it tried to have it both ways, advancing a social democratic agenda while at the same time trying to win the educated middle-class voters who supported candidates like Clinton and Warren. Running against Trump as a bigoted tyrant had the unintended effect of ignoring why it is that Trump beat Clinton. Nagle and Tracey are perfectly correct on this point as Sanders could have pushed much harder against bogus party initiatives like Russiagate and the half-hearted impeachment. After three years of liberal propaganda ended with the inconclusive Mueller Report, Sanders could easily have appealed to the public's common sense by admitting that the whole thing was a scam and that if Trump is to be impeached it should be for far more important reasons than snooping on Biden's Ukraine connections. He could also have addressed salient issues like the torture of Julian Assange or the attempts to invade Venezuela. In other words, Sanders could have made a distinction between leftist anti-corruption and liberal anti-Trumpism.

According to the authors, the Sanders campaign lurched too far towards the "self-contradictory morass of left-liberal groupthink" in order to give a progressive semblance to a campaign that fatally ignored what made Sanders popular in the first place (Nagle & Tracey). In order to pre-empt identity-related attacks, Sanders not only diversified his campaign staff, he also diversified the political culture that came to define the movement that supported him. They write:

> Over four years, this strain of turbocharged identity politics had turned the activist Left into an unnavigable minefield, which in the end made it more hospitable to destructive personalities and more alienating to ordinary members of the very demographics that the whole exercise was meant, in theory, to include.
> NAGLE & TRACEY

As the activist base reciprocally influenced his messaging and politics, liberals could blame his defeat on his Marxist class politics while democratic socialists could blame the corporate elite. The presumption, either way, is that the campaign adequately represented the interests of the American working class. The authors reiterate the findings of the 2016 exit polls, which indicated that the majority of the public is left of the status quo on economic issues and right (sic) of liberals on cultural issues. The activist and academic left ignores this and so ignores the interests of the working majority when it wages vindictive culture wars. What made Sanders different from Clinton in 2016 was not only his left-of-center platform, but his skepticism towards identity politics. Just as Warren and Harris suffered losses for pandering to identitarianism, so did Sanders. In contrast, Biden's outwardly flippant approach to woke sentimentality, like playing 'Despacito' on his iPhone for Hispanic voters in Florida, did not damage his candidacy.

Since 2016, the growth of interest in left politics has been reflected by the large number of Sanders supporters and the increase in DSA membership. The DSA is emblematic of what Nagle and Tracey refer to as the "fusionist left," meaning, the type of New Left that because of the Soviet fiasco combines reformist policies with the new cultural tendencies of civil rights, the student movement, feminism and other strands like environmentalism and prison abolition. Since around 2013, political correctness in activist circles has gone beyond the pale. The DSA, for instance, voted for a resolution to prohibit clapping so as to not disturb people with PTSD. The intra-elite signaling of the activist left put pressure on the Sanders campaign to adopt unpopular, youth-focused causes, pushing a left ideological resurgence back into banal bipartisan predictability. The authors conclude: "In the end, Bernie may well be the last domino to fall for the entire Cold War-era Left fusion of social democratic economics mixed with radical liberal culture wars" (Nagle & Tracey). Similar problems have afflicted the U.K.'s Labor Party (Devitt). One consequence of the rise of this so-called fusionism, they say, is that an open intellectual culture is no longer allowed on the American left.[5]

Nagle and Tracey's article is absolutely correct that in 2020 the Sanders campaign increasingly focused on intersectional messaging. It seemed at times that the candidate and his staff were on different planets, and further, that their politics were surreptitiously sabotaging his. To some extent, Sanders' openness to the culture of the people who support him is a testament to his democratic values and social movement sensibility. However, at the same time, as a career politician, Sanders seemed oblivious to the transformations that can be ascribed to postmodern theory, post-structuralism, difference politics, intersectionality, privilege theory and similar academic trends that interact with not only post-Fordist social conditions, but the new culture war orientations that have taken up nefarious and micro-fascist ideological dimensions.

While in the 1980s the education wars were more or less clear-cut in terms of left and right orientation, it is today less obvious that Republican lawmakers who want to protect the disciplines and scientific objectivity are altogether wrongminded. By promoting the anti-universalism of woke intersectionality, the postmodern left has given the right the pretext that it needs to litigate against anything that does not reinforce its right-wing agenda. Authorities are not at fault for insisting that schools should not be indoctrinating youth to think that one race is superior to another, that the U.S. is an inherently racist and sexist society, that groups of individuals are accountable for the past deeds of people of the same sex or race, or that people should be shamed and even given lower grades on account of their privileged identity (Schwartz 2021; Cassimeda). The fact that the liberal left has not more actively rejected the

---

5 On the problems of call-out culture and cancel culture, see Fisher 2013; Burgis 2021; Kovalik 2021. Nagle's 2018 article against open borders solicited a great deal of negative press, leading some to suggest that she has been canceled. See Nagle 2018.

reactionary aspects of seemingly 'progressive' scholarship legitimizes the conservative defense of constitutional rights. Progressives must now defend free speech, the freedom of thought as well as the political, intellectual and cultural legacy of the socialist left if it is not to reinscribe postmodernism. If they escalate the culture war by only defending trends like critical race theory, they will lose public support and further strengthen the fascist right.

As the author of *Kill All Normies*, Nagle is one of the few scholars who has troubled herself to take stock of the problems of identitarianism (Nagle 2017). The importance of her book, from a broad sociological perspective, is less the details about what the alt-right thinks and does, but the fact that what drives this movement is a reactionary appropriation of countercultural logic. The alt-right participates in the cultural shift from bourgeois definitions of culture to the hegemony of petty-bourgeois culture and ideology. Since the postwar period, society has avoided modernist utopianism and big ideological projects as a matter of course. Avant-gardism has been replaced with postmodern irony, lifestyle consumerism, anti-humanism and also what Marshall McLuhan referred to as right-brain ecological thinking, where for instance, structure is more important than agency. Replacing text with context-subtext, intention with chance, form with process, meaning with intertextuality, the postmodern has more readily fallen under the spell of the system. As Perry Anderson argues, its de-differentiating impulses have led the capitalist corruption of ethics and aesthetics (Anderson 1998: 135).

Nagle identifies as left-wing and Tracey as Trotskyist. Her work in particular has been the object of criticism on the left (Cummings). Nagle and Tracey's article on the Sanders campaign received a perhaps unsurprising critique in *Jacobin* by trade unionist Dustin Guastella (Guastella 2020c). Guastella was one of the guests on *Jacobin*'s early pandemic Stay at Home YouTube series, with an insightful report on the differences between "internally mobilized" political parties and "externally mobilized" third parties (Jacobin Magazine 2020e). Whereas the former have a decentralized catch-all orientation that seeks supporters and donors to win elections, the latter have a centralized ideological orientation that recruits members and whose purpose is to mobilize the masses into a constituent power bloc. As an organization with close ties to the Democratic Party, the DSA is nested somewhere between these two types of organization.

Guastella's article, "We Need a Class War, Not a Culture War," is a lengthy reply to Nagle and Tracey. One of the issues that he raises is the fact that they do not mention labor organizations, which is odd for authors who write as leftists, but which nevertheless does not invalidate their ideology critique. Guastella agrees that the concerns of the woke left are by and large distant from the struggles of everyday workers. However, he is not convinced that "fusionism" is the cause of Sanders' defeat. He interprets their article to suggest that what they are calling for is better leadership, which he refers to in pseudo-postmodern terms as a "grand narrative" that "puts a clear protagonist on the center stage of world history: intellectuals, media professionals, and other members of the chattering class" (Guastella 2020c). This distinction between pragmatic insiders and idealist outsiders is unfortunately the sort of device that is commonly used to marginalize radicals and to downplay the importance of leadership. Guastella strikes a populist note by focusing on working people rather than the Sanders campaign staff and supporters. He then suggests that because Nagle and Tracey focus on Twitter rather than left-wing political movements, they have more in common with the woke left than they might care to admit. He counters that one reason Sanders did not win is because there does not exist enough labor unions and mass political organizations. He offers as a counterpoint some historical evidence of what a genuine defeat looks like. All in all, Sanders demonstrated the potential of a future American left in the context of its near absence. Again, it is not the fault of socialists if much of the new social movement left has bought into the technological determinism that replaces labor organizing with hashtag activism. One should not target authors like Jodi Dean, Christian Fuchs, Nick Dyer-Witheford and myself, who have helped to elucidate these problems (Dean 2010, Fuchs, Dyer-Witheford, Léger 2018).

Guastella agrees with Nagle and Tracey that there is no point attributing too much agency to the ultra-liberal online activist set. To focus on campaign messaging as the cause of political outcomes, he argues, is to participate in irrelevant cultural activity. He adds to this the fact that Trotskyism focuses too much on the role of political leaders, which then makes leftists obsess over failures of leadership. "The result," he says, "is a blinkered tendency to read history as a succession of great leaders, an ideal perspective for fringe sectarians, isolated polemicists, and progressive NGO hustlers alike" (Guastella 2020c). In this, Guastella is taking the discussion back to what caused him to be interviewed by *Jacobin* magazine in the first place, which was the directive given by Sunkara to avoid third parties and sectarian politics.

Guastella agrees with Nagle and Tracey that if there was a sizeable self-conscious working-class movement, hyper-liberal opportunists would have less influence. They are therefore correct, he argues, that the culture war should be left behind: "couldn't we strive to capitalize on Bernie's popular economic agenda and ditch the Left side of the culture war?" (Guastella 2020c) Sadly, Reed later made an equally reductive criticism of Nagle and Tracey's article, suggesting that their "going out of their way" to criticize the identitarian aspect of the 2020 Sanders campaign somehow depreciates his contribution to reviving a social democratic agenda in the U.S. (Michael Brooks Show 2020a). In comparison, Žižek argued that Nagle and Tracey were correct to note that one of the reasons for Sanders' defeat in the Democratic Party nomination race was the shift from ideological class insurgency to culture wars. Eager to please the Democratic Party's liberal left, Žižek argues, Sanders "subordinated class insurgency to cultural topics" and shifted his focus from global capitalism to Trump's fascism, a game that was played equally well by Biden (Žižek 2020c). Guastella argues that toxic developments like privilege theory are political liabilities and that candidates adopt them only insofar as they resonate with the public. He suggests that leftists must find a way to prove that they are unpopular among social-democratically inclined working-class voters. This would be difficult if not impossible to do, according to Guastella's own reasoning, since earlier in his article he criticizes Nagle and Tracey for not understanding the fact that the Sanders campaign was not an attempt to save the American left, but to build it. The same should go for cultural theory: the purpose of radical culture is not simply to save culture but to build the proletarian culture of the future. Guastella is more than correct to say that the left can afford to avoid ultra-left culture. He writes: "For the Bidens and Trumps of the world, the culture war is a necessity, to divert and distract from the divide between the rich and the rest of us. For the left, it's a choice." "Thankfully," he adds, "after decades of mystifying and misdirection, we now know the answer" (Guastella 2020c). Knowing the problems with woke identitarianism, identified as fusionist or not, is accepted as a necessary step towards building a genuine American left.

Guastella has the correct answer about postmodernism on the left but seems unaware of how it is that we have come to know this. We know this thanks in part to writers like Nagle who have risked ostracism by providing unorthodox cultural analysis and ideology critique. Like other Marxists before her, she has become a target of postmodern leftists who are strong on identity, but weak on politics. Guastella adds that we should avoid the pitfall of countering identitarianism with social conservatism: "Working-class voters don't want candidates to use ultra-liberal rhetoric but neither do they want them to tear up the important gains of the 1960s Rights Revolution" (Guastella 2020c). He raises the specter of an intolerant and regressive working class but at the same time says that this group is more liberal on social issues than in any other country. His solution to all of these problems is to focus on political economy and socialist politics rather than cultural commentary. "A simple message built around destroying the obscenity of inequality and providing universal public goods would likely do well to unite workers across race, gender, region, and ideology; it just can't be paired with an alienating 'woke' aesthetic" (Guastella

2020c). As it happens, that is exactly what Occupy Wall Street tried to do, until it came under attack from various quarters for not being woke enough. In less than a decade, the problem of economic inequality has worsened, but the socialist left is now admonished to tilt at windmills like whiteness, which presents obstacles to the politics that Guastella advocates (Choonara & Prasad; Cassell).

Guastella is perhaps too much of a political scientist or labor activist to have a strong sense of what has been happening in the humanities in the last two decades. In postmodern academia, tearing up the Rights Revolution goes back not only to the 1960s but to the 1860s. At least three generations of intellectuals have been trained in semiotics, structuralism, post-structuralism, deconstruction, discourse theory and related methods (Chibber 2017). Whereas in the 1980s many humanities scholars were concerned about the dismantling of the disciplines, the postmodernists carried the torch of something like a cultural revolution. There are now so few Marxists around who are literate in both the radical tradition and continental theory that people like Guastella do not know how to appreciate someone like Nagle. The cadres of pseudo-radical postmodernists are stacked quite high, making it such that the pressure to conform to variants of liberal pluralism or postmodernism is nowadays endemic to the arts, humanities and even the social sciences.

In the past there was not one revolutionary leader who did not appreciate the importance of culture. Today, both politics and culture have been reduced to social constructionism, which teaches that anything someone does not like is the product of power relations that have been naturalized. Intellectual phenomena like discursive historicism cannot simply be wished away but have to be critiqued and demystified. When it is done effectively, critique can be very useful to radicals. For example, there are very few people around the DSA who understand culture and politics as well as Leon Trotsky did in his day. In 1922 and 1923, after the civil war, the leader of the Red Army found the country in economic tatters and its political leader on his death bed. Trotsky nevertheless took the time to write *Literature and Revolution*, a work that not only demonstrates his awareness of what was being debated in the arts, but offered a graded schema of the least and most promising tendencies. Trotsky argued that culture was not secondary to politics but was, as a human need, of a potentially higher significance (Trotsky 2005). Responding to this assertion, Ronald Suny writes in *Jacobin*:

> There's a funny anecdote which is probably not true, but it's illustrative. Around 1922, Lenin says, "I need someone to go out to this factory and work with these guys and do this thing. Trotsky, can you do that?" Trotsky

turns him down, saying "Oh, you know, Vladimir Ilyich, I have to write my article right now on literature and revolution." Stalin says, "I'll do it." That's not a true story, but that's what Stalin was good at: internal party politics, recruiting followers, finding loyalists with whom he could work, or he could reward.

cited in MAISANO 2021

This statement was posted a few days after several high-ranking DSA members had been exposed for celebrating Ramon Mercader on Twitter, the Stalinist agent who assassinated Trotsky. Although Suny understands perfectly well that Stalin was the gravedigger of the revolution, celebrating his organizational skills at the expense of everything else is not a good model for today's advocates of class struggle. Democratic socialists have as much difficulty as arts scholars understanding why so many people pursue arts degrees when the chances of living from your work in the U.S. is one out of 40,000. One of Fidel Castro's first acts as revolutionary leader was to bring literacy and arts classes to peasant communities (Gordon-Nesbitt). Today, the U.S. has practically the lowest literacy rates in the developed world and its culture thrives on cruelty and political disorientation.

The culture war and the class war must be analytically distinguished so that the radical movement has a better understanding of the structural and class forces that are at work in today's networked culture. However, the two cannot be completely separated because, as Reed and others have shown, the culture war, like culture more generally, has a class character. Artists and intellectuals are cultural workers and cultural workers today are trained to be fusionists. One must reject the assumption that culture is not a serious subject for politics or that artists do not contribute to social and political movements. Guastella claims that the left does not need broadsides with bold sans serif words like 'vanguard' and 'proletariat' on their covers (Guastella 2020b).[6] What it needs instead, he argues, are news shows like the defunct *Rising*, which he otherwise criticizes for its right and left populism, which he says is not very different from the views of establishment liberals. It is Guastella who comes across as a populist in this case, oblivious to what it means to champion the proletariat and the avant garde in a post-political context. His stance is out of step with the radical tradition.

---

6 Incidentally, I am the author of a book titled *Vanguardia*, whose cover font is in bold sans serif. See Léger 2019. See also Oskar Negt and Alexander Kluge's defense of the use of the term proletariat in Negt & Kluge.

Philistinism contributes to the degradation of left politics. It is true that the working class tends to get by on popular culture, but even within popular culture there are radical energies that combine with excellence. On this count, the 2020 Sanders campaign should be credited for winning the support of many high-profile artists. Boots Riley, the frontman for The Coup and director of the notable debut film *Sorry to Bother You* (2018), made the unexpected decision to forego his usual rejection of bourgeois elections and vote for Sanders. He multi-tweeted:

> I have never voted for a candidate in my life. But I will be voting for Bernie Sanders in the democratic primary and the general election. ... The politicians are beholden to the ruling class ... by taking the wealth that we create with our labor and controlling industry, controlling markets. ... In order to get some of the reforms that Bernie Sanders' campaign platform calls for – Medicare for All, the Green New Deal, free university and trade school tuition, building 10 million more homes in an effort to address homelessness – it's going to take movement tactics. ... I'm not voting for Bernie because I don't disagree with him on things ... What I am endorsing is the movement that has grown around him that involves millions of people who are willing to consciously and openly engage in class struggle in order to make these reforms happen. These struggles will radicalize millions of people and has the potential to organize the working class in the U.S. to a point we haven't seen before.
> cited in DARVILLE

Rock and Roll Hall of Famer Neil Young decided in 2019 to send in the required paperwork so that he could become an official citizen of the U.S. and exercise his voting rights. On his *Neil Young Archives Times-Contrarian* website, Young posted an open letter to Trump, denouncing his policies and values, and saying that he is a disgrace to the country. Young wrote:

> One of your opponents has the answers I like. He is aiming at preserving our children's future directly. He is not popular with the democratic establishment because unlike all the other candidates, he is not pandering to the industries accelerating Earth's Climate Disaster, the end of the world as we know it. He is truly fighting for the USA. His initials are BS. Not his policies. We are going to vote you out and Make America Great Again.
> YOUNG

Young's letter was commented on extensively by media outlets because Trump had used the song 'Rockin' in the Free World' at his rallies, something that Young denounced in his statement.

Another heavy hitter in the Sanders camp was Chuck D from Public Enemy, who performed as Public Enemy Radio at a Sanders rally in Los Angeles on March 1. During his performance, Chuck D emphasized the importance of voting: "You have to get your ass up and vote for something. You're a human being, use your mind, don't be a robot. Listen to somebody, be grown, make yourself important in your locale." He added: "I know damn well there ain't gonna be no messiah Jesus in the White House of the Unites States of America. But you know what? I certainly can recognize a motherfucking Hitler" (Sanders Channel 2020j). The artists concluded the set with 'Fight the Power.' Musicians Bon Iver and Vampire Weekend also performed at Bernie events in Iowa and The Strokes performed in New Hampshire. Other musicians who supported his campaign include Joyce Manor, Jack Johnson, Cardi B, Jack White, Killer Mike, Kim Gordon, Thurston Moore, Juliana Barwick, Jello Biafra, Jackson Browne, Belinda Carlyle, Brad Corrigan, Miley Cyrus, Ani DiFranco, Ariana Grande, Norah Jones, M.I.A., Ozomalti, Cat Power, Pussy Riot, Buffy Sainte-Marie, Michael Stipe and Roger Waters. Among notable artist, activist and scholar supporters were Naomi Klein, Krystal Ball, Glenn Greenwald, Paul Mason, Linda Alcoff, Robert Brenner, Noam Chomsky, Nancy Fraser, Barbara Ransby, Keeanga-Yamahtta Taylor, Yanis Varoufakis, Slavoj Žižek, Chapo Trap House, Chris Kraus, Martha Rosler, Hito Steyerl, Zoe Beloff, Kara Walker, John Cusack, Danny DeVito, Danny Glover, Tim Robbins, Mark Ruffalo, Chloë Sevigny, Dick Van Dyke and Joe Rogan.

In her essay on "The Cuteness of the Avant-Garde," Sianne Ngai reflects on how cuteness can be redeployed against the culture industry tendency towards objectification (Ngai). Avant-garde artists, she argues, can at times mobilize positive affect without at the same time conceding to what Marcuse referred to as the affirmative function of culture in a world of reified exchange. Along these lines, Werner Herzog's appearance at a Sanders campaign event in Los Angeles in December was certainly a surprise. Usually indirect in his political commentary, Herzog was in the company of Cornel West, Tim Robbins, Kim Gordon, Danny DeVito and Danny Glover. Arguing that people should not panic about Trump and should remain optimistic, Herzog was as absurdist about becoming a Bernie Bro as he was in response to *The Mandalorian* puppet Baby Yoda, about which the Bavarian auteur stated: "It's heartbreakingly beautiful. It looked absolutely convincing. It made you cry when you saw it" (Sharf). Also in this heteroclite collection, the brilliant songwriter Natalie Mering, whose stage name, Weyes Blood, is derived from a bizarre Flannery

O'Connor novel, took a selfie with Sanders on January 21 in which she is seen wearing a t-shirt from Disney World's Epcot Center. Sanders is credited with having pressured Disney to raise their minimum wage to $15.

Insofar as artists and intellectuals maintain a difficult relation to both dominant elites and society at large, the avant-garde aspects of popular culture can sometimes make transformative messaging seem more aesthetic than didactic. According to Renée Silverman, broad-based socio-political aims require popular culture's connection with everyday life (Silverman 2015: 11–21). With instantaneous mass distribution through social media, art gains a closer relationship to politics, causing even the most independent of artists to weigh in on issues. Jim Jarmusch, who was among the signatories of the Artists4Bernie list, had this to say in June 2019:

> I like some things about Elizabeth Warren. I, of course, like Bernie Sanders. I really like what's his name, the governor of Washington State who's the only really environmentally conscious one. And, of course, I like AOC; she's too young. But I'm trying to stay away from it right now because that Joe Biden thing makes me deeply depressed.
> cited in EBIRI

In his zombie movie, *The Dead Don't Die* (2019), Jarmusch had his Steve Buscemi character wear a MAGA-type hat that says Keep American White Again, which is neither racially nor grammatically feasible. Nor is his character very successful as a racist redneck as he chums up to the Danny Glover character in the diner where the "coffee zombies" played by Iggy Pop and Sara Driver later get their cup of joe. As the policemen played by Adam Driver and Bill Murray hack away at the horde of zombies at the end of the film, the takeaway is something like Chris Hedge's statement to the effect: I don't fight Nazis because it's inevitable that I'll win; I fight Nazis because they're Nazis.

5 Role Model Ideology

Exit polls are conducted after federal elections in order to better understand how and why various groups voted. Based on interviews with some 15,000 voters, they are continuously recalibrated over the course of election night. Exit polls can influence policy as well as future election campaigns (Bronner & Rakich). Aside from the question of accuracy due to the circumstances of the pandemic, the 2020 polls had several startling revelations when compared to 2016 (NYT Editors). The 2016 exit polls indicated that almost half of Americans were concerned primarily with economic insecurity. Identity issues and immigration registered at less than one percent. What is surprising about the 2020 results, especially as the coronavirus pandemic was contributing to unemployment and the closure of small businesses, is that an average of only 35 percent of the voters considered economic issues to be the reason for deciding who was their candidate of choice. Racial inequality came in second at 20 percent, the pandemic at 17 percent, crime at 11 percent and health care at 11 percent.

What is most striking about the 2020 exit polls is less the issues that were chosen for candidate choice, which were influenced by a new set of questions, than the sectarian and partisan divide that is evident in the answers given. On the economy, votes averaged out to 35 percent saying it is "good" and 31 percent "not so good." These numbers are not the same among Republican and Democratic voters. Two thirds of Republican supporters said they are better off after four years of Trump and the same percentage of Biden voters said that they are worse off. This is possibly due to the fact that between 2017 and 2019, some voters did receive better wages and some regions experienced decreased unemployment (Analysis News 2020). Of those who considered the economy to be their main concern, 82 percent were Trump supporters and 17 percent were Biden supporters. The fact that Sanders ran on a bread and butter issues campaign makes this about-face among Democratic Party voters quite remarkable. It represents, within the Democratic voter bloc, an ideological victory for the PMC that promoted progressive neoliberalism much in the same way that Thatcher and Reagan promoted authoritarian nationalism and individual responsibility.

The conclusion to be drawn from the 2020 exit polls is not that voting patterns reflect reality, but rather that establishment support for the racialist-identitarian agenda helped to make people oblivious to the problems caused by government policies. The other four items listed in the exit polls are indirectly correlated in two pairs of issues. Only 14 percent of Trump voters considered the pandemic to be a concern, as opposed to 82 percent of Biden voters. This correlates with 36 percent of Trump voters who cited health care as a reason to vote and 63 percent for Biden voters. Similarly, when one considers the reactionary politicization of the BLM protests by the Trump administration, only 8 percent of Trump voters considered racial inequality to be an issue, against 91 of Biden supporters. More exactly, 70 percent of Biden voters considered racism to be the most important problem in the U.S., in contrast to 28 percent of Trump voters. Those who considered racism to be a minor problem are 82 percent among Trump voters and 16 percent among Biden voters. When the question of racism is broken into four degrees – the most important problem, one of many important problems, a minor problem and not a problem – the results show that an average of 51 percent consider racism to be one of many important problems, 20 percent consider it the most important problem, 17 percent consider it a minor problem and only 9 percent consider it to be not a problem at all. These numbers extend to the issue of whether people think that the criminal justice system treats all people fairly, with 83 percent of Trump voters in agreement to only 15 percent of Biden voters. On whether or not black people are treated unfairly, 17 percent of Trump voters agree to 81 percent of Biden voters. This then correlates to some extent to the importance given to crime and safety, chosen by 71 percent of Trump voters to only 28 percent of Biden voters. The latter is substantiated by 20 percent of Trump voters having a favorable view of the BLM movement to 78 percent of Biden voters.

Most of the other exit poll questions also show a stark partisan divide. Only 29 percent of Trump voters consider global warming to be a serious problem, to 68 percent of Biden voters. The abortion issue remains divisive, with 72 percent of Biden voters in favor of its legality to 24 percent of Trump voters. A badly worded question asks people if Obamacare should be kept as it is, to which 80 percent of Biden voters said yes and 78 percent of Trump voters said it should be overturned. On the question of ecology and health care, what the numbers indicate is that Democratic Party voters are far more logical and rational than Republican voters. This fact intensifies the ideological problem around issues of class and identity. Democratic Party ideologues and capitalists understand that reasonable people oppose discrimination and make the most that they can of this fact to avoid questions of reform and wealth redistribution. Republicans assist them in this effort by heightening the reactionary character of the culture war, which conservatives associate with the struggle against socialism. Centrists then disassociate themselves from the dirty socialist bath water to protect the anti-discrimination baby. This by and large is the purpose that is served by concepts like institutional racism and racial capitalism. This paradigm alone explains how it is that someone who has as bad a track record on anti-racism and anti-sexism as Joe Biden could manage to beat Bernie Sanders. The crisis of democracy in the U.S. can be summed up with the two statements that Biden made in the run-up to the election: "I beat the socialist" and "If you have a problem figuring out whether you're for me or Trump, then you ain't black" (Kaplan; Herndon & Glueck).

The jump from less than 1 percent on identity issues to 20 percent is undoubtedly the most notable change from 2016. Oddly enough, it went unremarked by most of the media, right and left, perhaps because it tends to contradict the fact that Trump did better in 2020 with every demographic other than white men. From 2016, Trump's support with white men went down 5 points, with white women up 2 points, with black men up 4 points, with black women up 4 points, with Latino men up 3 points, with Latino women up 3 points, and with others up 5.3 points. Trump increased his share of the African-American male vote from 13 percent in 2016 to 18 percent in 2020. Among African-American women, Trump doubled his share from 4 to 8 percent. Most of these black Trump voters are among the wealthy. The same phenomenon occurred among Latino voters. Among non-white voters, Trump turned in the best results for the Republicans since the 1960s. Trump tripled his support among LBGT voters, from 14 percent in 2016 to a remarkable 28 percent in 2020. The Democrats increased their support among educated and affluent white suburban voters. However, what tilted the scales in Biden's favor was an increase of support for the Democrats among the working class and lower middle class whose lives have been affected by the pandemic. This gave Biden a 7 million lead in the popular vote, some 81 million to Trump's 74 million. Biden also won 8.6 million more male votes than Clinton had in 2016, and 5 percent more white votes than Clinton, increasing the Democratic vote by 23.4 percent from Clinton in 2016 (London 2020b).

If one ignores the reasons why people may not have voted and considers that the voter turnout was the highest it has been since 1900, the exit poll results show not only the influence of the BLM protests but also how virtue signaling by the media and the neoliberal establishment has succeeded in framing politics around identity. Without a mass political movement on the left, substantive social change around issues like economic inequality, climate change, militarism, unemployment, homelessness and the lack of affordable health care for millions of Americans are not linked to the question of policing and incarceration. The "war on racism," Touré Reed argues, can be thrown into the same pile of ruling class rubbish as the War on Drugs and the War on Terror (Park Center). The question of economic inequality was overlooked as a topic for the exit polls. Without a sense of the class nature of race issues, Americans are blinded by the obscenity of police violence. Far from being the product of the black left, the concern shown for racial inequality has been set by the neoliberal agenda, as expressed in the speechifying of black celebrities who are transforming the world history of slavery into another version of American exceptionalism. This sleight of hand shifts attention away from class solidarity and the critique of political economy towards the exoticism of a moral agenda, black authenticity, racial uplift, biological determinism, cultural politics that have no political orientation, the communitarian adventurism of grassroots protest and woke posturing.

Virtue signaling by mediocratic politicians has no political relevance and no limits. One week before the November election, Biden gave a speech on national healing in Warm Springs, Georgia, in which, like Louis Bonaparte, he wrapped himself in the legacy of Franklin D. Roosevelt, who went to Warm Springs to convalesce from polio paralysis. The stunt led pundits to look for the similarities and differences between these two men, coming up with little more than their low grades and frequent gaffes (Alter). After being elected, Biden arranged the decorations in the Oval Office around a large portrait of FDR. He also included in the room bronze busts of MLK, Cesar Chavez, Rosa Parks and Eleanor Roosevelt. Biden was following the marching orders given to him by Bill Clinton to build unity in the country and the party. As people like Ocasio-Cortez were willing to entertain the prospect that maybe Biden is not so bad after all, even the left began to show amnesia regarding Biden's long record of corruption. Biden lied about WMDs and instigated regime change wars in the Middle East. A man who mixes intimidating attacks on the public with smirks about screwing over working people was now being compared to FDR. As late as May 2020, when it was obvious to everyone that the comparison was inappropriate, it was said that unlike Sanders, who is given to revolutionary talk, Biden is the proper kind of FDR since what he is looking to do is save the capitalist system (Cassidy).

Joe Biden served 36 years in the Senate and 8 years as Obama's Vice President. According to Allen and Parnes, his election strategy rested entirely on winning the black vote and electing a woman as VP (Allen & Parnes 2021: 401–17). It made some sense since in June 2019, 76 percent of black voters already preferred Biden on account of his association with Obama. Biden otherwise has a record of collaboration with segregationists like James Eastland and the South Carolina reactionary Strom Thurmond. He supported Clinton's 1994 Crime Bill. He has advocated cuts to Social Security and Medicare for 40 years. In order to make up for his track record on race issues, he has invented stories about participating in sit-ins to desegregate movie theaters. Biden's association with right-wing segregationists makes him more of a Republican than a Democrat (Marcetic 2020a). Al Sharpton did not endorse him and neither did Obama, who favored Hillary Clinton in 2016 and Beto O'Rourke in 2020. In 2020, Obama was quoted saying to another party nominee: "You know who really doesn't have it? Joe Biden" (cited in Thompson).

As someone who is all about image, Obama was correct about Biden. On the campaign trail, Biden slurred his speech and said things that made him seem to be approaching senility. He scrambled Lincoln quotes and the words of the Constitution. He made gaffes about websites like Joe 30330 that do not exist and told confused stories about a thug called Corn Pop and stacking spaghetti sauce. He at times did not seem to know the difference between the ACLU and the KKK, or between his wife and his sister. Apologists would of course seek to make lemonade out of yet another lemon. Talk radio host Dom Giordano argued that Biden proved that senility is superior to socialism. Biden himself, to show that he was fit to be president, accused a man of being fat and challenged him to a push-up contest. He assured the *Los Angeles Times*: "I want to be clear, I'm not going nuts" (Manchester). Biden was popular with ageing baby boomers who confused the pragmatism that made sense during the golden age of economic prosperity with the twenty-first century realities of precarity. Sanders won the majority of votes from people under the age of 40 and approximately 70 percent for voters under 24. However, the generation gap that was apparent between the two candidates had nothing to do with their age and everything to do with their values and policies. The under 45 group is most likely to consult online media and to mistrust the mainstream press. This cohort, which was not impressed with Biden's facelifts, dental work and hair implants, were not weaned on Cold War ideology. It is highly ironic that the generation gap was the baby boomer generation's explanation for changes in values in the age of Civil Rights, the anti-war movement and the sexual revolution. The other half of that story is the way that this generation's idealism was destroyed by the recession of the 1970s, after which most boomers bought into the business values of the previous generation, as represented for example in the 1983 film *The Big Chill*. In the end, although the counterculture brought significant cultural changes, it did very little to redistribute wealth and move society beyond those needs that could be satisfied through consumerism (Frank 1997; Turner).

When it comes to comparisons with FDR and New Deal social welfare policies, the difference could not be greater. Biden has advocated raising the age of retirement and supported GOP attacks on social spending. His economic vision of cuts to federal programs is essentially the Reagan and Clinton-era neoliberal policies that have decimated the livelihoods of the average American worker. Biden takes credit for creating the Consumer Financial Protection Bureau when in actuality he supported laws that made it more difficult for people to declare bankruptcy, including students and those with medical debts. Biden was the Senator for Delaware, which is the headquarters of half of the publicly traded companies in the U.S. and the headquarters of 64 percent of Fortune 500 companies. They choose Delaware as a tax haven and a state that does not enforce stringent regulations. It is also the headquarters of major credit card companies, including MBNA, the largest credit card company in the U.S. Biden's son, Hunter Biden, was executive vice-president of MBNA before it was bought out by Bank of America. Biden supported the 2008 bailout of Wall Street as well as the $1.5 trillion stock market injection of March 2020, which evaporated as quickly as it was invented. Obama and his sidekick bailed out banks and CEOs while they allowed everyday people to lose their homes, their pensions, their wages and other necessities. Biden supported Obamacare because it protected the interests of the health insurance industry. He opposed Medicare for All, despite the fact that it is cost-effective. He helped pass legislation like the Comprehensive Crime Control Act, the Anti-Drug Abuse Act and the Violent Crime Control and Law Enforcement Act, which increased capital punishment, sentencing for drug possession and racial discrimination in the criminal justice system. He continues to oppose the legalization of marijuana. He helped to militarize domestic policing and supports NSA spying on citizens as well as other abuses of civil rights and liberties. Along with the former 'deporter in chief,' Biden is responsible for the deportation of hundreds of thousands of immigrants and has encouraged the arrest of undocumented workers.

In terms of foreign policy, Biden has difficulty admitting that he is directly responsible for the war in Iraq, which has killed more than one million people and cost trillions of dollars. He is one of the architects of the War on Terror and the regime change wars that have devastated the Middle East. He advocated ethnic cleansing in Iraq by dividing the country into three religiously and ethnically separate regions. His brother has received millions in government contracts to build homes in Iraq. Biden voted for the PATRIOT ACT, the Authorization to Use Military Force and the program of assassination by drones, which is responsible for killing countless non-combatant citizens. As a member of the Senate Foreign Relations Committee, Biden was a proponent of the U.S. intervention in the former Yugoslavia. He approved Bush's torture regime, awarding the former war criminal the Liberty Medal. During the Egyptian Revolution of 2011, he defended the dictator Hosni Mubarak as a faithful servant of the U.S. in the region. With Obama, Biden expanded the theater of regime change operations to Libya and Syria. Biden has lied about being responsible for the Paris Climate Accord. In actuality, Biden has shown no concern at all about climate change. He claims that he supports ending oil and gas fracking but will not commit to this. He accepts the support of the fossil fuel industry. While his son was being paid tens of thousands of dollars to serve as an American contact on the board of a fossil fuel company in Ukraine, Biden garnered a D grade from Greenpeace (Martin 2019a).

One of the more despicable aspects of Biden's virtue signaling is his hokey pandering as a populist, from the No Malarkey campaign slogan to epithets like Uncle Joe. But Jake is a fake. Biden has always staked his fate on the middle class, who have rewarded him for his mediocrity. In his run for the presidency in 1987–88, Biden plagiarized his campaign speeches from British labor leader Neil Kinnock. He lied about being the first person in his family to go to college and said he graduated at the top of his class. In actuality he finished at the bottom of his cohort and not unsurprisingly plagiarized his academic work. Biden is known to brag about the worst things he has done (Robinson 2020). According to Marcetic, Biden has spent his entire career showing concern and empathy for the working class while simultaneously pursuing conservative policies (Marcetic 2020b). Biden's special brand of politics is confusing people with misdirection. Thanks to decades of cronyism, he went from being a poor Senator to a multi-millionaire, joining the Martha's Vineyard yacht club by giving hundred-thousand-dollar speeches to his capitalist donors (Martin 2019b). He makes fun of the Sanders movement and the young people who call for a political revolution. Biden is an enemy of the people. If he had lived during the French Revolution, his head would be in a basket.

In addition to all of this, Biden served as a litmus test on the state of gender politics in the MeToo era. In his service on the Senate Judiciary Committee, Biden approved conservative Supreme Court nominees like Antonin Scalia and Clarence Thomas, whom he sheltered from accusations of sexism. He also voted for the Defense of Marriage Act and refuses to defend Roe vs. Wade. His virtue signaling about his plans to hire a woman Vice President helped to cover over his history of inappropriate behavior towards women. In 2019, Lucy Flores accused Biden of disrespectfully sniffing her hair and kissing her head before endorsing her at a 2014 campaign event (Taylor 2019). Biden conveniently forgot the incident. Then there was Tara Reade, a former Biden Senate staffer, who came forward in March 2020 with accusations of sexual harassment and assault (Brewster). That Bill Clinton was impeached for much less and that Donald Trump has not been impeached for much worse can only cause people to be confused about how questions of morality inform politics among the elite. Reade's objections were against Biden for his personal attack on her individual liberty, and not against the Democratic Party, which, like its Republican counterpart, routinely attacks the rights, freedoms and lives of people worldwide as a matter of policy. Her demand for justice was legitimate but it was also more personal and less politically relevant than many people made it out to be. The refusal of MeToo advocates to take her case seriously is what made it into a political issue. An article by Linda Hirshman in the *New York Times* went so far as to say that no matter how legitimate Reade's case against Biden may be, she nevertheless prefers the lesser of two evils. Hirshman described this as "the importance of owning an ugly choice" (Hirshman). And they accuse Marxists of masculinism.

As with the appeals to the legacy of FDR, the acceptance of Biden as a better choice for the leadership than Sanders is rarely made directly. It leads one to ponder the meaning of progress in today's America. The crux of the problem is neoliberalism's mediation of identity and class. Consider, in this regard, the way that the two campaigns addressed this issue. We could take as emblematic of progressive neoliberalism, the presentation given by the young African-American poet Amanda Gorman at Biden's inauguration ceremony. Whereas previous presidents have called on consecrated laureates to honor the swearing in of the new leader at Inauguration Day ceremonies – Robert Frost, Maya Angelou, Miller Williams, Elizabeth Alexander, Richard Blanco – the Biden administration selected the first National Youth Poet Laureate. The choice of Gorman was no doubt meant to seal the rift that was created when Kamala Harris went after Biden as "that little girl" he ignored as a casualty of *de facto* segregation. Gorman delivered a poem titled "The Hill We Climb" at the ceremony on January 20, 2021. Despite all of the cheap symbolism they had to report on, the media could not decide whether they were more impressed by her writing, which was nothing special in terms of either form or content, or her tiara-like Prada headband.

After the event, in an instance of what Olivier Driessens refers to as celebritization, where a somewhat unknown or unremarkable individual is made into a celebrity, Gorman was lionized by establishment media through rituals of media commodification (Driessens). After the inauguration, Gorman signed a modeling contract with IMG Models. She was then invited by the National Football League to read one of her poems during the Super Bowl. In February, *Time* magazine showed Gorman on its cover and celebrated the Harvard graduate as part of a Black Renaissance. The issue included an essay by the racialist scholar Ibram X. Kendi, who associates cultural revival with the liberation of black artists from the "white gaze" (Kendi 2021b). Whereas the Harlem Renaissance and the Black Arts Movement were weighted down by racism, today's black artists, he argues, have the newfound ability to express their true selves.

Fanon long ago rejected the neurotic effort to either live up to or refute the stereotypes that whites had of black people in postwar Europe. Fanon preferred instead to "reach out for the universal" (Fanon 1967: 197). It is worth citing here some well-known lines from *Black Skin, White Masks*:

> I am a man and what I have to recapture is the whole past of the world. I am not responsible solely for the [slave] revolt in Santo Domingo. Every time man has contributed to the victory of the dignity of the spirit, every time a man has said no to an attempt to subjugate his fellows, I have felt solidarity with his act. In no way should I derive my basic purpose from the past of the peoples of color. In no way should I dedicate myself to the revival of an unjustly recognized Negro civilization. I will not make myself the man of any past. I do not want to exalt the past at the expense

of my present and my future. (...) My black skin is not the wrapping of specific values. (...) Have I no purpose on earth, then, but to avenge the Negro of the seventeenth century? (...) I as a man of color do not have the right to hope that in the white man there will be a crystallization of guilt toward the past of my race. I as a man of color do not have the right to seek ways of stamping down the pride of my former master. I have neither the right nor the duty to claim reparations for the domestication of my ancestors. There is no Negro mission; there is no white burden. (...) Let us be clearly understood. I am convinced that it would be of the greatest interest to be able to have contact with a Negro literature or architecture of the third century before Christ. I should be very happy to know that some correspondence had flourished between some Negro philosopher and Plato. But I can absolutely not see how this fact would change anything in the lives of the eight-year-old children who labor in the cane fields of Martinique or Guadeloupe. (...) The body of history does not determine a single one of my actions. I am my own foundation.

FANON 1967: 226–31

By reducing the artists of the past and the present to his racialist obsessions, Kendi misinterprets Lacan and shores up the black capitalism promoted by politicians like Barack Obama, celebrities like Oprah and intellectuals like Ta-Nehisi Coates. Not only were most of the black artists of the Harlem Renaissance and the Black Arts Movement universalists, many were also associated with the radical left (Niemuth). It is neoliberal politics and not the white gaze that distinguishes today's so-called black Renaissance. To reinforce Gorman's status as a symbol of the Obama legacy and the future of black neoliberalism, Gorman is interviewed in the *Time* issue by Michelle Obama, who celebrated the confidence she exuded onstage as "a young black woman helping to turn the page to a more helpful chapter in American leadership" (Obama).

The ill-conceived redefinition of culture and politics along racial lines was in evidence when the following March, Gorman's translator, Marieke Lucas Rijneveld, was forced to resign. Although chosen by Gorman herself on the basis of her status as a winner of the Booker Prize, if not for her youth and transgender identity, the Dutch author was dissuaded from translating Gorman's poetry since her white race disqualified her from being able to properly understand blackness. Who knew that intersectionality consists of a set of one-way streets? Afterwards, Gorman appeared on the Apple TV+ series *The Oprah Conversation*, where Oprah dittoed Michelle Obama's superlatives. Like football games and Oscar nominations, her participation at the ceremony was treated like history in the making. She also appeared on the Hillary Clinton podcast, whom Gorman refers to affectionately as grandma. She then appeared on an International Women's Day panel with Clinton and Nancy Pelosi. She has been on most of the mainstream talk shows and some news shows, where like many other black celebrities she is expected to pay due homage to black radicals like Martin Luther King or her African ancestors. Even before they go to press, her books, like the memoirs of Barack and Michelle Obama, are already bestsellers.

By April, a somewhat gaunt Gorman graced two covers of *Vogue* magazine, with the headline "The Rise and Rise of Amanda Gorman, Poet, Activist, Phenomenon." On one cover she wears a Dior haute couture dress and on the other a Louis Vuitton blanket, which celebrates artistic director Virgil Abloh's African heritage. Both covers were photographed by Annie Liebovitz. Other images in the magazine show her wearing dresses by Alexander McQueen, Y/Projects and Studio 189. In her interview for the issue, Gorman discusses the pressures that have come from choosing to be a role model (St. Félix). Should it not be other people who decide that she is a role model? The article describes how Gorman first came to attention as a spoken-word poet and then to prominence in 2017 after the toy company Mattel invited the 18-year-old freshman to do a reading for the launch of a black doll that was marketed as 'Girl of the Year.' Gorman says she did it for the sake of black girls who would buy the company's new doll. Having since then turned down $17 million in brand endorsement offers, she says to her *Vogue* interviewer: "I'm not a BRAND AMBASSADOR or anything!" You will not find any negativity in her social media, she says, because she hopes one day to be president. Is Gorman the willing victim of media manipulation and is she being made into an emblem of something she is not? Despite her youth, she seems a willing standard bearer of corporate ideology.

How different is this ambassador of progressive neoliberalism from Briahna Joy Gray, the young black activist who was chosen to be the press secretary of the 2020 Sanders campaign and advocate of progressive populism? After the Sanders defeat, we heard a great deal from those who maintain a footing in the Democratic Party about how the left must do everything it can to hold the government to account. In response to the wokewashing of neoliberal policy, Gray has gone on after the Sanders campaign to appear on several media platforms, mainstream and independent, to question the uses of identity politics for the sake of 'centrist' goals. Her growing status as a spokesperson for the left is problematic, however, insofar as she seeks to salvage identity politics for progressive purposes. Since very few people on the left actually question identity politics, her media appearances have met with little to no scrutiny by platform hosts. She is co-host of the *Bad Faith* podcast along with Virgil Texas, a member of the Chapo Trap House group of leftist indie pundits. Gray earned a law degree at Harvard University and worked as a corporate lawyer before joining *The Intercept* and then the magazine *Current Affairs*. In 2020, she was considered by *Fortune* magazine to be among 40 of the most influential Americans under the age of 40. The magazine credits her for having fought off attacks by moderate Democrats and for operating a press machine that crafted a progressive message that "nearly propelled" Sanders to the Democratic nomination. She is also credited by *Fortune* for refusing to endorse Biden, writing that "her conviction gained her new followers on the far left and secured her place as a progressive lighting rod" (Fortune).

By January 2020, the Sanders campaign was resorting to demographics and woke messaging, thereby distorting the universalist and socialist thrust of his politics. Gray is not responsible for the defeat of the Sanders campaign. Her role as the Sanders campaign press secretary nevertheless points to tensions on the left that must be identified, elucidated and resolved. Gray's politics as a progressive Democrat are not by themselves socialist politics and so her self-identification as an advocate of leftism depends a great deal on definitions. This would be clear enough to any genuine radical, but the issue is confused by the question of identity, which Gray has incorporated into her politics in order to position herself as a spokesperson for the left after Sanders. Gray reflexively brands herself a rising star of the left, playing on her cuteness and 'weaponizing' her own identity in the service of the cause. The point here is not to use Gray's race and gender against her or against anyone else. It is, however, to make distinctions between leadership on the left and compromise formations that function more smoothly within mainstream and independent media networks.

On the news show *Democracy Now*, Gray discussed the effort to unify the Democratic Party by reaching out to the left through diversity nominees who have crowned their achievement as the 'first' of its kind within their minority group and as the result of the struggles of their families and communities (Democracy Now 2020c). None of Biden's administration picks, Gray argues, represent progressive politics. For instance, Neera Tanden, who was selected as Biden's director of the Office of Management and Budget, was openly antagonistic towards Sanders, assaulting his campaign manager when he was an editor at *ThinkProgress*. As the daughter of East Indian immigrants, Tanden serves the establishment as a symbol of progress in the areas of race and gender. While Gray is clear in her denunciations of Tanden's class politics, she also faults her for not representing the women and people of color that she can be identified with. As Gray puts it, "These people are assumed to represent the groups they themselves embody" (Democracy Now 2020c). Gray's position on race and political representation is neither universalist nor socialist but seems to derive from postmodern ideas like Cornel West's cultural politics of difference or Stuart Hall's politics of cultural representation. In the context of a pragmatic left that avoids resolving these issues, her thoughts on the matter tend to come across haphazardly.

Although Gray is correct to reject the kind of post-race ideology that allows people to trade on their identity in arbitrary and opportunistic ways, that is, to use it to their advantage but to avoid any disadvantages that may accrue on account of histories of discrimination, she is wrong to think that gender and race leaders in various fields are the authentic sources of group uplift. What seems to be a rejection of role model ideology and respectability politics actually confirms it. Her critique is not a leftist class politics but is, to date, a variant of the progressive liberalism of the professional-managerial class. Confusion on these issues is hardly unique to her and one can only hope that her leftism will develop. Since the 1960s, the culturalization of politics has created a situation where the concept of universal progress has been modified and substituted for intra-group alternatives that leave the totality of global capitalism intact. Wittingly or not, and despite her acumen as a news commentator, Gray plays on the chimera of having your identity politics and eating it too – or as Rocha refers to it, walking and chewing gum at the same time. Even if the profile in *Fortune* magazine is an embarrassment to her, and even if it ignores the troubles she has endured for defending the democratic socialist left, there is no doubt that this double game is what allows her to rank among the elect (Scahill). Turning a double bind into a double advantage, however, is not the solution to a class contradiction.

Gray took a still more explicit position on identity politics in her discussion of this topic with Saagar Enjeti on the morning news show *Rising* (The Hill 2020a). Enjeti opened the segment by saying that although Biden made good on his promise to create a diverse administration, many in the party's left wing were worried that his appointees have very little substance. "When you make diversity and quotas the only criterion that matters," he says, "you ignore substantive policy issues. The corporate left and right have been promoting identity issues to cover up the fact that they have the same policy consensus as some of the worse neoliberal politicians over the last three decades." Gray replies:

> I was really heartened to see some representational politics happening. I don't think that representational politics has no value whatsoever. But the most important thing, the principal concern should be whether or not the people picked for these positions represent the interests of the

group that they physically represent. There has been so much conversation about 'the first' in this group of appointees, which is hopeful, and frankly an indictment of the homogeneity of past picks, but that doesn't cure some very substantive defects here.

She goes on to discuss Tanden, who is on record for wanting to cut Social Security and Medicare entitlements. Half of African Americans rely on Social Security for 90 percent or more of their retirement income. Gray says: "It's a little hypocritical to be speaking that way and representing yourself as in the best interest of people of color, when in fact your stated policy positions are to the contrary." Enjeti replied that he has an East Indian background but that he is not heartened that Harris has been chosen to be Vice President. It is nice to see, he admits, but that is hardly what matters if a politician is working to cut Social Security. "I oppose all of that because it's going to hurt poor black people and poor white people as well – anybody who's poor." He says that this contradiction is apparent in the area of national defense. "What solace will that bring to people who are killed in foreign wars?" Gray replies:

> It is literally a meme, widely enjoyed by the left, that we don't need more female drone pilots, or the cartoon of people pointing to the sky, about to be bombed, saying: "I'm so proud that a woman is going to drop this bomb on me." That's not how the world works, and, you know, I want to be careful because I do understand that these are individuals, and that people, you know ... There are young children who aspire differently when they see role models that are in front of them. Every Democrat understands that representation isn't everything when the person has an R next to their name – when it's someone like Clarence Thomas, right, or Candace Owens. But for some reason there's a great deal of myopia when it comes to people on our quote-unquote side of aisle. Particularly in this case, I've been noticing how this rollout has happened, and it really does feel like the emphasis on the identity characteristic of these candidates is being very purposefully wielded to cut off any criticism.

Gray says that we should not be comfortable with the kind of politics that prevent us from criticizing politicians because of their identity, as was the case with a *New York Times* reporter who reproached the Sunrise Movement for calling out Louisiana congressman Cedric Richmond on his environmental record because he is black. She also disputes a *New York Times* report, which suggested that if the Biden team had sought to find appointees to satisfy the Sanders wing of the party, and who were not beholden to the Washington corporatist machine, they would not have been able to find candidates of color. She says:

> I think the overwhelming diversity of the Squad is a testament to the fact that as long as the progressive movement has been painted as a predominantly white movement – it is incredibly diverse – the history of radical left politics in this country has largely been one that has been in lock-step with the African-American experience and the experience of many other marginalized groups in this country. So it's really insulting, frankly, to pretend as though there is any kind of trade-off between diversity and progressivism.

It is a thoroughly conservative position to advocate the worst outcomes for the sake of equality. Confusion emerges when the extreme right is made into an alibi for neoliberal politics, and neoliberalism is made into an alibi for the democratic left. This explains the limited value if not the deficit of needing to remind oneself and others that the working class is multiracial and multigendered, as though countering liberal attacks against the 'white working class' is in and of itself a radical left perspective.

Radical left politics has been in lock-step with the radical left around the world since at least the First International. Likewise, imperialist forces have attacked revolutionary movements everywhere they have emerged. No fewer than 13 countries assailed the Red Army after the Bolshevik Revolution of 1917. The issue for the socialist left is not the trade-off between diversity and progressivism, but between radical leadership and self-appointed race leaders, whose politics of racial uplift, in keeping with W.E.B. Du Bois's notion of the 'Talented Tenth,' can be criticized as race reductionist abstract universalism (Du Bois). As race leadership devolves from internationalist anti-colonialism to postmodern race brokerage, its petty-bourgeois, PMC character comes to the surface. In some cases, what this does is transform a historically informed and theoretically dense political program into role-playing. As long as leftists talk as though they are serious and do their part to sway the less educated in a more progressive direction, then people like Gray can say they are contributing to movement building. Unlike a solid communist, who can explain the foundations of bourgeois ideology, a woke demagogue acts more like an activist, mobilizing left populism as a brand that is preferable to that of the corrupt establishment. The emphasis on attitude, which is an asset of the mediagenic executant petty bourgeoisie, has less to do with the left and more to do with the pressures placed on media professionals. While Gray is without doubt a social democrat of some sort, her notion of politics as responsibility to groups of ascriptive identification is a source of confusion.

The confusion expressed by Gray regarding class politics and identity politics was further demonstrated during her appearance on a lengthy episode of the online Katie Halper Show (Halper 2020c). This is one of many chat shows on the emerging streamer left. While these shows serve as progressive media that runs counter to more mainstream versions, the talk show aspect of these programs reinforce the casualization of seriousness that is a feature of the culture industries more generally. As Halper herself put it, the episode with Gray and Rania Khalek was a "freewheeling conversation" about "bad people" whose politics are shrouded in identity. Such programs showcase the lifestyles of activists, journalists and intellectuals, presenting impromptu encounters with people while they are in their pyjamas or pumping iron. The public display of the home life of the educated culturati potentially adds to the burdens that are imposed on young scholars who are increasingly expected to demonstrate to employers their online presence as well as their network of friends, contacts and colleagues. Of course, by complying with such demands, they subject themselves to increased scrutiny and termination if their views conflict with the wishes of those in power.

A certain amount of reflexivity about the logic of celebrity – where details about someone's personal life are folded back into their public persona and vice versa – was noted by Gray in her discussion of Kamala Harris:

> I want to at least like her on an individual level. I don't spend my life thinking about wanting to ruin her. The fact that she flip-flops all over the place is deeply frustrating, but also is an opportunity for us to push her on the commitments she has made in the past. I appreciate that at least she signed on to the Medicare for All bill. Now, it doesn't help me very much right now, but it's something that we can use as leverage going forward. I don't think she is the worst. My problem with her is that she's so cringe because she just won't be herself. When she's herself she can be very delightful. The last clip that I saw that she made, before she dropped out, was a clip of her and Mindy Kaling. She was so charming. They were in her kitchen talking ... and they were having a great culture talk of the moment. They were genuinely cute. And they seemed genuinely excited about each other, and I think the fact that Kamala Harris genuinely loves to cook, is good at it and gets a lot of joy out of it, and I like to see people do what they love and what they're good at. Being a politician isn't one of those things for Kamala Harris.

Discussing also Hillary Clinton's fashion sense, the conversation included many indications that Gray approaches politics as entertainment. "Watching all of our friends, like David Sirota, compete so aggressively," she says, "really ranking with a lot of these folks who have, are coming from forums where they had a lot of mainstream buy-in, is really heartening." The celebritization of sports and entertainment has long been one of the means through which African Americans have recalibrated the black agenda to the requirements of black capitalism. This process in no way excludes the realm of politics, especially now that Obama's forays into entertainment will likely continue to affect the public sphere for years to come. In this sense, Gray presents herself as a cosplay radical:

> People are playing different roles. I'm not saying that every person in Congress needs to go hard on the paint in the same exact way. But for those of us who are free agents, I don't understand why there are so many leftists who entertain these long, winding conversations about what is good strategy, and spend twice as much time on that than talking about educating people on what these things actually mean. Somebody has to occupy the space of the 'far left' to exert the kind of pressure that you need to bring anybody even remotely close to the 'middle,' which is really where the left, where most Americans are. You gotta go big.

Going big should not imply pretending to be a Marxist. To do so may have less to do with socialism and more to do with creating the kind of world that would make the middle class comfortable again. Gray laughingly complains that after graduating she had to make monthly student loan payments of $2300. Earning $60,000 annually at that time, she is well-placed to appreciate how it is that indebted students avoid activist rebellion in favor of survival, and how, at the other end of the scale, the purchase of a $1 million-dollar home would have allowed her to deduct the interest payments on her loan as tax deductions. How is one to tackle this inequality? According to a *Bad Faith* podcast that Gray did with comedian Roy Wood Jr., the goal of the left should be, in addition to "identity stuff" and "coms" that are "for no one in particular," creating a homogeneity of left talking points to counter those of the center and right. One might like to know what radical movement is implicated in Gray's politics other than the cohort of lefty journalists around the DSA that she belongs to. While this sector is cause for some principled complaint, it is worth considering how a restricted alternative media space filters issues and construes left strategy.

On the race and class issue, Halper and Gray palaver with the kind of equanimity that is suited to the open and live format of streaming shows. Like Starbucks environments that curate sophomoric smarts along with cozy comforts, such shows combine what Arthur Kroker referred to as the "recline of the West" with the "will to virtuality" (Kroker 1994: 4–26). How much of this is useful information and how much of it is the soft ideology of tech-hype and cyber-control, sucking social energy into the retro-Darwinian vacuum of the liberal-fascist state? The *Left Bitches* podcast that Rania Khalek started hosting provides a similar combination of young female host with leftist politics. It will likely be more to the point than the soft cooing of the hosts of the *Red Scare* podcast. The modus operandi is to not paint yourself into a corner and keep as many progressive channels open as possible so as to increase your audience. The strategy is not unlike winning elections and it is not surprising that these emerging sites of discussion favor the government-oriented left more than the anarchist left, which prefers to work in small collectives if not in clandestine and anonymous ways. Sectarians, for their part, also function behind closed doors, working out their strategies and policies before presenting them to the public. A more open and processual format discourages decisiveness since its broad range of topics prevents too much specialization and because its political outlook and economic considerations emphasize inclusiveness.

Halper begins a discussion about Adolph Reed and says that she does not worry about being considered a class reductionist. At the same time, she also says, she does not want to be thought of as a being in denial about racism, sexism or homophobia. "We just gotta figure out what we're doing," she says. Gray replies:

> The reason I wouldn't call myself a class reductionist is because I do think that – all things being equal – there is value to representation on some level. I want to roll my eyes, but there were some little kids in 2008 who were like: "I never really thought I could be president, but now I can be." And there is utility in that. Women grow up seeing ourselves not represented in certain fields, and we don't even think that they're available to us, even if our parents are actively messaging you can do it, subconsciously these things affect you. … All of these kinds of things have an effect. I do think there's a value, but representational value comes so far down below substantive value. That's the line, when you're talking to people and trying to recruit people to our cause … Half of my family still has an Obama key. … Even if it's only cynical, even if it's only because you want to recruit people and make them like us, I think that the left should be a little bit more sensitive to the fact that this stuff still means

something to somebody else. We want to adjust their priorities more than say identity doesn't matter.

Halper then says:

> Identity stuff is important because racism is bad and we should fight against it. But also, I do tend to think that most of the things that we should be prioritizing are structural things that are not identity-based. Not because I don't have any problem with that, but because I don't think that's the way you actually will uplift most people, and of course that's disproportionately non-straight-white-people, whether that's Social Security, Medicare for All, whatever. We don't go up to people and identify ourselves as class reductionist. We all have different roles to play also. Adolph Reed has real problems with disparity discourse. I agree with him. The goal is not to have a more representative, exploitative system, where whites are as well-represented among the poor as black people are, percentage-wise. Not having Medicare for All disproportionately harms people of color. That's not only important morally, but it's an important organizing tool – a gateway argument. There's so much discourse about how race stuff, and gender stuff, on the one hand, and economic stuff are mutually exclusive, or not connected. Because so many people start there it would be useful to say: look at how these things, which people pretend have nothing to do with racism, look how intrinsically related they are to that. From there you can say: now that you're on board with that, let's actually fight beyond just making it more representative. Let's try to get rid of poverty.

Gray then adds:

> Adolph Reed's critique of disparity politics I think is spot on, but we also live in a world where we have been indoctrinated for generations to perceive things through that lens, so, you know, there are people on the 'far left' who were frustrated with me during the campaign because I would tweet so much about racial disparities in student loan debts, and all this stuff. (...) I'm coming to human beings, not ideas. These were human beings who I'm trying to connect to, who fully know how to use this lingo. No one ever says that about farmers. If Bernie gets on a stage in Iowa and talks about agricultural subsidies or something, no one says: oh, that's identity politics. If I go to a coastal town and talk about erosion, no one is like: ah, how dare you pander to my identity as a coastal, you know,

gulf worker, or whatever. And they shouldn't – mechanics, white working class – all these people have aggregate interests that they can use collectively to get power. And racial groups are no different, especially since we live in a country that has specifically marginalized people on the basis of race. You can't do that for hundreds of years and then turn around and say: let's not think about that again. That political identity was encoded on us, forced upon us ... You forced us to be this thing. We don't have an alternative. I don't know where my ancestors are from. Don't get mad at us for having this identity that's been put on us. Instead, be happy that there is a political hook for you to use. Let's be honest and clear about it and try to expand people's sense of identity so that we can grow a bigger coalition. But don't alienate people by acting as though the identity they have, which is the only thing they have, politically, to grasp on to, doesn't matter.

If the Soviet Union was an incentive for the U.S. to desegregate and if Gray's favorite law professor helped her to realize that Obama's politics were bad politics, Gray has not learned a great deal from Adolph Reed and she has done next to nothing to expose the limits of identity politics from the perspective of the left. There are many facets to the left critique of identity politics. However, even the most cursory examination of Reed's thoughts, as expressed for instance in *Class Notes*, allows us a quick corrective.

Although Reed's pragmatic and empirical definition of material interests can be criticized from a radical Marxist, or dialectical materialist, perspective, his criticism of over-reliance on symbolic events and electoral candidacies provides a helpful account of the weakness of the left after decades of retreat and defeat. Political pressure to reject radicalism leads to both an intense ideological vigilance on the part of sectarians, he argues, as well as naïve desires to access popular constituencies on the part of academics. Class struggle has thus been replaced with the contingent open-endedness of postmodern and poststructuralist scholarship. Among the features of this shift are: 1) the supposedly liberatory significance of marginal groups, 2) the preference for strategies of resistance to institutions and the transgression of conventions, and 3) the building of radical politics around identity groups whose goal is to recognize and preserve the integrity of their respective differences (Reed 2000: xiv). Reed is of course not arguing against efforts to curtail discrimination or against the fact that people understand themselves through their various identities. What he is arguing against is the notion that ascriptive identities have anything to do with left politics. The notion that women or African Americans have interests and that on this basis may have common interests does not ratify the PMC politics according to which identity groups can be defined outside of and independently of political considerations across the spectrum. As Barbara and Karen Fields have argued, only circular reasoning uses politics to confirm identity and identity to "hijack" politics (Fields 2012: 6). The same can be said for culture.

The efforts of governments and scholars to advance the status of minority groups in the postwar period has coincided with efforts to demobilize the communist left and replace class solidarity with the career ambitions of an upwardly mobile class of race representatives. Although the politics of identity groups sometimes comes into conflict with the postmodern commitment to decenter totalizing projects, the two tend to reinforce the kind of standpoint epistemology which argues that classification as a woman or person of color gives someone special insight into the understanding of that class of people. Positionality and group consciousness abstracts from other considerations like social class, social status, family status, career orientation, and much else that cuts across race and gender categories. The fact that a great deal of attention has been given to black women and to queer and trans people in recent years is evidence of the reduction of politics to identity markers, and further, to the re-establishment of discredited forms of positivism and scientific racism, as in the DNA research into genetic ancestry and the proliferation of classifications of sexuality. Even if Gray would like to give more attention to substantial issues than to identity issues, the now popular concept of class reductionism is not something that Halper or any well-meaning leftist could agree with because it is a concept that Marxists reject. What class reductionism does is distort Marxist theory and so its attribution by race brokers with the views of Adolph Reed is mistaken. What Reed has done is demystify this notion so as to reject it. One might not learn this from freewheeling online reporting.

In addition to these problems, Reed mentions that the intersectional analysis of compound forms of oppression leads to the presumption that the greater the oppression associated with a group, the greater is the assumed insight into moral and political claims. In reaction to increased specialization in the analysis of oppression and privilege, the right puts forward a narrow and reactive definition of universality, which then reshapes liberal politics around the elite brokerage of identity politics and the designation of popular individuals as representatives of groups. The case of Rachel Dolezal shows how someone with the correct politics but the wrong body could not be thought of as solidaristic with black interests (Reed 2015). This sort of pseudo-radicalism gains traction, Reed says, because it does little more than ratify what already exists and because it reinforces liberal politics. Moreover, it gives a privileged role to people who are deemed to be specialized interpreters of the interests of identity groups. The "absurd nattering" of petty-bourgeois intellectuals, he argues, gives a radical-sounding patina to what amounts to liberal pluralism.

Unlike Reed, Gray and Halper do not argue that class has the kind of "functional location in the system of social reproduction" that constitutes the social relation through which identities are constituted in the political economy (Reed 2000: xxvi). To do so would open onto questions having to do with post-Fordism, the creative and knowledge industries, globalization and the neoliberalization of government. This might be too much reflexivity for YouTube chats and softball spots on mainstream media, where the new generation of left pundits easily make a meal of the inanities of people like Jordan Peterson or the depravities of the Washington swamp. Their special talent, like that of sports announcers, is to relay all of the moves and background information about the players in a game that most people know works against them. And like the readers of the astrology column that Theodor Adorno described in his *Minima Moralia*, their followers approach politics as though a superstition that justifies the system (Adorno).

In January 2021, Alexandria Ocasio-Cortez told the DSA flagship magazine *Democratic Left* that the Biden administration is pushing the party in a progressive, "almost radical" direction (McIntosh). The main difficulty for the establishment, AOC argued, is the "bad faith" criticism of "predominantly white" "class essentialists," which she denounced as "privileged" because such criticism thwarts human rights and Biden's efforts to help the poor. After Eric London criticized her claims in this interview, Gray came to the defense of AOC and the DSA, chastising London for what she perceived as misrepresentation (London 2021). What mattered to Gray in this minor scandal, which received a fair amount of press, was to defend the DSA, if not the left wing of the Democratic Party, against the criticisms of the SEP. Whereas *Bad Faith* podcast co-host Virgil Texas confessed that he had not read London's articles about the AOC interview, Gray mockingly referred to WSWS counter-reporting as "big news" and insisted that "in our circles" criticism of OAC from the left would not be tolerated (Bad Faith). Gray gave credit to Biden, who only a few months later reversed course on his promises to increase taxes on corporations.

What change did the 2020 Sanders campaign bring to the Democratic Party? Many, like Naomi Klein, were satisfied with the spectacle of Bernie's aloof posture at the Inauguration Day ceremony. As she put it,

> the slouch, the crossed arms, the physical isolation from the crowd. The effect is not of a person left out at a party but rather of a person who has no interest in joining. At an event that was, above all, a show of

cross-partisan unity, Bernie's mittens stood in for everyone who has never been included in that elite-manufactured consensus.

KLEIN 2021

But even that was too much socialism for the woke American public. The fact that the meme of Sanders with his arms crossed went viral caused an indignant high school teacher to come out and accuse his mittens of manifesting white, male and class privilege: "A wealthy, incredibly well-educated and privileged white man, showing up for perhaps the most important ritual of the decade, in a puffy jacket and huge mittens" (Seyer-Ochi). A Twitter user commented: "Apparently it is … NOT privilege to wear expensive designer clothing while the media talk about ensembles like it's a red carpet event." Another tweeted that the privilege was "being able to publish a bad faith opinion piece in a newspaper with a paywall" (Garger).

Conclusion

> We do not fight racism with racism. We fight racism with solidarity. We do not fight exploitative capitalism with black capitalism. We fight capitalism with basic socialism. And we do not fight imperialism with more imperialism. We fight imperialism with proletarian internationalism.
>
> BOBBY SEALE, *Seize the Time*

∴

Pundits were bewildered by the extent to which Donald Trump fumbled his chance to beat Joe Biden. The Trump reelection campaign could easily have used the same strategy that it used to beat Hillary Clinton, making populist promises regarding people's economic worries as the U.S. headed into Depression-era levels of unemployment. Instead, the GOP tabled a bailout plan that would cut Social Security. After Trump had deployed federal troops across the country to quell BLM protests and some civil unrest, a Fox News interviewer felt compelled to ask the would-be dictator if he would accept the results of the November election. Months before the January 6 coup riot, it was apparent that Trump, whose approval ratings were nosediving, was thinking of imposing a state of emergency to maintain his grip on power. Why did Trump seem sleepier than the man he derided as Basement Joe? Did he want to even the odds with the bumbling Biden for the sake of a more entertaining election match – like they do in the National Hockey League playoffs? Did Trump's Reality TV ethos run deeper in its irrational madness than even his political antagonists give him credit for? Was he doing poorly because his ego really is so fragile that he felt unappreciated for the way he mishandled the pandemic? Or could it be that there really is not much of a difference between the Dems and the GOP, save for the diversity window dressing? Is the bipartisan agenda gamed to that extent?

On Wednesday, November 4, while general election votes were still being counted, Trump declared: "Frankly, we did win this election. ... So, we'll be going to the U.S. Supreme Court. We want all voting to stop" (Chalfant & Samuels). The Trump campaign filed lawsuits in Georgia, Michigan and Pennsylvania to stop the counting of ballots and also demanded a recount in Wisconsin. This led to the use of a reactionary hashtag called #StoptheCount, which was accompanied by armed Trump supporters and protesters interfering with election offices and vote-counting facilities. Brown shirt vigilantism substantiated Trump's comments at the presidential debate in late September to Proud Boys that they should "stand back and stand by" (Nix). The order to stand by turned out to be a reference to his anticipated refusal to accept the outcome of the election. But it was Americans and the world who were standing by to see what would unfold once the vote was determined. As Barry Eidlin reported, given the likelihood that Biden had won, the refusal of the Democrats to put forward a compelling alternative vision for American politics implied that some form or other of Trumpism was going to be there when the U.S. got 'back to brunch' with Biden (Eidlin).

Bernie Bros Gone Woke has argued that there is no reason to avoid the problems that affect not only the Bernie Sanders campaigns but the American and international left. The post-politics that define progressivism in the twenty-first century have a complex history that relates questions of class struggle to political, economic and cultural issues. Whereas the organized left made great strides in the first half of the twentieth-century, by the postwar period the anti-communist policy of containment had led the younger generation in the U.S. to opt for social change through lifestyle and identity rather than armed insurrection. As Jodi Dean has it, those who consider that any evocation of communism should come with qualifications and apologies for past excesses and violence probably belong to the liberal and democratic camp and should be grouped in the same set as capitalists and conservatives (Dean 2012: 7–8). As a counterpoint, Žižek adds the notion of philosophical vigilance police regarding the potential catastrophes that are invented by intellectuals, like those for example who seek to deconstruct the moral foundations of our societies (Žižek 2008a: s22). Civil Rights, the women's movement, student radicals, the anti-war movement, gay liberation, Black Power liberation, the Chicano movement, the American Indian Movement and radical ecologists transformed the revolutionary tradition that was based on proletarian internationalism and diversified the theories of oppression. As these groups were either absorbed by the mainstream or failed to win popular support, the politics of identity became more closely aligned with the ideology of liberal pluralism. Postmodern discourse theory changed the meaning of power at a 'molecular' level, or so it seemed, until black capitalism, green capitalism, red capitalism and corporate feminism defined group solidarity on the same terms as the rest of class society. Today's intersectionality, whiteness studies, privilege theory, critical race theory and the like derive from these previous transformations. As the left attempts to regroup and organize around a common vision and program to fight against economic inequality and corporate domination, progress is stymied by woke culture wars.

In conclusion to this study of the way that the 2020 Sanders campaign came up against the limits of radicalism on the American left, the influence of postmodern post-politics and the pitfalls of strategic voting through appeals to demographics, I present an analysis of the fascist authoritarianism that prevails when mainstream liberals and the professional-managerial class avoid democratic radicalization and instead do the bidding of the billionaire class. Laments about political polarization on the extreme left and right tend to ignore the mediocracy of the virtue-signaling middle, which dilutes the radical praxis of the left and replaces it with advocacy for diversity. Against flawed efforts to play one against the other, or to combine the two in a synthesis without a subject, Marxist materialism reveals their contradictory mediations.

1 The Bipartisan Endgame

The state of American democracy in 2021 reflected the strength of its progressive movement. The way that the Democratic Party handled the Trump coup attempt speaks volumes about the weakness of the left. On Wednesday, January 6, after a Trump 'Save America Rally,' the U.S. Capitol was stormed by a mob of some 5,000 Trump supporters and right-wing militias, including Proud Boys, Oath Keepers, the National Socialist Movement, New York Watchmen, Three Percenters, QAnon supporters, white supremacists, anti-immigrant hate groups and neo-Nazis. In an effort to prevent the validation of Biden's 306-to-232 Electoral College majority, hundreds of rioters mobbed the Capitol police, breached the building and led an armed standoff outside the House of Representatives. Members of Congress were evacuated, many of them fearing for their lives. During the incident, the mob was heard chanting "take the building," "stop the steal" and "hang Mike Pence." At the rally, Trump had incited them to do just that, saying that the vote was a fraud and that when you catch someone cheating you are allowed to play by a different set of rules. He then instructed them to "fight like hell," saying that if they did not do so, they would no longer have a country. He instructed them to march on the Capitol to give the Republicans the backup they need to stop the steal.

The notion that Vice President Mike Pence had the authority to stop the vote was another one of Trump's deceptions. His fascist supporters were more than indifferent to the legality of the matter, as evidenced by the fact that the mob planned to use deadly force. The rioters were found to be in possession of plastic ties for handcuffing hostages, Molotov cocktails, bear spray, pepper spray, explosives, assault rifles, long guns, handguns, knives, brass knuckles, sledgehammers, pipes, baseball bats, hockey sticks, gas masks, rope tied in nooses, encrypted communication equipment, ballistic helmets, bulletproof vests and police shields. A civilian discovered that the rioters had planted pipe bombs at Democratic and Republican Party headquarters so as to divert police away from the Capitol building. Panic buttons in congressional offices were later found to have been disabled and it was discovered that far-right militias posing as tourists had before January 6 been shown the tunnels and the safety passageways of the Capitol building by Republican officials, including Colorado Republican Lauren Boebert. The attack led to five deaths, four among the rioters and one U.S. Capitol Police officer. More than 140 Capitol Police suffered injuries and House representatives have been treated for PTSD.[1]

Far from being the work of a bitter and resentful 'white working class,' the January 6 coup attempt was carried out with the assistance of countless government and security officials. These include:

- *The former President of the United States, Donald Trump*: months before the January 6 coup, acting U.S. President Donald Trump encouraged a plot to kidnap and assassinate Gretchen Whitmer, the Governor of Michigan; on June 1, 2020, Trump declared himself the "president of law and order" and used police to remove peaceful protesters who were demonstrating in Lafayette Square against police violence; throughout the 2020 election campaign, Trump had cast doubt on the legitimacy of the vote, refusing to promise that he would honor the results if he did not win; when the polls closed, Trump denied the results and began to litigate recounts and other forms of obstruction; on January 3, Trump and his cabinet met with Secretary of Defense Christopher Miller and Chairman of the Joint Chiefs of Staff Mark Milley to discuss the use of National Guard troops on January 6, with Trump indicating that they should "take whatever action is needed as events unfold"; after the meeting with Trump, Milley and Secretary of the Army Ryan McCarthy curtailed the ability of designated officials to deploy the National Guard; before January 6, Trump summoned tens of thousands of supporters to Washington D.C. for a rally that he promised "will be wild" and misinformed the public with the lie that Congress has the power to overturn the electoral votes of the contested states; Trump repeatedly invoked the use of violence to settle the results of the election; at the January 6 rally, Trump whipped up a right-wing mob to take back their country by fighting like hell;

---

1 A video of the riot that was shown during the second Trump impeachment is available at C-SPAN 2021.

after the rally, Trump retreated to the White House, where he approvingly watched the riot on television; while watching the riot unfold, Trump called a senator to urge him to delay the certification proceedings so that his followers had more time to interfere with the deliberations; while watching the riot Trump was called by House Minority Leader Kevin McCarthy, who asked Trump to call off the attack – Trump responded with the statement: "well Kevin, I guess these people are more upset about the election than you are"; on January 5 and 6, Trump was accompanied by his Oath Keeper bodyguard, Roberto Minuta, who was later charged for participating in the riot and attacking Capitol police; Trump associates Roger Stone and Alex Jones have ties to Proud Boys and Oath Keepers, whose membership is dominated by active and former police and military; the leadership of the Proud Boys and Oath Keepers has been charged with conspiracy in the January 6 attack on the Capitol; as late as March, 2021, Trump defended the rioters as people who "love our country" and who posed "zero threat" to the congresspeople they were equipped to kidnap and kill; for several months after the riot, Trump maintained the lie that he was the true winner of the 2020 election, denouncing Mike Pence and Mitch McConnell for not being faithful to his dictates

- *Trump allies, aides and White House officials*: among Trump aides who conspired in the riot are Trump political advisor Stephen Miller, National Security adviser Michael Flynn (and also his brother, Lt. General Charles A. Flynn, a former Defense Intelligence Agency head under Obama), Trump campaign consultant Roger Stone (who is connected to fascist militias) and former Navy officer and political strategist Stephen Bannon (who sent 400,000 automated text messages encouraging people to attend the rally); White House staffers were scheduled to be on site during the demonstration; 15 members of Trump's inner circle (including Donald Trump Jr., Eric Trump, Rudy Giuliani, Michael Flynn, Peter Navarro, Tommy Tuberville, Corey Lewandowski, David Bosse, Adam Piper, Daniel Beck, Michael Lindell) met on January 5 to discuss the next day's events; Trump aide and former Marine Federico Klein, a man with FBI clearance, was arrested for unlawful entry, violent conduct, obstructing Congress and assaulting Capitol police; an FBI official confirmed that an unnamed "Trump associate" was in contact with Proud Boys in the days leading up to the riot

- *Save America Rally organizers*: Arizona representatives Andy Biggs and Paul Gosar, Alabama representative Mo Brooks, far-right activist Ali Alexander, billionaire Robert Mercer and his daughter Rebekah Mercer (an associate of Stephen Bannon); around half a dozen people in staff positions for the Save

America Rally (including Megan Powers, Caroline Wren, Maggie Mulvaney, Tim Unes) were paid thousands of dollars by the Trump 2020 reelection campaign (as noted by a National Park Service permit granted to the pro-Trump non-profit group Women for America First)
- *government officials*: many government officials have aided and abetted Trump in his deceptions and plotting of the coup riot, including Senate Majority Leader Mitch McConnell, House Minority Leader Kevin McCarthy, Missouri senator Joshua Hawley, Texas senator Ted Cruz, Tennessee lawmaker Terry Lynn Weaver, State senator Amanda Chase, Michigan representative Matt Maddock, Pennsylvania state senator Doug Mastriano, Missouri state representative Justin Hill, Colorado congresswoman Lauren Boebert, Pennsylvania representative Scott Perry, Georgia representative Marjorie Taylor Greene, Florida representative Matt Gaetz, Ohio representative Jim Jordan, Georgia representatives Andrew Clyde and Jody Hice; many government officials support or are connected to the far-right groups who participated in the January 6 coup and related activities; Paul Douglas Irving, the Sergeant at Arms of the U.S. Congress (who resigned January 7, 2021) gave a directive on January 5 to the Architect of the Capitol to remove 500 bike racks that served as security barricades around the Capitol building
- *Department of Defense*: two days before January 6, Secretary of Defense Christopher Miller disarmed the National Guard, ensuring that soldiers (if called upon) would be unable to protect themselves (with weapons, helmets, body armor or riot control agents) without his approval; Christopher Miller is a far-right former Special Ops commander who was assigned by Trump to purge the Pentagon of civilian leaders, including Mark Esper, who was replaced by Miller after refusing to invoke the Insurrection Act against anti-police-violence protests; Miller was appointed by Trump on November 9, 2020, after Biden was declared the winner of the November 3 election
- *Pentagon and military officials*: December 31, 2020, U.S. Army and military officials unprecedentedly blocked a standard request from D.C. Mayor Muriel Bowser for a contingent of National Guard troops to help with traffic and crowd control on January 6 (this decision was backed by Secretary of the Army Ryan McCarthy, who said that the 340 troops requested would not be needed unless there were more than 100,000 Trump demonstrators); the memo related to this decision by McCarthy also stated that all federal agencies should be exhausted before the National Guard can be deployed; the decision was eventually accepted by Secretary of Defense Christopher Miller and Chairman of the Joint Chiefs of Staff Mark Milley with the condition that troops be unarmed and have no contact with pro-Trump demonstrators; on

January 5, the Pentagon stripped the DC National Guard Commander, Major General William J. Walker, of his authority to dispatch troops to secure the Capitol, making him answerable to Ryan McCarthy and Christopher Miller; McCarthy denied intelligence about threats to the Capitol (he left office January 20, 2021); FBI documents contradict claims by McCarthy that the Pentagon had no intelligence showing that the Capitol was the target of a planned attack; Miller and McCarthy ignored Walker's and the D.C. police's urgent request to deploy National Guard troops (the request was made at 1:49 p.m. and was given the go-ahead at 5:08 p.m.); Walker has testified that as few as 155 soldiers would have been enough to secure the perimeter of the Capitol building; the Pentagon (military and civilian officials, including Lt. General Charles Flynn and Lt. General Walter Piatt) ignored D.C. National Guard Commander Walker, Capitol Police Chief Steven Sund and Washington D.C. Police Chief Robert Contee's report of a Capitol breach and prevented the Washington D.C. National Guard from being deployed until Pentagon official Elissa Slotkin contacted General Mark Milley of the Joint Chiefs of Staff; Flynn and Piatt later told Congress that their delay to send National Guard troops was due to the fact that there were no 'standing plans' in existence for defending the Capitol from attack; a supporter of far-right forces and QAnon, Flynn had previously advocated the military occupation of swing states that voted for Biden and holding new elections at gunpoint; Flynn upheld the view that Trump won the election long after the January 6 coup; Piatt has said that he did not want to use federal troops against what he deemed were protesters exercising their constitutional rights; the Pentagon delayed for 90 minutes on a request by Maryland Republican governor Larry Hogan to send in the Maryland National Guard; the Pentagon blocked the deployment of a quick reaction force at Maryland's Joint Base Andrews; since he could not reach Trump, Mike Pence, who was trapped in a secure location, made a call to Christopher Miller at 4:08 p.m., demanding the Pentagon "clear the Capitol"; Senate Majority Leader Chuck Schumer, House Speaker Nancy Pelosi and House Majority Leader Steny Hoyer made calls to Milley and other Pentagon officials before the Senate chamber was breached, accusing the Pentagon of knowing about the planned assault; by 3:37 p.m. the Pentagon had security forces guarding the homes of defense leaders but not the Capitol; Christopher Miller gave the approval to Walker to send in the National Guard at around 4:40 p.m., about 25 minutes after Trump tweeted to his followers "go home and go in peace"

- *F.B.I.*: FBI officials denied advance notice of the coup plot and failed to issue an intelligence bulletin or threat assessment prior to January 6, despite notice given by memo by FBI agencies in Norfolk and Virginia, one day before the coup, which indicated that Trump supporters had maps of Capitol tunnels and were planning to wage war and take hostages; the Norfolk memo was shared with the FBI Washington Field Office's Joint Terrorism Task Force on January 5 and was posted on the Law Enforcement Enterprise Portal, which is shared with law enforcement agencies throughout the country, including Capitol Police; the FBI received more than 50 reports of plans for violence at the Capitol from the social media company Parler, which is used by fascist and white supremacist groups; FBI Director Christopher Wray denies having had knowledge of this information and has prevented requested information being sent to the House Committee on Oversight and Reform; the FBI did issue warnings of potential violence on January 6 and deployed three tactical teams thanks to an aide of Mitch McConnell who ignored the chain of command; Wray confirmed that the agency failed to issue a threat assessment in advance of the vote ratification session; retired Navy Commander and Oath Keeper leader Thomas Caldwell, who was charged for his participation in the riot, had FBI clearance; Proud Boys chairman Enrique Tarrio possibly acted as an FBI informant against the riot, which reveals prior awareness of the planned coup; Florida Proud Boys leader Joe Biggs also had connections with the FBI; FBI official Jill Sanborn made the unreliable statement that the FBI did not monitor social media posts by militia groups before the riot; a Proud Boys organizer who was charged for conspiracy and obstruction of Congress in the riot was an FBI informer against "antifa networks"; Wray denied allegations that there were left-wing protesters masquerading among the Trump supporters; the House Committee on Oversight and Reform later deemed the FBI intelligence failure to be a mistake

- *Department of Justice*: the DOJ was staffed by Attorney General William Barr, the reactionary advocate of presidential authority; the DOJ denied prior knowledge of the coup plot, despite the fact that a few days before the riot Trump pressured Attorney General Jeffrey Rosen to reverse the Georgia certification (Trump also pressured Georgia Secretary of State Brad Raffensberger to find the votes he needed to overturn Biden's victory); Rosen refused to follow Trump's orders and planned a mass resignation at the DOJ in the eventuality of forced sedition; ten days before the riot, Jeffrey Clark, head of the Civil Division, drafted a letter urging the Georgia legislature to overturn the results of the vote; Clark prepared similar letters for the five other contested states won by Biden but controlled by pro-Trump Republicans; Clark had worked with Trump to remove Rosen and use the DoJ to pressure legislatures in battleground states; the DOJ and the FBI

later assisted the Biden administration to drop charges on hundreds who invaded the Capitol so as to limit prosecution to those who were linked to violent acts; under the Biden administration, the DOJ has refused to comply with requests for information regarding the January 6 coup attempt made by the House Committee on Oversight and Reform
- *Department of Homeland Security*: the Office of Intelligence and Analysis of the DHS avoided making a threat assessment of the planned January 6 rally, though such assessments are typically made before left-wing protests and despite the fact that I&A had received ample evidence of plans to attack the Capitol to prevent the vote certification; the DHS ignored January 4 information, available through fusion centers, about threats posed by the Trump rally; 50 armed members of the DHS, who failed to deploy on January 6, were seen loitering 13 blocks away from the Capitol during the riot; on account of the warnings issued by the FBI, the DHS could have certified the threatened session of Congress as a National Special Security Event; the Acting Director of the DHS, Chad Wolf, later resigned; a report by senator Gary Peters, the chairman of the committee that investigated the DHS, indicated that under the Trump administration, the DHS downplayed the threat posed by white supremacist and anti-government groups and exaggerated the role of "groups" like antifa
- *National Guard*: National Guard troops that were stationed 20 minutes from the Capitol could have deployed after 2:00 p.m.
- *Capitol Police*: in 2018 and 2019, Capitol Police (USCP), with the approval of CP Chief Steven Sund, spent $90,000 to hire Northern Red, a neo-Nazi contractor (also employed by the FBI, local police and the U.S. military), to train the CP's emergency response unit (CERT) in techniques used by US Special Ops death squads in war zones; on January 6, the CERT team refused to deploy; according to the Senate Homeland Security and Rules committee, the CP were aware as early as December 21 that Trump protesters planned to bring guns and other weapons to the January 6 demonstration and use these against any law enforcement preventing their access to the Capitol; a leaked January 3 intelligence report from the CP indicated awareness of the scenario that played out three days later, including the fact that Members of Congress were the target, the size of the crowd, the right-wing character of the crowd, the militia members involved and the weapons they would have with them; the DHS sent the CP a map of the Capitol that was in the possession of the coup plotters; the January 3 report was shared with all CP command staff by intelligence unit director Jack Donohue; on January 5, a CP official shared information about an increase in visitors to a website called

WashingtonTunnels.com; CP intelligence determined on January 5 that there was no threat of a violent attack on the Capitol; CP abandoned their posts and many were nowhere to be seen during the riot; some CP posed for photographs with rioters and facilitated their entry to the Capitol; CP leaders refused calls from Democratic congresswoman Zoe Lofgren, chair of the House Administration Committee which oversees Capitol operations; Chief of Capitol Police Steven Sund lied to Lofgren that the National Guard were on hand; Sund hung up the phone on congresswoman Maxine Waters when during the riot she called for help; Sund saw the January 3 memo and the only order he gave was to expand the police perimeter around the Capitol; Sund neglected to send the January 3 memo to the DHS; Sund said he assumed that the Pentagon would call in the National Guard; Sund resigned in March, 2021; 35 CP were given paid leave while being investigated for collaborating with the mob; 6 CP officers were suspended for code of conduct violations; an April 2021 report and Capitol Police Inspector General Michael Bolton confirmed that the leadership of the CP department facilitated the attack through a concerted stand-down and the refusal to deploy crowd control munitions (one excuse being resentment of left-wing criticism of the misuse of such weapons by police against BLM protesters); the Capitol Police Civil Disturbance Unit designed to handle aggressive crowds, which was led by Eric Waldow, who fought off the mob rather than issuing commands, was prevented from using its crowd control weapons, riot shields in particular, which are commonly available to local police throughout the country; rank-and-file police were not briefed on intelligence warnings of attacks on Congress on January 6; unlike previous protests, CP failed to pre-position ammunition caches within the Capitol or set up a decontamination area for officers attacked with chemicals; Inspector Bolton confirmed that CP were aware of 200 Proud Boys militiamen moving towards the Senate wing of the Capitol but no counter-surveillance teams were sent to monitor them; hundreds of Proud Boys on Capitol grounds were not monitored; in comparison, CP did monitor 3–4 anti-Trump demonstrators setting up props on Third Street; CP failed to gather intelligence on suspicious activity during the riot, making only three reports on January 6 (at 2:18 a.m., 6:19 a.m. and 6:20 a.m.); however, an FBI document revealed that CP and DC Metro police monitored fascist groups, including Proud Boys, in real time through radio on January 6; CP leadership abstained from issuing commands and when they did they gave conflicting and confused orders during the riot, including "take appropriate action" and "we don't know what to do"; many CP officers were sent home after their morning shift; a CP rank-and-file officer reported that "we

had no clue what was going on" and that CP were instructed to watch out for anti-Trump demonstrators; Waldow and several USCP leaders later received a no-confidence vote from rank-and-file police
- *Metropolitan D.C. Police*: Senate hearings demonstrated that Metro police had intelligence reports warning of a planned attack; Metro Police Chief Robert Contee had received the January 5 FBI memo about planned attacks on the Capitol; D.C. police were seen leaving the scene of the riot
- *active duty, off-duty and veteran police officers, members of the military and firefighters*: dozens of police officers and soldiers from across the U.S. participated in the riot; some 40 police and law enforcement officials from 17 states were eventually identified (one of them was charged for threatening to kill AOC); of those charged with offenses, 21 were members of the military; Navy veteran, Vets for Trump founder and QAnon supporter Joshua Macias has been charged; according to retired military officer Thomas Kolditz, thousands of officers in the Department of Defense view the coup favorably
- *citizens*: the Republican Attorneys General Association and the Rule of Law Defense Fund paid for and authorized January 5 robo-calls across the country to "patriots like you" to "fight to protect the integrity of our elections"; prominent business executives and business owners participated in the riot (Brian Sicknick, the Capitol policeman who died during the riot, was likely killed by the bear spray used by two restaurant owners); fascist podcast host Alex Jones participated in the riot (Jones distanced himself from Trump in August 2021 after Trump recommended taking the COVID-19 vaccine); Oath Keeper founder Stewart Rhodes

As the insurrection unfolded, not one Democratic leader denounced the coup and no emergency press conference was called. Barack Obama and the Clintons said nothing on the day of the coup. In an act of utter cowardice, Biden called on Trump – the leader of the coup – to appear on television and defend the Constitution. In what is rather an act of complicity, Biden called on the leader of the fascist coup attempt to "step up" and "end this siege" (Choi). The day of the riot, Biden and the media called for bipartisan unity and healing. Afterwards, Obama praised those of his Republican colleagues who spoke out against the fascist coup. In press conferences two days later, Nancy Pelosi denounced Trump as a tool of Russian President Vladimir Putin and completely ignored the rise of fascism in the U.S. She said:

> And the message that it sent to the world, a complete tool of Putin, this President is. Putin's goal was to diminish the role of – the view of

democracy in the world. That's what he has been about. ... With you, Mr. President, all roads lead to Putin. Putin wants to undermine democracy.
PELOSI

Despite Pelosi's wild accusation, Biden did not call for Trump's co-conspirators to resign. Pelosi could just as easily have said that Biden is a tool of Trump and that she herself is a tool of Putin.

Even as fascist militias were planning another riot on Inauguration Day, the Million Militia March, Biden called for bipartisan unity and demonstrated that he would not hold anyone accountable, including McConnell, who had given cover to Trump's narrative of a stolen vote. "We need a Republican Party," he said, "we need an opposition that is principled and strong" (Closing Bell). Biden also said that he did not support the impeachment of Trump and did not call for his resignation. He was supported in this by neoliberal governments in Europe, Canada, Mexico and Australia. So did left media, including *Jacobin, Rising, Secular Talk, Consortium News, Marx21* and the journalist Glen Greenwald downplay the seriousness of the riot, mostly in defense of civil liberties. The Trump coup attempt and the attempt to overturn the election on the claim that the vote was stolen by irregularities in four swing states, where the minority vote prevailed, was supported by more than 140 Republican congressmen and 8 senators, many of whom were threatened by Trump and his cronies with retaliation. The 'big lie' of a stolen election was repeated by right-wing media outlets like Fox News, Breitbart and Newsmax. Although the hoax of a stolen election is thought to have been believed by only 23 million Americans, disinformation tends to gain credibility the more often it is repeated. Six Republican state legislators took part in the riots, including West Virginia delegate Derrick Evans. One indication that the Democratic establishment did take the fascist threat seriously is that it announced there would be 25,000 National Guard soldiers deployed throughout Washington D.C. during the inauguration – more than all the soldiers deployed in the Middle East. On the other hand, this could be interpreted as Biden taking his turn with a similar show of force. For the most part, the left was more obsessed with the danger posed by the removal of Trump from Facebook and Twitter than with the task of removing him from government office.

Among the thousands of people who participated in the Capitol riot, 610 individuals were arrested and 579 people were charged with federal crimes. Most of these were released before trial. More than 200 were charged with the felony crime of obstructing an official proceeding, leading to 8 guilty pleas and 25 misdemeanors. As of March, 2021, the Department of Justice and U.S. Attorney for the District of Columbia have rejected charges of sedition. Among those arrested, 52 were members of the Proud Boys, Oath Keepers and other extremist groups. Among these, 45 have links to law enforcement agencies and 37 have links to the military. Four active U.S. soldiers were also charged. Far-right groups worked with the Trump White House, the Republican Party as well as the police and military to coordinate the riot of January 6. More than 200,000 tips were eventually given to police by people who recognized participants on Internet videos. Had rioters wore COVID-19 masks – which they could easily have used as a pretext to be masked – they would not likely have been identified. Early on, a lower number of arrests had been compared to the peaceful June 1 Rose Garden protests against police violence, which led to 326 immediate arrests by the D.C. Metro Police. This allowed the corporate media to define the insurrection in racialist terms as a problem of white privilege and racism. Calling for more policing of extremists, Hillary Clinton blamed the coup attempt on white people and white-supremacist grievances (Folley). Such accusations are typically used by the establishment against the working class. A writer at *Vox* stated: "Whiteness is at the core of the insurrection" (Cineas). Ibram X. Kendi tweeted: "White privilege is on display like never before in the U.S. Capitol" (Kendi 2021a). Gerald Horne, the author of *The Counter-Revolution of 1776*, used some rather twisted reasoning to comment: "I'm not convinced that class-based remedies, like a Green New Deal, higher minimum wage and Medicare for All, would be enough to buy off the non-elite Trump supporters, unless you can say that it's for whites only" (Analysis News 2021). Universal programs are not designed as bribes for fascists.

The mediocratic incompetence of the Democratic establishment in their response to the coup belies several weeks of advance notice that disruptions were planned. As Biden called for healing and a peaceful transition of power, Trump defined his speech at the rally as "totally appropriate" and warned Biden against impeachment, threatening him to "be careful what you wish for" (McKelvey). Two days before the Inauguration Day ceremony, Biden's chief of staff, Ron Klain, welcomed coup plotters Josh Hawley and Ted Cruz to the proceedings. As he boarded Air Force One during his departure ceremony in Palm Beach, and as a DJ played 'Macho Man,' 'Billie Jean' and 'My Way,' Trump promised his supporters: "we will be back in some form" (Crisp).

One week after the coup riot, Congress voted to impeach President Trump on charges of "incitement of insurrection." The choice was made as an alternative to an investigation and as a mostly symbolic gesture, which allowed Trump to remain in power until January 20. Regardless, 197 out of 211 Republicans voted against impeachment. Although Congress is required by Article One to investigate plots to subvert the Constitution, the involvement of so many government officials made the task all too damning. Trump could have been expelled with recourse to the 14th Amendment, which bars from office any officeholder who takes part in an insurrection or rebellion against the country. However, the charge would have applied to the other Republicans who supported Trump's effort to overturn the vote through the illegal use of force. Although representative Cori Bush resolved to pursue this course, no lawmaker has been expelled since the Civil War. Led by a motion introduced by senator Paul Rand, 45 out of 50 Senate Republicans flouted constitutional norms and voted to prevent the impeachment. Democratic senators and 5 opposed GOP senators blocked the motion. Only 10 of the 211 congressional Republicans voted in favor of the impeachment. The 80-page impeachment brief that was filed proved irrefutably that Trump was guilty of advocating, planning and inciting an armed attack on Congress on January 6 so as to overturn the results of the election.

Trump's second impeachment trial began on February 9 and concluded February 13. In a foregone decision, 43 Republican senators acquitted the man they would have allowed to overthrow the separation of powers and install himself as a dictator. Among the jurors were people who had opposed the certification of the election results, including Mitch McConnell, Josh Hawley, Ted Cruz, Tommy Tuberville, Rick Scott and Cindy Hyde-Smith. Without even worrying themselves to present a credible defense, Trump's lawyers argued that the riot was an appropriate response to the George Floyd protests. The Democrats practically ignored what had taken place in the Capitol building and how the event was allowed to transpire. Unlike Watergate or the Iran-Contra hearings, none of the people involved in the insurrection were interrogated. Legal professionals consider that the Democrats sabotaged their own case so that they could focus on more important business. Echoing Biden, Pelosi concluded: "We need a strong Republican Party" (Elizabeth). In other words, what Pelosi was actually saying is: The billionaire class needs fascists in government if it is to continue to dominate the American population and the rest of the world. The Republicans vowed to censure the seven senators in their party who voted against Trump and lawmakers went on a spree with voter suppression legislation as well as anti-left anti-protest laws, such as anti-riot bills passed in Florida and Oklahoma that give legal immunity to counter-protesters who kill people with their vehicles (Hill; Baptiste).

Whereas the first Trump impeachment lasted close to three months, the second procedure was over in less than a week. The senators then took a week of holidays and Trump went golfing. The purpose and effect of the second impeachment, which was focused on preventing Trump from running for the presidency again in 2024, was to give amnesty to Trump's co-conspirators in and around the Republican Party. Preventing the punishment of those who commit serious crimes, Biden gave a repeat performance of Obama's handling of the banking crisis and the Bush torture program. The mishandling of the Trump coup attempt gives further evidence that by refusing to legitimize working-class demands and implementing reforms, the New Democrats contribute to the rise of fascist tendencies and the demonization of the left.

Impeachment was not the only means that American citizens had at their disposal to convict Trump and his co-conspirators on criminal charges. In late February, Senate committees held hearings on Capitol security but avoided connecting the dots between intelligence failures and government corruption. On March 15, Pelosi called for a bipartisan '9/11-style commission' to investigate the attack on the Capitol. Such a commission would have as its purpose the delay and indefinite postponement of further revelations of conspiracy and charges of sedition. This hypothesis is reinforced by the fact that former national security officials, many of them war criminals, wanted the commission to be designed like the 9/11 commission, which concealed the connections between the Al Qaeda hijackers and U.S. intelligence agencies. One month later, as he imposed a new round of economic sanctions against Russia, Biden announced a national emergency, alleging that Russia interfered with the 2020 presidential election! According to a 15-page U.S. National Intelligence Report, Russians spread misleading claims about Biden. The report denies that Russia attempted to alter the outcome of a single vote. Putin may as well have said that Biden is a good friend.

Unlike 9/11, it would be redundant to suggest that the January 6 coup attempt was an inside job. For this reason, the Republicans demanded that a commission should give Republicans 50/50 representation, veto power on the commission's findings and a mandate for subpoenas on George Floyd protesters. Despite having a majority in both houses, in Congress and the Senate, the Democrats conceded on all but the last point, which would have turned the commission into a witch hunt against left-wing protesters. In May, the House Homeland Security Committee announced that H.R.3233, a bill for a bipartisan commission agreement, had been drawn to form a commission on the domestic terrorism attack of January 6. It was agreed that partisan politics would be kept out of the inquiry, which would focus on the security breach at the Capitol. Pelosi introduced the legislation along with a $1.8 billion security plan to increase, among other things, the annual $510 million budget of the U.S. Capitol Police force, which altogether ignores the facts of the incident. The bill was approved 252-to-175 in the House of Representatives but was blocked by Mitch McConnell and Republican senators after Trump called on House

Minority Leader Kevin McCarthy to shut down the proposed commission. The Democrats responded with more pleas for bipartisan unity. Most of what is known about the coup attempt has been confirmed by reports issued by the Capitol Police Inspector General, the House and Senate committee and the Senate Homeland Security and Rules committee.

One cannot ignore the fact that the January 6 riot, the impeachment charade and the negotiations around the commission occurred as hundreds of thousands of Americans had died from the coronavirus pandemic – 350,000 in January, 2021, and by June, around 600,000. Switching from one big lie to another, the Biden administration launched a propaganda campaign to resurrect the idea that the virus originated in a Chinese laboratory in Wuhan, the city where SARS-CoV-2 was first detected. Whereas World Health Organization scientists had determined in March 2020 that there is no evidence that the virus originated in a lab, the White House flexed all of its "diplomatic" muscle on the basis of a 2019 State Department claim that three employees of the Wuhan Institute of Virology had shown symptoms that were consistent with common seasonal illnesses. Although the State Department officials who made this claim were never identified, their report was weaponized by Trump to concoct a 'kung flu' hypothesis, which sought to blame China for the existence of the virus and deflect attention from his willful mishandling of the pandemic (P. O'Connor). While the mainstream media denounced Trump for what they deemed was a conspiracy, the narrative was turned 180 degrees when Biden became president and reanimated the Wuhan lab leak hypothesis along with allegations of genocide of the Uyghur ethnic minority, which was later discredited as the propaganda work of the Uyghur World Congress, a CIA-backed separatist group with ties to terrorist organizations, and the Uyghur American Association, a militia-led group that supports Trump's far-right politics (Xin & Lingzhi; Singh 2021). The Biden administration intentionally ignored the fact that the WHO inquiry had in effect ruled out the deliberate bioengineering of COVID-19. By comparing COVID-19 to similar viruses identified in bats, the WHO concluded that its origin is consistent with other naturally occurring viruses.

The U.S. government, like many other capitalist powers, promoted a 'herd immunity' policy that protected corporate profits over human lives and livelihoods. It also hoarded vaccines in a policy of "vaccine diplomacy," while at the same time delivering a snail-pace roll-out of the vaccine to its own citizens. To detract from these and other failings, the Biden administration adapted scientific research to its foreign policy agenda of economic and military conflict with China. The reissue of the Wuhan lab theory under Biden has the same characteristics as other government-generated conspiracies and fake news, like the Weapons of Mass Destruction lies that were used by Bush to invade Iraq. Tom Cotton, the fascist senator from Arkansas who started the lab leak conspiracy under Trump, and who also claims that the election was stolen, was later hailed by the mainstream media as having been correct all along.[2] In addition to stoking anti-Asian and anti-vaccine violence, the conspiracy is an attack on science and democracy. The lab leak theory was reignited by a May 25 article written by Glenn Kessler for the *Washington Post* (Damon 2021b). Journalists had previously uncovered the fact that the theory was manufactured by Stephen Bannon's associate, the billionaire Miles Guo, an anti-communist business partner of the 2016 Trump campaign and ally of the right-wing newspaper *Epoch Times*, which is associated with the Falun Gong religious sect. The story was first "reported" in January 2020 by Chinese columnist Wang DingGang, an associate of Bannon, Guo and Rudolph Giuliani. The story was then repeated by Guo's *G News*, by Bannon's *War Room Pandemic* podcast and then by the *Washington Post*. The only official source that is mentioned by the *Post* article is a former Israeli intelligence officer, Lt. Col. Dany Shoham. Further articles by the *Post* indicated that the lab leak theory was weak and no further research could be carried out at the lab itself, a convenient factor since disproving the lab leak theory would require evidence that does not exist. In other words, reporting that is untrustworthy at best became the basis for National Security officials to claim there was evidence for the leak theory and cause enough to blame the Chinese Communist Party for creating, if not spreading the virus, and for impeding further investigation.

By summer 2020, Trump was routinely referring to COVID-19 as the 'Chinese virus.' By November, a non-peer reviewed article by researcher Li-Meng Yan, which defended the notion that the virus was man-made, was discredited as a Bannon and Guo concoction. Regardless, in May 2021, the invention of the lab leak hypothesis by the far right had disappeared from mainstream media reporting. As it happens, the May 23, 2021, article in the *Wall Street Journal* that revived the story and that was used by Biden and the United Nations Health and Services Secretary to call for a new inquiry, which this time would exclude Chinese scientists, not only did not present new evidence, but was co-authored by Michael R. Gordon, who in 2002 co-authored with Judith Miller an article

---

2 Reporting by Saagar Enjeti on the show *Rising* and then *Breaking Points* was particularly pernicious in confusing the matter of science with partisan politics. Along similar but not hawkish lines, Matt Taibbi dismissed the issue as a partisan and epistemic standoff. See Breaking Points; Useful Idiots.

which asserted that Saddam Hussein was seeking to build nuclear weapons (Damon 2021a; Gordon, Strobel & Hinshaw). The claim by Gordon and Miller was invented by the office of former Vice President Dick Cheney and given to the *New York Times* reporter, who consequently lost his job at the *Times* but kept working as a Pentagon correspondent. The errors of the report on WMDs was only retracted by the *Times* in 2004.

In addition to this dubious article by Gordon and his conspirators, most of the mainstream news articles that revived the lab leak hypothesis were based on a May 5 article published in the *Bulletin of the Atomic Scientists*. The article, which has served as the basis of propaganda pieces in the *Washington Post*, *New York Times*, *New Yorker* and *Wall Street Journal*, asserts that a leading Chinese expert on bat viruses received funding from the National Institute of Health to collaborate with Peter Daszak to manipulate bat coronaviruses – a fact that by itself has no bearing on COVID-19. None of the articles in the mainstream media mention the fact that the author of that article, Nicholas Wade, is the author of *A Troublesome Inheritance: Genes, Race and Human History*, a 2014 book that advocates racist pseudo-science and that was denounced by more than 140 human development biologists (Damon 2021e). They also do not mention the fact that Wade's book was celebrated by KKK Grand Wizard David Duke. The scientists whose work was misused by Wade denounced his book in a letter written to the *New York Times*, the same newspaper that on May 31 defined Wade's lab leak article as a "landmark essay" (Damon 2021e). Contradicting the findings of the February 2021 report of the WHO, which argues that the virus mutated in a living organism with an immune system, Wade ignores the fact that there is no evidence of COVID-19 at the Wuhan Institute of Virology, either in human hosts or in coronavirus test samples, all of which were tested when the virus was first discovered in the Hunan market. There is no scientific validity to the potential for the mutation to have been simulated at the WIV because the lab does not have the capacity for that to be possible. Information provided by WIV scientist Dr. Shi Zhengli indicates that human genome sequences have more in common with pigs than the bat viruses they were studying in December 2019 have in common with SARS-CoV-2 (Mateus). Note also that Daszak, who was president of the Ecohealth Alliance, along with Anthony Fauci, the director of the National Health Institute, and Kristian G. Andersen, the director of Infectious Disease Genomics at Scripps Research Translational Institute, has definitively rejected the genetically-engineered lab leak theory in favor of either natural selection in an animal host before zoonotic transfer or natural selection in humans following zoonotic transfer. Other scientists, like Dan Samorodnitsky, have referred to the lab leak theory as an anti-science conspiracy invented by compliant scientists, civilians and government officials. Whereas the zoonotic spillover hypothesis explains everything, the lab leak hypothesis is a *deus ex machina* that seeks to blame specific individuals, or political regime, and has no scientific value (Damon 202d).

Journalist historian Thomas Frank approvingly cited the Wade article, suggesting in *The Guardian* that the lab leak theory, if proven to be true, would shatter belief in the very notion of truth. Instead of questioning the motives of the Biden administration, Frank chose to question scientists on the non-scientific basis that: 1) lab leaks happen, 2) the Wuhan lab studied bat coronaviruses and was funded by the American national medical establishment, 3) some labs use "gain of function" methods to make viruses more virulent for the sake of research (Frank 2021). Frank suggested that the news media cannot always be trusted, but in this instance, was doing just that. He failed to mention that the scientists at the WIV denied conducting any gain of function research. The furin cleavage site (FCS) that was used by Wade to assert human manipulation was rejected by Andersen as both an improbable strategy for a 'gene jockey' and something that has never been used in CoV experiments. The biologist David Baltimore eventually retracted his earlier speculation that the FCS may be evidence of manipulation. Frank also failed to mention that not only did Facebook censor early lab leak stories but that it was later censoring anti-lab leak stories like those referenced here. Frank's pontificating about human foibles did not help get to the truth of the matter. If the American public wanted to ponder conspiracies, the complicity of vast sectors of the establishment in the fascist January 6 coup was a far less dubious story, right at its doorstep, that had yet been settled. Biden preferred to project conflict onto an external enemy.

The reality of viruses like COVID-19 is that they are a product of the shared commons of public health created and compromised by the worldwide supply of exotic foods, industrialized land use, imperial extractivism, capitalized corporate and public management structures, agribusiness, large-scale animal farming and animal trading, the deregulation and subcontracting of food inspection, the criminalization of ecological and animal rights activists, capital-led deforestation, global warming and global travel. The accelerated evolution of pathogen virulence is directly related to the production of genetic monocultures, which weaken genomic firewalls. The next issue to be considered is the means to prevent cascades of infection when they occur. For full protection one would need to nationalize hospitals, supercharge testing, socialize pharmaceuticals, enforce protection for medical staff, force companies to produce ventilators and personal protective equipment when needed and establish a corps of pandemic workers. The only problem is that these are aspects of what is otherwise a socialist economy (Wallace et al). That the politicians who were first advised about the virus chose to focus on dumping personal stocks before alerting the public is only one reason why the lab leak theory inspired so much corporate media drivel. In the interim, the most basic facts were ignored.

In March 2021, the WHO, which is the official United Nations public health agency, issued a report on the origins of COVID-19 that drew upon the research of thousands of scientists in hundreds of countries (Damon 2021c). The investigative team included scientists from China, the U.S., Russia, Japan, Germany, Denmark, the Netherlands, Vietnam and Qatar. The scientists investigated thousands of samples from Wuhan and dismissed the lab leak hypothesis as "extremely unlikely" since no virus or genomes of the sort existed in any lab before December 2019. The report acknowledged that the first major outbreak emerged in Wuhan and the Hunan seafood market but could not determine that Wuhan was the origin of the virus. The report examined the similar bat and pangolin viruses that could cause COVID-19 and that resemble the SARS pandemic of 2000. The difference between these and COVID-19 was determined to be an animal intermediary. The WHO hoped to extend the research to the health data of 76,000 Chinese people with flu-like illnesses before December 2021.

In mid-August the *Ralph Nader Radio Hour* hosted Andrew Kimbrell, a public interest attorney with the Center for Food Safety who opposes gain of function research (Ralph Nader Radio Hour 2021). Confusing his policy agenda with the conspiracy, Kimbrell credited Wade and denounced Daszak. A few days later, an article written by the science authors of the March WHO report, which includes Daszak along with 10 other scientists, was published in the journal *Nature* (Koopmans). Giving due deference to those who want to believe the leak hypothesis, the group reiterates the fact even if a lab leak is possible there is no evidence that the virus emerged in a lab and that further research on zoonotic infection or introduction in the Wuhan region would at this stage yield diminishing returns. This article in *Nature* further confirms the zoonotic spillover hypothesis presented by the 21 scientists who published their findings in July, 2021 (Holmes). One need not wait on the *Wall Street Journal* to make good on these findings.

Against the counsel of scientists, the WHO came under U.N. pressure to maintain the lab leak hypothesis, which was supported by U.S. allies in the U.K., where Boris Johnson was reported saying in October 2020, "No more fucking lockdowns, let the bodies pile high in their thousands," and in India, where neglect by the Hindu supremacist Modi government had by May 2021 led to anywhere between 250,000 and one million deaths (Waugh). The main proponent of the lab leak theory in the U.K. is former M16 chief Richard Dearlove, who supported Secretary of State Mike Pompeo's claims in June 2020 that there was enormous evidence of a leak, but added that the data has probably been destroyed. Dearlove helped the Blair government justify the war against Iraq with WMD claims and was judged dishonest by the Chilcot Inquiry (Hyland). Due to Biden flip-flopping on campaign promises, Democratic Party supporters on the left and the right, who feared the prospect of another Trump term, sheltered the Biden administration's bellicose decision to condemn the WHO study and demonize the malleable Fauci for the sake of its desperate Great Power Conflict agenda to save U.S. hegemony.

2   Meanwhile, Back in Wokeville

In an article on American imperialism and regime change operations, Vijay Prashad racalls that on September 15, 1970, Richard Nixon and Henry Kissinger used the power of the U.S. government to do everything it could to undermine the socialist president of Chile, Salvador Allende (Prashad). Their goal, according to a declassified CIA report, was to "make the (Chilean) economy scream." After Allende nationalized the copper industry, which was celebrated by Chileans with the creation of the National Day of Dignity, companies like Pepsi and Kennecot demanded that the U.S. intervene through military means to organize a regime change. After Allende was killed, the country that was now headed by the military dictatorship of Augusto Pinochet was turned over to the interests of transnational monopolies. The U.S. today has similar intentions towards Venezuela, Iran and Myanmar.

Prashad outlines twelve steps through which a regime change typically takes place: 1) poor countries are trapped within structures already in place and become dependent on the export of specific commodities, like sugar or oil; 2) poor countries are prevented from controlling the prices at which their products sell, which places them at the mercy of more powerful countries; 3) the workers of poor countries are outproduced by industrial mechanization in more powerful countries; 4) transnational corporations disregard the rule of law and rob these poor countries; 5) the victims of plunder become indebted to the more powerful countries; 6) due to declining revenues, a crisis develops in public finances; 7) due to the unreliability of international governments and financiers, the governments of poor countries are forced to cut social spending; 8) the poorest of the people from poor countries are forced to migrate; 9) corporate media control the narrative, show no sympathy towards the countries that are devastated and defend right-wing dictators who impose reforms that serve the transnationals; 10) for the regime change to occur, foreign powers create a situation where an unelected proxy, who is not popular with the people, can nevertheless undermine the existing government of the poor country; 11) sanctions are used to make the economy scream and the poor country is depicted as a threat to the security of foreign invaders; 12) the powerful countries go to war against the poorer ones. Prashad says that none of this inevitable. Those who continue to defend their revolution against the imperialists can say no to regime change interventions. His conclusion is that there is no middle ground.

One might think that today's woke wars are 'first world problems' in comparison with the problems of the poor in the Global South. That would be true only if one also considered that the fate of the latter is not tied up with the power of the organized left in the Global North. Yet the progress of the left in the developed West is today tied to the vicissitudes of identity politics and its transmutation through postmodern discourse theory and new social movements. What is sometimes referred to as 'the great awokening' is premised on a critique of Enlightenment universalism and a rejection of Marxist communism (Yglesias). The ensuing woketivism, and its cancel culture tactic, has led to legitimate skepticism about this phenomenon that is associated with the left. While woketivists may sincerely believe that what they are doing is progressive, their zealotry is often an affront to common sense and to human rights, which the activists are typically unconcerned with since they, in pseudo-Marxist terms, associate rights discourse with bourgeois ideology. Rejection of new social movement fanaticism by the broader polity sometimes makes conservatives out of people who would otherwise have much more in common with the activists than with Walmart shareholders or Academi investors. As wokesters carry on with their agonism, believing themselves to be the vanguard of a cultural revolution and-or renaissance, many people, who are neither innocent nor guilty of anything in particular, are being tried in kangaroo courts of what passes for public opinion and summarily dismissed from their jobs and careers, which they likely worked towards for most of their adult lives.

The Columbia University linguist John McWhorter has been known to collect emails sent to him by people who have been canceled for whatever minor infraction of the new, ever more stringent codes of political correctness (Foundation). The perverse character of woke wars is that many people, on account of their whiteness, or other traits, are considered "guilty" in advance and irredeemable. The fact that this conflict is untenable, which causes outlets like *Harper's* magazine to appeal to reasonable norms of social tolerance, makes little difference to people whose anti-foundationalism matches their will to power (Harper's Editors). A second figure to address this problem is Helen Pluckrose. Although she once identified as Marxist, Pluckrose now says that on economic issues she is socialist, or social democratic, but that she otherwise adheres to political liberalism. She would, on these terms, have nothing in common with latter-day Foucauldians, who on the whole have become neoliberals. Pluckrose has made valid criticisms of the "applied postmodernism" of the social justice "left," which may or may not have anything much in common with the 'French theorists' who developed what has come to be known as post-structuralism. However, by separating her analysis from the Marxist critiques of postmodernism that already exist, she has produced a critique of woke wars that is what Prashad refers to as middle of the road. Her new advocacy group, called *Counterweight*, which provides support and advice for people who have been canceled, is framed in the terms of liberal ideology and defends individualism, universalism as well as diversity.[3] McWhorter is even more conservative.

A middling approach, however helpful it may be in the short term, is not necessarily the solution to our problems. Like the postmodern activists who combine anti-Enlightenment anti-universalism with discursive historicism for the sake of identity politics, woke activists are motivated by the sense of grievance and resentment, which they project onto their victims. In an article on the dangers of today's 'great awakening,' Žižek writes:

> One has to make an effort so that this awakening would not turn into just another case where political legitimization is based on the subject's victimhood status. Is the basic characteristic of today's subjectivity not the weird combination of the free subject who experiences itself as ultimately responsible for its fate and the subject who grounds the authority of its speech on its status as a victim of circumstances beyond its control? ... Today's logic of victimization is today universalized, reaching well beyond the standard cases of sexual harassment or racist harassment. ... This notion of the subject as an irresponsible victim involves the extreme Narcissistic perspective from which every encounter with the Other appears as a potential threat to the subject's precarious imaginary balance. As such, it is not the opposite, but, rather the inherent supplement of the liberal free subject. In today's predominant form of individuality,

---

3   See the *Counterweight* website at https://counterweightsupport.com.

> the self-centred assertion of the psychological subject paradoxically overlaps with the perception of oneself as a victim of circumstances.
>
> ŽIŽEK 2017

In one instance of this not so great awakening, the Canadian actress and director Michelle Latimer was deemed to be not indigenous enough to represent First Nations issues. Because of this she was prevented from working and stripped of her accomplishments (Dowling). Is the greatest danger in cases like this one that Latimer will turn to liberalism to solve her problems? Would the self-interest of someone like her not pale in comparison to the narcissism of those who have nihilistically attacked her and the cowardice of those in the CBC and the media who have gone along with the travesty? Latimer had the resources – and the DNA – to fight her case (Barrera). No doubt many of the hundreds of individuals who have contacted McWhorter and Pluckrose have been thrown under the bus by people in much the same way that capitalist society constantly makes people into losers of some sort. Those who might reach out for help are perhaps those who are aware of the new kinds of prevarication that woke wars are inspiring, which did not exist only a few years ago. In the 1980s, the critics of political correctness were mostly neoconservatives. Today the situation has changed, and McWhorter is correct to say that people should not be cowed against criticism of woke fanaticism by the fear that in doing so they make themselves seem like supporters of Trump and the alt-right. However, one need not resort to conservative defenses of universal rights. Note that in 2021 Pluckrose's colleague, James Lindsay, shifted his criticism of 'cultural Marxism' from postmodern social justice warriors to the more foundational figure of Hegel as the "operating system" of the old left, the new left and woke activism (Boyce; New Discourses). Ironically, this move has left him without an emancipatory perspective and his economic liberalism begins to resemble the discourse theory he otherwise rejects. One can better criticize woke agonism and micro-fascism from the perspective of emancipatory left universalism.

As bohemian anti-bourgeois attitudes have long ago become the petty-bourgeois presuppositions of much of the professional-managerial class, and as countercultural attitudes have become the stock-in-trade of contemporary reactionaries, what ultimately matters in culture and politics is the kind of world we want to build. Relying on human rights standards is not a reactionary bourgeois position, as argued by people like Wendy Brown and Judith Butler, but is as socialist as the right of self-defense and the 8-hour workday. Since the Trump coup attempt, many on the left were quick to warn that right-wing extremism should not be the motivation to pass new laws or to censor neo-fascist groups since the repressive means of the state could soon be turned against the left. One response to this is that the poor were living a state of emergency well before the coup attempt. Research has revealed that only about 12 percent of those who participated in the January 6 storming of the Capitol building were anonymous members of the working class. The rest were mostly professionals with military and police training, right-wing politicians and businesspeople. The social justice movement's obsession with the racism and sexism of the majority is an elite neoliberal politics that reanimates outdated postmodern theories after the moment of their eclipse. Obama once said that African Americans can no longer count on the guilt feelings of white liberals to advance their interests. However, this neoliberal scold was referring to yesterday's Civil Rights strategies. Today's new social movement radicals are much more disoriented and far less concerned with civil society. There is no ideological filter on accelerationist immanentism or whatever singularity. Its schizoid post-politics is unmoored from principles, program and leadership. The post-political horizon of today's social justice movement researchers, academics, artists and activists is social democratic at best. Their mission is to make the unwoke scream, and as Ben Burgis adds, while the world burns. The task of the left is simply to refuse the blackmail of woke neoliberalism and to instead lead the struggle against the billionaire class.

When concepts become banalized, like for example the Marxist proletariat or the Freudian unconscious, they lose their meaning and are reconfigured as pop cultural phenomena. One word that has animated discussions around class and identity is reductionism. A back-and-forth exchange between Ben Burgis and Noah Berlatsky qualified the concepts of class and identity against the notion of reductionism. Burgis opened the debate with an article from November 17, 2020, titled "Racial Essentialism and the 2020 Election: We should think of America's divisions more in terms of class and ideology, and less in terms of race" (Burgis 2020b). This was followed by Noah Berlatsky's article on the same website, titled "Why Class-First Leftists Are Wrong: Defining leftism based on economics while excluding identity is theoretically, empirically, and ethically misguided" (Berlatsky). Much to his discredit, Berlatsky's arguments were mostly bluster and Burgis had no difficulty taking the strands of his article apart in his December 6 rejoinder, "Noah Berlatsky's Critique of My Alleged 'Class First Leftism'" (Burgis 2020a).

Although Burgis uses the term (race) essentialism rather than (race) reductionism, the concept of (class) reductionism was used in Berlatsky's retort as he attempted to expose and undo his opponent. The concepts of race reductionism and race essentialism are not the same and would have different implications in a discussion of politics.[4] However, it is fair to say that Burgis was talking about race reductionism. In the case of such reductionism, the identity in question could refer to sex, gender, race, sexuality, nationality, religion, ability or other aspects of social stratification. The problem of reductionism has been discussed fairly extensively in Marxist literature, in particular, in the debate between Adolph Reed and Ellen Meiksins Wood (Davis 2006). The class reductionism critique has been challenged by reputed scholars like Vivek Chibber, David Harvey, Barbara Foley, Alain Badiou, Terry Eagleton, Adolph and Touré Reed, Walter Benn Michaels, David Walsh, Étienne Balibar, Cedric Johnson, Jacques Rancière, Daniel Zamora, Fredric Jameson, Jodi Dean, Bruno Bosteels and Nancy Fraser. Contrary to what David Roediger suggests in his book *Class, Race, and Marxism*, the number of "class-splainers" is somewhat restricted, however, even if the aforementioned are prominent public intellectuals (Roediger 2017a: 44). They are easily outnumbered by the army of left scholars who also fall under categories like identity and queer activists, diversitarians, racialists, post-structuralists or identity brokers. Among the latter are scholars like Roediger himself, Michael D. Yates, Sara Ahmed, Asad Haider, Simon Critchley, Glen Sean Coulthard, Robin D.G. Kelley, Angela Davis, Chris Chen, Gerald Horne, Richard Seymour and Nikhil Pal Singh. Although there are countless Marxist scholars who have addressed identity issues under the rubric of materialism and class analysis, least of all Marx and Engels, few of these have engaged with the problem of so-called primary and secondary contradictions, or the question of universalism and particularism as it informs Marxist theory. The broader categories of social studies, sociology, Cultural Studies, postmodernism and post-structuralism have more adherents today than any group that could wrongly be identified as "class reductionists." Regardless, this small grouping plays a decisive role with regard to the rest, elucidating the contemporary conjuncture in the terms of radical left praxis.

Although Burgis does a good job of countering Berlatsky's accusation of class reductionism, he leaves the concept of reductionism itself unexamined. Not unlike the term political correctness, the concept of reductionism has a history as a term of opprobrium on the left. Marxism distinguishes between the terms reduction and reductionism. *Reductionism* explains the relations between the elements within a complex system with reference to their root causes. Such reductionism defines the relation between the parts and the whole in a mechanistic way that has very little to do with Marxist materialism.

---

4 Whereas Touré Reed takes credit for inventing the term "race reductionism" (Park Center), the more or less same concept was used by Leon Trotsky in his rejection of the "zoological materialism" of Nazi ideology. See Trotsky 1944.

The notion of *reduction*, in contrast, allows for flexibility, for example, between elements of the economic base and the ideological superstructure – in other words, without presuming a direct and mechanical continuity between these elements. Although the notion of reduction is concerned with causes, the advanced and unpredictable characteristics of a system, or a society, are not reducible to earlier or more 'essential' forms (Kangal). We can speak therefore of a non-reductionist materialism, which is precisely what the Reeds and the Fields have accomplished in their respective ways with regard to the study of race and class in American history and politics. Non-reductionism is not to be confused or conflated with eclecticism, randomness, chaos, relativism, will or force.

Whereas the aspect of complexity in dialectics is summed up with the terms negation, contradiction, unevenness and overcoming, a historical demonstration of dialectical contradiction helps to make a more convincingly Marxist argument. This contrasts with the empirical, metaphysical, phenomenological, existentialist, structuralist and deconstructionist tendencies in contemporary theory. For example, the uses of Hegelian dialectics and the theory of contradiction in Marxism finds Žižek asserting that the logic of today's free market capitalism is demonstrated in the tendency of the state to strengthen authoritarian forms of control. Analogously, in terms of identity issues, contemporary mores are similarly sustained by regulatory mechanisms. As Žižek puts it:

> Today's celebration of "minorities" and "marginals" *is* the predominant majority position; even alt-rightists who complain about the terror of liberal political correctness present themselves as protectors of an endangered minority. Or take the critics of patriarchy – those left-wing cultural theorists who focus their critique on patriarchal ideologies and practices: they attack them as if patriarchy were still a hegemonic position, ignoring what Marx and Engels wrote 170 years ago, in the first chapter of *The Communist Manifesto*: "The bourgeoisie, wherever it has got the upper hand, has put an end to all feudal, patriarchal, idyllic relations." Is it not the time to start wondering why patriarchal phallogocentrism was elevated into a main target of criticism at the exact historical moment – ours – when patriarchy definitely lost its hegemonic role, when it began to be progressively swept away by the market individualism of "rights"? … This means that *the critical statement that patriarchal ideology continues to be today's hegemonic ideology* is *today's hegemonic ideology*: its function is to enable us to evade the deadlock of hedonistic permissiveness, which is effectively hegemonic.
>
> ŽIŽEK 2019b: 14–6

Along these lines, it would have been good to know what it is exactly that former Zero Books editor Douglas Lain implied in his vlog on this reductionism debate (Zero Books). Since Lain suggested that Burgis does not prioritize an abstract class-first politics but is concerned with all forms of oppression, it is odd that his video propounds Marxist theory by framing the reductionism debate in the terms of the conflict between Democratic Party centrists and Democratic Party progressives. What kind of non-reductionist materialism might one expect to find among Democratic Party progressives that one does not find among centrists? Walter Benn Michaels has sought to avoid this dilemma by simply accepting the term class reductionism (Jacobin 2021a). As noted in the introduction, this accepts the particularity of the working class but not its universality as the gravedigger of capitalism. It is a picturesque view that has always been comfortable to the middle class, regardless of how charitable, reformist and progressive it may be.

Class-first politics is no more or less abstract and no more or less concrete than capitalism. As questions of identity and ontology replace questions of politics, belief and commitment, politics itself is redefined as a matter of tolerance or prejudice. Yet, as Žižek reminds us, tolerance is an ideological category (Žižek 2008b). Its purpose is to transform problems of inequality and exploitation into matters of cultural difference. This "culturalization of politics," he argues, rests on two paradoxes: the first relates to the difference between being determined by one's culture and choosing one's culture; the second has to do with the problem of choice, which potentially renders the particularized individual intolerant towards others. The paradox, for Žižek, is that any free choice is a meta-choice that violently tears someone out of their particular cultural lifeworld. In political terms, this means conferring to others more than condescending tolerance of difference from ourselves. Beyond the certainty of ontology, the paradox of universality is that identity, like the Cartesian *cogito*, is experienced as something that is entirely contingent. While for Badiou, ontology is infinitely multiple, and for that reason irrelevant to the immanent truths of science, love, art and politics, for Žižek it is perennially out of joint. Those postmodernists who oppose Enlightenment universalism so as to critique essentialism tend to affirm capitalism. What seems to be a matter of cultural inequality, cultural domination and cultural superiority is in actuality a matter of class struggle. The question is not simply who decides and who benefits, as it were, but what universality will emerge? Abstraction is defined by how concrete individuals relate to others and to social life. In this sense, universality, autonomy, freedom and equality are not simply illusory or hegemonized by particular interests. The tension in all of these articulates the forms of social life. Democracy cannot be exported through gunboat diplomacy. Privilege cannot be redistributed through persecution.

As the U.S. is currently declining as a world economic power, and certainly as a democracy, something more than woke intersectionality is going to be required to offset the rise of right-wing populism and fascism, especially now that Republicans are openly attacking critical race theory along with civil liberties and voting rights (Henninger; Johnson 2021). The communist lawyer Mike Macnair made the important point that what Kimberlé Crenshaw's first studies of intersectionality demonstrated is less the fact that specific court cases brought forward by black women can be shown to be biased in favor of either black men or white women than the fact that they are obviously biased in favor of the employer (Communist Party of Great Britain). Against this, all that Macnair's critics need to say in reply is that he is a racist and/or sexist male. This is how 'reductionism' gets bandied about without much concern for what the word means and becomes an artefact of political correctness, contributing to anti-communism and strengthening the right.

Unless we want to become the slaves of our own concepts, as Norbert Weiner would have said, we need to better understand the critical theory that informs the radical tradition, which would relieve us of at least one humiliating task, which is to either affirm or deny that we are class reductionists. The best antidote to this is better and more rigorous left analysis, which includes work on the development and refinement of concepts. Otherwise, words like reductionism take on a life of their own and function as the trendy accessories of the kinds of socialists who are bereft of Marxism.

3 Political Revolution Inside

In the mid-1970s, after the strikes of May 68 had failed to result in any significant social progress, Henri Lefebvre wrote several works on the theory of the state. One of these is *Hegel, Marx, Nietzsche, Or the Realm of Shadows* (Lefebvre 2020). Lefebvre presented the trajectory Hegel-Marx-Nietzsche as a kind of roadmap for the left that would bypass the baneful influence of structuralism and discourse theory, but that allowed for revolutionary romanticism to be combined with Marx's critique of civil society and Hegel's notion of telos. With Hegel, Lefebvre examines how it is that the straitjacket of the nation state masks the realities of the global market. Nowhere is this more evident than in the state's ability to define the terms of civil society. The state becomes the measure and the limitation of consciousness. This is not a world of real people, but of historical contradictions. All sense of realism, pragmatism and materialism is subordinated to the power of the state, which, despite rampant economic inequality, embodies the interests and the ideology of the bourgeois middle class. The state therefore undertakes to define the terms of class struggle. The function of the professional-managerial class is to manage, mediate and direct this conflict. The pinnacle of this structure is the technocracy.

With Marx, Lefebvre demonstrates how modern society is preoccupied with economic growth. In their relation to production, workers are not self-directed but are directed by the state. What are the means and relations of production in what is now referred to as 'late stage' capitalism? Reading Marx through Hegel, the conflicts of the social base are contained by the unity of the state in the world system. This is what is known as History, which is not to be conflated with Super Bowl matches and Oscar nominations. The corporatized sense of 'history in the making' that comes from sporting events, if not from electoral politics, is severed from self-production. In this regard, voting for Biden is not very different from rooting for your favorite sports team.

Unlike Hegel, Marx had no sympathy for the bourgeois state as the definition of the movement of History. The state cannot live up to the role that we might assign to it. The notion of overcoming (*aufhebung*) represents for Marx the withering of the state and its replacement by a higher stage in human development. This means, concretely, a rupture with the ideology and philosophy of the bourgeois class. Neverminding economic inequality, unemployment, homelessness and ongoing wars, the crisis of global warming by itself announces the end of property relations as we know it (Klein 2014). But the middle class does not want to know it. Its social function is to make us forget. The bourgeois state achieves this more or less successfully by keeping up with and guiding new developments in technology, management, education, sports, culture, and so on. That is why the view of Trump as exceptionally evil masks the fact that he is not so different from other neoliberal politicians. His sideshow antics, however dangerous, are there to obscure rather than reveal the authoritarian character of liberal democracy. And that is why the Democratic Party has done so little to oppose him. The bigger problem is that the extreme center threatens human survival, which paradoxically makes the state apparatus more necessary than ever before.

With Nietzsche, Lefebvre discusses how the will to change the world is directed against the definition of society in the singular terms of economic productivity. Unable to change society, protest and contestation are delimited to realm of culture and intellectual production, where the tendency to absurdity or the fantasy of superhuman qualities betray the deadlocks of mass society. Social contradictions that cannot be overcome and a collective social project that cannot be realized devolves into war, violence, barbarism and genocide. For the "last men," humanity becomes little more than a theological platitude. If God is dead, as Nietzsche proclaimed, then so is History and so is Humanity. Biden and Trump reflect perfectly this ghastly transformation of reason into randomness. Nothing about history evokes in them the sense of collective necessity. Instead, historical becoming is deemed immanent to the state of things. Humanity looks to the past, with hokey 50s slogans like 'No Malarkey' and boastful verbiage like 'Make America Great Again.' All of this is a mark of uncertainty. Out of this complete relativism emerges the creative individual, whose elite capacities, or what Nietzsche referred to as the Gay Science, opposes Hegelian Absolute Knowing. The will to power of those who are now referred to as yuccies – young urban creatives – replaces logic, morality and ethics with self-love. The folly of self-affection is not all for the worse since it opposes the technocrats who destroy the world. It aesthetically resolves social conflict with an art of living – healthy naturalism, sensual pleasures and what has otherwise been encapsulated by the idea of counterculture. The Nietzschean impulse rejects objectivism in favor of a subjectivism that transcends reality. However, it does so by destroying reason and what is human at the same time, resulting in a pathological anti-civilization. This brings us to Freud, who retrospected that God is dad.

By itself Nietzscheanism is no more legitimate than the world it denounces. Its limits bring us back to the idea and the concept of history. When radicalized, history is remade into meta-politics. Knowledge can have no certainty except the knowledge of the necessity to act in a way that advances rather than impedes social progress. The Marxist science of praxis is the result of this triad, which advances the transition from capitalism to communism. For Marx, contrary to today's postmodernists, the movement towards communism does not and cannot progress without the notion of human rights that Nietzscheans and now also the corporate state believe they can dispense with. That is why Marxists have little interest in the pessimistic prognostics of post-everything. Rather, Marxism announces the end of the state of things: the end of art as we know it, the end of politics, the abolition of wage labor, the abolition of prisons, the abolition of billionaires, the abolition of the state, the end of capitalism, and with it, the end of History.

If Marx refused to prophecy what comes after capitalism, he did focus on what it is that would lead the way: creative and productive activity based on new ideas, new works and new institutions. Not much of this is possible through an apologia for the violence and inequality that is perpetrated by the U.S. government and the Democratic Party. The militias that Trump called upon to overturn the results of the 2020 election are not so different from the soldiers that successive Republican and Democratic Party administrations have sent overseas.

Like most advertising, the injunction to vote for Biden was an uneasy persuasion. We all knew what a mistake it would be but absolute knowing came too late. One might think the same thing about an advertisement put out by the Friends of Bernie Sanders in May 2021, which shows how the co-owner of Klavon's Ice Cream Parlor could not fill 16 (mostly temporary summer) positions and so increased employee wages from $7.25 to $15 an hour. After receiving 1000 applications in one week, filling the positions overnight, keeping prices the same and still making profit, the story was hailed by progressive media as a rebuttal to Chambers of Commerce claims that federal $300/week COVID relief benefits should be stopped on account of the fact that they disincentivize job searching (Sanders Channel 2021). The Fight for $15 agenda that was added to the Sanders platform in 2016 affects 17 million Americans. It was nevertheless removed from the February 2021 American Rescue Plan. As COVID-19 wiped out approximately half of small businesses in the U.S., large retailers looked for new ways to automate their services. Higher minimum wages will not settle the contradiction between the means of production and the relations of production. Nor will they solve the contradiction that the most powerful and richest nation in the world defines minimum wage increases as a means to address racial inequality.

The culture war is a displaced class war. What makes the relationship between the two difficult to disentangle is the similarity between morality and politics. There is nevertheless no direct connection between economic justice and racial or gender justice. That is why capitalism can make use of both racism and anti-racism. Conservative populists understand this better than the postmodern left. The contemporary struggle against sexism, racism and homophobia is a disavowed form of class struggle. More often than not, it is waged against the working class or against people who are deemed normal, against which petty-bourgeois elements desperately seek to distinguish themselves. Inverting the terms changes nothing of this essential problem. Identity and class issues can be combined in different ways, as we have seen with ageing black voters in the Southern states and elsewhere, or with Latino voters in different parts of the country, whether they are from California, Nevada, Texas or Florida.

When a political constituency is addressed as an identity group, even in places where racism is structurally omnipresent, the level of class consciousness is not automatically raised. The 'wages of wokeness' was an open secret of the Sanders campaign. It allowed his team to appeal to different voter demographics among the working class without frightening them away with the language of class struggle. Allyship is uncomplicated in the sense that you either already have it or you can achieve it through moral conversion. A job, a living wage, a career, free post-secondary education, universal health care, clean drinking water, a healthy planet, world peace – such things are harder to come by. Since the countercultural 50s and 60s, a petty-bourgeois class that was ideologically shaped by Cold War anti-communism and that benefited from the postwar economic boom made cultural distinction and lifestyle concerns into a new hegemonic formation that is now global in scope. The Cold War liberalism that peaked with postmodernism and Cultural Studies is now in crisis and decline. The moribund conversation around identity politics is desperately kept alive with trendy new concepts like toxicity, trolls, snowflakes, privilege, call-out culture, cancel culture, safe spaces and killjoys. They are as relevant to radical left politics as McDonald's restaurants, hula hoops and nudist beaches. By the time the anti-globalization movement got underway in the 1990s, socialist parties and labor unions in the West had been decimated. Aware that neoliberalism was wreaking havoc in every sphere of social life, activists assumed that anti-system protests and the valorization of difference could combine as a force of disruption and disobedience. These strategies have ceded control of the state to the neoliberal technocrats whose devastating austerity policies have in turn fueled right-wing reaction. A global structural transformation is underway that has very little to do with identity. If the left does not understand this it will have no ability to shape the future.

Bibliography

Abrajano, Marisa A. 2010. *Campaigning to the New American Electorate: Advertising to Latino Voters*. Stanford: Stanford University Press.

AcTVism Munich. 2020. "Richard D. Wolff on Bernie Sanders endorsing Joe Biden & Voting for Lesser of Two Evils." *YouTube*, April 18. https://www.youtube.com/watch?v=R2wtVDrhe3E.

Adorno, Theodor. 1994. *The Stars Down to Earth, and Other Essays on the Irrational in Culture*, ed. Stephen Cook. London: Routledge.

Al Jazeera English. 2016a. "Noam Chomsky on the new Trump era | UpFront special." *YouTube*, November 25. https://www.youtube.com/watch?v=jB54XxbgIoE.

Al Jazeera English. 2016b. "Zizek: Electing Trump will 'shake up' the system – UpFront." *YouTube*, November 16. https://www.youtube.com/watch?v=qfgnAU-6Tvo.

Alexander, Michelle. 2010. *The New Jim Crow: Mass Incarceration in the Age of Colorblindness*. New York: The New Press.

Ali, Tariq. 2015. *The Extreme Centre: A Warning*. London: Verso.

All Urban Central. 2019. "Cardi B Pulls Up On Bernie Sanders." *YouTube*, July 30. https://www.youtube.com/watch?v=gS7pNmcVrLM.

Allen, Jonathan and Amie Parnes. 2021. *Lucky: How Joe Biden Barely Won the Presidency*. New York: Crown.

Alter, Charlotte. 2020. "How Joe Biden Is Positioning Himself as a Modern FDR." *Time*, October 28. https://time.com/5904569/joe-biden-fdr/.

American Bridge 21st Century. 2019a. "Pennsylvania: Mark." *YouTube*, November 12. https://www.youtube.com/watch?v=2VB6uE4ERoM.

American Bridge 21st Century. 2019b. "Wisconsin: David." *YouTube*, November 12. https://www.youtube.com/watch?v=mKwhB0D4KUg.

Analysis News, The. 2020. "Economics Not Culture Wars Drove Most Trump Voters – Thomas Ferguson." *YouTube*, November 25. https://www.youtube.com/watch?v=azd21dCriFE.

Analysis News, The. 2021. "Racism and a Failed Coup – Gerald Horne." *YouTube*, January 10. https://www.youtube.com/watch?v=QB2OMidTOqk.

Anderson, Perry. 1998. *The Origins of Postmodernity*. London: Verso.

Anderson, Perry. 2013. "Homeland." *New Left Review* #81 (May-June): https://newleftreview.org/issues/II81/articles/perry-anderson-homeland.

Arceneaux, Michael. 2016. "Bernie Sanders still says class is more important than race. He is still wrong." *The Guardian*, November 22. https://www.theguardian.com/commentisfree/2016/nov/22/bernie-sanders-identity-politics-class-race-debate.

Bad Faith. 2021. "Has AOC Really Sold Out the Left?" *YouTube*, March 29. https://www.youtube.com/watch?v=xFrZ5R3edoM.

Badiou, Alain. 2005 [1988]. *Being and Event*, trans. Oliver Feltham. London: Continuum.

Badiou, Alain. 2013 [2010]. *Philosophy and the Event*, trans. Louise Burchill. Cambridge Polity Press

Baptiste, Nathalie. 2021. "The Wave of GOP Anti-Protest Bills Will Criminalize Protesters – and Sabotage Police Reform, Too." *Mother Jones*, May 7. https://www.motherjones.com/crime-justice/2021/05/the-wave-of-gop-anti-protest-bills-will-criminalize-protesters-and-sabotage-police-reform-too/.

Barabak, Mark Z. and Melanie Mason. 2019. "Trump raises a new menace – socialism – and Democrats can't agree how to respond." *The Los Angeles Times*, February 15. https://www.latimes.com/politics/la-na-pol-trump-socialism-democrats-20190215-story.html.

Barrera, Jorge. 2021. "Michelle Latimer breaks silence, presents ancestry report following questions about Indigenous identity." CBC *News*, May 17. https://www.cbc.ca/news/indigenous/michelle-latimer-ancestry-report-expert-1.6024508.

Barthes, Roland. 1972 [1957]. *Mythologies*, trans. Annette Lavers. New York: Farrar, Strauss & Giroux

Beauchamp, Zach. 2020. "The raging controversy over 'Bernie Bros' and the so-called dirtbag left, explained." *Vox*, March 9. https://www.vox.com/policy-and-politics/2020/3/9/21168312/bernie-bros-bernie-sanders-chapo-trap-house-dirtbag-left.

Beauchamp, Zach. 2021. "Biden's America First hangover." *Vox*, May 1. https://www.vox.com/policy-and-politics/22408089/biden-trump-america-first-policy-immigration-vaccines.

Beijer, Carl. 2019. "Bernie Has Been Vetted, and He Can Beat Trump." *Jacobin*, September 16. https://www.jacobinmag.com/2019/09/bernie-sanders-2020-presidential-election-not-vetted-media.

Benjamin, Walter. 1968 [1955]. *Illuminations: Essays and Reflections*, trans. Harry Zohn. New York: Schocken Books.

Berlatsky, Noah. 2020. "Why Class-First Leftists Are Wrong." *Arc Digital*, December 6. https://arcdigital.media/why-class-first-leftists-are-wrong-fc768d0666d8.

Bhambra, Gurminder K. 2017. "Brexit, Trump, and 'methodological whiteness': on the misrecognition of race and class." *The British Journal of Sociology* (November 8): https://onlinelibrary.wiley.com/doi/full/10.1111/1468-4446.12317.

Biden, Joe. 2020. "Michelle Obama's Closing Argument | Joe Biden For President 2020." *YouTube*, October 6. https://www.youtube.com/watch?v=5l_Xz2MIh4s.

Bishin, Benjamin G. 2009. *Tyranny of the Minority: The Subconstituency Politics Theory of Representation*. Philadelphia: Temple University Press.

BKB | Het Campagnebureau. 2020. "BKB Lunch Lecture – Campaigning during COVID-19 with Arun Chaudhury." *YouTube*, June 8. https://www.youtube.com/watch?v=jN3CF7qkfdk.

Bohrer, Ashley J. 2020. *Marxism and Intersectionality: Race, Gender, Class and Sexuality Under Contemporary Capitalism*. New York: Columbia University Press.

Bourdieu, Pierre. 1984 [1979]. *Distinction: A Social Critique of the Judgement of Taste*. Translated by Richard Nice. Cambridge: Harvard University Press.

Boyce, Benjamin A. 2021. "WOKEBUSTERS! (live with Lindsay & Wokal)." *YouTube*, May 27. https://www.youtube.com/watch?v=j6IufYLMrqM.

Bray, Mark. 2020. "Antifa isn't the problem. Trump's bluster is a distraction from police violence." *The Washington Post*, June 1. https://www.washingtonpost.com/outlook/2020/06/01/trump-antifa-terrorist-organization/.

Breaking Points. 2021. "Saagar Enjeti: Fauci Emails REVEAL LIES On Lab Leak Hypothesis." *YouTube*, June 7. https://www.youtube.com/watch?v=cxtzHfmnG7U.

Brewster, Jack. 2020. "A Timeline of Tara Reade's Sexual Assault Allegations Against Joe Biden." *Forbes*, May 24. https://www.forbes.com/sites/jackbrewster/2020/05/07/a-time-line-of-tara-reades-sexual-assault-allegations-against-joe-biden/?sh=3129848c79d1.

Bridge Project. 2019. "Michigan: Lori." *YouTube*, November 21. https://www.youtube.com/watch?v=phyiOnMBQRk.

Bronner, Laura and Nathaniel Rakich. 2020. "Exit Polls Can Be Misleading – Especially This Year." *FiveThirtyEight*, November 2. https://fivethirtyeight.com/features/exit-polls-can-be-misleading-especially-this-year/.

Brown, Ellen. 2020. "The Fed's Baffling Response to the Coronavirus Explained: The next time the country's largest banks become insolvent, rather than bailing banks out, Congress should nationalize them." *Common Dreams*, March 11. https://www.commondreams.org/views/2020/03/11/feds-baffling-response-coronavirus-explained.

BTV SB College. 2021. "THE MATERIAL EXISTENCE OF IDEOLOGY | SLAVOJ ZIZEK." *YouTube*, May 18. https://www.youtube.com/watch?v=s_9eWgRSN4Y.

Bugden, Sebastian. 2021. "The Last Man Takes LSD: A letter from the editor." *Verso Blog*, April 13. https://www.versobooks.com/blogs/5053-the-last-man-takes-lsd-a-letter-from-the-editor.

Burgis, Ben. 2020a. "Noah Berlatsky's Critique of My Alleged 'Class First Leftism'." *Arc Digital*, December 6. https://benburgis.medium.com/noah-berlatskys-critique-of-class-first-leftism-c9a738caf77a.

Burgis, Ben. 2020b. "Racial Essentialism and the 2020 Election." *Arc Digital*, November 17. https://arcdigital.media/racial-essentialism-and-the-2020-election-dac4810f2deb.

Burgis, Ben. 2020c. "We Don't Need a Culture War. We Need a Class War." *Jacobin*, December 18. https://www.jacobinmag.com/2020/12/culture-war-class-polarization-medicare-for-all.

Burgis, Ben. 2021. *Canceling Comedians While the World Burns: A Critique of the Contemporary Left*. Winchester: Zero Books.

Buttigieg, Pete. 2019. "Big Ideas | Pete Buttigieg for President." *YouTube*, November 29. https://www.youtube.com/watch?v=uTuMYr1YeQE.

C-SPAN. 2021. "Senate Impeachment Trial: January 6 Video Montage." *YouTube*, February 9. https://www.youtube.com/watch?v=ivVOPWrFfW4.

Carr, Jemma. 2020. "Statues of the philosopher Voltaire and a colonial military figure are vandalised in Paris as movement to take down monuments linked to slavery spreads across France." *Daily Mail*, June 22. https://www.dailymail.co.uk/news/article-8446749/Statues-philosopher-Voltaire-colonial-military-figure-vandalised-Paris.html.

Cashmore, Ellis. 2006. *Celebrity/Culture*. New York: Routledge.

Cashmore, Ellis. 2012. *Beyond Black: Celebrity and Race in Obama's America*. London: Bloomsbury Academic.

Cassell, Jessica. 2017. "Marxism vs. Intersectionality." *Fightback*, July 12. https://www.marxist.ca/article/marxism-vs-intersectionality.

Cassidy, John. 2021. "Biden's Great Economic Rebalancing." *The New Yorker*, May 3. https://www.newyorker.com/news/our-columnists/joe-bidens-great-economic-rebalancing.

Cassimeda, Renae. 2021. "Republican-led states enact fascistic laws that ban the teaching of 'divisive concepts'." *World Socialist Web Site*, June 21. https://www.wsws.org/en/articles/2021/06/22/crit-j22.html.

CBC. 2021. "Trudeau vows to tackle 'she-cession' after new report says pandemic has been worse for working women." *CBC*, March 8. https://www.cbc.ca/news/politics/report-trudeau-international-women-s-day-1.5941674.

Central Intelligence Agency. 2021. "Humans of CIA." *YouTube*, January-May. https://www.youtube.com/results?search_query=humans+of+cia.

Ceron, Ella. 2020. "Kentucky's Attorney General Slams Celeb Reactions to Breonna Taylor News." *Teen Vogue*, September 24. https://www.teenvogue.com/story/daniel-cameron-breonna-taylor-celebrities.

Chalfant, Morgan and Brett Samuels. 2020. "Trump prematurely declares victory, says he'll go to Supreme Court." *The Hill*, November 4. https://thehill.com/homenews/campaign/524404-trump-says-hell-go-to-supreme-court-to-stop-votes-from-being-counted.

Chibber, Vivek. 2013. *Postcolonial Theory and the Specter of Capital*. London: Verso.

Chibber, Vivek. 2017. "Rescuing Class from the Cultural Turn." *Catalyst* 1:1 (Spring): https://catalyst-journal.com/2017/11/cultural-turn-vivek-chibber.

Choi, Matthew. 2021. "'President Trump, step up': Biden calls on Trump to rebuke Capitol rioters." *Politico*, January 6. https://www.politico.com/news/2021/01/06/capitol-rioters-biden-response-trump-455595.

Choonara, Esme and Yuri Prasad. 2014. "What's Wrong with Privilege Theory?" *International Socialism*, April 2. http://isj.org.uk/whats-wrong-with-privilege-theory/.

Chotiner, Isaac. 2019. "The Disturbing, Surprisingly Complex Relationship Between White Identity Politics and Racism." *The New Yorker*, January 19. https://www.newyorker.com/news/q-and-a/the-disturbing-surprisingly-complex-relationship-between-white-identity-politics-and-racism.

Cineas, Fabiola. 2021. "Whiteness is at the core of the insurrection." *Vox*, January 8. https://www.vox.com/2021/1/8/22221078/us-capitol-trump-riot-insurrection.

Clinton, Hillary Rodham. 2016. *What Happened*. New York: Simon & Schuster.

Closing Bell. 2021. "Biden: We need a Republican party that is principled and strong." *CNBC*, January 8. https://www.cnbc.com/video/2021/01/08/biden-we-need-a-republican-party-that-is-principled-and-strong.html.

Clover, Joshua. 2016. *Riot. Strike. Riot: The New Era of Uprisings*. London: Verso.

Clover, Joshua. 2020. "The Two Politics: 2020 So Far." *Verso Blog*, July 16. https://www.versobooks.com/blogs/4796-the-two-politics-2020-so-far.

Coates, Ta-Nehisi. 2017. *We Were Eight Years in Power: An American Tragedy*. New York: One World Press.

Collins, Chuck. 2021. "Global Billionaires See $5.5 Trillion Pandemic Wealth Surge." *Institute for Policy Studies*, August 11. https://ips-dc.org/global-billionaires-see-5-5-trillion-pandemic-wealth-surge/.

Communist Party of Great Britain. 2018. "Mike Macnair: The dead end of intersectionality." *Vimeo*. https://vimeo.com/300339126.

Coppins, McKay. 2020. "Why Romney Marched." *The Atlantic*, June 8. https://www.theatlantic.com/politics/archive/2020/06/mitt-romney-black-lives-matter/612808/.

Cozzarelli, Tatiana. 2020. "Class Reductionism Is Real, and It's Coming from the Jacobin Wing of the DSA." *Left Voice*, June 16. https://www.leftvoice.org/class-reductionism-is-real-and-its-coming-from-the-jacobin-wing-of-the-dsa.

Crenshaw, Kimberlé. 1989. "Demarginalizing the Intersection of Race and Sex: A Black Feminist Critique of Antidiscrimination Doctrine, Feminist Theory and Antiracist Politics." *University of Chicago Legal Forum* #140 [Vol.1989, Issue 1, Article 8]: 139-67.

Crisp, Elizabeth. 2021. "Donald Trump, in Final Farewell Speech, Says 'We Will be Back in Some Form.'" *Newsweek*, January 20. https://www.newsweek.com/donald-trump-final-farewell-speech-says-we-will-back-some-form-1563025.

Critchley, Simon. 2013. *Infinitely Demanding: Ethics of Commitment, Politics of Resistance*. London: Verso.

Cummings, Jordy. 2017. "I Know Who Else Was Transgressive: Teen Vogue has better politics than Angela Nagle." *Red Wedge*, August 2. http://www.redwedgemagazine.com/online-issue/nagle-review.

Dabashi, Hamid. 2016. "Why Chomsky and Zizek are wrong on the US elections." *Al Jazeera*, November 30. https://www.aljazeera.com/indepth/opinion/2016/11/chomsky-zizek-wrong-elections-161129090634539.html.

Daggett, Cara. 2015. "Drone Disorientation: How 'Unmanned' Weapons Queer the Experience of Killing in War." *Internationalist Feminist Journal of Politics* (August): 361-79.

Damon, Andre. 2021a. "Author of Wall Street Journal 'Wuhan lab' story wrote lies about Iraqi 'Weapons of Mass Destruction'." *World Socialist Web Site*, June 1. https://www.wsws.org/en/articles/2021/06/01/wuha-jo2.html.

Damon, Andre. 2021b. "How the US media declared the 'Wuhan lab' lie 'credible'." *World Socialist Web Site*, May 30. https://www.wsws.org/en/articles/2021/05/31/wuha-m31.html.

Damon, Andre. 2021c. "Science vs propaganda: World Health Organization report exposes 'Wuhan laboratory' lie." *World Socialist Web Site*, March 30. https://www.wsws.org/en/articles/2021/03/31/pers-m31.html.

Damon, Andre. 2021d. "Scientists take a stand against 'Wuhan lab' witch hunt." *World Socialist Web Site*, June 3. https://www.wsws.org/en/articles/2021/06/03/wuha-jo3.html.

Damon, Andre. 2021e. " 'Wuhan lab' theory proponent Nicholas Wade pushed racist pseudo-science in 2014 book." *World Socialist Web Site*, June 7. https://www.wsws.org/en/articles/2021/06/07/wade-jo7.html.

Darville, Jordan. 2020. "The Coup's Boots Riley says his first-ever vote will be for Bernie Sanders." *The Fader*, February 19. https://www.thefader.com/2020/02/19/the-coups-boots-riley-says-his-first-ever-vote-will-be-for-bernie-sanders.

Davis, Angela. 2017. "An Interview on the Futures of Black Radicalism." In *Futures of Black Radicalism*, eds. Gaye Theresa Johnson and Alex Lubin, 583-603. London: Verso.

Davis, Diane E., ed. 2006. *Political Power and Social Theory*. Bingley: Emerald Publishing Limited.

Davis, Mike. 2017. "The Great God Trump and the White Working Class." *Catalyst* 1(1) (Spring): https://catalyst-journal.com/vol1/no1/great-god-trump-davis.

Davis, Mike. 2020. "Trench Warfare: Notes on the 2020 Election." *New Left Review* #126 (November-December): 11-14.

Dean, Jodi. 2009. *Democracy and Other Neoliberal Fantasies: Communicative Capitalism and Left Politics*. Durham: Duke University Press.

Dean, Jodi. 2010. *Blog Theory: Feedback and Capture in the Circuits of Drive*. Cambridge: Polity.

Dean, Jodi. 2012. *The Communist Horizon*. London: Verso.

Dean, Jodi. 2019. *Comrade: An Essay on Political Belonging*. London: Verso.

Dean, Mitchell and Daniel Zamora. 2021. *The Last Man Takes LSD: Foucault and the End of Revolution*. London: Verso.

Delaney, Samuel. 2015. *Mad Men and Bad Men: What Happened When British Politics Met Advertising*. New York: Faber & Faber.

Democracy Now. 2020a. "Feminist Scholar Barbara Smith on Identity Politics & Why She Supports Bernie Sanders for President." *Democracy Now*, February 12. https://www.democracynow.org/2020/2/12/barbara_smith_identity_politics_bernie_sanders.

Democracy Now. 2020b. "How Bernie Sanders changed his views on identity politics." *YouTube*, February 12. https://www.youtube.com/watch?v=eUhE9MLXo1k.

Democracy Now. 2020c. "Where Are the Progressives? Briahna Joy Gray on Neera Tanden & Other Biden Picks for Economic Team." *Democracy Now*, December 2. https://www.youtube.com/watch?v=Ll5a49h2iLI.

Deneault, Alain. 2018 [2015/2016]. *Mediocracy: The Politics of the Extreme Centre*, trans. Catherine Browne. Toronto: Between the Lines.

Derysh, Igor. 2019. "Joe Biden to rich donors: 'Nothing would fundamentally change' if he's elected." *Salon*, June 19. https://www.salon.com/2019/06/19/joe-biden-to-rich-donors-nothing-would-fundamentally-change-if-hes-elected/.

Devitt, Liam. 2021. "How Britain's Red Wedge Tried to Bring Pop Into Politics and Politics Into Pop." *Jacobin*, June 26. https://www.jacobinmag.com/2021/06/red-wedge-uk-labour-party-80s-youth-vote-bragg-weller-kinnock-political-concerts.

Di Liscia, Valentina. 2020. "Statue of Black Lives Matter Activist Replaces Toppled Monument of Enslaver." *Hyperallergic*, July 15. https://hyperallergic.com/576935/marc-quinn-jen-reid-statue-bristol/.

Dixon, Bruce A. 2018. "Looking Down That Deep Hole: Parasitic Intersectionality and Toxic Afro-Pessimism." *Black Agenda Report*, February 1. https://www.blackagendareport.com/looking-down-deep-hole-parasitic-intersectionality-and-toxic-afro-pessimism-part-2.

Dovere, Edward-Isaac. 2019. "As Bernie Sanders Leans Into Socialism, His Rivals Laugh." *The Atlantic*, June 12. https://www.theatlantic.com/politics/archive/2019/06/bernie-sanders-socialism-trump/591493/.

Dowling, Amber. 2020. "Michelle Latimer's Identity Crisis Is Raising Impossible Questions for Canada's Indigenous Filmmakers." *Variety*, December 23. https://variety.com/2020/film/global/michelle-latimer-indigenous-trickster-inconvenient-indian-1234873888/.

Driessens, Olivier. 2013. "The Celebritization of Society and Culture: Understanding the Structural Dynamics of Celebrity Culture." *International Journal of Cultural Studies* 16(6): 641-59.

Du Bois, W.E.B. 2007 [1903]. *The Souls of Black Folk*. Oxford: Oxford University Press

Dugyala, Rishika. 2020. "MSNBC's Chris Matthews quits." *Politico*, March 2. https://www.politico.com/news/2020/03/02/chris-matthews-quits-msnbc-hardball-119042.

Dyer-Witheford, Nick. 2015. *Cyber-Proletariat: Global Labour in the Digital Vortex*. London/Toronto: Pluto Press/Between the Lines.

Dyson, Michael Eric. 2016. *The Black Presidency: Barack Obama and the Politics of Race in America*. Boston: Houghton Mifflin Harcourt.

Ebiri, Bilge. 2019. "Jim Jarmusch Believes in the Teens, But Not Joe Biden." *Vulture*, June 17. https://www.vulture.com/2019/06/jim-jarmusch-interview-the-dead-dont-die.html.

Edsell, Thomas B. 2021. "Should Biden Emphasize Race or Class or Both or None of the Above?" *The New York Times*, April 28. https://www.nytimes.com/2021/04/28/opinion/biden-democrats-race-class.html.

Ehrenreich, Barbara. 1990. "The Professional-Managerial Class Revisited." In *Intellectuals: Aesthetics, Politics, Academics*, ed. Bruce Robbins, 173-85. Minneapolis: University of Minnesota Press.

Ehrenreich, Barbara and John. 1979. "The Professional-Managerial Class." In *Between Labor and Capital*, ed. Pat Walker, 5-45. Boston: South End Press.

Ehrenreich, Barbara and John. 2013. *Death of a Yuppie Dream: The Rise and Fall of the Professional-Managerial Class*. New York: The Rosa Luxemburg Foundation.

Eidlin, Barry. 2020. "Whoever Wins, This Election Is Not the End of Trumpism." *Jacobin*, November 5. https://www.jacobinmag.com/2020/11/election-trumpism-trump-biden.

Eisenstein, Hester. 2018. "Querying Intersectionality." *Science & Society* 82(2): 248-61.

Ellefson, Lindsey. 2021. "Socialist Magazine Current Affairs Fires Most of Staff for Trying to Start a Worker Co-Op." *The Wrap*, August 18. https://www.thewrap.com/current-affairs-fires-staffers/.

Elizabeth, Lauren. 2021. "According to Nancy Pelosi, We Need a 'Strong' Republican Party." *Medium*, February 14. https://medium.com/discourse/according-to-nancy-pelosi-we-need-a-strong-republican-party-97fb9ef8e271.

Ember, Sydney. 2020a. "Bernie Sanders Predicted Revolution, Just Not This One." *The New York Times*, June 19. https://www.nytimes.com/2020/06/19/us/politics/bernie-sanders-protests.html.

Ember, Sydney. 2020b. "The Democratic Establishment Suddenly Loves Bernie Sanders." *The New York Times*, April 12. https://www.nytimes.com/2020/04/16/us/politics/bernie-sanders-joe-biden-democrats.html.

Endnotes. 2015. "Brown v. Ferguson." *Endnotes* (October): https://endnotes.org.uk/issues/4/en/endnotes-brown-v-ferguson.

Endnotes. 2020. "Onward Barbarians," *Endnotes* (December): https://endnotes.org.uk/other_texts/en/endnotes-onward-barbarians.

English, Micah and Joshua Kalla. 2021. "Racial Equality Frames and Public Policy Support: Survey Experimental Evidence." *Race and Class* (April 26): https://osf.io/tdkf3/.

Ettinger, Leonie. 2017. "Slavoj Žižek, Donald Trump, and the Left." *Platypus Review* #99 (September): https://platypus1917.org/2017/08/29/slavoj-zizek-donald-trump-left/.

Evelyn, Kenya. 2020. "Hillary Clinton says 'nobody likes' Bernie Sanders and criticizes 'culture around' him." *The Guardian*, January 21. https://www.theguardian.com/us-news/2020/jan/21/hillary-clinton-bernie-sanders-nobody-likes-him-hulu-documentary.

Ewen, Stewart. 2001 [1976]. *Captains of Consciousness: Advertising and the Social Roots of Consumer Culture*. New York: Basic Books

Fanon, Frantz. 1963 [1961]. *The Wretched of the Earth*, trans. Constance Farrington. New York: Grove Press.

Fanon, Frantz. 1967. *Black Skin, White Masks*, trans. Charles Lam Markmann. New York: Grove Press.

Fawbush, Esq., Joseph. 2020. "Vermont Law School Sued for Removing Artist's Murals." *Findlaw*, December 3. https://www.findlaw.com/legalblogs/greedy-associates/vermont-law-school-sued-for-removing-artists-murals/.

Fields, Karen and Barbara. 2012. *Racecraft: The Soul of Inequality in American Life*. London: Verso.

Finkel, Eli J., et al. 2020. "Political sectarianism in America: A poisonous cocktail of othering, aversion, and moralization poses a threat to democracy." *Science* 370(6516) (October 30): 533-6.

Finn, Daniel. 2020. "An Open Letter from SDS Veterans Haranguing Young Socialists to Back Biden Was a Bad Idea." *Jacobin*, April 17. https://www.jacobinmag.com/2020/04/sds-new-left-joe-biden-letter.

Fisher, Mark. 2009. *Capitalist Realism, Is there No Alternative?* Winchester: O Books.

Fisher, Mark. 2013. "Exiting the Vampire Castle." *Open Democracy*, November 24. https://www.opendemocracy.net/en/opendemocracyuk/exiting-vampire-castle/.

Fitzgerald, David and Gabriel Black. 2020. "Support for socialism jumps by nearly 10 percent among US youth amid pandemic depression." *World Socialist Web Site*, October 22. https://www.wsws.org/en/articles/2020/10/23/soci-o23.html.

Florida, Richard. 2002. *The Rise of the Creative Class, And How It's Transforming Work, Leisure, Community and Everyday Life*. New York: Basic Books.

Folbre, Nancy. 2021. *The Rise and Decline of Patriarchal Systems: Intersectional Political Economy*. London: Verso.

Foley, Barbara. 2018. "Intersectionality: A Marxist Critique." *Science & Society* 82:2 (April): 269-75.

Folley, Aris. 2021. "Clinton backs Trump impeachment but warns it 'won't remove white supremacy'." *The Hill*, January 11. https://thehill.com/blogs/blog-briefing-room/news/533674-clinton-backs-trump-impeachment-but-warns-it-wont-remove-white.

Ford, Glen. 2020. "The Corporations and Their Media Strangled Bernie, and Older Black Voters Tied the Knot." *Black Agenda Report*, March 12. https://www.blackagendareport.com/corporations-and-their-media-strangled-bernie-and-older-black-voters-tied-knot.

Fortune. 2020. "Briahna Joy Gray." *Fortune.* https://fortune.com/40-under-40/2020/briahna-joy-gray/.

Foundation for Individual Rights in Education. 2021. "Americans are really, really worried, says John McWhorter [audio]: So to Speak podcast." *YouTube,* January 28. https://www.youtube.com/watch?v=LLCX71sk_MU.

Frank, Thomas. 1997. *The Conquest of Cool: Business Culture, Counterculture, and the Rise of Hip Consumerism.* Chicago: University of Chicago Press.

Frank, Thomas. 2004. *What's the Matter with Kansas? How Conservatives Won the Heart of America.* New York: Metropolitan Books.

Frank, Thomas. 2016. *Listen, Liberal, or, What Ever Happened to the Party of the People?* New York: Henry Holt.

Frank, Thomas. 2020. *The People, NO: A Brief History of Anti-Populism.* New York: Metropolitan Books.

Frank, Thomas. 2021. "If the Wuhan-leak hypothesis is true, expect a political earthquake." *The Guardian,* June 1. https://www.theguardian.com/commentisfree/2021/jun/01/wuhan-coronavirus-lab-leak-covid-virus-origins-china.

Frase, Peter. 2014. "Stay Classy." *Jacobin,* June 26. https://jacobinmag.com/2014/06/stay-classy.

Fraser, Andrea. 2017. "Toward a Reflexive Resistance." *X-TRA* 20(2) (Winter): 21-37.

Fraser, Nancy. 2017. "From Progressive Neoliberalism to Trump – and Beyond." *American Affairs* 1(4) (Winter): 46-64.

Fraser, Nancy and Liza Featherstone. 2020. "Why Bernie Is the True Feminist Choice." *Jacobin,* February 10. https://jacobinmag.com/2020/02/bernie-sanders-feminism-2020-democratic-race-women.

Frazer, Charise. 2020. "Diddy Once Told Black America To #VoteOrDie. Now He's Flirting With The Idea of Staying Home In November." *Madame Noire,* April 29. https://madamenoire.com/1161384/diddy-once-told-black-america-to-voteordie-now-hes-flirting-with-the-idea-of-staying-home-in-november/.

Freeman, Hadley. 2016. " 'Don't play identity politics!' The primal scream of the straight white male." *The Guardian,* December 2. https://www.theguardian.com/commentisfree/2016/dec/02/identity-politics-donald-trump-white-men.

Friedersdorf, Conor. 2016. "Among the Pure at 'Bernie or Bust'." *The Atlantic,* July 27. https://www.theatlantic.com/politics/archive/2016/07/among-the-pure-at-bernie-or-bust/493094/.

Fuchs, Christian. 2014. *Digital Labour and Karl Marx.* London: Routledge.

Fukuyama, Francis. 2018. *Identity: The Demand for Dignity and the Politics of Recognition.* New York: Farrar, Straus and Giroux.

Gabbard, Tulsi. 2020. "Presidential candidates must also condemn election interference by US intelligence agencies." *The Hill,* February 27. https://thehill.com/blogs/congress-blog/politics/485051-tulsi-gabbard-presidential-candidates-must-also-condemn-election.

Garger, Kenneth. 2021. "San Francisco teacher writes in op-ed: Bernie Sanders' mittens a 'lesson in white privilege'." *New York Post*, February 2. https://nypost.com/2021/02/02/teacher-calls-bernie-sanders-mittens-lesson-in-white-privilege-in-op-ed/.

Gautney, Heather. 2018. *Crashing the Party: From the Bernie Sanders Campaign to a Progressive Movement*. London: Verso.

Gentzler, Sara. 2020. "AG Barr praises killing of Portland suspect Reinoehl in 'effort to restore law and order'." *The Olympian*, September 4. https://www.theolympian.com/news/local/crime/article245495910.html.

Gerbaudo, Paulo. 2017. *The Mask and the Flag: Populism, Citizenism and Global Protest*. Oxford: Oxford University Press.

Gilroy, Paul. 2002. *Against Race: Imagining Political Culture Beyond the Color Line*. Cambridge: Harvard University Press.

Gindin, Sam. 2004. "Unmaking Global Capitalism." *Jacobin*, June 1. https://jacobinmag.com/2014/06/unmaking-global-capitalism.

Girigharadas, Anand. 2019. "Bernie Sanders Wants to Change America. But He May Have to Change Himself First." *Time*, June 6. https://time.com/longform/bernie-sanders-2020/.

Glasser, Susan B. 2019. "Trump's Dark Preview of His 2020 Campaign." *The New Yorker*, February 6. https://www.newyorker.com/news/letter-from-trumps-washington/trump-vows-to-stop-america-from-turning-into-a-venezuelan-socialist-hellscape.

Glover, Michael. 2019. "Kara Walker's Monument to Monstrousness." *Hyperallergic*, October 5. https://hyperallergic.com/520353/kara-walkers-monument-to-monstrousness/.

Gordon, Michael R., Warren P. Strobel and Drew Hinshaw. 2021. "Intelligence on Sick Staff at Wuhan Lab Fuels Debate on COVID-19 Origin." *The Wall Street Journal*, May 23. https://www.wsj.com/articles/intelligence-on-sick-staff-at-wuhan-lab-fuels-debate-on-covid-19-origin-11621796228.

Gordon-Nesbitt, Rebecca. 2015. *To Defend the Revolution Is to Defend Culture: The Cultural Policy of the Cuban Revolution*. Oakland: PM Press.

Gorz, André. 1982 [1980]. *Farewell to the Working Class: An Essay on Post-Industrial Socialism*, trans. Michael Sonenscher. London: Pluto Press

Gouldner, Alvin W. 1979. *The Future of Intellectuals and the Rise of the New Class*. London: Macmillan.

Graeber, David. 2020. "The Center Blows Itself Up: Care and Spite in the 'Brexit Election'." *The New York Review of Books*, January 13. https://www.nybooks.com/daily/2020/01/13/the-center-blows-itself-up-care-and-spite-in-the-brexit-election/.

Gray, Briahna Joy. 2017a. "Bernie Sanders Doesn't Have a Black Problem – He Has a Pundit Problem." *Paste*, July 27. https://www.pastemagazine.com/articles/2017/07/bernie-sanders-doesnt-have-a-black-problemhe-has-a.html.

Gray, Briahna Joy. 2017b. "How Identity Became a Weapon Against the Left." *Current Affairs*, September 3. https://www.currentaffairs.org/2017/09/how-identity-became-a-weapon-against-the-left.

Greenwald, Glenn. 2016. "The 'Bernie Bros' Narrative: A Cheap Campaign Tactic Masquerading as Journalism and Social Activism." *The Intercept*, January 31. https://theintercept.com/2016/01/31/the-bernie-bros-narrative-a-cheap-false-campaign-tactic-masquerading-as-journalism-and-social-activism/.

Greenwald, Glenn. 2020. "Democrats and Their Media Allies Impugned Biden's Cognitive Fitness. Now They Feign Outrage." *The Intercept*, March 9. https://theintercept.com/2020/03/09/it-was-democrats-and-their-media-allies-who-impugned-bidens-cognitive-fitness-yet-now-feign-outrage/.

Guardian staff. 2019. "Democratic candidates reject Obama's warning of going too far." *The Guardian*, November 17. https://www.theguardian.com/us-news/2019/nov/17/democratic-candidates-obama-warns-going-too-far-left.

Guastella, Dustin. 2020a "Like It or Not, If We Run a Third Party, We Will Lose." *Jacobin*, April 17. https://www.jacobinmag.com/2020/04/third-party-bernie-sanders-democratic-socialism-elections.

Guastella, Dustin. 2020b. "The Populist Pundits." *Jacobin*, February 23. https://jacobinmag.com/2020/02/hill-tv-rising-populists-guide-2020-krystal-ball-saagar-enjeti-review.

Guastella, Dustin. 2020c. "We Need a Class War, Not a Culture War." *Jacobin*, May 25. https://www.jacobinmag.com/2020/05/we-need-a-class-war-not-a-cultural-war.

Guastella, Dustin. 2021. "Everyone Hates the Democrats." *Jacobin*, February 8. https://jacobinmag.com/2021/02/everyone-hates-the-democrats.

Haider, Asad. 2018. *Mistaken Identity: Race and Class in the Age of Trump*. London: Verso.

Halper, Katie. 2020a. "Chris Hedges & Gerald Horne + David Sirota on Amy Coney Barrett + Arun Gupta Live in Portland." *YouTube*, September 30. https://www.youtube.com/watch?v=SGpk1xSeqoI.

Halper, Katie. 2020b. "Matt Christman! Noam Chomsky! Michael Moore!" *YouTube*, October 28. https://www.youtube.com/watch?v=h8zkZ1PSW8A.

Halper, Katie. 2020c. "Woke Imperialism With Rania Khalek & Briahna Joy." *YouTube*, November 22. https://www.youtube.com/watch?v=IiI4xnRCOT8.

Hall, Stuart. 1988. "Brave New World." *Marxism Today* 39(10) (October): 24-9.

Hamilton, Conrad and Matt McManus. 2021. "In Defense of Slavoj Žižek." *Jacobin*, June 11. https://www.jacobinmag.com/2021/06/slavoj-zizek-leftist-philosophy-ideology-postmodernism-neoliberalism.

Hardt, Michael and Antonio Negri. 2000. Empire. Cambridge: Harvard University Press.

Hardt, Michael and Antonio Negri. 2017. *Assembly*. New York: Oxford University Press.

Harper's Editors. 2020. "A Letter on Justice and Open Debate." *Harper's*, July 7. https://harpers.org/a-letter-on-justice-and-open-debate/.

Harris, Meena. 2020. "Over 20,000 People Want to Rename the High School Maya Angelou Attended – After Her." *Glamour*, July 7. https://www.glamour.com/story/rename-george-washington-high-school-maya-angelou.

Harvard College Students for Bernie. 2020. "Cornel West, Philip Agnew, Michael Brooks, Esha Krishnaswamy | Class Warfare | Harvard." *YouTube*, January 31. https://www.youtube.com/watch?v=LVTDahs2gFQ.

Heath, Joseph and Andrew Potter. 2004. *The Rebel Sell: Why the Culture Can't Be Jammed*. Toronto: Harper Collins.

Hedges, Chris. 2010. *Death of the Liberal Class*. New York: Nation Books.

Henninger, Daniel. 2021. "Banning Critical Race Theory." *The Wall Street Journal*, June 2. https://www.wsj.com/articles/banning-critical-race-theory-11622670206.

Hepburn, Bob. 2021. "Can Green Party recover from racist-tinged charges?" *The Toronto Star*, April 7. https://www.thestar.com/opinion/star-columnists/2021/04/07/can-green-party-recover-from-racist-tinged-charges.html.

Herndon, Astead W. and Katie Glueck. 2020-21. "Biden Apologizes for Saying Black Voters 'Ain't Black' if They're Considering Trump." *The New York Times*, May 22/January 20. https://www.nytimes.com/2020/05/22/us/politics/joe-biden-black-breakfast-club.html.

Hill, Corey. 2021. "Florida just signed into law one of the most dangerous bills in America." *The Independent*, April 19. https://www.independent.co.uk/voices/florida-desantis-riot-bill-republicans-blm-b1833996.html.

Hill, The. 2020a. "Briahna Joy Gray: The Problem With Biden's Diverse Corporatist Appointments." *YouTube*, December 2. https://www.youtube.com/watch?v=qxLaA3NUSHM.

Hill, The. 2020b. "Cardi B endorses Joe Biden in livestream with Bernie Sanders." *YouTube*, April 14. https://www.youtube.com/watch?v=aQRuf_-TNhQ.

Hill, The. 2020c. "Diddy's SHOCKING message to Biden on behalf of Black Voters: 'I will hold vote HOSTAGE'." *YouTube*, April 30. https://www.youtube.com/watch?v=HkQTzLcRh68.

Hill, The. 2020d. "Krystal and Saagar: Andrew Yang SMEARED As Sexist For Telling Pelosi To Take Stimulus Deal." *YouTube*, October 13. https://www.youtube.com/watch?v=xmzyEF6GP2o.

Hill, The. 2020e. "Krystal Ball: Biden so WEAK establishment already blaming Bernie for his loss." *YouTube*, April 2. https://www.youtube.com/watch?v=B5UkNoCJGg4.

Hill, The. 2020f. "Krystal Ball: Why the left can't just roll over for Joe Biden, even if Bernie asks us to." *YouTube*, April 15. https://www.youtube.com/watch?v=dWxyEiTQGKA.

Hill, The. 2020g. "LIVE: Hill TV's Super Tuesday 2020 Results Coverage – HOUR ONE." *YouTube*, March 3. https://www.youtube.com/watch?v=qIPimoA2dVs.

Hirshman, Linda. 2020. "Opinion: I Believe Tara Reade. I'm Voting for Joe Biden Anyway." *The New York Times*, May 6. https://www.nytimes.com/2020/05/06/opinion/tara-reade-joe-biden-vote.html.

Hockett, Jeremy. 2005. "Brand 'W' and the Marketing of an American President: Or, Logos as Logos." *Westminster Papers in Communication and Culture* 2(2): 72-96.

Hofstadter, Richard. 2015. "Reflections on Violence in the United States" (1970). *The Baffler*, July. https://thebaffler.com/ancestors/reflections-violence-united-states.

Holberg Prize. 2019. "Slavoj Žižek: 'Why I Am Still a Communist'. The 2019 Holberg Debate with Slavoj Žižek & Tyler Cowen." *YouTube*, December 7. https://www.youtube.com/watch?v=bgPqk8-HPGQ.

Holmes, Edward C. et al. 2021. "The Origins of SARS-CoV-2: A Critical Review." *Zenodo*, July 7. https://zenodo.org/record/5075888#.YSfJky2cYW0.

Holtz-Bacha, Christina and Lynda Lee Kaid. 2006. "Political Advertising in International Comparison." In *The Sage Handbook of Political Advertising*, eds. Lynda Lee Kaid and Christina Holtz-Bacha, 3-13. London: Sage.

Hyland, Julia. 2021. "UK: Former MI6 chief behind faked 'evidence' for Iraq war leading anti-China Wuhan lab conspiracy." *World Socialist Web Site*, June 10. https://www.wsws.org/en/articles/2021/06/10/wuuk-j10.html.

Illing, Sean. 2021. " 'Wokeness is a problem and we all know it': James Carville on the state of Democratic politics." *Vox*, April 27. https://www.vox.com/22338417/james-carville-democratic-party-biden-100-days.

IntelligenceSquared Debates. 2020. "Identity Politics Debate: John McWhorter & Michael Eric Dyson." *YouTube*, December 14. https://www.youtube.com/watch?v=4YE8NMx2lY0.

Intercept, The. 2020a. "Mehdi Hasan and Noam Chomsky on Biden vs. Trump." *YouTube*, April 17. https://www.youtube.com/watch?v=39902cn5lX8.

Intercept, The. 2020b. "System Update With Glenn Greenwald – Liz Franczak and Kyle Kulinski." *YouTube*, April 1. https://www.youtube.com/watch?v=y3VGDDErnmk.

Ivey, Justin. 2020. "Diddy Blocks Kenny Burns On Instagram For Disagreeing With His Joe Biden Agenda." *HipHopDX*, April 29. https://hiphopdx.com/news/id.55660/title.diddy-blocks-kenny-burns-on-instagram-for-disagreeing-with-his-joe-biden-agenda.

Jackson, Peter. 1993. "Towards a Cultural Politics of Consumption." In *Mapping the Futures: Local Cultures, Global Change*, edited by Jon Bird et al., 207-28. London: Routledge.

Jacobin. 2021a. "Antiracism Can't Overcome Capitalism – Adolph Reed and Walter Benn Michaels." *YouTube*, August 5. https://www.youtube.com/watch?v=QYuzFZfsxEY.

Jacobin. 2021b. "What Did the Racial Reckoning Achieve? – Cedric Johnson." *YouTube*, June 25. https://www.youtube.com/watch?v=mldXcOhctKo.

Jacobin Magazine. 2020a. "Adolph Reed, Cedric Johnson, Willie Legette & Michael Brooks 'Bernie, South Carolina & Black Voters'." *YouTube*, April 10. https://www.youtube.com/watch?v=qwnb0xParBM&list=PLxlNhP2fokUKLSP2cQ38b9xymXZInHzRn&index=3&t=0s.

Jacobin Magazine. 2020b. "Leo Panitch on the Political Thought of His Mentor, Ralph Miliband (Stay At Home #29)." *YouTube*, April 27. https://www.youtube.com/watch?v=0BJR3xfmgA4.

Jacobin Magazine. 2020c. "Walter Benn Michaels & Jennifer Pan on the Trouble with Diversity." *YouTube*, July 3. https://www.youtube.com/watch?v=HT41gzsN7Ik.

Jacobin Magazine. 2020d. "What Bernie accomplished & where we go next with Amber Frost, Michael Brooks, Meagan Day & Matt Karp." *YouTube*, April 8. https://www.youtube.com/watch?v=qzTdnvkvUJo.

Jacobin Magazine. 2020e. "What's Unique About The American Party System and How Socialists Can Beat It (Stay At Home #24)." *YouTube*, April 21. https://www.youtube.com/watch?v=YEwAaE5jquw.

Jameson, Fredric. 1992. *The Geopolitical Aesthetic: Cinema and Space in the World System*. Bloomington: Indiana University Press.

Jardina, Ashley. 2019. *White Identity Politics*. Cambridge: Cambridge University Press.

Johnson, Cedric. 2016. "Fear and Pandering in the Palmetto State." *Jacobin*, February 29. https://www.jacobinmag.com/2016/02/sanders-clinton-south-carolina-primary-black-voters-firewall/.

Johnson, Cedric. 2017. "The Panthers Can't Save Us Now." *Catalyst* 1(1) (Spring): https://catalyst-journal.com/vol1/no1/panthers-cant-save-us-cedric-johnson.

Johnson, Cedric. 2020a. "Don't Let Blackwashing Save the Investor Class." *Jacobin*, June 24. https://jacobinmag.com/2020/06/blackwashing-corporations-woke-capitalism-protests.

Johnson, Cedric. 2020b. "The Triumph of Black Lives Matter and Neoliberal Redemption." *Nonsite*, June 9. https://nonsite.org/editorial/the-triumph-of-black-lives-matter-and-neoliberal-redemption.

Johnson, Jason. 2021. "Critical Race Theory Is a Convenient Target for Conservatives." *Slate*, June 12. https://slate.com/news-and-politics/2021/06/critical-race-theory-ibram-kendi-racism-racists.html.

Jones, Elliott. 2020. "Op-Ed: Which Monuments Should Come Down And What Should Replace Them?" *SFist*, July 20. https://sfist.com/2020/07/27/op-ed-taxpayers-continue-to-fund-racist-symbols-and-messaging/.

Jordan, Roger. 2020a. "Trudeau exploits coronavirus crisis to strengthen Canada-US imperialist alliance." *World Socialist Web Site*, March 14. https://www.wsws.org/en/articles/2020/03/14/trud-m14.html.

Jordan, Roger. 2020b. "Why is Canada's ruling elite deploying the military amid the COVID-19 pandemic?" *World Socialist Web Site*, May 8. https://www.wsws.org/en/articles/2020/05/08/caco-m08.html.

Kaid, Lynda Lee. 2006. "Political Advertising in the United States." In *The Sage Handbook of Political Advertising*, eds. Lynda Lee Kaid and Christina Holtz-Bacha, 37-51. London, Sage.

Kangal, Kaan. 2020. "Engels's Emergentist Dialectics." *Monthly Review*, November 1. https://monthlyreview.org/2020/11/01/engelss-emergentist-dialectics/.

Kaplan, Thomas. 2020. "Biden's response to voters concerned about socialism: 'I beat the socialist.'" *The New York Times*, September 22. https://www.nytimes.com/2020/09/22/us/politics/bidens-response-to-voters-concerned-about-socialism-i-beat-the-socialist.html.

Kendi, Ibram X. 2021a. *Twitter*, January 6. https://twitter.com/dribram/status/1346903075597000705?lang=en.

Kendi, Ibram X. 2021b. "This Is the Black Renaissance." *Time*, February 3. https://time.com/5932842/ibram-kendi-black-renaissance/.

KETKnbc. 2020. "George W. Bush calls for care and compassion during pandemic." *YouTube*, May 3. https://www.youtube.com/watch?v=knykOfcsYKE.

Khachaturian, Rafael. 2020. "The Emancipation of All: Marxism in the Age of Identity Politics." *Verso Blog*, July 29. https://www.versobooks.com/blogs/4808-the-emancipation-of-all-marxism-in-the-age-of-identity-politics.

Klein, Naomi. 2007. *The Shock Doctrine: The Rise of Disaster Capitalism*. Toronto: Random House.

Klein, Naomi. 2014. *This Changes Everything: Capitalism vs. The Climate*. Toronto: Knopf.

Klein, Naomi. 2021. "The Meaning of the Mittens: Five Possibilities." *The Intercept*, January 21. https://theintercept.com/2021/01/21/inauguration-bernie-sanders-mittens/.

Koopmans, Marion et al. 2021. "Origin of SARS-CoV-2: window is closing for key scientific studies." *Nature*, August 25. https://www.nature.com/articles/d41586-021-02263-6.

Kovalik, Dan. 2021. *Cancel This Book: The Progressive Case Against Cancel Culture*. New York: Hot Books.

Kracauer, Siegfried. 1998 [1930]. *The Salaried Masses: Duty and Distraction in Weimar Germany*. Translated by Quintin Hoare. London: Verso.

Kroker, Arthur. 1994. *Data Trash: The Theory of the Virtual Class*. Montreal: New World Perspectives.

Kuznetsov, Dmitry and Milan Ismangil. 2020. "YouTube Praxis? On BreadTube and the Digital Propagation of Socialist Thought." *tripleC* 18(1): 204-18.

Laclau, Ernesto. 1979. *Politics and Ideology in Marxist Theory: Capitalism, Fascism, Populism*. London: Verso.

Laclau, Ernesto and Chantal Mouffe. 1985. *Hegemony and Socialist Strategy: Towards a Radical Democratic Politics*. London: Verso.

Lancaster, Roger. 2020. "How Not to Tackle COVID-19: Butler's Anticapitalism." *Nonsite*, April 10. https://nonsite.org/editorial/how-not-to-tackle-covid-19-butlers-anticapitalism.

Lantier, Alex and Andre Damon. 2020. "The response of the ruling elite to the coronavirus pandemic: Malign neglect." *World Socialist Web Site*, March 14. https://www.wsws.org/en/articles/2020/03/14/pers-m14.html.

Lefebvre, Henri. 1976. *De l'État. 1 L'État dans le monde moderne*. Paris: Union Générale d'Éditions, 10/18.

Lefebvre, Henri. 2020 [1975]. *Hegel, Marx, Nietzsche, Or the Realm of Shadows*. Translated by David Fernbach. London: Verso Books

Léger, Marc James. 2018. *Don't Network: The Avant Garde after Networks*. Wivenhoe: Minor Compositions.

Léger, Marc James. 2019. *Vanguardia: Socially Engaged Art and Theory*. Manchester: Manchester University Press.

Leigh, Genevieve. 2020. "Democratic Socialists of America goes all in for Biden." *World Socialist web Site*, October 16. https://www.wsws.org/en/articles/2020/10/17/dsoc-o17.html.

Lenin, Vladimir. 1988 [1902]. *What Is to Be Done? Burning Questions of Our Movement*, trans. George Hanna. London: Penguin Books

Lenin, Vladimir. 2014 [1917]. *State and Revolution*. Chicago: Haymarket Books

Lewis, Hollis. 2016. *The Politics of Everybody: Feminism, Queer Theory, and Marxism at the Intersection*. London: Zed Books.

Lilla, Mark. 2017. *The Once and Future Liberal: After Identity Politics*. New York: HarperCollins.

Liu, Catherine. 2021. *Virtue Hoarders: The Case Against the Professional-Managerial Class*. Minneapolis: University of Minnesota Press.

Lizza, Ryan. 2019. "Waiting for Obama: The Democratic establishment is counting on him to stop Trump and, perhaps, stave off Bernie as well. But can his cerebral politics still galvanize voters in an age of extremes?" *Politico*, November 26. https://www.politico.com/news/magazine/2019/11/26/barack-obama-2020-democrats-candidates-biden-073025.

Lock, Samantha. 2020. "Top Defender: What did Donald Trump say about Kyle Rittenhouse." *The Sun*, September 1. https://www.thesun.co.uk/news/12548981/donald-trump-defends-kyle-rittenhouse-gunman/.

London, Eric. 2016. "The myth of the reactionary white working class." *World Socialist Web Site*, November 12. https://www.wsws.org/en/articles/2016/11/12/pers-n12.html.

London, Eric. 2020a. "The end of Sanders' campaign deepens crisis in Democratic Socialists of America." *World Socialist Web Site*, April 11. https://www.wsws.org/en/articles/2020/04/11/sand-a11.html.

London, Eric. 2020b. "2020 election results explode the identity politics narrative." *World Socialist Web Site*, November 6. https://www.wsws.org/en/articles/2020/11/06/pers-no6.html.

London, Eric. 2021. "Alexandria Ocasio-Cortez and 'bad faith actors'." *World Socialist Web Site*, March 30. https://www.wsws.org/en/articles/2021/03/31/resp-m31.html.

Lopez, German. 2017. "The battle over identity politics, explained." *Vox*, August 17. https://www.vox.com/identities/2016/12/2/13718770/identity-politics.

Los Angeles Times. 2020. "Sarah Silverman supports Bernie Sanders in Los Angeles." *YouTube*, March 2. https://www.youtube.com/watch?v=U-KepKr_lio.

Lowrey, Annie. 2020. "The Fed Did Not Just 'Spend' $1.5 Trillion." *The Atlantic*, March 13. https://www.theatlantic.com/ideas/archive/2020/03/federal-reserve-trying-stop-financial-crisis/607987/.

Lury, Celia and Alan Warde. 1997. "Investment in the Imaginary Consumer: Conjectures Regarding Power, Knowledge and Advertising." In *Buy This Book: Studies in Advertising and Consumption*, eds. Mica Nava et al., 87-102. London: Routledge.

Lütticken, Sven. 2018. "Cultural Marxists Like Us." *Afterall* 46(1) (September): 66-75.

Maclean's Editors. 2020. "Governor General Julie Payette's 2020 Throne Speech: Full transcript." *Maclean's*, September. https://www.macleans.ca/news/throne-speech-2020-governor-general-julie-payette-transcript/.

Maisano, Chris. 2019. "Democracy's Morbid Symptoms." *Catalyst* 3:2 (Summer): https://catalyst-journal.com/vol3/no2/democracys-morbid-symptoms.

Maisano, Chris. 2020. "No, the Racial Justice Protests Are Not at Odds With Class Politics." *Jacobin*, June 26. https://jacobinmag.com/2020/06/ross-douthat-nyt-racial-justice-protests-bernie-sanders/.

Maisano, Chris. 2021. "How Joseph Stalin Became a Bolshevik: An Interview with Ronald Suny." *Jacobin,* May 29. https://www.jacobinmag.com/2021/05/stalin-ronald-suny-book-interview-passage-to-revolution-georgia-russian-revolution.

Malik, Abdullah and Bushan D. Sudhakar. 2014. "Brand Positioning Through Celebrity Endorsement – A Review Contribution to Brand Literature." *International Review of Management and Marketing* 4(4): 259-75.

Manchester, Julia. 2019. "Biden tells supporters: 'I'm not going nuts'." *The Hill*, August 26. https://thehill.com/homenews/campaign/458817-biden-tells-supporters-after-flub-im-not-going-nuts.

Marcetic, Branco. 2019a. "Actually, the Democrats Don't Care About Identity." *Jacobin*, March 9. https://jacobinmag.com/2019/03/democratic-party-identity-politics-ilhan-omar-bernie-sanders.

Marcetic, Branco. 2019b. "Yet Another Round of Clinton Smears." *Jacobin*, December 10. https://jacobinmag.com/2019/12/hillary-clinton-howard-stern-interview-bernie-sanders.

Marcetic, Branco. 2020a. "Joe Biden Has Built a Career on Betraying Black Voters." *Jacobin*, March 5. https://www.jacobinmag.com/2020/03/joe-biden-black-voters-african-americans-betrayal.

Marcetic, Branco. 2020b. *Yesterday's Man: The Case Against Joe Biden*. London: Verso.

Marchese, David. 2020. "Henry Gates Jr. on what really happened at Obama's 'beer summit'." *The New York Times*, February 3. https://www.nytimes.com/interactive/2020/02/03/magazine/henry-louis-gates-jr-interview.html?auth=login-email&login=email.

Marcuse, Herbert. 1977. *The Aesthetic Dimension: Toward a Critique of Marxist Aesthetics*. Boston: Beacon Press.

Marcuse, Hebert. 2009. "The Struggle Against Liberalism in the Totalitarian View of the State." (1934). In *Negations: Essays in Critical Theory*, trans. Jeremy J. Shapiro, 1-30. London: MayFly Books.

Martin, Patrick. 2019a. "Hunter Biden made $850,000 on board of Ukraine gas company." *World Socialist Web Site*, October 1. https://www.wsws.org/en/articles/2019/10/01/bide-o01.html.

Martin, Patrick. 2019b. "Joe Biden: A familiar face, a deeply reactionary record." *World Socialist Web Site*, September 23. https://www.wsws.org/en/articles/2019/09/23/bide-s23.html.

Masket, Seth. 2020. *Learning from Loss: The Democrats, 2016-2020*. Cambridge: Cambridge University Press.

Mateus, Benjamin. 2021. "How science demolishes the right-wing fiction of a Wuhan 'lab leak' as the source of coronavirus." *World Socialist Web Site*, June 21. https://www.wsws.org/en/articles/2021/06/21/sci1-j21.html.

Marx, Karl. 1978. "Critique of the Gotha Program" (1891). In *The Marx-Engels Reader*, ed. Robert C. Tucker, 525-41. New York: W.W. Norton.

McIntosh, Don. 2021. "Talking Socialism | Catching up with AOC." *Democratic Left*, March 19. https://www.dsausa.org/democratic-left/aoc/.

McKelvey, Tara. 2021. "Capitol riots: Trump says his speech was totally appropriate." *BBC News*, January 12. https://www.bbc.com/news/world-us-canada-55638017.

McWhorter, John. 2021. *Woke Racism: How a New Religion Has Betrayed Black America*. New York: Random House.

Mealy, Dominic. 2020. "'To Halt Climate Change, We Need an Ecological Leninism': An Interview with Andreas Malm." *Jacobin*, June 15. https://www.jacobinmag.com/2020/06/andreas-malm-coronavirus-covid-climate-change.

Mediasanctuary. 2020. "Chris Hedges 'The Politics of Cultural Despair'." *YouTube*, October 18. https://www.youtube.com/watch?v=GxSN4ip_F6M.

Meyer, David. 2019. "'A Pathological Liar:' Bernie Sanders Attacks Trump as He Officially Launches His 2020 Run." *Fortune*, February 19. http://fortune.com/2019/02/19/bernie-sanders-2020-campaign-launch/.

Meyerson, Gregory. 2000. "Rethinking Black Marxism: Reflections on Cedric Robinson and Others." *Cultural Logic* #6 (Spring): https://ojs.library.ubc.ca/index.php/clogic/article/view/192628/189186.

Meyerson, Gregory. 2009. "Post-Marxism as Compromise Formation." *Cultural Logic* #16 (January): https://ojs.library.ubc.ca/index.php/clogic/article/view/191554.

Michael Brooks Show, The. 2020a. "UNLOCKED PANEL 2 THE MICHAEL BROOKS TRIBUTE SERIES Harvey Kaye, Adolph Reed Jr., Touré Reed." *YouTube*, December 15. https://www.youtube.com/watch?v=eMLotiB-VwQ.

Michael Brooks Show, The. 2020b. "Special: Third-Party Politics? Part 1 ft. Adolph Reed Jr." *YouTube*, April 16 https://www.youtube.com/watch?v=EcXxwar9Z9Y.

Michaels, Walter Benn. 2004. *The Shape of the Signifier: 1967 to the End of History*. Princeton: Princeton University Press.

Michaels, Walter Benn. 2006. *The Trouble with Diversity: How We Learned to Love Identity and Ignore Inequality*. New York: Metropolitan Books.

Michaels, Walter Benn and Adolph Reed Jr. 2020. "The Trouble with Disparity." *Nonsite*, September 10. https://nonsite.org/the-trouble-with-disparity/.

Michallon, Clémence. 2019. "Michael Moore says Michelle Obama should run against Trump in 2020." *The Independent*, August 1. https://www.independent.co.uk/arts-entertainment/films/news/michael-moore-michelle-obama-donald-trump-presidential-election-2020-run-a9035126.html.

Miller, Jenni. 2016. "Sarah Silverman Remains Baffled by 'Bernie or Bust' Folks." *The Cut*, October 1. https://www.thecut.com/2016/10/sarah-silverman-baffled-by-bernie-or-bust-supporters.html.

Mills, C. Wright. 1951. *White Collar: The American Middle Classes*. New York: Oxford University Press.

Moller-Nielsen, Thomas. 2012. "What Is Žižek For?" *Current Affairs*, October 18. https://www.currentaffairs.org/2019/10/what-is-zizek-for.

Moran, Marie. 2018. "Identity and Identity Politics: A Cultural Materialist History." *Historical Materialism* 26(2) (July): http://www.historicalmaterialism.org/articles/identity-and-identity-politics.

Moreno, J. Edward. 2020. "Obama praises Sanders in Biden endorsement." *The Hill*, April 14. https://thehill.com/homenews/campaign/492708-obama-praises-sanders-in-biden-endorsement.

Morris, Meaghan. 1988. "Banality in Cultural Studies," *Discourse* 10(2): 3-29.

Mouffe, Chantal. 2018. *For a Leftist Populism*. London: Verso.

Murray, Douglas. 2019. *The Madness of Crowds: Gender, Race and Identity*. London: Bloomsbury.

Nagle, Angela. 2017. *Kill All Normies: Online Culture Wars from 4chan and Tumblr to Trump and the Alt-Right*. Winchester: Zero Books.

Nagle, Angela. 2018. "The Left Case Against Open Borders." *American Affairs* 2(4) (Winter): https://americanaffairsjournal.org/2018/11/the-left-case-against-open-borders/.

Nagle, Angela and Michael Tracey. 2020. "First as Tragedy, Then as Farce: The Collapse of the Sanders Campaign and the 'Fusionist' Left." *American Affairs* IV(2) (Summer): https://americanaffairsjournal.org/2020/05/first-as-tragedy-then-as-farce/.

Nash, Jennifer C. 2014. "Institutionalizing the Margins." *Social Text* 32(1) (Spring): 45-65.

Negt, Oskar and Alexander Kluge. 1993 [1972]. *Public Sphere and Experience: Toward an Analysis of the Bourgeois and Proletarian Public Sphere*, trans. Peter Labanyi et al. Minneapolis: University of Minnesota Press

New Discourses. 2021. "Hegel, Wokeness, and the Dialectical Faith of Leftism." *YouTube*, May 28. https://www.youtube.com/watch?v=uf4R0gX7g3w.

New York Times Editors. 2020. "National Exit Polls: How Different Groups Voted." *The New York Times*, November 4. https://www.nytimes.com/interactive/2020/11/03/us/elections/exit-polls-president.html.

Ngai, Sianne. 2005. "The Cuteness of the Avant-Garde." *Critical Inquiry* 31(4) (Summer): 811-47.

Nguyen, Lananh and Tyler Pager. 2019. "Elizabeth Warren Starts Winning Begrudging Respect on Wall Street." *Bloomberg News*, July 3. https://www.bloomberg.com/news/articles/2019-07-03/elizabeth-warren-wins-respect-in-unlikeliest-place-wall-street.

Niemuth, Niles. 2021. "Time magazine and Ibram X. Kendi promote a race-obsessed, money-hungry 'Black Renaissance'." *World Socialist Web Site*, February 16. https://www.wsws.org/en/articles/2021/02/17/time-f17.html.

Nix, Naomi. 2020. "Trump Tells Violent, Far-Right Group: 'Stand Back and Stand By'." *Bloomberg*, September 30. https://www.bloomberg.com/news/articles/2020-09-30/trump-proud-boys-debate-stand-back-stand-by.

Nogales C., Pamela C. 2020. "The Cancel Wars: The Legacy of the Cultural Turn in the Age of Trump." *Platypus* #131 (November): https://platypus1917.org/2020/11/01/the-cancel-wars-the-legacy-of-the-cultural-turn-in-the-age-of-trump/.

North, David and Thomas Mackaman, eds. 2021. *The New York Times' 1619 Project and the Racialist Falsification of History*. Oak Park: Mehring Books.

Not Bill Murray. 2020. *Twitter*, March 28. https://twitter.com/StayWonked/status/1243906297721913346.

Obama, Michelle. 2021. " 'Unity With Purpose.' Amanda Gorman and Michelle Obama Discuss Art, Identity and Optimism." *Time*, February 4. https://time.com/5933596/amanda-gorman-michelle-obama-interview/.

O'Connor, Brendan. 2021. "When the Party's Over: Organizing after Bernie." *The Baffler* #57, May 2021. https://thebaffler.com/salvos/when-the-partys-over-oconnor#footnote1.

O'Connor, Patrick. 2021. "Australia's Murdoch media and the Wuhan COVID-19 lab conspiracy theory." *World Socialist Web Site*, June 9. https://www.wsws.org/en/articles/2021/06/09/mark-j09.html.

Palast, Greg. 2020. *How Trump Stole 2020: The Hunt for America's Vanished Voters*. New York: Seven Stories Press.

Palma, Bethania. 2020. "Did Activist Shaun King Say 'White Jesus' Statues Should Come Down?" *Snopes*, June 24. https://www.snopes.com/fact-check/shaun-king-jesus-statue/.

Parenti, Christian. 2020. "The Surprising Geography of Police Killings: Back-of-the-Napkin Calculations on Race, Region, and Violence." *Nonsite*, July 9. https://nonsite.org/the-surprising-geography-of-police-killings-back-of-the-napkin-calculations-on-race-region-and-violence/.

Park Center for Independent Media. 2021. "Recognize Race Reductionism with Scholars of Sociology, History." *YouTube*, May 26. https://www.youtube.com/watch?v=nwCSsoT5Tbk.

Parton, Heather Digby. 2020. "Donald Trump unmasked: Culture-war nihilism is his last line of defense." *Salon*, May 29. https://www.salon.com/2020/05/29/donald-trump-unmasked-culture-war-nihilism-is-his-last-line-of-defense/.

Pelosi, Nancy. 2021. "Press Release: Transcript of Pelosi Weekly Press Conference Today." *Speaker.gov*, January 7. https://www.speaker.gov/newsroom/1721-1.

Pengelly, Martin. 2021. "Nancy Pelosi rebukes Ilhan Omar for tweet on Israel, Hamas and Taliban." *The Guardian*, June 10. https://www.theguardian.com/us-news/2021/jun/10/ilhan-omar-democrats-harassment-silencing-israel-hamas-taliban.

People's Forum NYC, The. 2020. "Dr. Michael Hudson: Economic Lessons for 2020." *YouTube*, January 10. https://www.youtube.com/watch?v=nluLNA30e8k.

Peterson, Jordan B. 2019. "Marxism: Zizek/Peterson: Official Video." *YouTube*, May 15. https://www.youtube.com/watch?v=lsWndfzuOc4.

Phillips, Steve. 2016. *Brown Is the New Black: How the Demographics Revolution Has Created a New American Majority*. New York: The New Press.

Pitner, Barrett Holmes. 2016. "The White Entitlement of Some Sanders Supporters." *The Daily Beast*, June 16. https://www.thedailybeast.com/the-white-entitlement-of-some-sanders-supporters.

Pluckrose, Helen and James Lindsay. 2020. *Cynical Theories: How Activist Scholarship Made Everything About Race, Gender, and Identity – and Why This Harms Everybody*. Durham: Pitchstone Publishing.

Pod Save America. 2020. "Barack Obama on 2020." *Crooked*, October 14. https://crooked.com/podcast/barack-obama-on-2020/.

Polanyi, Karl. 1944. *The Great Transformation*. New York: Farrar & Rinehart.

Political Science SDSU. 2020. "What Is Left of American Democracy on the Eve of the 2020 Elections? David North & Adolph Reed." *YouTube*, October 29. https://www.youtube.com/watch?v=Ibzsr81XhnQ.

Politics and Prose. 2018. "Bernie Sanders, 'Where We Go From Here.'" *YouTube*, November 29. https://www.youtube.com/watch?v=7Q_3qPWlX2s.

Pountain, Dick and David Robins. 2000. *Cool Rules: Anatomy of an Attitude*. London: Reaktion Books.

Prashad, Vijay. 2019. "The U.S. 12-Step Method to Conduct Regime Change." *Common Dreams*, February 1. https://www.commondreams.org/views/2019/02/01/us-12-step-method-conduct-regime-change.

Press, Michael. 2020. "Who Really Owns the Hagia Sophia?" *Hyperallergic*, July 28. https://hyperallergic.com/578925/who-really-owns-hagia-sophia/.

Ralph Nader Radio Hour. 2020. "How To Fix Our Broken Democracy." *YouTube*, July 4. https://www.youtube.com/watch?v=NWBnarQkA6s.

Ralph Nader Radio Hour. 2021. "Eugenics/Wuhan Lab Leak?/Donziger Update." *YouTube*, August 14. https://www.youtube.com/watch?v=rytcwf-zYPQ.

Rancière, Jacques. 2004 [2000]. *The Politics of Aesthetics*, trans. Gabriel Rockhill. London: Continuum

Re, Gregg. 2019. "Ocasio-Cortez says Trump 'scared' after he vows America will 'never be a socialist country'." *Fox News*, February 5. https://www.foxnews.com/politics/trump-vows-america-will-never-be-a-socialist-country.

Real Time with Bill Maher. 2020. "New Rule: Take the Money and Run | Real Time with Bill Maher (HBO)." *YouTube*, March 6. https://www.youtube.com/watch?v=mTbfxNoRDBU.

Reed Jr., Adolph. 2000. *Class Notes: Posing as Politics and Other Thoughts on the American Scene*. New York: The New Press.

Reed Jr., Adolph. 2015. "From Jenner to Dolezal: One Trans Good, the Other Not So Much." *Common Dreams*, June 15. https://www.commondreams.org/views/2015/06/15/jenner-dolezal-one-trans-good-other-not-so-much.

Reed Jr., Adolph. 2016a. "Adolph Reed on Sanders, Coates, and Reparations." *New Politics*, February 5. https://newpol.org/adolph-reed-sanders-coates-and-reparations/.

Reed Jr., Adolph. 2016b. "Splendors and Miseries of the Antiracist 'Left'." *Nonsite*, November 6. https://nonsite.org/editorial/splendors-and-miseries-of-the-antiracist-left-2.

Reed Jr., Adolph. 2016c. "Vote for the Lying Neoliberal Warmonger: It's Important." *Common Dreams*, August 18. https://www.commondreams.org/views/2016/08/18/vote-lying-neoliberal-warmonger-its-important#.

Reed Jr., Adolph. 2018. "Which Side Are You On?" *Common Dreams*, December 23. https://www.commondreams.org/views/2018/12/23/which-side-are-you.

Reed Jr., Adolph. 2019. "The Myth of Class Reductionism." *The New Republic*, September 25. https://newrepublic.com/article/154996/myth-class-reductionism.

Reed Jr, Adolph. 2021. "Why Black Lives Matter Can't Be Co-opted." *Nonsite*, July 23. https://nonsite.org/why-black-lives-matter-cant-be-co-opted/.

Reed Jr., Adolph and Merlin Chowkwanyun. 2012. "Race, Class, Crisis: The Discourse of Racial Disparity and Its Analytical Discontents." *Socialist Register*, 149-75.

Reed, Touré F. 2020a. *Toward Freedom: The Case Against Race Reductionism*. London: Verso.

Reed, Touré F. 2020b. "Why I'm Still Thinking About the Amy Cooper 'Black Birder' Episode in Central Park." *Jacobin*, June 4. https://www.jacobinmag.com/2020/06/christian-cooper-amy-central-park-racism-black-birder.

Relman, Eliza. 2019. "Obama indirectly rebukes Bernie Sanders and Elizabeth Warren by warning donors not to be 'deluded' into thinking voters want radical change." *Business Insider*, November 18. https://www.businessinsider.sg/obama-warns-donors-not-be-deluded-pushing-radical-change-2019-11/.

Rice, Susan. 2020. *Twitter*, March 2. https://twitter.com/ambassadorrice/status/1234575446714523654?lang=en.

Robinson, Nathan J. 2019. *Why You Should Be a Socialist*. New York: Macmillan.

Robinson, Nathan J. 2020. "Democrats, You Really Do Not Want to Nominate Joe Biden." *Current Affairs*, March 7. https://www.currentaffairs.org/2020/03/democrats-you-really-do-not-want-to-nominate-joe-biden.

Rocha, Chuck. 2020. *Tío Bernie: The Inside Story of How Bernie Sanders Brought Latinos to the Political Revolution*. Washington, D.C.: Strong Arm Press.

Roediger, David. 1991. *The Wages of Whiteness: Race and the Making of the American Working Class*. London: Verso.

Roediger, David. 2017a. *Class, Race, and Marxism*. London: Verso.

Roediger, David. 2017b. "Who's Afraid of the White Working Class? Joan C. Williams's 'White Working Class: Overcoming Class Cluelessness in America'." *Los Angeles Review of Books*, May 17. https://lareviewofbooks.org/article/whos-afraid-of-the-white-working-class-on-joan-c-williamss-white-working-class-overcoming-class-cluelessness-in-america/.

Salem, Sara. 2016. "Intersectionality and Its Discontents: Intersectionality as traveling theory." *European Journal of Women's Studies* 25(1): 1-16.

Sanders, Bernie. 2010. "Bernie Sanders: The U.S. Must Stop Being an Apologist for the Netanyahu Government." *The New York Times*, May 14. https://www.nytimes.com/2021/05/14/opinion/bernie-sanders-israel-palestine-gaza.html.

Sanders, Bernie. 2016. *Our Revolution: A Future to Believe In*. New York: St. Martin's Press.

Sanders, Bernie. 2017. *Bernie Sanders Guide to Political Revolution*. New York: Henry Holt.

Sanders, Bernie. 2018. *Where We Go From Here: Two Years in the Resistance*. New York: Thomas Dunne.

Sanders Channel, Bernie. 2016a. "America | Bernie Sanders." *YouTube*, January 21. https://www.youtube.com/watch?v=2nwRiuh1Cug.

Sanders Channel, Bernie. 2016b. "It's Not Over | Bernie Sanders." *YouTube*, February 11. https://www.youtube.com/watch?v=Syln8IkOIqc.

Sanders Channel, Bernie. 2016c. "Sons of New York | Bernie Sanders." *YouTube*, April 16. https://www.youtube.com/watch?v=oXRxZyTVOUI.

Sanders Channel, Bernie. 2019a. "Bennett College Town Hall." *YouTube*, September 20. https://www.youtube.com/watch?v=tW9V7eWbZbg.

Sanders Channel, Bernie. 2019b. "Bernie x Cardi B." *YouTube*, August 15. https://www.youtube.com/watch?time_continue=1&v=p1ubTsrZFBU.

Sanders Channel, Bernie. 2019c. "Bernie & Killer Mike: 2020." *YouTube*, August 29. https://www.youtube.com/watch?v=EHps9UsJsko.
Sanders Channel, Bernie. 2019d. "Big Us | Bernie Sanders." *YouTube*, November 26. https://www.youtube.com/watch?v=tg5gfKqcFv8.
Sanders Channel, Bernie. 2020a. "A Different Kind of Campaign." *YouTube*, March 3. https://www.youtube.com/watch?v=phajOtD6L7o.
Sanders Channel, Bernie. 2020b. "Arab Americans in Michigan Are All in for Bernie." *YouTube*, March 8. https://www.youtube.com/watch?v=jYnW89T_OVY.
Sanders Channel, Bernie. 2020c. "Barbara Smith Endorses Bernie Sanders for President." *YouTube*, February 3. https://www.youtube.com/watch?v=6hMOP2-iVpY.
Sanders Channel, Bernie. 2020d. "Dalhi | Bernie Sanders." *YouTube*, February 18. https://www.youtube.com/watch?v=FLGC_GzdnVU.
Sanders Channel, Bernie. 2020e. "Hear the Bern Episode 43 | Origin of Identity Politics (w/ Barbara Smith)." *YouTube*, February 7. https://www.youtube.com/watch?v=avP9VbFxDVU.
Sanders Channel, Bernie. 2020f. "Hear the Bern Episode 44 | Big Tents & Iowa." *YouTube*, February 13. https://www.youtube.com/watch?v=Ao7_eY1SFqo.
Sanders Channel, Bernie. 2020g. "Investing in HBCUs." *YouTube*, February 28. https://www.youtube.com/watch?v=ShApSYt7zlc.
Sanders Channel, Bernie. 2020h. "Laura Gómez Endorses Bernie." *YouTube*, March 17. https://www.youtube.com/watch?v=Zj1AXRmpBwg.
Sanders Channel, Bernie. 2020i. "Let's Elect the First Jewish President." *YouTube*, February 24. https://www.youtube.com/watch?v=1IK1tQdtV1Y.
Sanders Channel, Bernie. 2020j. "LOS ANGELES RALLY WITH PUBLIC ENEMY RADIO." *YouTube*, March 1. https://www.youtube.com/watch?v=Tz48E8hzUX4.
Sanders Channel, Bernie. 2020k. "Matt McGorry Endorses Bernie." *YouTube*, February 14. https://www.youtube.com/watch?v=aH1IpfG0FOw.
Sanders Channel, Bernie. 2020l. "Mayor Chokwe Antar Lumumba Endorses Bernie." *YouTube*, March 9. https://www.youtube.com/watch?v=-sfU3vAWUeE.
Sanders Channel, Bernie. 2020m. "Pramilla | Bernie Sanders." *YouTube*, February 26. https://www.youtube.com/watch?v=QP5Og_qwUjI.
Sanders Channel, Bernie. 2020n. "Sarah Silverman Endorses Bernie." *YouTube*, March 11. https://www.youtube.com/watch?v=927gpuWAGkk.
Sanders Channel, Bernie. 2020o. "Town Hall on Racial and Economic Justice: Live from Flint, MI." *YouTube*, March 8. https://www.youtube.com/watch?v=tACugTo2btg.
Sanders Channel, Bernie. 2020p. "Trump Is a Fraud and a Liar." *YouTube*, February 18. https://www.youtube.com/watch?v=63WsTf-jCgM.
Sanders Channel, Bernie. 2020q. "Trump's Worst Nightmare." *YouTube*, February 2. https://www.youtube.com/watch?v=3ocneQiSE94.

Sanders Channel, Bernie. 2020r. "Vampire Weekend Endorses Bernie." *YouTube*, March 17. https://www.youtube.com/watch?v=E9HX0BL_RFE.

Sanders Channel, Bernie. 2020s. "We're Building the Coalition to Beat Trump." *YouTube*, February 16. https://www.youtube.com/watch?v=Q8dG_Jp-IX8.

Sanders Channel, Bernie. 2020t. "With These Hands." *YouTube*, March 3. https://www.youtube.com/watch?v=IckwaUkr2Dc.

Sanders Channel, Bernie. 2021. "Raise wages to end labor shortage." *YouTube*, May 21. https://www.youtube.com/watch?v=ZUQLITQAwt0.

Sarmiento, Isabella Gomez. 2019. "Why Senator Bernie Sanders Lost My Support." *Teen Vogue*, February 20. https://www.teenvogue.com/story/bernie-sanders-lost-my-support.

Savage, Luke. 2019. "The Real Barack Obama Has Finally Revealed Himself." *Jacobin*, November 27. https://www.jacobinmag.com/2019/11/obama-socialism.

Sawant, Kshama. 2020. "#DemExit: Time to Launch a New Party Of, By, and For Working People." *Socialist Alternative*, March 11. https://www.socialistalternative.org/2020/03/11/demexit-time-to-launch-a-new-party-of-by-and-for-working-people/.

Sawant, Kshama. 2021. "Why I'm Joining Democratic Socialists of America." *Socialist Alternative*, February 26. https://www.socialistalternative.org/2021/02/26/why-im-joining-democratic-socialists-of-america/.

Scahill, Jeremy. 2020. "We Are Not Your Firewall: Nina Turner and Briahna Joy Gray on South Carolina and the Attacks They Endure." *The Intercept*, January 25. https://theintercept.com/2020/02/25/we-are-not-your-firewall-nina-turner-and-briahna-joy-gray-on-south-carolina-and-the-attacks-they-endure/.

Schwartz, Ian. 2020. "Susan Rice On Violence At Floyd Protests: 'This Is Right Out Of The Russian Playbook." *RealClearPolitics*, June 1. https://www.realclearpolitics.com/video/2020/06/01/susan_rice_on_violence_at_floyd_protests_this_is_right_out_of_the_russian_playbook.html.

Schwartz, Sarah. 2021. "8 States Debate Bills to Restrict How Teachers Discuss Racism, Sexism." *Edweek*, April 15. https://www.edweek.org/policy-politics/8-states-debate-bills-to-restrict-how-teachers-discuss-racism-sexism/2021/04.

Science & Society Editors. 2018. "Intersectionality: A Symposium." *Science & Society* 82(2) (April): 248–91.

SDS, Former leaders of. 2020. "An Open Letter to the New Left From the Old New Left." *The Nation*, April 16. https://www.thenation.com/article/activism/letter-new-left-biden/.

Secular Talk. 2020. "Obama Blames Democratic Voters For His Failures." *YouTube*, October 19. https://www.youtube.com/watch?v=2CxeXMYkWD4.

Segers, Grace. 2019. "Obama says average American doesn't think we have to 'tear down the system and remake it.'" *CBS News*, November 16. https://www.cbsnews.com/news/obama-says-average-american-doesnt-think-we-have-to-tear-down-the-system-and-remake-it/.

Seyer-Ochi, Ingrid. 2021. "S.F. high school students get a lesson in subtle white privilege." *San Francisco Chronicle*, January 30. https://www.sfchronicle.com/opinion/openforum/article/S-F-high-school-students-get-a-lesson-in-subtle-15909700.php.

Shali, Saurabh Kumar. 2020. "Bernie or Bust? Well, Democrats chose bust!" *National Herald*, March 5. https://www.nationalheraldindia.com/india/bernie-or-bust-well-democrats-chosebust.

Sharf, Zack. 2020. "Werner Herzog Directs Baby Yoda on 'Mandalorian' Set As If the Puppet Was Real." *IndieWire*, April 23. https://www.indiewire.com/2020/04/werner-herzog-direct-baby-yoda-real-1202226850/.

Shields, Rob. 1992. "Spaces for the Subject of Consumption." In *Lifestyle Shopping: The Subject of Consumption*, ed. Rob Shields, 1-20. London: Routledge.

Silverman, Renée M., ed. 2015. *The Popular Avant-Garde*. Leiden: Rodopi.

Singh, Ajit. 2021. " 'Wipe out China!' US-funded Uyghur activists train as gun-toting foot soldiers for empire." *The Grayzone*, March 31. https://thegrayzone.com/2021/03/31/china-uyghur-gun-soldiers-empire/.

Singh, Nikhil Pal and Joshua Clover. 2018. "The Blindspot Revisited." *Verso Blog*, October 12. https://www.versobooks.com/blogs/4079-the-blindspot-revisited.

Sivanandan, Ambalavaner. 1990. "All That Melts into Air Is Solid: The Hokum of New Times." *Race & Class* 31(3) (Jan/March): 1-23. https://www.versobooks.com/blogs/3082-all-that-melts-into-air-is-solid-a-sivanandan.

Smiley, Tavis and Cornel West. 2012. *The Rich and the Rest of Us: A Poverty Manifesto*. New York: Hay House.

Smith, Sharon. 1994. "Mistaken identity – or can identity politics liberate the oppressed?" *International Socialism* 2(62) (Spring): https://www.marxists.org/history/etol/newspape/isj2/1994/isj2-062/smith.htm.

Sprunt, Barbara. 2021. "The History Behind 'When The Looting Starts, The Shooting Starts." *NPR*, May 29. https://www.npr.org/2020/05/29/864818368/the-history-behind-when-the-looting-starts-the-shooting-starts.

St. Clair, Jeffrey. 2016. *Bernie and the Sandernistas: Field Notes From a Failed Revolution*. Petrolia: CounterPunch.

St. Félix, Doreen. 2021. "The Rise and Rise of Amanda Gorman." *Vogue*, April 7. https://www.vogue.com/article/amanda-gorman-cover-may-2021.

Sternhell, Zeev. 1986. *Neither Left Nor Right: Fascist Ideology in France*. Translated by David Maisel. Princeton: Princeton University Press.

Sullivan, Sean, Michael Scherer and David Weigel. 2020. "Bernie Sanders says he's staying in the presidential race. Many Democrats fear a reprise of their 2016 defeat." *MSN*, March 31. https://www.msn.com/en-us/news/elections-2020/bernie-sanders-says-hes-staying-in-the-presidential-race-many-democrats-fear-a-reprise-of-their-2016-defeat/ar-BB11U5OR.

Sunkara, Bhaskar. 2019. *The Socialist Manifesto: The Case for Radical Politics in an Era of Extreme Inequality*. London: Verso.

Taylor, Brian and Tamara Keith. 2021. "Kamala Harris Tells Guatemalans Not To Migrate To The United States." *NPR*, June 7. https://www.npr.org/2021/06/07/1004074139/harris-tells-guatemalans-not-to-migrate-to-the-united-states.

Taylor, Jessica. 2019. "Former Nevada Candidate Accuses Biden of Unwanted Touching, Which He Doesn't 'Recall'." *NPR*, March 29. https://www.npr.org/2019/03/29/708232869/former-nevada-candidate-accuses-biden-of-unwanted-touching-which-he-doesnt-recal.

Taylor, Keeanga-Yamahtta. 2016. *From #BlackLivesMatter to Black Liberation*. Chicago: Haymarket Books.

Taylor, Keeanga-Yamahtta. 2020a. "Joe Biden's Success Shows We Gave Obama a Free Pass." *The New York Times*, March 4. https://www.nytimes.com/2020/02/05/opinion/Biden-Obama-2020.html?auth=login-email&login=email.

Taylor, Keeanga-Yamahtta. 2020b. "Reality Has Endorsed Bernie Sanders." *The New Yorker*, March 30. https://www.newyorker.com/news/our-columnists/reality-has-endorsed-bernie-sanders.

Thompson, Alex. 2020. "'The President Was Not Encouraging': What Obama Really Thought About Biden." *Politico*, August 14. https://www.politico.com/news/magazine/2020/08/14/obama-biden-relationship-393570.

Tietze, Tad. 2014. "What Privilege Theory Doesn't Explain." *Socialist Worker*, January 14. https://socialistworker.org/2014/01/14/what-privilege-theory-doesnt-explain.

Treene, Alayan and Stef W. Kight. 2021. "Biden's immigration tightrope." *Axios*, April 13. https://www.axios.com/bidens-immigration-tightrope-3c358702-5aae-41a9-9d25-44081b06914c.html.

Trotsky, Leon. 1944. "Fascism: What It Is and How to Fight It." https://www.marxists.org/archive/trotsky/works/1944/1944-fas.htm.

Trotsky, Leon. 2005 [1925]. *Literature and Revolution*. Chicago: Haymarket Books

Tumulty, Karen. 2019. "Branding 2020 Democrats as 'socialist' could be harder than Republicans think." *The Washington Post*, February 18. available at https://www.washingtonpost.com/opinions/branding-2020-democrats-as-socialist-could-be-harder-than-republicans-think/2019/02/18/6349c6c2-2fdc-11e9-813a-0ab2f17e305b_story.html?utm_term=.48a281845d29.

Turner, Fred. 2006. *From Counterculture to Cyberculture: Stewart Brand, the Whole Earth Network and the Rise of Digital Utopianism*. Chicago: University of Chicago Press.

Urie, Rob. 2020. "The Neoliberal Plague." *CounterPunch*, March 6. https://www.counterpunch.org/2020/03/06/the-neoliberal-plague/.

Useful Idiots. 2021. "Krystal Ball and Saagar Enjeti On Leaving Hill." *YouTube*, June 4. https://www.youtube.com/watch?v=wUUsnnsh188.

VandeHei, Jim and Mike Allen. 2020. "Joe Biden's governing plan." *Axios*, March 9. https://www.axios.com/joe-biden-cabinet-vice-president-picks-b17882ac-3953-450f-8afb-38a3c8dcda57.html.

Veblen, Thorstein. 1899. *The Theory of the Leisure Class: An Economic Study of Institutions*. New York, Macmillan.

VICE News. 2020. "Man Linked to Killing at a Portland Protest Says He Acted in Self-Defense." *VICE News*, September 4. https://www.vice.com/en_ca/article/v7g8vb/man-linked-to-killing-at-a-portland-protest-says-he-acted-in-self-defense.

Vogel, Lise. 1983. *Marxism and the Oppression of Women: Toward a Unitary Theory*. New Brunswick, NJ: Rutgers University Press.

Wallace, Rob, et al. 2020. "COVID-19 and Circuits of Capital." *Monthly Review*, May 1. https://monthlyreview.org/2020/05/01/covid-19-and-circuits-of-capital/.

Walters, Joanna and Lauren Gambino. 2020. "Sanders warns his loyalists it would be 'irresponsible' not to support Biden." *The Guardian*, April 15. https://www.theguardian.com/us-news/2020/apr/15/bernie-sanders-joe-biden-irresponsible-not-support.

Warren, Elizabeth. 2019. "Elizabeth Warren Stands Up to Billionaires (Warren for President Campaign Ad)." *YouTube*, November 23. https://www.youtube.com/watch?v=mNoa_ZhYjac.

Waugh, Paul. 2021. "Does Boris Johnson's 'Bodies' Remark Explain His Deadly Delay of the New Year Lockdown?" *The Huffington Post*, April 26. https://www.huffingtonpost.co.uk/entry/boris-johnson-bodies-analysis_uk_6087242ae4b02e74d21dcec4.

Weaver, Jeff. 2018. *How Bernie Won: Inside the Revolution that's Taking Back Our Country – And Where We Go From Here*. New York: Thomas Dunne Books.

Weigel, David. 2016. "Clinton in Nevada: 'Not Everything Is about an Economic Theory'." *The Washington Post*, February 13. https://www.washingtonpost.com/news/post-politics/wp/2016/02/13/clinton-in-nevada-not-everything-is-about-an-economic-theory/?utm_term=.234a7289e914.

Wernick, Andrew. 1991. *Promotional Culture: Advertising, Ideology and Symbolic Expression*. London: Sage.

Williams, Joan C. 2017. *White Working Class: Overcoming Class Cluelessness in America*. Boston: Harvard Business Review Press.

Wilson, Conrad and Kimberley Freda. 2020. "Racial justice protester suspected in Portland shooting death killed by law enforcement." *OPB*, September 3. https://www.opb.org/article/2020/09/04/michael-forest-reinoehl-protest-fatal-shooting-self-defense/.

Wolcott, James. 2017. "Why the Alt-Left Is a Problem, Too." *Vanity Fair/Hive*, March 3. https://www.vanityfair.com/news/2017/03/why-the-alt-left-is-a-problem?verso=true.

Wolin, Richard. 2004. *The Seduction of Unreason: The Intellectual Romance with Fascism, from Nietzsche to Postmodernism*. Princeton: Princeton University Press.

Wolin, Sheldon S. 2008. *Democracy Incorporated: Managed Democracy and the Specter of Inverted Totalitarianism*. Princeton: Princeton University Press.

Wood, Ellen Meiksins. 1995. *Democracy Against Capitalism: Renewing Historical Materialism*. Cambridge: Cambridge University Press.

Wood, Ellen Meiksins. 1998 [1986]. *The Retreat from Class: A New 'True' Socialism*. London: Verso

Wray, Ben. 2019. " 'We Have to Move to a Post-Capitalist System': An Interview with Walden Bello." *Jacobin*, October 28. https://jacobinmag.com/2019/10/walden-bello-interview-capitalism-china.

Wright, Bruce C.T. 2020. "Bernie Sanders' Press Secretary Under Fire For Tweet Responding To Kamala Harris." *Newsone*, March 31. https://newsone.com/3921360/bernie-sanders-press-secretary-briahna-joy-gray-kamala-harris/.

Wright, Erik Olin. 1985. *Classes*. London: Verso.

Wright, Erik Olin. 2015. *Understanding Class*. London: Verso.

Xin, Liu and Fan Lingzhi. 2020. "World Uyghur Congress a US-backed network seeking 'fall of China': US news website." *Global Times*, March 15. https://www.globaltimes.cn/content/1182641.shtml.

Yglesias, Matthew. 2019. "The Great Awokening." *Vox,* April 1. https://www.vox.com/2019/3/22/18259865/great-awokening-white-liberals-race-polling-trump-2020.

Young, Neil. 2020. "An Open Letter to Donald Trump." *Neil Young Archives Times-Contrarian*, February 18. https://neilyoungarchives.com/news/1/article?id=Viewpoint-Open-Letter-To-Trump-Page-1.

Zamora, Daniel. 2016. "Bernie Sanders and the New Class Politics: An Interview with Adolph Reed." *Jacobin*, August 8. https://www.jacobinmag.com/2016/08/bernie-sanders-black-voters-adolph-reed-trump-hillary.

Zamora, Daniel and Michael C. Behrent, eds. 2016 [2014]. *Foucault and Neoliberalism*. Cambridge: Polity Press,.

Zero Books. 2020. "Class Consciousness vs. the Fiction of 'Class First' Politics." *YouTube*, December 19. https://www.youtube.com/watch?v=bU5s7COxpl0.

Žižek, Slavoj. 1989. *The Sublime Object of Ideology*. London: Verso.

Žižek, Slavoj. 1998. "For a Leftist Appropriation of the European Legacy." *Journal of Political Ideologies* (February): https://www.lacan.com/zizek-leftist.htm.

Žižek, Slavoj. 1999. *The Ticklish Subject: The Absent Centre of Political Ontology*. London: Verso.

Žižek, Slavoj. 2000. "Class Struggle or Postmodernism? Yes, Please!" In Judith Butler, Ernesto Laclau and Slavoj Žižek, *Contingency, Hegemony, Universality: Contemporary Dialogues on the Left*, 90-135. London: Verso.

Žižek, Slavoj. 2004 [2000]. "Rancière's Lesson." In Jacques Rancière, *The Politics of Aesthetics*, trans. Gabriel Rockhill, 69-79. London: Continuum.

Žižek, Slavoj. 2006a. "Against the Populist Temptation." *Critical Inquiry* #32 (Spring): 551-74.

Žižek, Slavoj. 2006b. "Multiculturalism, or, The Cultural Logic of Late Capitalism." In *The Universal Exception: Selected Writings, Volume Two*, eds. Rex Butler and Scott Stephens, 151-82. London: Continuum.

Žižek, Slavoj. 2006c. *The Parallax View*. Cambridge: The MIT Press.

Žižek, Slavoj. 2008a. "Intellectuals, Not Gadflies." *Critical Inquiry* #34 (Winter): s21-s35.

Žižek, Slavoj. 2008b. "Tolerance as an Ideological Category." *Critical Inquiry* #34 (Summer): 660-82.

Žižek, Slavoj. 2010. *Living in the End Times*. London: Verso.

Žižek, Slavoj. 2012. *Less Than Nothing: Hegel and the Shadow of Dialectical Reason*. London: Verso.

Žižek, Slavoj. 2016. "Slavoj Žižek on Clinton, Trump and the Left's Dilemma." *In These Times*, November 7. https://inthesetimes.com/article/slavoj-zizek-on-hillary-clinton-donald-trump-and-the-lefts-election-dilemma.

Žižek, Slavoj. 2017. "A Great Awakening and Its Dangers." *The Philosophical Salon*, November 20. https://thephilosophicalsalon.com/a-great-awakening-and-its-dangers/.

Žižek, Slavoj. 2019a. "Donald Trump's Topsy-Turvy World." *The Philosophical Salon*, January 16, 2019. https://thephilosophicalsalon.com/donald-trumps-topsy-turvy-world/.

Žižek, Slavoj. 2019b. *The Relevance of the Communist Manifesto*. Cambridge: Polity, 2019.

Žižek, Slavoj. 2019c. "Was I right to back Donald Trump over Hillary Clinton? Absolutely." *The Independent*, June 26. https://www.independent.co.uk/voices/trump-hillary-clinton-populist-right-left-democratic-party-civil-war-a8975121.html.

Žižek, Slavoj. 2020a. "Global communism or the jungle law, coronavirus forces us to decide." RT, March 10. https://www.rt.com/op-ed/482780-coronavirus-communism-jungle-law-choice/.

Žižek, Slavoj. 2020b. *Pandemic! COVID-19 Shakes the World*. New York: OR Books.

Žižek, Slavoj. 2020c. "Power, Appearance, and Obscenity: Five Reflections." *The Philosophical Salon*, June 22. https://thephilosophicalsalon.com/power-appearance-and-obscenity-five-reflections/.

Žižek, Slavoj. 2021. "Class Struggle Against Classism." *The Philosophical Salon*, May 10. https://thephilosophicalsalon.com/class-struggle-against-classism/.

Zussman, Richard. 2019. "Former Liberal byelection candidate Karen Wang wants party to bring her back." *Global News*, January 17. https://globalnews.ca/news/4858602/karen-wang-liberals-return/.

Index

1619 Project   156

Abdelgader, Remaz   69–70
Abdullah, Melina   155
abortion   79, 183, 197, 202
Abrajano, Marisa A.   79
Abrams, Stacey   157
Academi   239
academia   7, 12, 38, 42, 56, 93, 94, 110, 113, 150, 160, 166, 181, 191
ACLU   199
activism   5, 7, 9, 38, 39, 46, 48, 54, 69, 70, 77, 88, 90, 94, 97, 110, 127, 130, 131, 133, 154–157, 165, 166, 173, 175, 181, 185–187, 189, 205, 209, 139, 241
Adorno, Theodor   216
advertising
  negative attack ads   8, 69, 74, 93, 101
  commercial advertising   20, 98–100, 150
  political advertising   20, 56, 60, 68, 69, 71, 79, 82, 84–86, 97–130, 148
  Sanders campaign ads   19, 20, 69, 71, 79, 103–130, 148
aesthetics   *See* culture
affect   53
affirmative action   15, 30, 31
Affordable Care Act   34, 64, 68, 135, 197, 201
Afghanistan   12, 33, 68, 86, 96
AFL-CIO   26, 27, 72, 174, 180
Africa   2, 134
African Americans   8, 26–29, 35, 36, 44, 57, 70–72, 74, 77, 79, 80, 90–94, 101, 113, 122, 125, 135, 137, 149, 154, 165, 168, 170, 172, 198, 199, 208–209, 211, 214, 242, 249
Afro-pessimism   162
Agnew, Philip   112–113, 125, 139
Ahmed, Sara   243
Alabama   75, 92, 136, 222
Alaska   72
Albright, Madeleine   70
Alcoff, Linda   194
Alexander, Ali   222
Alexander, Elizabeth   203
Alexander, Michelle   159n
Ali, Tariq   45

Allende, Salvador   238
Allen, Jonathan   82, 88, 91, 199
Allen, Woody   144
allyship   3, 55
Al Qaeda   232
alt-left   5
alt-right   5, 34, 59, 60, 81, 123, 188, 241, 244
alter-anti-globalization   *See* new social movements
American Israel Public Affairs Committee   129
American Bridge 21st Century   119
American Federation of Teachers   85
American Rescue Plan   249
anarchism   36, 76, 77, 98, 115, 160, 164, 174, 175, 179, 212
Anderson, Perry   34, 188
Angelou, Maya   165–166, 203
anti-communism   *See* communism
anti-Enlightenment   *See* Enlightenment
antifa   114, 151, 155, 226
anti-racism   *See* racism
anti-Semitism   55, 56, 119–122
anti-sexism   *See* sexism
Arab Americans   128–130
Arab Spring   97
Arbery, Ahmaud   164
Arizona   222
Arkansas   234
Arnautoff, Victor   166
Asian Americans   8, 9, 44, 72, 77
Assange, Julian   35, 59, 96, 186
Australia   229
authoritarianism   10, 11, 13, 43, 45, 81, 92, 111, 181, 196, 238, 239, 244, 247
authoritarian populism   11, 111

Badiou, Alain   108, 243, 245
Baldwin, James   29, 160
Balibar, Étienne   243
Ball, Krystal   171, 194
bank bailout   84, 151, 232
banks   6, 12, 25, 33, 34, 40, 64, 65, 84, 151, 153, 200, 232
Bannon, Stephen   81, 222, 234

INDEX   283

Barber, William   76, 156
Barr, William   169, 225
Barthes, Roland   99
Barwick, Juliana   194
Beck, Daniel   222
Beijer, Carl   82
Bello, Walden   45
Beloff, Zoe   193
Ben & Jerry's   99
Benjamin, Walter   162
Berlatsky, Noah   242–243
Bernays, Edward   99
Bernie Bros and Broads   4, 5, 60, 62, 70, 74, 80, 116, 194
Bernie or Bust   20, 141, 144, 146–147
Beshear, Andy   170
Beyoncé   101, 170
Bezos, Jeff   61, 183
Bhambra, Gurminder K.   44
Biafra, Jello   194
Biden, Hunter   200
Biden, Joe   7, 10, 13, 20, 21, 36, 54, 67, 69, 70, 76, 79, 80, 82, 85, 86, 88, 89, 91–93, 95, 96, 125, 126, 134–136, 140, 141, 147–150, 153–157, 162, 164, 168–172, 178, 182–186, 190, 195–203, 206, 207, 216, 218, 219, 224, 226, 228–230, 232–238, 248, 249
Biggs, Andy   222
Biggs, Joe   225
billionaires   *See* ruling class
bin Laden, Osama   34
bipartisanship   10, 11, 21, 32, 33, 82, 96, 157, 187, 220–238
Black Arts Movement   203–204
black capitalism   30–31, 34
blackface   162
Black Lives Matter   8, 13, 19, 21, 34, 58, 69, 70, 76, 79, 97, 108, 133, 154–159, 165, 166, 168, 169, 171, 196–198, 218, 227
Black Panther Party   134, 173
Black Power   29–30, 38, 57, 107, 134, 219
blacks   *See* African Americans
Blair, Tony   45, 112, 238
Blanchard, Tom   119–120, 123–124
Blanco, Richard   203
Bland, Sandra   69
Bloomberg, Michael   79, 82, 84, 88, 89, 91, 115, 145, 148

Boebert, Lauren   221, 223
Bohrer, Ashley   160
Bolsonaro, Jair   56, 139
Bolton, John   82, 157
Bolton, Michael   227
Booker, Cory   6n, 82, 89, 136
Bosse, David   222
Bosteels, Bruno   243
Bourdieu, Pierre   10, 37, 99, 160
bourgeoisie   *See* middle class
Bowman, Jamaal   75, 174
Bowser, Muriel E.   159, 223
Bragg, Billy   141
branding   35, 56, 77, 101, 102–103, 165, 166, 170, 176, 205, 206, 209
Brazile, Donna   73
Brecht, Bertolt   87
Brenner, Robert   194
Brexit (Leave)   44
Brock, David   60
Brooks, Michael   113, 176–177, 180–181, 190
Brooks, Mo   222
Browne, Jackson   194
Brown, Wendy   241
Bugden, Sebastian   167n
bureaucracy   24, 163
Burgis, Ben   22, 187n, 242–246
Burns, Kenny   149
Buscemi, Steve   195
Bush, Cori   75, 131
Bush, George H.W.   32–33
Bush, George W.   1, 9, 10, 12, 33–34, 102, 142, 153, 232
Butler, Judith   150, 241
Buttigieg, Pete   20, 82, 84–89, 91–93, 148

Caldwell, Thomas   225
California   72, 91, 249
Cameron, Daniel   170
Campbell, Naomi   101, 149
Canada   55–56, 84, 109, 151, 154, 229
cancel culture   42, 187n, 239, 242, 250
capitalism   9, 10, 12, 14, 16, 31, 38, 40, 42, 43, 47, 48, 52, 81, 107, 109, 115, 118, 128, 140, 199, 219, 245, 248
capitalist realism   52
Capitol, U.S.   *See* coup attempt

Cardi B   87, 170–171, 194
CARES Act   152
Carlyle, Belinda   194
Carter, Jimmy   2, 19, 31–32, 36, 92
Cashmore, Ellis   101–102
Cassell, Jessica   191
Castro, Fidel   12, 79, 192
Cat Power   194
celebrity   12, 20, 44, 48, 87, 101–103, 150, 168, 170, 198, 203–205, 210–211
Center for Popular Democracy   133
Chadhury, Arun   105, 122
Charlottesville   76, 120
Chase, Amanda   223
Chavez, Cesar   199
Chávez, Hugo   12
Chen, Chris   243
Cheney, Dick   88, 235
Chibber, Vivek   108, 191, 243
Chicago Monuments Project   157
Chile   45, 238
China   33–34, 84–85, 95, 174, 233–238
Chomsky, Noam   60–61, 179–180, 182–183, 194
Chuck D   194
Churchill, Winston   76
CIA   32, 56, 145, 233, 238
Citizens United   61, 65
civil rights   7, 9, 14, 26–30, 69, 70, 122, 139, 142, 154, 187, 190, 200–201, 219, 242
Clark, Jeffrey   225
class
    class analysis   13, 22–25, 51, 67, 108, 112, 140, 161, 167, 197
    class consciousness   18, 22–25, 31, 39, 42–43, 156, 159, 249
    class formation   18, 22–25
    class politics   16, 22–25, 61–62, 94, 118, 158–159, 167, 210, 243–245
    class structure   18, 22–25, 108
    class struggle   3, 12, 16, 18, 22–25, 38–39, 49, 94, 111–112, 137, 142, 158, 179, 184, 247, 249–250
    class war   3, 20, 67, 111, 159, 175, 188–189, 192
climate change   *See* ecology
Clinton, Bill   1, 6, 11, 19, 32–34, 45, 82, 106, 112, 152, 165, 199, 200, 202, 228

Clinton, Hillary   1, 3, 4, 5, 6, 8, 9, 12, 19, 34, 35, 41, 43, 44, 59, 60, 62, 69–74, 85, 86, 88, 90, 91, 93, 107, 124, 131, 144, 146, 147, 155, 179, 182, 185, 186, 198, 199, 204, 205, 211, 218, 228, 230
Clover, Joshua   52, 163–166
Clyburn, James   19, 71, 91, 157
Clyde, Andrew   223
Coates, Ta-Nehisi   41, 53–54, 204
Cohen, Ben   79, 99
COINTELPRO   29, 155
Cold War   26–27, 33, 38, 45, 70, 76, 82, 143, 187, 200, 250
colonialism   6, 142, 160, 209
Colorado   72, 223
colorblindness   5, 8, 56, 159n
Combahee River Collective   54, 106–107, 110–112
Combs, Sean   36, 149–150
communism   8, 10, 19, 26, 35, 42, 43, 45, 46, 49, 55, 81, 99, 107, 115, 139, 142–144, 160, 163, 174, 175, 178, 181, 183, 185, 209, 215, 219, 234, 246, 250
Communist Party of Great Britain   246
community   16, 29, 32, 38, 42, 47, 49, 133, 139, 198
Congress   9, 26, 28, 31, 33, 61, 67, 75, 223, 226, 230–232
Congress of Racial Equality   67, 110
Congressional Black Caucus   91, 95
conservatism   1, 5, 9–11, 15, 18, 27, 28, 33, 41, 48, 55, 59, 72, 77, 78, 84, 87, 91, 94, 98, 100, 109, 111, 112, 125, 140, 144, 146, 154, 157, 158, 161, 173, 176, 197, 202, 219, 249
Consumer Financial Protection Bureau   84, 145, 200
consumerism   99–100, 163, 176, 188, 200
Contee, Robert   224, 228
Corbyn, Jeremy   10, 51
Correct the Record   60
Corrigan, Brad   194
Cotton, Tom   234
Coulthard, Glen Sean   243
counterculture   38, 41, 100, 161, 163, 169, 176, 188, 200, 248, 250
Counterweight   240
coup attempt (January 6)   21, 95, 218–219, 220–233, 242

INDEX   285

COVID-19 pandemic   20, 21, 56, 95, 109, 114,
    151–154, 158, 164, 168, 171, 175, 183, 196,
    197, 218, 233–238, 249
Crenshaw, Kimberlé   54, 107, 156, 246
crime
    criminal justice policy   6, 33, 65, 69, 70,
        72, 80, 127, 134, 187, 201
    incarceration   29, 35, 65, 80, 159n, 198, 201
Critchley, Simon   42, 243
critical race theory   53, 160, 188
Cruz, Ted   223, 230–231
Cuba   8, 76, 174
Cullors, Patrice   76, 155
cultural competence   78, 80
cultural Marxism   4–5, 34, 47, 98, 158, 241
cultural politics of difference   *See* identity
    politics
Cultural Studies   100, 111, 161, 178, 243, 250
culture   32, 47, 53, 100, 108, 161, 185–195, 148
culture industry   5, 87, 99–100, 115
culture wars   3, 9, 20, 22, 31, 41, 53–59, 67, 74,
    81, 130, 151, 157, 188–190, 192, 197, 219,
    239, 241, 242
Cusack, John   193
cybernetics   50, 163, 246
Cyrus, Miley   194

Daggett, Cara   56
Damon, Andre   151, 234–237
Danielson, Aaron   169
Daszak, Peter   235, 237
Davis, Angela   108, 170, 243
Day, Meagan   176, 178
Dean, Jodi   55, 76, 184, 189, 219, 243
Dean, Mitchell   131, 167n
Dearlove, Richard   238
Debs, Eugene   174
debt   33, 40, 65, 66, 80, 95, 123, 137, 183, 200
deconstruction   50, 79, 191, 244
deficit   32–34
DeGeneres, Ellen   88
deindustrialization   29–30, 45, 118
Delaney, John   82
Delaware   200
delegates   8, 19, 71, 74, 91
democracy   14, 43, 46, 161, 245, 246
Democratic National Committee   2, 8, 19, 44,
    59, 60, 70, 73, 147

Democratic National Convention   8, 72, 74
Democratic Party   3, 8, 25–36, 46, 59–96, 103,
    104, 111, 116, 118, 119, 139, 141–144, 146–
    149, 151, 154, 162, 166, 170–180, 184, 185,
    196–198, 202, 205, 216, 220, 230–232,
    238, 245, 248, 249
democratic socialism   *See* social democracy
Democratic Socialists of America   53, 158,
    159, 174–178, 182, 184, 186, 188, 216
demographics   7, 14, 17, 19, 34, 69, 78, 79, 87,
    89, 92, 98, 105, 186, 197, 206, 250
Deneault, Alain   40
Douthat, Ross   158–160
Department of Defense   223, 228
Department of Homeland Security   226–227
Department of Justice   96, 154, 225–226, 230
deregulation   11, 31, 32, 33, 39, 83, 112,
    140, 236
determinism   *See* reductionism
Detroit Action   136–137
Devine, Mulvey and Longabaugh   104
DeVito, Danny   193
dialectics   113, 163, 167, 177, 244
DiAngelo, Robin   41
difference politics   *See* identity politics
DiFranco, Ani   194
Dimon, Jamie   148
DingGang, Wang   234
discourse theory   15, 50, 51, 77, 160, 167, 191,
    239–241, 246
discrimination   7, 85, 113, 116, 120, 121, 128,
    142, 207
disinformation   21, 60, 73, 90, 105, 199,
    233–238
Disney   195
disparity   31, 69, 70, 159, 213
diversity   3, 4, 6–9, 11, 13–15, 17, 20, 29, 42, 48,
    50, 53, 56, 59, 76–78, 93, 94, 109–111, 115,
    116, 128, 160, 209, 218, 245, 250
Dixon, Bruce   54
Dolezal, Rachel   215
donations   19, 20, 36, 66, 68, 69, 73, 83, 85,
    100, 101, 105, 119, 144–145, 185
Donohue, Jack   226
Dooley, Victoria   132, 135–136
Douglas, Stephen A.   157
Dream Defenders   112
Driessens, Olivier   203

Driver, Adam 195
Driver, Sara 195
drone warfare 57, 68, 88, 201
Du Bois, W.E.B. 57, 209
Dukakis, Michael 2
Duke, David 235
Duncan, Carol 157
Dyer-Witheford, Nick 189
Dyson, Michael Eric 90, 157

Eastland, James 199
ecology 3, 11, 13, 16, 32, 38, 49, 51, 61, 65, 82, 83, 93, 119–120, 170, 173, 180, 187, 193, 197, 201, 208, 219, 236
economics
   economic justice 7, 63
   economic policy 64, 74
   political economy 13, 29, 31, 42, 49, 100, 108, 152, 156, 162, 185, 198, 216
   redistribution 3, 11, 12, 13, 16, 45, 63, 159
Ecuador 59
education 6, 28, 34, 38–41, 65, 67, 80, 83, 85, 86, 123, 127, 135, 137, 183, 187, 247
Egypt 201
Ehrenreich, Barbara and or John 10, 18, 36–40, 174
Eidlin, Barry 219
Eisenhower, Dwight 26
Eisenstein, Hester 160
electability 8, 13, 46, 78, 93n, 147, 150
electoral college 5
Ellison, Keith 72
Ellison, Ralph 29
elitism 41, 46, 52, 62, 77, 103
emancipatory politics 4, 94, 110, 163, 167, 171, 181, 241
employment 25–29, 31, 39, 40, 64, 69, 150, 153, 158, 183, 196, 198, 247, 249, 250
Endnotes 14, 133
energy 35, 72, 80
Engels, Friedrich 42, 108, 243
English, Micah 8
Enjeti, Sagar 207–208, 234n
Enlightenment 10, 45, 47, 98, 113, 130, 157, 161, 163, 165, 239, 240, 245
entrepreneurialism 18, 30, 48, 116, 170
Epps-Addison, Jennifer 132–135
Esper, Mark 223

essentialism *See* reductionism
Eurocentrism 4, 134
Eurocommunism 49
Evans, Derrick 229
Evers, Medgar 27, 130
Ewen, Stewart 99
exceptionalism 46, 48, 176, 198
existentialism 48, 163, 244
exploitation 23, 95, 112, 128, 131, 157, 182
Extinction Rebellion 97, 156

Facebook 60, 68, 104, 153, 229, 236
Fanon, Frantz 108, 165, 203–204
Farrakhan, Louis 113
far right *See* fascism
fascism 4, 9–11, 18, 21, 25, 36, 43, 45–49, 76, 84, 90, 95, 115, 120–122, 132, 139, 140, 166, 168, 172, 183, 184, 188, 190, 219–234, 241, 242, 243n, 246, 248, 249
Fauci, Anthony 235, 238
FBI 27, 29, 155, 222, 224–226, 228
Featherstone, Liza 55
feminism
   feminism 11, 14, 23, 38, 39, 51, 55, 61, 70, 107, 160
   corporate 'lean-in' feminism 3, 13, 41, 48, 55, 56, 85, 116, 204, 205
Ferguson 134
Fields, Barbara and Karen 215, 244
filibuster 68
financialization 11, 31, 33
Fisher, Mark 52, 187n
Flint, Michigan 34, 131–133
Flint Rising 132
Flores, Lucy 202
Florida 81, 186, 223, 225, 231, 249
Florida, Richard 11
Floyd, George (protests) 8, 20, 95, 114, 150, 154–157, 164, 168–169, 171, 231, 232
Flynn, Charles A. 222, 224
Flynn, Michael 222
Folbre, Nancy 160
Foley, Barbara 109, 243
Foner, Eric 51
food stamps 27, 32
Ford, Glen 93n, 172–173
fossil fuels *See* energy
Foucault, Michel 50, 86

INDEX   287

Foundation for Individual Rights in
    Education   239
fracking   72, 183
France   85, 140
Frankfurt School   113
Frank, Thomas   11, 51, 140, 200, 236
Fraser, Nancy   11–13, 55, 194, 243
Frazer, Charise   149
Freeland, Chrystia   56
Freud, Sigmund   242, 248
Frost, Amber   176, 178
Frost, Robert   203
Fuchs, Christian   189
Fukuyama, Francis   148, 182
Furham, Jonah   23

Gabbard, Tulsi   79, 146
Gaetz, Matt   223
Garner, Erica   71, 105
Gates Jr., Henry Louis   115
Gautney, Heather   2–3, 63, 70, 74
gay rights movement   *See* LGBTQ+
Gaza   *See* Palestine
George Washington High School   165–166
Georgia   68, 136, 198, 218, 223, 225
Gerbaudo, Paolo   51
Germany   31, 237
Giammattei, Alejandro   169
Gilbert, Dan   137
Gillibrand, Kirsten   82
Gilroy, Paul   53
Gindin, Sam   31
Giordano, Dom   199–200
Giuliani, Rudy   222, 234
Glass-Steagall Act   25, 33, 64, 72
global capitalism   *See* capitalism
Glover, Danny   71, 139, 194, 195
Glover, Michael   161
Goldman Sachs   22, 36, 74, 76
Gómez, Laura   148
Gomez, Selena   170
Goodman, Amy   110–111
Goodstein, Scott   105
Gordon, Kim   194
Gordon, Michael R.   234–235
Gordon-Nesbitt, Rebecca   192
Gorman, Amanda   203–205
Gore, Al   180

Gorz, André   24
Gosar, Paul   222
Gouldner, Alvin   24
Graeber, David   121
Graham, Lindsey   82, 85, 157
Graham, Mark   119
Gramsci, Antonio   50, 87, 107
Grande, Ariana   194
Grant, Ulysses   166
Gray, Briahna Joy   6n, 72, 79, 106, 114, 125–
    126, 171, 205–216
Great Britain   85
Great Power Conflict   76, 84, 238
Great Society   1, 2, 27, 74, 139
Greene, Marjorie Taylor   223
Green, Ja'mal   126
Green New Deal   65, 80, 126, 193, 230
Green Party of Canada   56
Green Party USA   43, 73, 141, 175
Greenwald, Glenn   4, 172, 194, 229
Guaidó, Juan   56, 157
Guantánamo Bay   34
Guastella, Dustin   9, 162, 188–192
Guatemala   169
gun ownership   79
Gunnels, Warren   72
Guo, Miles   234

Habermas, Jürgen   86
habitus   36
hacking   59–61
Hagia Sophia   165
Haider, Asad   54, 166–168, 243
Halper, Katie   183–184, 210–216
Hall, Stuart   111, 207
Hamer, Fannie Lou   130
Hammoud, Abdullah   128–129, 133
Hardt, Michael   52, 160
Harlem Renaissance   203–204
Harper's free speech statement   240
Harrington, Michael   174
Harris, Kamala   6n, 20, 79, 82, 86, 89, 93,
    95, 136, 148, 165, 169, 171, 172, 186, 203,
    208, 210
Harris, Meena   165–166
Hart, Peter D.   81
Harvey, David   54, 243
Hasan, Medi   179

Hawaii 72
Hawley, Josh 223, 230–231
HBCUS 71, 125–126
health care 33–35, 64, 68, 72, 74, 79, 80, 83, 93, 96, 123, 124, 126, 132, 135–137, 151–154, 171, 178, 183, 197, 232–238, 250
Hedges, Chris 25, 45–46, 102, 183–184, 195
Hegel, G.W.F. 16, 113–114, 140, 163, 241, 244, 246–248
hegemony 11, 12, 21, 50, 112, 125, 244–245
Heng, Elizabeth 82
Herzog, Werner 194
heteronormativity 6, 57
Heyer, Heather 76
Hice, Jody 223
Hill, Justin 223
Hiroshima and Nagasaki 26, 47
Hirshman, Linda 202
Hispanics *See* Latinos
Hitler, Adolph 148
Hobsbawm, Eric 59
Hockett, Jeremy 102
Hofstadter, Richard 159
Hogan, Larry 224
Hollywood 11, 42, 101, 119, 125, 204, 247
Holocaust 15, 47, 53, 67
homelessness *See* housing
homophobia 6, 12, 41, 74, 81, 95, 103, 114, 126, 149, 157, 212, 249
Hoover, J. Edgar 29
Horne, Gerald 230, 243
House of Representatives *See* Congress
housing 29, 32, 33, 36, 38, 67, 137, 150, 198, 247
Hoyer, Steny 224
Huber, Anthony 169
Huerta, Dolores 70
human rights 14, 15, 21, 56, 113, 126, 160, 188, 241, 248
Hurricane Katrina 34
Hussein, Saddam 32, 235
Hyde-Smith, Cindy 231

Idaho 72
identity politics 3–8, 10, 13, 15–20, 31, 35, 38, 46–49, 52–58, 61, 62, 69, 70, 74, 76–78, 89, 93, 94, 97, 98, 106, 109–114, 116, 117, 131, 154–156, 160, 167, 168, 173, 178, 186, 188, 196–198, 210, 213, 214, 239, 240, 249–250
Ilitch, Mike 137
Illinois 157, 168
immigration 6, 12, 13, 26, 28, 30, 49, 61, 65, 72, 75, 78–80, 95, 111, 122, 129, 169, 170, 201
impeachment 21, 88, 202, 229–233
imperialism 27, 32, 33, 35, 43, 45, 56, 61, 76, 81, 85, 122, 129, 157, 209, 218, 236, 238, 239
Inauguration Day 35, 166, 203, 216–217, 229–230
India 45, 182
Indiana 72, 86
Indonesia 45
inequality 8, 11, 20, 23, 30, 33, 34–36, 40, 62, 63, 79, 104, 110, 111, 136, 139, 150, 152, 154, 191, 196, 198, 208, 238, 239, 247, 249
Institute for Policy Studies 151–152
institutional racism *See* racism
internationalism *See* socialism
International Workers of the World 159, 173
intersectionality 7, 17, 24, 51, 53, 54, 56, 77, 78, 94, 106, 107, 109, 110, 112, 114, 115, 158–161, 187, 204, 219, 246
Iowa 43, 69, 71, 73, 85, 88, 89, 91, 120, 121, 193, 213
Iran 61, 231, 238
Iraq 32, 33, 68, 96, 201, 234, 238
Irving, Paul Douglas 223
Islamophobia 69
Ismangil, Milan 181n
Israel 55, 57, 61, 68, 96, 129, 183
Iver, Bon 193

Jackson, Jesse 32, 140, 180
Jameson, Fredric 43, 243
Japan 31, 33, 85, 237
Jardina, Ashley 44
Jarmusch, Jim 195
Jayapal, Pramila 75, 116–119, 126–127
Jay-Z 170
Jealous, Ben 71
Jefferson, Thomas 51, 166
Jewish Americans 6–7, 67, 89, 110, 119–122, 129, 142
Jilani, Zaid 95

Jim Crow   *See* segregation
Johnson, Boris   142, 237
Johnson, Cedric   54, 72n, 159, 243
Johnson, Jack   194
Johnson, Lyndon B.   27–29, 139
Jones, Alex   222, 228
Jones, Jacqueline   101
Jones, Norah   194
Jordan, Jim   223
jouissance   57, 178
Justice Democrats   75

Kaling, Mindy   210
Kalla, Joshua   8
Kansas   72, 140
Kant, Immanuel   122
Kardashian, Kim   36
Karp, Matt   176–177
Kelley, Robin D.G.   243
Kendi, Ibram X.   41, 203–204, 230
Kennedy, John F.   27–29
Kennedy, Robert   30
Kentucky   72, 170
Kerry, John   82
Kerner Commission   30
Kerson, Sam   166
Kessler, Glenn   234
Keys, Alicia   170
Khachaturian, Rafael   166–168
Khlaek, Rania   210, 212
Khanna, Ro   75, 79
Killer Mike   88, 139, 194
Kimbrell, Andrew   237
King, Gail   89
King Jr., Martin Luther   27, 29–30, 32, 76, 88–89, 134–135, 199, 205
King, Loretta Scott   32
King, Shaun   76, 122–126, 155
Kinnock, Neil   201
Kissinger, Henry   238
Klain, Ron   230
Klavon's Ice Cream Parlor   249
Klein, Federico   222
Klein, Naomi   151, 194, 216–217, 247
Klobuchar, Amy   82, 89, 91–93, 144, 148
Kluge, Alexander   192n
Klu Klux Klan   199, 235
Koenig, Ezra   148

Kolditz, Thomas   228
Kracauer, Siegfried   37
Kraus, Chris   194
Kroker, Arthur   212
Kübler-Ross, Elisabeth   20, 141–142
Kulinski, Kyle   150, 172, 229

lab leak conspiracy   95, 233–238
labor politics and organizations   2, 12, 22–27, 31, 35, 63, 72, 79, 111, 145, 148, 159, 167, 176, 177, 183, 188, 189, 250
Labour Party (UK)   98, 111, 121, 187
Lacan, Jacques   14, 57, 98, 108, 178, 204
Laclau, Ernesto   50, 110
Lain, Douglas   245
Lancaster, Roger   150
Lascaris, Dimitri   56
Latimer, Michelle   241
Latin America   2, 96
Latinos   3, 6, 8, 12, 30, 36, 44, 70–72, 77–80, 88–89, 92, 113, 116, 186, 198, 219, 249
Lee, Spike   71
Lefebvre, Henri   43, 246–247
Léger, Marc James   189, 192n
Lenin, Vladimir (Leninism)   42, 174–175, 177, 191–192
Lewandowski, Corey   222
Lewinsky, Monica   33, 101
Lewis, Holly   108
Lewis, John   7, 55, 71
LGBTQ+   3, 8, 11, 14, 51, 54, 67, 77, 86, 110, 122, 134, 198, 204, 215, 219
Liberal Party of Canada   55–56
liberalism   11, 14, 18, 25, 29, 38, 43, 45–49, 52, 77, 83, 134, 142, 159, 162, 167, 185, 186, 219, 240, 241, 247
Libya   33, 34, 68, 201
Liebovitz, Annie   205
lifestyle   25, 31, 37, 47, 99, 101, 163, 188, 250
Lightfoot, Lori   157
Lilla, Mark   77
Lincoln, Abraham   157, 199
Lindell, Michael   222
Lindsay, James   130, 241
Lis, Hannan   129
Liu, Catherine   41
Lizza, Ryan   82
Lofgren, Zoe   227

London, Eric   175, 198, 216
Louisiana   208
Lumumba, Chokwe Antar   130, 140
Lury, Celia   98

Macias, Joshua   228
Macnair, Mike   146
Maddock, Matt   223
Maddow, Rachel   90
Maduro, Nicolás   80, 157
Maher, Bill   116–118, 143–148
Maine   72
Maisano, Chris   25, 158–160
Make America Great Again   1, 123, 152, 171, 193, 195, 248
Malburg, Lori   119
Malik, Abdullah   103
Mandela, Nelson   89, 149
Manning, Chelsea   15, 68
Manor, Joyce   194
March for Our Lives   97, 156, 171
March on Washington   27–28, 32, 67
Marcetic, Branco   6, 7, 90, 199, 201
Marcuse, Herbert   47–49, 100, 194
Margolin, Jamie   119–121
Marshall Plan   26
Marxism   16, 22–25, 37, 42, 47–49, 50–54, 77, 98, 100, 108, 109, 113, 127, 140, 158, 160–162, 165–167, 174–176, 184, 190, 191, 211, 214, 239, 240, 242–248
Marx, Karl   42, 51, 108, 113, 134, 176, 243, 246, 248
Maryland   69, 224
Masket, Seth   78
Mason, Paul   194
Massachusetts   72
Mastriano, Doug   223
materialism   23, 47, 50, 53–54, 77, 108, 128, 140, 158, 162–163, 167, 177–178, 243–244, 247
Matthews, Chris   90
May 1968   140, 246
May, Elizabeth   56
McCain, John   85
McCarthy, Kevin   222–223, 233
McCarthy, Ryan   221, 223–224
McConnell, Mitch   157, 222–223, 225, 229, 231–232
McCree, Floyd   136

McGorry, Matt   114–115
McKibben, Bill   72
McLuhan, Marshall   188
McWhorter, John   98, 239, 241
media
    concentration   66
    mainstream and corporate media   5, 6, 35, 42, 55, 59, 61, 70, 73, 83–84, 88, 90, 93, 95–96, 102–106, 118, 125, 129, 144, 146, 147, 149, 153, 156, 158, 162, 165, 169–173, 178, 179, 185, 189, 195, 197–199, 202, 204–208, 200, 217, 221n, 229, 230, 231, 234–237, 239, 240
    progressive media   5, 6, 110–111, 150, 156, 158–159, 165, 172, 175–178, 180–181, 183, 184, 188–189, 191, 194, 205–207, 211, 212, 216, 229, 230, 234n, 237, 245
    social media   3, 34, 48, 60, 68–69, 83, 88, 104, 117, 125, 149, 153, 178, 180, 181n, 189, 192, 195, 210–212, 216–217, 225, 229–230, 236
Medicaid   27, 32, 64, 135
Medicare   27, 64, 85, 135, 199, 208
Medicare for All   *See* universal health care
mediocracy   25, 86, 100, 157, 201, 219, 230
memes   4, 62, 70, 90–91, 216–217
men voters   5, 8, 60, 70, 118, 198
Mercader, Ramon   192
Mercer, Rebekah   222
Mercer, Robert   222
Mering, Natalie   194
meritocracy   11, 18, 40–41
Merritt, Lee   155
MeToo   34, 97, 156, 170–171, 202
Mexico   81, 84, 151, 169, 229
Meyer, Robinson   70
Meyerson, Gregory   49, 134
M.I.A.   194
Michaels, Walter Benn   24, 53–54, 243, 245
Michigan   43, 71–72, 117, 119, 128–129, 131–139, 155, 218, 221, 223
micro-politics   9, 77, 94, 127, 157
middle class   9, 10, 18, 22–25, 36–43, 45, 47, 50, 85, 108–109, 123, 126, 136, 153–154, 162, 170, 198, 244, 247
Middle East   2, 34, 85, 88, 93, 201, 229
militarism   3, 12, 13, 16, 26, 33–35, 56, 57, 66, 68, 74, 82, 84, 85, 93, 96, 126, 170, 198, 200, 201, 208, 219, 238, 239, 247, 250

millennials 7, 72, 74, 80, 92, 95, 156
Miller, Christopher 223–224
Miller, Judith 234–235
Miller, Stephen 222
Milley, Mark 221, 223–224
Million Militia March 229
Mills, C. Wright 37
Minnesota 43, 72
Minuta, Roberto 222
Mississippi 130
Missouri 223
Mitchell, Eve 160
mittens *See* Sanders
Modi, Narendra 237
Monáe, Janelle 170
Moore, Michael 82, 138
Moore, Thurston 194
Moran, Marie 109
Mouffe, Chantal 50–51, 110
Moyniha, Daniel Patrick 28–29
Mubarak, Hosni 201
Mueller, Robert *See* Russiagate
multiculturalism *See* diversity
Murray, Bill 195
Muslim Americans 128–130
Myanmar 238
Myers, Dalhi 125

NAACP 27
Nader, Ralph 85, 156, 175, 180, 237
NAFTA 6, 33, 68
Nagle, Angela 42, 185–191
National Action Network 76
National Guard 154, 168, 170, 223–224, 226–227, 229
nationalism 10, 12, 13, 18, 29, 43, 45, 47–50, 94, 111, 122, 159, 196
National Organization of Women 70
National Urban League 27
Nation of Islam 113
Native Americans 28, 65, 72, 219
NATO 33, 56
Navarro, Peter 222
Nebraska 72
Negri, Antonio 52, 160
Negro American Labor Council 28
Negt, Oskar 192n
neoliberalism 4, 9, 10, 12, 15, 16, 18, 21, 25, 31, 35, 40, 45, 46, 52, 56, 58, 76, 78, 86, 88, 102, 124, 127, 131, 139, 144, 151, 154, 158, 160, 166, 170, 176, 178, 180, 191, 198, 200, 204, 209, 216, 242, 247, 250
Netanyahu, Benjamin 56, 61, 68
Netherlands 237
Netroots National Conference 69, 79
Nevada 71, 73, 79, 89, 249
NeverBiden 156, 172
New Deal 1, 2, 18, 25–28, 31, 33, 36, 44–45, 74, 83, 130, 166, 200
New Democratic Party of Canada 55–56
New Democrats 11, 18, 19, 25, 36, 40, 45, 54, 59, 124, 232
New Hampshire 69, 71, 85, 89, 121, 194
New Left *See* new social movement
New Orleans 34
new social movements 10, 11, 13, 36, 38–39, 49–51, 111, 153, 160, 164, 167, 171, 174, 242, 250
Newton, Huey 29
New York State 72
Ngai, Sianne 194
NGOs 77, 133, 180, 189
Nietzsche, Friedrich 246–248
Nixon, Richard 30–31, 34, 139, 238
No Malarkey 92, 201, 248
normativity 57, 114–115, 170, 188, 249
North, David 156, 182
North Korea 76
Nuland, Victoria 95

Oath Keepers 220, 222, 225, 228, 230
Obama, Barack 1, 3, 6, 10, 12, 19, 21, 34–36, 40, 44, 54, 69, 72, 73, 76, 82–84, 86, 90–95, 102, 105, 106, 112, 124, 125, 139, 142, 145, 150, 152, 155, 157, 170, 171, 199–201, 204, 205, 211, 212, 214, 228, 232, 242
Obama, Michelle 54, 82, 204–205
objectivity 21, 41, 47–48, 107
Ocasio-Cortez, Alexandria 75, 80–82, 113, 174, 195, 199, 216, 228
Occupy Wall Street 12, 34, 40, 53, 97, 191
Ohio 43, 223
Oklahoma 72, 231
O'Malley, Martin 69
Omar, Ilhan 55, 75, 128
oppression 4, 14, 16, 18, 19, 23, 25, 31, 75, 108, 155, 158, 215
Orbán, Viktor 56, 139

Oregon 72, 169
O'Rourke, Beto 82, 199
Owens, Candace 208
Ozomalti 194

PACs *See* donations
Pacific Islanders 77
Packard, Vance 97
Paine, Thomas 51
Palast, Greg 68
Palestine 55–57, 68, 96, 126, 129
Palma, Bethania 162
pandemic *See* COVID-19
Parker, Deborah 72
Parks, Rosa 199
Parnes, Amie 82, 88, 91, 199
Paris Commune 42
particularism 13, 15, 16, 108, 113, 243
patriarchy *See* sexism
Patrick, Deval 82
patriotism 84–85, 94, 140
Paul, Annamie 56
peasantry 23, 49
Pelosi, Nancy 55, 82, 155, 157, 204, 224, 228–229, 231
Pence, Mike 157, 220, 222
Pennsylvania 43, 119, 218, 223
Pentagon 34, 76, 83, 223–224, 227, 235
Perez, Tom 70, 73, 82
Perry, Scott 223
Peters, Gary 226
Peterson, Jordan 98, 216
petty bourgeoisie 9, 10, 16, 18, 21, 22–25, 29, 36–42, 50, 100, 125, 127–128, 133, 163, 169, 177, 181–182, 188, 209, 216, 242, 250
Phenomenal Women Action Campaign 165
phenomenology 48, 50, 108, 244
philanthropy 38
Philippines 45
Phillips, Steve 78
Piatt, Walter 224
Pinochet, Augusto 39, 238
Piper, Adam 222
Pluckrose, Helen 130, 240–241
pluralism *See* diversity
Podemos 51
Polanyi, Karl 122
police
    Metropolitan D.C. Police 228, 230

policing 27, 29, 30, 154, 198, 201, 220–232
police violence 30, 155, 158–159, 168–170, 175, 183, 198, 223
police reform 19, 65, 95, 170
    United States Capitol Police 221–222, 224–228, 232
polarization 9, 22
political contributors *See* donations
political correctness 41, 77, 131, 144, 145, 161, 169, 187, 241, 243, 244, 246
political economy *See* economics
polls 8, 18, 21, 71, 81–82, 85–86, 88, 98, 186, 195–198
Pompeo, Mike 238
Pop, Iggy 195
Popular Front 115, 166
Poor People's Campaign 29, 76, 88, 156
populism 8, 11, 12, 13, 18, 19, 20, 25, 49–52, 62, 73, 75, 81, 103, 110–111, 140, 156, 161, 172, 176, 182, 184, 189, 209, 246, 249
Porter, Billy 95
post-Fordism 13, 24, 87, 187, 216
postmodernism 4, 7, 9, 10, 14, 15, 16, 17, 21, 47, 48, 53, 54, 77, 90, 93, 94, 98, 100, 108, 113, 122, 125, 127, 128, 130, 156, 158–162, 165, 166, 170, 177, 181, 187–191, 209, 214, 215, 240, 241, 243, 249, 250
post-Marxism *See* Marxism
post-politics 4, 7, 13–17, 41, 58, 77, 109, 219, 242
post-structuralism 54, 108, 115, 130, 160, 240, 243
Poulantzas, Nicos 37
Pountain, Dick 100
poverty *See* inequality
Prashad, Vijay 238–239, 240
precarity 13, 25
prefigurative politics 10
press *See* media
Pressley, Ayanna 75
Pride March 157
primaries 7, 8, 19, 43, 60, 71, 73, 83, 85, 89, 91, 122
privatization 39, 86, 143, 151
privilege 4, 5, 6, 58, 77, 115, 187, 190, 217, 219, 246, 250
professional-managerial class 9, 10, 12, 18, 21, 22–25, 29, 36–44, 49, 52–54, 58, 70, 87,

94, 97, 107, 155, 162, 177, 196, 207, 209, 214, 219, 241, 247
progressive neoliberalism   10, 11–13, 18, 19, 20, 49, 54, 56, 77, 80, 87, 97, 127, 140, 196, 205
progressive populism   *See* populism
proletariat   42–43, 113, 176, 190, 192n, 219, 242
protests   8, 10, 20, 154–157, 164–165, 168–169, 230–232, 250
Proud Boys   219–220, 222, 225, 227, 230
psychoanalysis   4, 14, 57, 98, 108–109, 141–142, 178, 242, 248
Public Enemy   194
Pussy Riot   194
Putin, Vladimir   59, 61, 144, 228–229, 232

QAnon   220, 224, 228
Qatar   237
Quebec student strike   97, 175
Queen Latifah   170

Rabin-Havt, Ari   79
race neutral, *see* colorblind
racial capitalism   108, 133–134
racism   4, 6, 8, 11, 12, 16, 23, 26–30, 33, 41, 44, 47, 51, 54–57, 74, 81, 90, 103, 107, 109, 112, 114, 118, 123, 126, 128, 134, 148, 149, 154, 156–159, 161, 168, 169, 196, 197, 212, 218, 242, 246, 249
radical democracy   4, 24, 49–52, 62, 77, 127
radicalism   3, 10, 18, 21, 26, 31, 37–39, 76, 89, 94, 115, 137, 181, 185, 189, 193, 219, 242
Raffensberger, Brad   225
rainbow coalition   32, 140, 158
Rancière, Jacques   13, 108, 243
Rand, Paul   231
Randolph, A. Philip   28, 174
Ransby, Barbara   194
Reade, Tara   202
Reagan, Ronald   9, 31–32, 34, 39, 77, 101, 112, 196, 200
reason   21, 48
recognition (politics of)   13, 15, 159
redistribution   *See* economics
reductionism
    class reductionism   4, 16, 18, 24, 50–53, 108–109, 158, 213, 215, 216, 242–246
    economic reductionism   50–52, 108, 177, 242–246

race or identity reductionism   51–52, 108, 156, 163, 198, 209, 242–246
technological reductionism   34, 50, 189
Reed Jr., Adolph   2–3, 6, 14, 18, 24, 42, 52–54, 107, 130–131, 139–140, 180–182, 192, 212–213, 243–244
Reed, Touré   29, 156, 198, 243–244
reformism   7, 10, 61, 74, 187
regime change operations   2, 68, 80, 83, 186, 199, 238–239
Reid, Harry   92
Reinoehl, Michael   114, 169
reparations   53, 64, 154, 204
Republican Party   21, 30, 46, 59, 74, 77, 95, 104, 118, 145, 151, 173, 183, 187, 196–198, 200, 202, 218, 221, 229–232, 246, 249
resentment   15, 44
respectability   35, 125, 150, 207
responsibility   33
revolution   10, 13, 17, 38, 73, 76, 83, 93, 94, 109, 158, 165, 173, 202, 246
Revolution Messaging   104–105
Rhode Island   72
Rhodes, Stewart   228
Rice, Susan   153–155
Rice, Tamir   155
Richmond, Cedric   208
Riegle, Don   136
rights and freedoms   21, 31, 116, 140, 202, 229
Rihanna   170
Rijneveld, Marieke Lucas   204
Riley, Boots   193
riots   27, 29–30, 114, 155, 164, 220–233
Risher, Richard   155
Rittenhouse, Kyle   114, 168–169
Robbins, Tim   194
Robeson, Paul   29
Robins, David   100
Robinson, Cedric   108
Robinson, Nathan   177, 202
Rocha, Chuck   78–80, 88–89, 104, 207
Roediger, David   44, 54, 57, 243
Rogan, Joe   194
Romney, Mitt   155
Roosevelt, Eleanor   199
Roosevelt, Franklin D.   25, 77, 105, 143, 199–201
Roosevelt, Theodore   84
Rosenbaum, Joseph   168

Rosen, Jeffrey   225
Rosler, Martha   194
Ross, Tracee Ellis   170
Ruffalo, Mark   194
ruling class   3, 16, 19, 30, 44, 46, 59, 61, 66, 80, 84, 85, 93, 103, 133, 137, 147, 150, 151, 152, 159, 173, 176, 177, 183, 184, 202, 220, 222, 231, 234, 242, 248
Rumsfeld, Donald   88
Russia   61, 76, 84–85, 144–146, 232, 237
Russiagate   35, 60–61, 124, 186
Rustin, Bayard   28–29, 174

Saatchi, Charles and Maurice   98
Sainte-Marie, Buffy   194
Saint-Just, Louis Antoine Léon de   1
Samorodnitsky, Dan   235
Sanborn, Jill   225
Sanders, Bernie
   Bernie Sanders Guide to Political Revolution   74–75
   Bernie Sanders YouTube Channel   88, 103–140, 142, 148–149, 194, 249
   biography   7, 67–68
   campaign advertising   97–130, 148
   heart attack   80, 90
   Hear the Bern   106, 109–110, 114
   mittens   216–217
   Not Me, Us   80, 103, 133, 149
   Our Revolution (organization)   75, 176
   Our Revolution: A Future to Believe In   63–68, 103
   policy agenda   63–68, 74–76
   Rallies and town hall meetings   68–69, 131–140
   Sanders 2016 campaign   3, 17, 19, 61, 63–76
   Sanders 2020 campaign   7, 10, 13, 17, 78–92, 103–130, 148, 157
   Town Hall on Racial and Economic Justice   131–139
   Where We Go From Here   75–76
   Where We Go From Here speech   61
Sartre, Jean-Paul   165
Saudi Arabia   129
Save America Rally   *See* coup attempt
Sawant, Kshama   173, 178
Scalia, Antonin   202

Schultz, Debbie Wasserman   73
Schumer, Chuck   155, 224
scientific management   163
Scott, Rick   231
Seale, Bobby   29, 218
sectarianism   173–178, 181, 184, 189, 196, 212
secularism   45
segregation   26–28, 67, 79, 87, 102, 159n, 199, 214
SEIU   72
semiotics   50
senior citizens   70, 208
separatism   12, 13, 38, 107
Serbia   33, 68
settler colonialism   *See* colonialism
Sevigny, Chloë   194
Seymour, Richard   243
sexism   6, 8, 12, 16, 23, 41, 47, 54, 55, 70, 74, 79, 81, 82, 90, 95, 103, 114, 118, 148, 149, 157, 169, 197, 202, 240, 242, 244, 246, 249
Shakir, Faiz   79
Shariff, Nayyirah   132
Sharpton, Al   102, 169
Shields, Rob   100
shock doctrine   151, 155
Shoham, Dany   234
Show Up For Racial Justice   114
Sicknick, Brian   228
Silicon Valley   11, 86
Silverman, Renée   195
Silverman, Sarah   141–142, 144–146, 148
Simon and Garfunkel   104
simulation   14, 15
Singh, Jagmeet   55–56
Singh, Nikhil Pal   52, 243
single-payer health care   *See* universal health care
Sirota, David   211
Sivanandan, Ambalavaner   111–112
slavery   15, 53–54, 102, 118, 135, 159, 166
Slotkin, Elissa   224
Smiley, Tavis   36
Smith, Barbara   106–107, 109–111, 114
Smith, Jada Pinkett   170
Smith, Liz   88
Smith, Sharon   112, 160
SNCC   27
Snowden, Edward   68

Snyder, Brandon 136–137
Soborowicz, David 119
social constructionism 50, 162, 191
social democracy 5, 11, 16, 20, 28, 45, 51, 66, 76, 77, 81, 88, 94, 136, 144, 153, 168, 182, 184, 190, 192, 207, 210, 240
socialism 4, 7, 9, 11, 15, 16, 21, 29, 46, 47, 50, 51, 75, 77, 81, 82, 88, 93, 94, 108, 110–112, 114, 123, 127, 132, 139, 140, 142–144, 146, 150, 156, 157, 159, 161, 163, 173–182, 185, 200, 207, 209, 238, 240, 246, 250
Socialist Alternative 173
Socialist Equality Party 175, 178, 182
social justice warrior See culture wars
Social Security 25, 64, 68, 85, 93, 103, 199, 208, 213, 218
Solange 170
solidarity 10, 31, 69, 92, 110, 116, 156, 159, 160, 170, 180, 198, 215
Solidarity Strategies 78–79, 104
Somalia 96
Soth-Rethel, Alfred 127
South Carolina 7, 8, 19, 71, 72n, 79, 91–92, 125, 148
South Korea 162
Soviet Union 32, 45, 47, 174, 181, 186, 214
Spain 140
Spain, Christale 71
Sprunt, Barbara 155
Stalin, Joseph (Stalininsm) 12, 47, 174, 177, 192
standpoint epistemology 50, 77
statues 157, 162, 166
St. Clair, Jeffrey 1–2, 73–74
Stein, Jill 43, 73, 141
Steinem, Gloria 70
Stephanopoulos, George 88
stereotype 5, 13, 32, 39, 55, 123, 125, 162
Stern, Howard 90
Steyerl, Hito, 194
Steyer, Tom 82
Stone, Roger 222
Stipe, Mike 194
Street, Paul 54
strikes 26, 29, 31, 85, 164
Strokes, The 193
structural adjustment 32
structuralism 108, 163, 191, 244, 246

structural racism See racism
students 12, 31, 38, 40, 49
Students for a Democratic Society 38–39, 174, 179
suburbs 27, 41, 74, 170
Sudhakar, Bushan D. 103
Sund, Steven 224, 226–227
Sunkara, Bhaskar 176–177
Sunrise Movement 208
Suny, Ronald 191–192
Super Tuesday 19, 72, 79, 85, 91–93, 119, 130, 136, 172
Supreme Court 26, 91, 202, 218
surveillance 34, 96, 183, 227
symptom 4, 25, 114, 118
Syria 33, 34, 51, 68, 96, 201

Taibbi, Matt 234n
Taft-Hartley Act 26
Tanden, Neera 95, 206, 208
Tarrio, Enrique 225
Taylor, Breonna 164, 170
Taylor, Keeanga-Yamahtta 92, 159n, 171, 194
taxation 9, 27, 31–32, 34, 59, 64, 72, 80, 96
technocracy 1, 11, 15, 40, 51, 109, 166, 248, 250
Tennessee 223
Texas 79, 91, 95, 102, 249
Texas, Virgil 205–206, 216
Thailand 45
Thatcher, Margaret (Thatcherism) 39, 51, 98, 111–112, 196
Theoharis, Liz 156
third party 11, 20, 43, 151, 156, 171–181, 184, 188–189
Thomas, Clarence 202, 208
Thompson, Tessa 170
Thurmond, Strom 199
Till, Emmett 27
Tlaib, Rashida 75, 128, 174
Tomson, Chris 148
totalitarianism 46, 48
totality 47–48, 108, 215
toxic masculinity 150
Tracey, Michael 185–190
Trans-Pacific Partnership 72
Trotsky, Leon (Trotskyism) 39, 173–174, 176, 178, 180, 182, 188–189, 191–192, 243n
Trudeau, Justin 55–56, 109

Truman, Harry   26
Trump, Donald   1, 4–14, 18, 21, 35, 41, 43–44, 48, 55, 59–61, 71–77, 79–82, 84–85, 88–93, 95–96, 98, 101, 103–104, 106, 114, 117–120, 122–125, 127, 139, 141–142, 145–146, 148, 150–152, 154–156, 166–167, 169, 171–172, 175, 179–180, 184–186, 190, 193, 196–197, 218–219, 220–232, 234, 242, 247–249
Trump, Eric   222
Tuberville, Tommy   222, 231
Turner, Fred   200
Turner, Nina   71, 79, 126, 139
Twitter   3, 6, 55, 69, 75, 83, 88, 117, 149, 152–153, 189, 192–193, 213, 217, 224, 229–230

Ukraine   84, 95, 144, 186
Underground Railroad   166
unemployment   *See* employment
unions   *See* labor politics and organizations
United Arab Emirates   96
United Auto Workers   85, 136
United Mine Workers of America   182
United States-Mexico-Canada Trade Agreement   84, 151
Universal Basic Income   64, 79, 153
universal health care   1, 6, 28, 34, 41, 72, 110, 135–136, 142, 170, 180, 193, 201, 210, 213, 230, 250
universalism   4, 6–7, 12, 13, 15–17, 19, 20, 21, 31, 41, 47–49, 51, 59, 62, 67, 76, 77, 79, 85, 89, 92, 94, 98, 107–110, 112, 113, 121, 125, 130, 138, 154, 156, 158, 162, 163, 167, 179, 187, 190, 204, 206, 207, 240, 241, 243, 245
upper class   *See* ruling class
Urie, Rob   152
Utah   72
Uyghurs   95, 233

Vampire Weekend   148, 193
Van Dyke, Dick   194
VANghazi   73
Varoufakis, Yanis   194
Veblen, Thorstein   99
Venezuela   8, 56, 76, 80, 157, 186, 238
Vermont   1, 18, 67, 72, 128, 166, 175
Vermont Law School   166
victim politics   5, 15, 112, 156, 162, 240, 241
Vietnam   29, 32, 67, 110, 174, 237

Virginia   225
virtue signaling   19, 20, 40–42, 95, 115, 198, 201
Vogel, Lise   108
Voltaire   162
voting
  lesser evil voting   1, 2, 20, 73, 139, 141, 182
  strategic voting   82
  voting rights   65, 68, 70–71, 74, 246

Wade, Nicholas   235
Waldow, Eric   227–228
Walker, Kara   162
Walker, William J.   224
Wall Street   11, 17, 30, 35, 40, 60, 64, 68, 74, 75, 80, 83, 84, 86, 119, 145, 152
Walmart   151, 239
Walsh, David   243
Walton, India   174
Wang, Karen   56
Wark, McKenzie   22
War on Crime   11, 32, 33
War on Drugs   30–31, 65, 198
War on Poverty   27–29
War on Terror   32, 76, 198, 201
Warren, Elizabeth   8, 20, 41, 79, 82–84, 87, 89–93, 122, 145, 164, 177, 185–186, 195
Washington, George   157, 166
Washington State   72, 195
Watergate   231
Waters, Maxine   227
Waters, Roger   194
weapons of mass destruction   234–235, 238
Weather Underground   175
Weaver, Jeffrey   60, 63, 69–70, 79, 104
Weaver, Terry Lynn   223
Weiner, Norbert   246
welfare   31–33, 38, 45, 63–64, 116, 131, 143, 184, 200
Wells, Ida B.   130
Wernick, Andrew   100, 105
West, Cornel   36, 72, 94, 113, 131, 137–140, 174, 184, 194, 207
West, Kanye   150
West Virginia   72, 122, 229
white
  white Americans   88, 91, 123
  white identity   44
  whiteness   57, 191, 219, 230, 239

white privilege, *see* privilege
white savior   6
white supremacy   1, 9, 12, 23, 44, 53, 76, 95, 133, 137, 138, 154, 230
white working class   3, 8, 55, 57, 92, 110, 123, 168, 221
White, Jack   194
Whitmer, Gretchen   221
WikiLeaks   19, 59, 61, 73, 146
Williams, Joan C.   44
Williams, Miller   203
Williams, Pharrell   170
Winfrey, Oprah   39, 101, 170, 204
Wisconsin   43, 72, 117, 119, 122, 168, 169, 218
woke
   wokeism   53–58, 62, 92, 127, 150, 158, 162, 188, 190, 191, 198, 209, 217, 239–241
   woke war,   *See* culture war
   wokewashing   90, 97, 170
Wolf, Chad   226
Wolff, Richard   184
Wolin, Richard   130
Wolin, Sheldon   46
Women's March   75, 97, 156, 157, 171
women's movement   *See* feminism
women voters   5, 8, 19, 34, 44, 74, 77, 92, 116, 117, 119, 137, 197, 198
Wood, Ellen Meiksins   16, 49, 54, 118, 243
Wood Jr., Roy   211
Woods, Tiger   101
working class   12, 18, 22–25, 32, 37, 41–44, 49, 75, 94, 108, 109, 118, 119, 124, 136, 140, 148, 151, 176, 182, 183, 186, 190, 193, 198, 209, 230, 242, 245, 249

World Health Organization   233–237
World Trade Organization   39
Wray, Christopher   225
Wright, Erik Olin   18, 22–25
Wright, Richard   29
Wuhan Institute of Virology   21, 95, 233–237
Wyoming   72

xenophobia   7, 12, 35, 41, 61, 74, 76, 81, 95, 103, 126, 128, 129, 148, 149
X, Malcolm   29–30
Xi Jinping   144

Yang, Andrew   55, 79, 89, 114
Yan, Li-Meng   234
Yates, Michael D.   243
Yemen   34
Yippies   174
Young, Neil   83, 193–194
youth voters   *See* millennials
YouTube   87–88, 103–140, 148–149, 194, 249
yuccies   248
Yugoslavia   201
Yúlin-Cruz, Carmen   79
yuppies   39

Zahr, Amer   129
Zamora, Daniel   7, 131, 167n, 243
Zedong, Mao (Maoism)   10, 80
Zhengli, Shi   235
Žižek, Slavoj   13–17, 60, 94, 98, 109, 127, 140, 141, 145–146, 148, 153–154, 161, 177–180, 182, 190, 194, 219, 240–241, 244–245
Zogby, Jim   72

www.ingramcontent.com/pod-product-compliance
Lightning Source LLC
Chambersburg PA
CBHW070911030426
42336CB00014BA/2367